CRITICAL READINGS:
MORAL PANICS AND THE MEDIA

ISSUES in CULTURAL and MEDIA STUDIES

Series editor: Stuart Allan

Published titles

CRITICAL READINGS:
MORAL PANICS AND THE MEDIA

Edited by
Chas Critcher

OPEN UNIVERSITY PRESS
Maidenhead

Open University Press
McGraw-Hill Education
McGraw-Hill House
Shoppenhangers Road
Maidenhead
Berkshire
England
SL6 2QL

email: enquiries@openup.co.uk
world wide web: www.openup.co.uk

and Two Penn Plaza, New York, NY 10121–2289, USA

First published 2006

A catalogue record of this book is available from the British Library

ISBN 10: 0335 21807 5 (pb) 0335 21808 3 (hb)
ISBN 13: 978 0335 21807 3 (pb) 978 0335 21808 0 (hb)

Library of Congress Cataloging-in-Publication Data
CIP data applied for

61756725

Typeset by YHT Ltd, London
Printed in Poland by OZ Graf.S.A.
www.polskabook.pl

CONTENTS

In memory of Bob, miscueing no more.

SERIES EDITOR'S FOREWORD

To unravel the notion of 'moral panic' in conceptual terms, Chas Critcher's perceptive introduction to this volume reminds us, it is helpful to consider its initial formulation in Stanley Cohen's book, *Folk Devils and Moral Panics: The Creation of the Mods and Rockers*, first published in 1972. Cohen, having borrowed the phrase from a colleague (Jock Young's study of the social meaning of drug-taking), proceeded to elaborate a general theory of what constitutes a moral panic, and how they operate. The oft-quoted opening passage of his book offers a succinct description of its principal features:

> Societies appear to be subject, every now and then, to periods of moral panic. A condition, episode, person or group of persons emerges to become defined as a threat to societal values and interests; its nature is presented in a stylized and stereotypical fashion by the mass media; the moral barricades are manned by editors, bishops, politicians and other right-thinking people; socially accredited experts pronounce their diagnoses and solutions; ways of coping are evolved or (more often) resorted to; the condition then disappears, submerges or deteriorates and becomes more visible. Sometimes the object of the panic is quite novel and at other times it is something which has been in existence long enough, but suddenly appears in the limelight. Sometimes the panic passes over and is forgotten, except in folklore and collective memory; at other times it has more serious and long-lasting repercussions and might produce such changes as those in legal and social policy or even in the way the society conceives itself.

Of interest to Cohen was the potential explanatory power of the 'moral panic' concept as a means to better understand the emergence of 'Mods' and 'Rockers' as subcultural styles in Britain during the 1960s. As a result, he explored the ways in which the occasionally violent clashes between these two groups of young people, as well as their attitudes toward sex, vandalism and drug-taking, became the subject of intense media controversies over 'deviancy'.

Mods or 'modernists' were stereotyped as being fashion-conscious (wearing neat, colourful suits, usually well-groomed with short hair), listened to ska, rhythm and blues, were fond of 'pep pills' and rode motor-scooters. Stereotypes of the Rockers, in sharp contrast, suggested that they preferred black leather jackets and jeans, listened to rock and roll music, were more likely to be low-paid, 'unskilled' workers than (semi-skilled, white collar) Mods, and rode noisy motor bikes. Members of both groups were involved in a series of confrontations at various seaside towns, beginning with one in Clacton, a small holiday resort on the east coast of England, in 1964. This event, which set the pattern for the others to follow, saw both groups defined as rampaging menaces. In the words of one newspaper editor at the time: '... they were something frightening and completely alien ... they were visitors from a foreign planet and they should be banished to where they came from.' As such, in the eyes of some establishment figures, the Mods and Rockers were folk devils whose delinquent activities endangered the very foundations of society.

The actual risk to society posed by these groups of young people, according to Cohen's investigation, was grossly exaggerated by the news media. Citing the admission of an Assistant Editor at the *Daily Mirror* that the initial incident at Clacton between the Mods and Rockers had been 'a little over reported', Cohen pointed to how that newspaper and some of its rivals deliberately distorted the seriousness of the events. Journalists' use of sensational headlines and melodramatic vocabulary, as well as the repeated embellishment of certain facts (the numbers taking part, the degree of the violence and its effects, and so forth), served to create a fundamentally misleading picture of what was happening. As Cohen stated, the 'regular use of phrases such as "riot", "orgy of destruction", "battle", "attack", "siege", "beat up the town" and "screaming mob" left an image of a besieged town from which innocent holidaymakers were fleeing to escape a marauding mob.' Highly dubious evidence provided the basis for some news accounts, while others rested on unconfirmed rumours.

In very little time, the Mods and Rockers came to symbolise a threat to traditional, decent values of law and order. Indeed, the very words 'Mod' and 'Rocker' acquired what Cohen called 'symbolic powers' through three processes of symbolization: 'a word (Mod) becomes symbolic of a certain status (delinquent or deviant); objects (hairstyle, clothing) symbolize the word; the objects themselves become symbolic of the status (and the emotions attached to the status).' These two words, at one time denoting little more than different consumer styles, promptly acquired wholly negative meanings on the pages of the press. This process, Cohen argued, allowed for 'full-scale demonology and hagiology to develop: the information had been made available for placing the Mods and Rockers in the gallery of contemporary folk devils.'

The faces may have changed in today's gallery of folk devils, but moral panics continue to revolve around the ways in which certain 'deviant' individuals or groups are stigmatised as threatening to tear the social fabric of 'our' everyday lives. In taking Cohen's 1972 study as the point of departure for this volume, editor Chas Critcher proceeds to show why several of the issues which it helped to elucidate are very much alive in certain places around the world. At the heart of *Critical Readings: Moral Panics and the Media*, therefore, is the pressing need to investigate the extent to which the media, in particular, give shape to the normalisation of 'us' versus 'them' dichotomies as an acute form of prejudice. Herein lies the value of this unique volume. Across the diverse range of topics represented by its twenty-two chapters, produced by leading researchers in five countries, the relative strengths and limitations of a number of theoretical and methodological approaches are explored. Many of these chapters would not otherwise be easily accessible because they are out of print or take some finding in journal archives. In any case, however, all of them have been chosen by Critcher for the significance of their contribution, as well as for their potential to further encourage this area of study to develop in new and challenging directions.

The *Issues in Cultural and Media Studies* series aims to facilitate a diverse range of critical investigations into pressing questions considered to be central to current thinking and research. In light of the remarkable speed at which the conceptual agendas of cultural and media studies are changing, the series is committed to contributing to what is an ongoing process of re-evaluation and critique. Each of the books is intended to provide a lively, innovative and comprehensive introduction to a specific topical issue from a fresh perspective. The reader is offered a thorough grounding in the most salient debates indicative of the book's subject, as well as important insights into how new modes of enquiry may be established for future explorations. Taken as a whole, then, the series is designed to cover the core components of cultural and media studies courses in an imaginatively distinctive and engaging manner.

Stuart Allan

ACKNOWLEDGEMENTS

This book took a lot longer to produce than originally intended owing to the vagaries of (middle-aged) life. I was thus grateful for the forbearance of commissioning editor Chris Cudmore. Series editor Stuart Allan provided excellent advice which I did not always take. Four anonymous reviewers provided pointed but invariably constructive suggestions. My wife, children, dog and sense of humour have all survived another book, though not necessarily in that order of priority.

I would like to be able to say that my understanding of moral panics has been advanced by the many national and international conferences at which I have been asked to speak. Alas, there have been none such though I remain available – at very reasonable rates. And for bar mitzvahs.

And finally a goodbye. After fifteen years of working with me, Pam Hibberd eventually found a better alternative. Her contribution to this book has been, as usual, indispensable, including the tedious task of retyping bibliographies in the required format. She also tracked down more than one obscure reference. My working life will never be the same without her.

Postscript. During the final edit of this book in July 2005 home-grown terrorism struck at the heart of London with devastating consequences. It seems unlikely that moral panic analysis has the capacity to encompass the global conflict underlying terrorism though folk devils are already much in evidence. How easily we forget the observation of the poet W.H. Auden: 'Those to whom evil is done, do evil in return.'

ACKNOWLEDGEMENTS FOR READINGS

The editor and the publisher wish to thank the following for permission to use copyright material:

Part I

Cohen, S. (1973) *Folk Devils and Moral Panics*, Chapter 1, pp. 1–16. Reprinted by permission of Routledge.

Hall, S., Critcher, C., Jefferson, T., Clarke, J. and Roberts, B. (1978) *Policing The Crisis: Mugging, the State and Law and Order*, Chapter 8, pp. 220–7. Reprinted by permission of Macmillan Publishers.

Goode, E. and Ben-Yehuda, N. (1994) *Moral Panics: The Social Construction of Deviance*, Chapter 3, pp. 31–53. Reprinted by permission of Blackwell Publishing.

Thompson, K. (1998) *Moral Panics*, Chapter 1, pp. 16–21. Reprinted by permission of Routledge.

Part II

Weeks, J. (1989) 'AIDS, the intellectual agenda', pp. 1–13, in P. Aggleton, G. Hart and P. Davies (eds) *AIDS: Social Representations, Social Practices*. Reprinted by permission of The Falmer Press.

Jenkins, P. and Maier-Katkin, D. (1992) 'Satanism: myth and reality in a contemporary moral panic', Kluwer Academic Publishers *Crime, Law and Social Change*, 17: 53–73, with kind permission from Springer Science and Business Media.

Chiricos, T. (1996) 'Moral panic as ideology: drugs, violence and punishment in America', pp. 19–48 in M. Lynch and B. Patterson (eds) *Justice with Prejudice: Race and Criminal Justice in America*. Reprinted by permission of Criminal Justice Press.

Stockwell, S. (1997) 'Panic at the Port', *Media International Australia*, 85(November): 56–61.

Kitzinger, J. (1999) 'The ultimate neighbour from hell? The media representation of paedophilia', pp. 207–20 in B. Franklin (ed.) *Social Policy, the Media and Misrepresentation*. Reprinted by permission of Routledge.

Ost, S. (2002) 'Children at risk: legal and social perceptions of the potential threat that possession of child pornography poses to society', *Journal of Law and Society*, 29(3): 436–60. Reprinted by permission of Blackwell Publishing.

Welch, M. and Schuster, L. (2005) 'Detention of asylum seekers in the UK and US: deciphering noisy and quiet constructions', *Punishment and Society: An International Journal of Penology*, 7(4): 397–417. Reprinted by permission of Sage Publications.

Meylakhs, P. (2004) 'The discourse of the press and the press of discourse', *Journal of Sociology and Social Anthropology*, 4 (28) vii: 135–51.

Part III

Best, J. (1990) *Threatened Children: Rhetoric and Concern about Child Victims*, Chapter 2, pp. 22–41. Copyright 1990 by University of Chicago Press via the Copyright Clearance Center.

Williams, P. and Dickinson, L. (1993) Fear of crime: read all about it? *British Journal of Criminology*, 33(1): 33–56. Reprinted by permission of Oxford University Press.

Kepplinger, H.M. and Habermeier, J.H. (1995) 'The impact of key events upon the presentation of reality', *European Journal of Communication*, 10(3): 371–90. Copyright Sage Publications, 1995, reproduced by permission of Sage Publications Ltd.

Altheide, D.L. (2002) *Creating Fear: News and the Construction of Crisis*, Chapter 8, pp. 175–83. Reprinted by permission of Transaction Publishers.

Part IV

Watney, S. (1988) 'AIDS, "moral panic" theory and homophobia', pp. 52–64 in P. Aggelton and H. Homans (eds) *Social Aspects of AIDS*. London: Falmer Press. Reproduced from 'Practices of Freedom: Selected Writings on HIV/AIDS', by Simon Watney, Rivers Oram Press, London, 1994, and Duke University Press, Durham, NC, 1994.

McRobbie, A. and Thornton, S.L. (1995) 'Re-thinking "moral panic" for multi-mediated social worlds', *British Journal of Sociology*, 46(4): 559–74. Reprinted by permission of Blackwell Publishing.

de Young, M. (1998) 'Another look at moral panics: the case of satanic day care centers', *Deviant Behavior*, 19(3): 257–78. Reprinted by permission of Taylor & Francis Group, http://taylorandfrancis.com

Ungar, S. (2001) 'Moral panic versus the risk society: the implications of the changing sites of social anxiety', *British Journal of Sociology* 52(2): 271–91. Reprinted by permission of Blackwell Publishing.

Hier, S. P. (2003) 'Risk and panic in late modernity: implications of the converging sites of social anxiety', *British Journal of Sociology*, 54(1): 3–20. Reprinted by permission of Blackwell Publishing.

INTRODUCTION:
MORE QUESTIONS THAN ANSWERS
Chas Critcher (2005)

The purpose of this reader is to make more widely and readily available a selection of significant extracts on moral panics, including those without which I could not have written *Moral Panics and the Media* (2003). In adopting a review format which would simultaneously provide an entry point for those new to the area and a refresher course for those already familiar with it, I eventually settled on the Frequently Answered Questions Format. Encountered on websites, FAQs often seem to miss what I need to know while covering what I already know or have no interest in knowing. I can only hope this is not true of my own efforts. The key questions are listed below, after which follow my attempts to answer them. An outline of the book's contents is provided at the end of the introduction.

1. What exactly is a moral panic?
2. Why study moral panics at all?
3. What are moral panics about?
4. Are some issues more likely to become moral panics than others?
5. Who or what starts and ends moral panics?
6. How much do moral panics vary historically and geographically?
7. When is a moral panic not a moral panic?
8. What is the current status of moral panics in social science?

1. What Exactly is a Moral Panic?

Not all definitions are helpful. Here is one for moral panic from a (generally excellent) dictionary of media and cultural studies. 'Individuals and social groups can by their very activities emerge as a basis for outrage expressed by influential members of society who perceive these activities as seriously subverting the mores and interests of the dominant culture' (Watson and Hill 2003: 196). The same source tells us that 'mores' are 'those social rules concerning acceptable behaviour that is considered wrong to break' (2003: 196). We have here a description of what is happening which does not clarify the status of the term 'moral panic'.

Moral panic is a concept, an abstraction which enables us to trace similarities between otherwise apparently very different phenomena. It specifies the common characteristics of those social problems which suddenly emerge, cause consternation among powerful institutions and seem to require exceptional remedies. Cohen's massively influential version ([1972] 2002) concentrates on the processes a moral panic passes through as the threat emerges, is caricatured and disseminated by the mass media, seized upon by moralists, dissected by experts and eventually resolved through the adoption of special measures. The construction of a folk devil by the media appears crucial. In Goode and Ben-Yehuda's (1994) version, moral panics can be recognized because they exhibit five carefully defined criteria or attributes. Four of these are concern, hostility, consensus, and volatility but it is disproportionality which is the key. Moral panics are by definition disproportionate reactions to perceived threats.

Such definitions seek to describe rather than explain moral panics. As Erich Goode has emphasized, moral panic should be appreciated as a concept not a theory:

> There is no moral panics 'theory'. The moral panic is a sociological phenomenon, an analytical concept much like stratification, interaction, deviance and social movements. Examining the moral panic no more makes one the advocate of moral panics 'theory' than studying gender makes one the advocate of gender 'theory'. Among students of the moral panic, there are advocates of a diversity of 'theories'. And all sociological concepts are social constructs. The important thing is, do they have real-world referents? And do those referents manifest interesting and revealing patterns in social life? (Goode 2000: 551)

Moral panics can consequently be theorized from almost any established framework in sociology. Cohen's original approach was based on a symbolic interactionist theory of identity as the outcome of negotiations with others. The idea that labelling and punishing deviance contributes to social solidarity was being recognized within the theoretical framework of structural functionalism (Lauderdale 1976). A famous later study of mugging (Hall et al. 1978) used an explicitly Marxist theory to explain moral panics as forms of hegemony. Goode and Ben-Yehuda (1994) use several theoretical frameworks, including that of collective behaviour, to help explain the irrationality of moral panics. Many writers on child abuse adopt a feminist perspective (Kitzinger 2004), seeing the distortions of moral panics as helping to shore up male power. In short, a whole range of social scientists have been willing to insert the moral panic concept into their own theoretical perspectives.

When we say that this or that issue was or is a moral panic, we are saying it belongs in a distinct category of such problems where we expect to find specific attributes or processes – not necessarily each and every one but enough for the case to qualify. This judgement is not a neutral one; it is implicitly negative. It implies that the problem is being distorted and exaggerated, that it is being hyped up by the media and other interest groups, that unspeakable monsters are being manufactured and that the end result will be the adoption of measures out of all proportion to the actual threat. The moral panic classification does not imply rational appraisal, considered reaction or appropriate remedies. As the words connote, what we are contemplating is a state of panic where emotion rules over reason. It is, moreover, focussed on an issue about moral order. Where either reaction stops short of a panic or the problem is not integral to the moral order, then we do not have a moral panic. Campaigns about food safety, for example, are unlikely to be categorized as either moral or a panic.

2. Why Study Moral Panics at All?

There are at least four reasons for studying moral panics. First, moral panics are around us all the time. A lot depends, of course, exactly where and when you are. The reader will no doubt be able to nominate their own list of issues which seem to have followed the moral panic trajectory. As I first drafted this, in the middle of pre-election fever in Britain in March 2005, the list of such issues was substantial – binge drinkers and cannabis smokers; gypsies and immigrants; asylum seekers and terrorists – all against a background of some moral panics which were ongoing, such as paedophilia, and some which had never quite taken off, such as gun culture. If there is a better guide than the moral panic concept to what links all these issues together, then it has yet to be discovered.

A second reason for studying moral panics is that they have assumed increasing political importance, at least in Britain. Most of the issues I have just listed were produced early in 2005 by Conservative newspapers and politicians in an unsuccessful effort to prevent the Labour Party from being elected for a third consecutive term. According to the Conservative Party's Australian election strategist, they were 'dog whistle' issues, so called because they call forth an automatic response from the electorate. Cultivating prejudice has become a political ploy. There is nothing very new about this but the implications are greater in a political environment where basic economic and political principles divide the main political parties less and less. In such a context, issues about the moral state of the nation might become a way for the political right to become distinctive, especially if it feels (with some justification) that other parties have largely stolen its economic polices. A moral panic has yet in Britain to bring a government down but they can make its life very uncomfortable.

This relates to the third reason for studying moral panics: they reveal a lot about the workings of power, specifically who has the capacity to define a social problem and prescribe appropriate action. Here we can identify those groups who potentially have this power, especially when they form alliances with each other:

- the press and broadcasting
- pressure groups and claims makers
- politicians and government
- police and law enforcement agencies
- public opinion.

These are the five powerful Ps of moral panics. If they all pull together on an issue, their power is truly awesome. Opposition will be swept aside in the urge to action, generally a law authorizing draconian new powers to deal with the problem.

Yet this does not always happen every time a new social problem or folk devil is identified. If it did, then democratic states would resemble totalitarian ones, so many freedoms would have had to be forsaken in order to label and capture whoever has been identified as the enemy. There is always potential conflict over the precise definition of the issue and the remedial action required to deal with it. There are also always potential conflicts of interest between significant groupings around a moral panic. The press, for example, is always looking for flaws in the government of the day.

Such difficulties were very evident in Britain in the first three months of 2005 over two issues: binge drinking and terrorism. Binge drinking refers to the habit of otherwise respectable 16–25-year-olds getting very drunk, very fast, each weekend producing spectacle and nuisance in city centres. The issue exhibited two contradictions. The first was gender. Male binge drinkers were easy to vilify. Young men in a drunken state can easily be presented as potentially violent and thus a threat to public order. The same could not be said of young women. The alleged novelty of binge drinking was precisely that young women were now involved, getting drunk quickly by consuming 'alcopops' (spirits mixed into soft drinks). However, it could not be alleged that drunken young women were likely to get into fights with each other or nightclub bouncers, as young men might. Another suggestion, that binge drinking might make women sexually vulnerable, seemed no more credible. In fact, all that can be said against binge drinking by young women was that it was, well, unladylike.

The second contradiction around binge drinking emerged between a government committed to deregulating leisure and a police force convinced that alcohol causes disorder. The furore over binge drinking occurred at precisely the moment when the government announced its intention of liberalising licensing hours so that some pubs and bars would be able to stay open 24 hours. The grounds for this, like similar moves over casinos, were that governments had no right to regulate commercial leisure unless some demonstrable harm could be shown. The police welcomed the abolition of 'chucking out time' when all licensed premises shut at the same time, creating potential for disorder. Yet they had reservations because extended drinking hours could bring a demonstrable harm: more trouble on the city streets. Thus on this issue the law creators did not share exactly the same agenda as the law enforcers. This was one of several reasons why binge drinking could not take off as a fully-fledged moral panic.

In the case of terrorism, the conflict was between the government and the legal establishment, notable the judiciary, over the appropriateness of the laws aimed at terrorists. The government had originally assumed powers of indefinite detention without trial on the word of the Home Secretary, which eventually the Law Lords declared to be in breach of the Human Rights Act. The government then proposed to substitute what was effectively house arrest for imprisonment, again sanctioned by the Home Secretary. The objections came from senior members of the judiciary, still prominent in the half-reformed House of Lords. They repeatedly sent back the new law on the grounds that judges, not politicians, should make such decisions. Eventually a compromise was reached but the government had been forced into several concessions. The threat of terrorism was accepted by all but the differences emerged over how far this threat could justify suspending the established principles of legal procedure.

The threat of terrorism is unlikely to fade away but that from binge drinking (in fact, a rerun of a minor previous panic in 1997–98 over 'alcopops') will eventually do so. Indeed, immediately after the General Election, binge drinking was subsumed into a wider panic about 'yob culture'. The entirely predictable outcome was a proposed new law, the

Violent Crime Reduction Bill. Drunken brawls featured alongside possession of knives and guns as objects of increased powers for the police and courts. The specifics of each example do matter but so equally do the lessons to be deduced from them. Here it is that a consensus on the definition of a social problem and the remedies appropriate to it does not emerge automatically; it has to be achieved. For every moral panic where that achievement can be smoothly managed, there are two or three where its passage is very rough indeed.

A fourth and final reason for studying moral panics is that they require us to face up to some awkward questions about truth in relation to social problems. In sociology this is an unfashionable enterprise. Extreme forms of constructionism and postmodernism subscribe to the idea that there is no knowable social reality outside constructions or representations. Anything, even or especially a statistic, is a social construction not a fact, so can only be assessed as a representation. Like much postmodernist thought, this takes an old idea (that reality is socially constructed), gives it a new twist (the advent of a multi-mediated world where we constantly encounter representations) and then inflates it so grandly that everything else is obscured (we have to give up on explaining society).

An example may illustrate. A sharp awareness about paedophilia is by now common to most Anglophone and Western European nations. If it is to be judged a moral panic, then, according to Goode and Ben-Yehuda's criteria, it will show signs of disproportionality. There will be an exaggeration and distortion of the actual incidence of the problem, with dramatic and distressing cases treated as if they were typical of a wider problem.

To test this out, we need to know more about the actual rates of sexual abuse of children. Unfortunately, like a lot of sexual violence, much of this remains unknown. This is not because, as some versions of postmodernism/constructionism would opine, that it is unknowable. It is because much, perhaps most, sexual abuse of children goes unreported and undetected. Random surveys of adults asked if they experienced such abuse as children founder on the problem of defining abuse precisely and the unreliability or even denial of adult recollections.

So we do not know how much 'real' abuse of children there is. (And, amazingly, those who fund British social science research have apparently no interest in finding out.) As a result, we cannot judge if the concern over paedophilia is disproportionate or not. However, we do know something about an alternative measure to make judgement of a sort. All child murders are reported. As recent appalling British cases have demonstrated, some accidental deaths have been wrongly classified as murders. It may equally be that some murders are reported as accidental. But the level of official investigation into the death of a child is such that statistics should normally be reasonably reliable. We cannot know how many children are sexually abused but we can know how many children are murdered, who murders them and whether it is sexually motivated (Pritchard and Stroud 1999). Thus, from statistics for England and Wales, Scottish figures being recorded separately, we 'know' that

- the number of child murders is small and declining;
- children most at risk are under one year of age;
- victims are most likely to be murdered by their mother or father;
- the numbers murdered by strangers for sexual motives is tiny.

That by no means resolves the issue of disproportionality over paedophilia. Most paedophile attacks do not result in murder, so we still have no adequate measure of those. We have established that the rape and murder of a child is extremely rare but that does not mean that we should do nothing to prevent it. Nevertheless, if a group or an individual says or implies that such murders are frequent or on the increase, we know that to be a misrepresentation of the 'truth' about paedophile murders. Those who feel unable to use such terms will have to remain silent. (For an example of this kind of approach applied to newspaper coverage of all British homicides, see Peelo et al. 2004, and to TV coverage of US school shootings, see Killingbeck 2001.)

3. What Are Moral Panics About?

Moral panics are ostensibly about new forms of troubling behaviour which society appears unable to control. The troubling behaviour may stem from an identifiable group (whether long-standing or incoming) or be associated with a particular object (anything from the internet to a drug in powder or tablet form). Moral panics then are a reaction to changes: bad things are happening which didn't used to.

There are four ways of thinking about the relationships between moral panics and social changes, what Goode and Ben Yehuda (1994) posed as questions about the target, timing and content of moral panics. The first is that there is a reasonably direct and transparent relationship between the cause of the panic and its focus. As an example, a moral panic about an illegal drug, say, crack or ecstasy, is a direct response to a genuinely new development, the rise of drug taking among young people.

The second view is that the focus of moral panics might have a much more tenuous relationship with their sources. In this version the underlying dynamics of moral panics are to be found in generalized feelings about the rapid and uncontrolled nature of social change characteristic of late modern societies. The old certainties of life – work, neighbourhood, family life – crumble away. Individuals and groups are disoriented and experience social anxiety. In our example, drug taking is seen as a general symptom of the moral decline of society most obvious among young people. Such resentment can be focussed on an outgroup or activity which has little or nothing to do with the troubling changes. Social security 'scroungers' or 'illegal' immigrants are blamed for the general experience of decline. This is a familiar psychological process in which anxieties are 'displaced' from their often complex original sources and projected onto misleadingly simple targets. Those who are anxious or insecure prove ready recruits to campaigns which promise to restore order and security.

In the third version of the relationship between a moral panic and social change, the object of the panic is selected because it appears to challenge some of the central values of mainstream society. Simon Watney, in this volume, for example, argues that the advent of AIDS promoted attacks upon homosexuality which were in effect attempts to preserve the core values it seemed to subvert: heterosexuality and the family unit. Pursuing our example of drug taking, the value being attacked here is that of hedonism, the pursuit of extreme pleasure for its own sake. The value defended is the traditional view of pleasure as something to be enjoyed in moderation and only as a reward for hard work.

Perhaps the most transparent example of this 'value inversion' is the case of gypsies, otherwise known as Romanis or travelling people. Wherever they are found, they provoke hostility at all levels of society. This cannot be because they constitute a real threat to the moral order; at most they may be a nuisance, by definition a temporary one. The hostility seems much more related to their way of life as inverting mainstream values. The objections to gypsies reveal these cherished values (see Table 1.1).

It is easy to see how gypsies represent what anthropologist Mary Douglas (cited in Lupton 1999a: 43) defines as 'pollution' which in all societies requires cleansing work. They defile the social environment, so must be vilified and cast out. This requires, among other ploys, reducing quite varied communities to one single homogeneous group and then exaggerating the differences between 'them' and 'us' (Acton 1994; Campbell and Clark 2000). Social solidarity is increased by the pursuit of an illusory enemy.

A fourth position stresses the complexity of the relationships between the moral panic and its social context. de Young (2004), for example, argues

Table 1.1 Gypsies as outsiders

Gypsies	Mainstream society
mobile: 'out of place'	static: 'in place'
not working, evading tax, claiming welfare benefits	working, paying tax, not claiming benefits
dirty	clean
child-neglecting	child-caring
thieving	honest
aggressive	polite
on the margin	in the centre

that the ritual abuse day care panic in the USA in the early 1980s did reflect some real tensions around child care and the changing role of women but it distorted them into an illusory problem. This was partly down to the way issues were culturally mediated by what she calls master symbols. 'As the object of the moral panic, day care ritual abuse stood for the deep and unsettling concerns in 1980s America signified by the master symbols of that decade: the vulnerable child, the menacing devil, and the psychological trauma model' (de Young 2004: 192). So the panic was shaped by both actual social change and by prevailing cultural myths. Its timing, target and content were thus explicable.

Whatever the relationship between a particular moral panic and its social context, all moral panics are ultimately about reconfirming moral values. Sometimes it doesn't seem to matter who has been defined as the outgroup. Drug-takers, sex offenders or immigrants are very different targets of hostility but each may ultimately serve the same function for the social order. Defining, labelling and punishing their unacceptable behaviour confirm who we are, what we believe in or stand for and where we draw the boundary around our community. The need for such confirmation increases whenever established moral certainties no longer hold:

> When a society's moral boundaries are sharp, clear, and secure, and the central norms and values are strongly held by nearly everyone, moral panics rarely grip its members – nor do they need to. However, when the moral boundaries are fuzzy and shifting and often seem to be contested, moral panics are far more likely to seize the members of society. (Goode and Ben-Yehuda 1994: 52)

The suggestion is that the more a society is unsettled about its core moral values, the more we can expect to find moral panics as a means of restoring moral certainty. For this to work effectively, the enemy must be cast in terms which brook no ambiguity. Evil is the most effective category for this role (Burns and Crawford 1999).

4. Are Some Issues More Likely to Become Moral Panics than Others?

As has been noted, judgements about whether an issue has become a moral panic are sometimes made too slickly:

> the identification of a moral panic can be no more than the start of an analysis, not its conclusion ... the moral panic idea has tended to function as something of a taxonomy: once the criteria for a moral panic are checked off, central questions of how constituencies are mobilized for and against or why moral entrepreneurs are successful or unsuccessful in generating a panic are often left undeveloped. (Adam 2003: 260)

Clearly, we need to make more complex assessments. This is not primarily a matter of deciding whether an issue was or was not a moral panic. The degree to which an example deviates from the moral panic ideal type may be useful to establish but even more so is how and why it differs. This is when the ideal type is most productive in enabling us to specify the missing dimension, thwarted trajectory or strategic intervention which changes the course of the moral panic.

Accumulating evidence from a range of case studies, such as those represented in Part II of this volume, has enabled us to specify which conditions are most crucial to the outcome of a potential moral panic. On that basis we can outline which types of issues are more, and which less, likely to become moral panics.

A moral panic is more likely to proceed where there is present:

- a convincing portrait of a new threat with a highly connotative label;
- unanimity among the media about the seriousness of the problem and appropriate remedies;
- an effective alliance among at least two of the five Ps (politicians and government, pressure groups and claims makers, police and judiciary, press and broadcasting, public and audiences);
- claims makers who become accredited in the media as experts;
- consensus among elites about the seriousness of the problem and appropriate remedies;
- the availability of attainable remedies which can be presented as effective.

These conditions seem to be most likely to be present in such issues as: child abuse, especially by strangers (paedophilia); the presence of alien groups who do not 'belong' in the host society (gypsies, asylum seekers); or street crime threatening innocent victims anywhere at any time (mugging).

Conversely, a moral panic is most likely to be derailed by one or any combination of the following five factors:

- a failure to establish an issue as sufficiently new or threatening to provoke the formulation of a new label or the resuscitation of an old one;
- a lack of media unanimity in accepting the legitimacy of the label and its connotations;
- an attempt to brand as folk devils groups whose social status precludes such vilification;
- opposition to the moral panic from an alliance of effectively organized pressure groups (counter-claims makers);
- divisions among elite groups over the seriousness of the problem or its causes and remedies when its seriousness is agreed;
- the absence of available and effective remedies.

These negative conditions seem most likely in the following types of issues: AIDS and other sexually transmitted diseases because their medicalization cedes ground to experts and/or the victims resist demonization; gun culture and related problems such as crack cocaine which can be ghettoized in black communities and thus do not normally pose a threat to white communities; road rage, binge drinking and other outbursts by ordinary citizens because the perpetrators cannot be made into folk devils.

To assess a particular issue as more or less likely to generate a moral panic by no means guarantees this outcome. This is because moral panics are unpredictable by nature. Often it is only in retrospect that their underlying dynamic becomes clear. Even then, it is difficult to extract consistent patterns from what often seem to be the unique characteristics of each moral panic. Nowhere is this more evident than in the problem of how moral panics start or end.

5. Who or What Starts and Ends Moral Panics?

A moral panic might start with the emergence of a genuinely new condition, such as a disease or media technology. There may well be a key event, usually of a tragic nature, which serves to quicken media interest. But sometimes this occurs well into the panic rather than at the beginning. In theory, any one or combination of significant actors (the five Ps) can instigate a moral panic. It can start inside the state apparatus or outside it. Pressure groups can activate or be activated by press interest. Public opinion can be central or peripheral. Some potential moral panics never quite get started; they bubble beneath the surface. For some time child pornography on the Internet has been in this category. In that instance, the reason may be the lack of any simple solution to the problem.

In any individual case factors precipitating moral panic are often combined in a unique way. This is much less true of the ends of moral panics. The most frequent denouement remains a significant change in the law or its application. Since that has often been the objective of the panic, agitation falls away once it has been achieved. Less important, though still of some significance, is that the media will tire of a specific issue unless there is a new story or fresh angle. Occasionally the moral panic ends because the condition which sparked it off goes away or is revealed to have been an illusion.

Serial moral panics start and end more than once. Child abuse, drugs and crime all seem to have serial status in many developed societies across the world. All it takes is a new kind of abuse, type of drug or form of violent crime, as symbolized by a key event, claimed by a law enforcement agency or revealed by a commissioned report. The cycle is played out all over again until there is introduced a new law, reform of an existing one or change in the activities of enforcement agencies. Then the topic is dropped – until the next time.

The effects of moral panics vary enormously, much as Cohen originally noted. They may involve minor adjustments of law enforcement, entirely new laws or new types of law which breach long-standing constitutional principles. Whatever their legal status, such reforms may be used effectively against the folk devils or they may serve a mainly symbolic purpose. Moral panics also have a discursive legacy. They establish the terms in which this issue has to be debated now and for the foreseeable future. Recurrent episodes will be mapped onto the established discursive framework often connoted by a phrase: 'child abuse' or the 'war on drugs'. It becomes extremely difficult to shift the terms of the immediate and subsequent debates.

In addition to individual and serial moral panics, we need to consider the effects of an apparently endless succession of moral panics. The impression is created that the key moral values of society, if not those of civilization itself, are under attack from all sides. Since evil is everywhere, we must be eternally vigilant and cede to the authorities the additional powers they need to deal with these threats. Moral panics invite us to endorse authoritarian responses to our primeval fears. This is, it should be insisted, a discourse originating and rooted in the public sphere. In their private lives, citizens are unlikely to encounter any of these villains. They are potential or symbolic threats rather than actual or material ones. But fear and anxiety need not be rational or proportionate to be prevalent.

This idea, that moral panics feed off public anxiety which then increases as moral panics proliferate, is attractive but difficult to verify. We can analyse and measure the degree of fear and anxiety in the mass media and other parts of the public sphere. But how far these are shared by the public at large is difficult to determine. It is analogous to the problem about risk consciousness. It is easy to trace discourses about risk in the public sphere where they seem to be pervasive. It is much harder to show that in their daily lives people do constantly worry about risks to the environment at large or to their own futures or identities.

It seems at least plausible that most of us on a day-to-day basis simply block out environmental or existential dilemmas. We have our own pre-occupations and relate only indirectly to what interests and motivates journalists or politicians. If you take the view, as I do, that moral panics do not require public support to be successful, then it does not matter very much just how interested the public really are. Yet even that view cannot sidestep the distinct possibility that the long-term cumulative effect of a constant stream of moral panics is to invite fear of evil as a reflex response to any group or activity regarded as deviant. If moral panics do make us more fearful and anxious, then we become more receptive to the next folk devil to be paraded as the embodiment of evil. In such circumstances we are unlikely to recognize that, as US President Roosevelt once famously said, the only thing we have to fear is fear itself.

6. How Much Do Moral Panics Vary Historically and Geographically?

A study of crime and drugs policy in the Netherlands argued that problems like deciding how moral panics start and end can only be resolved by 'shifting the analysis of moral panics towards comparative research' (Baerveldt et al. 1998: 43). They suggest comparing minor with major moral panics or successful with failed ones. Their own study is also a contribution to a different kind of comparison, across nations. The moral panic concept also seems to have registered in France (Bonnet 2004). Wood (1999) has argued that New Zealand provides a very different political context for moral panics from Britain, despite their close cultural affinity. As yet, we do not have evidence from enough parts of the globe or periods of history to judge whether a propensity to moral panics is a universal feature of human societies.

We can perhaps hazard two hypotheses. One is that moral panics seem to be an especially effective way to confirm the core values or normative boundaries of society. That being so, then any society anywhere at any time experiencing social strain might well produce a moral panic: medieval Europe (Goode and Ben-Yehuda 1994), seventeenth-century Massachusetts (Erikson 1966), eighteenth-century England (Pearson 1983). These three examples occurred in societies without mass media. Instead the Church monopolized the public sphere, acting simultaneously as claims maker, moral entrepreneur, legislator, prosecutor and executioner. This should qualify but not invalidate our second hypothesis, that moral panics seem to flourish most in those societies where the public sphere and civil society are most developed, with an elaborate state apparatus, elected government, formally free press and institutionalized pressure groups.

These are not the conditions of predemocratic societies or dictatorships. Moral panics are unlikely in such societies. There will be moral crusades against perceived symbolic threats but these will be stage-managed to remain within the control of the state apparatus. Moral panics are not so predictable. They may for a time be steered but they cannot be directed. They depend upon an arena for open contest over social problem definition which they seek to dominate. That is why when moral panics do succeed – over paedophilia, immigrants or terrorists, for example – then it feels a bit like living under a dictatorship because there is only one 'party line' permissible. In that sense, moral panics are totalitarian products of democratic systems.

We can never be sure of any of this because democracies produce both moral panics and sociologists. There may be other kinds of societies with moral panics but, unless there are social scientists to document them, they remain unknown to us. Interestingly, as Eastern Europe emerges from years of Soviet domination, it seems to be engendering both moral panics and critical analysts (Kitzinger 2000; Meylakhs this volume).

In an increasingly globalized world, moral panics in different countries cannot remain independent of each other. Some panics may even be exported from one country to another. The USA is thought to play a pivotal role here (Richardson 1997; Victor 1998). It exports its moral panics along with other kinds of cultural products. It is also monitored by other countries as prefiguring the way their own society is developing. This diffusion argument is complex and there is evidence to support it. But there are substantial objections to the diffusion thesis (Atmore 1997).

First, moral panics may occur in different countries at around the same time because the same problem is presenting itself in each society. AIDS and recreational drugs are two obvious examples. Second, many societies, especially in Western Europe, do not copy American reaction, their own being much less punitive and more rehabilitative. This is the case for both AIDS and recreational drugs. Adam (2003) has argued that the conservative political culture of the USA generally shapes attitudes towards homosexuality. Third, the nature of the public sphere – its political, judicial and media system – is likely to be different in each country. Indeed, the USA is less a model for other countries than an example to be avoided, especially when it comes to the influence of religious fundamentalism and credulousness about outrageous claims of all kinds. Fourth, other societies panic about things which Americans largely do not, while Americans panic about things which other societies do not. Other societies are much more concerned about new media technologies or the availability of guns, neither of which apparently trouble many Americans. By contrast, the American obsession with conspiracies to abduct, abuse and even murder children is unmatched in any other country, as is their denial that gun ownership is a dangerous habit.

This is not to say that the USA will never be able to export its moral panics, only that there are many points of resistance to this happening. The big exception is paedophilia where without doubt America did export the label, the diagnosis and the remedy, all in one package. Other societies may have been vulnerable because they had for too long been in a state of denial about the sexual abuse of children, so had no indigenous definitions or procedures as alternatives to the American model.

There is much work to do in comparing moral panics across time and space to establish their necessary preconditions, universal characteristics and local variations. It might prove instructive to compare panics with related themes but in different times and places. For example, Sutherland's classic study of a panic producing sexual psychopath laws in the USA during the late 1930s and the 1940s might be compared with Kohn's (2001) more accessible account of a panic about white girls, oriental or black men and cocaine in Britain of the 1920s. There would seem to be enough issues which look like moral panics in different times and places to suggest that the model is not merely relevant to twenty-first-century democracies. Such societies generate moral panic entrepreneurs and moral panic debunkers. We cannot, however, be sure that analysts are entirely disinterested in their decisions about what counts as a moral panic.

7. When Is a Moral Panic Not a Moral Panic?

Moral panic is inherently a label of disapproval. This raises the question of whether there are moral panics which can be supported. Goode and Ben Yehuda (1994: 50–1) argue that moral panic analysis can be applied just as well to liberal as conservative causes; it is ideologically agnostic. Campaigns over pollution, smoking or pornography might turn out to be moral panics if they fail the crucial tests. This ignores the fact that in practice moral panics are mounted by conservative forces as a reaction to social change and that their ultimate function is to shore up the existing moral order. Usually moral panics are conservative in their concerns and functions. Are all moral panics wrong or only those which offend liberal sensibilities? Does the collective social scientific view alter, if the underlying problem and its remedies are genuine?

Two tests cases come to mind: child abuse and gun control. On the whole, one might accept preventing child abuse and controlling gun use as civilized aims. One might as a consequence be prepared to turn a blind eye to some doubtful practices by campaigners, if the end justifies the means. What happens, then, when moral panic analysts address these two issues?

In the case of child abuse the dilemma has been most acutely felt and most carefully resolved by feminist writers (e.g. Atmore 1999; Kitzinger 2004). Their position is clear. For a long time feminists have campaigned for more attention to be paid to all forms of male sexual violence, whether against women or children. Reaction to key events and organized campaigns have over the past 20 years raised awareness about abuse and some limited legal reforms have been secured. All this has been welcomed but the price has been high: a systematic misrepresentation of who the main abusers are. The focus on 'stranger danger' directs attention away from the home as the most likely location of abuse and the male relative as the most likely perpetrator. Hence it is perfectly consistent to appreciate the small gains made while using moral panic as one way to denounce the distorted way the issue has been represented.

No such consistent resolution of the dilemma is available in the case of gun control. It would seem hypothetically possible for a moral panic to produce legislation to control gun use and ownership. What, then, would the moral panic analyst have to say? We do not have to speculate, for something very like this has already happened in Australia.

In April 1996 in the Australian state of Tasmania Michael Bryant shot dead 35 people and wounded 18 others in an apparently random attack. This proved to be the turning point in a long-running campaign for national gun control. Within months the federal government had introduced laws which, among other measures, banned all ownership of semi-automatic weapons and required ownership of all other guns to be registered. From the key event embodying a problematic condition through to the measures resorted to, it bears a superficial resemblance to a moral panic.

This is more or less confirmed in an account written by an academic prominent in the campaign for gun control.

> My main interest in writing the book was to capture the nature of the public discourse on gun control that the Port Arthur killings unleashed and which framed the way that the issue came to be defined by ordinary people throughout the country and by the politicians who were now forced to act. (Chapman 1998: ix)

His book is a manual for, depending on how you look at it, running an effective campaign against the forces of conservatism or setting out to create a moral panic.

Chapman is quite open about the need to exploit a highly emotive event for political ends. 'The question is how can advocates exploit the huge public and political interest these disasters generate when they occur?' (Chapman 1998: 7). Years had been spent arguing with evasive politicians to no avail. Here was an opportunity not to be missed. It could not be allowed to matter that the event itself was wholly untypical of the actual gun problem. The death toll was exceptional, equivalent to the annual average number of homicides in the state of Tasmania or half the figure for Australia as a whole. The most frequent use of the gun to kill in Australia was in fact for suicide with the next most frequent for domestic homicide. Shooting strangers, as Bryant did, was wholly untypical. No matter; the chance could not be missed.

Chapman and others in the gun control lobby exploited the interest of the mass media in the event and the issue; asserted claims about gun usage and cited expert studies from across the world; directly pressurized the newly elected government and opposition parties to sign up for gun control legislation. Generally, they behaved like moral entrepreneurs, successfully advocating gun control laws as 'sensible, easily understood and above all the course that any decent society committed to public safety should adopt' (Chapman 1998: 5).

Was this, then, a moral panic and, if so, does it demonstrate that there can after all be moral panics for good causes? If we follow the model of Goode and Ben-Yehuda (see *Reading 4*), then most of the five requirements seem to be met. The Bryant shootings prompted widespread *concern*. *Consensus* about the gun problem was eventually achieved across political parties, among media commentators and in public opinion about the problem of unregulated gun ownership, despite organized opposition from the gun lobby. There was *hostility* though not, as Goode and Ben-Yehuda assume, towards a folk devil but rather towards an object, the gun, especially semi-automatic weapons. The issue was *volatile* since the agitation was quite short-lived though based on years of preparatory work. *Disproportionality* is difficult to assess. As an incident, Port Arthur was as exceptional as the Dunblane mass murder in Scotland just one month before. The actual use of guns was of an altogether different kind. The 560 Australian deaths a year in which guns were implicated might have justified intervention; it all depends on what you compare the figure with.

Cohen's model (see *Reading 2*) is also a rough kind of fit, with all the basic processes visible. A *newly recognized condition* of unregulated gun ownership did emerge as a threat to society. There was no human *folk devil* here; the object of attention was the gun. The killer Bryant was *stylized and stereotyped* but, if Chapman is to be believed, there was a genuine and rational debate in the media. *Moral leaders* – newspaper editors and columnists, politicians and clergy – did pronounce in favour of gun control. *Experts* turned out in practice to be the control lobby who had substantial research to back their case. *The means resorted to* was classic: a new law to control the problematic behaviour.

This looks and feels very much like a moral panic according to Cohen's model. If that is so, then we might have to conclude that this is a rare example of a moral panic justified by the impeccable motives of the claims makers to reduce deaths and injuries resulting from easy access to guns. (Stockwell in *Reading 9* outlines the moral panic about video nasties following the Port Arthur killings, which Campbell does not mention at all.) How could we possibly object to this situation?

> Australia is now a country where anyone now owning an illegal gun or being an unlicensed shooter faces the prospects of large fines and/or prison sentences; where near universal awareness exists that semi-automatic weapons are illegal; and where community support for gun control remains higher than practically any other single issue in public affairs. (Chapman 1998: 169)

And yet we may have missed something. In their opening two chapters Goode and Ben Yehuda distinguish between moral crusades and moral panics. In a crusade the campaigners are genuinely concerned about a real issue; in a moral panic the issue is symbolic of a wider sense of threat. Crusades are created by moral entrepreneurs or social movements while panics require an alliance of previously divergent groupings. Discussing the ambiguous case of the anti pornography movement (2004: 45–7), they suggest that it is a moral crusade if campaigners are genuinely concerned about pornography and they accurately represent its effects; but if their interest is politically opportunistic and they misrepresent the known facts, then it is a moral panic.

Further distinctions emanate from the specification of what in practice disproportionality means: exaggerating figures, fabricating statistics, ignoring other equally harmful conditions and misrepresenting historical trends. On all these grounds, the gun control campaign would be absolved from mounting a moral panic but the judgement is a fine one. What seems to be happening here is that a scale of rationality and integrity (are these people logical and well intentioned?) has been substituted for a political judgement (is this a conservative or liberal cause?). If we do stress exaggeration and distortion, stereotyping and sensationalizing as the ultimate distinguishing characteristics of a moral panic, then the Australian gun control campaign does not qualify.

In the USA the construction of – and inaction over – mass shootings have been quite different, even for the 1999 Columbine school massacre (Burns and Crawford 1999; Springhall 1999; Killingbeck 2001). Then there was no moral panic. It almost might have been better for there to have been one. The same may apply to gun crime in Britain (Bennett and Holloway 2004; McGlagan 2005). Perhaps Cohen's (2002: xxxiii) mischievous suggestion that he wants more moral panics but about different issues is accurate. It all depends on whether it matters not just whether your arguments prevail but how.

Moral panic analyst Philip Jenkins found himself in a similar quandary when he wrote a book about the dangers of child pornography on the Internet:

> Having spent a decade arguing that various social menaces were vastly overblown – that serial killers did not lurk behind every tree, nor paedophile priests in every rectory – I now find myself in the disconcerting position of seeking to raise public concern about a quite authentic problem that has been neglected. (Jenkins 2001: 9)

He does not, perhaps wisely, tell us if he would approve of a moral panic on the subject. His careful concluding discussion of appropriate measures would absolve him on Goode and Ben-Yehuda's criteria. Yet the irony is that action on many social issues is more likely to happen when there is a notoriously unrepresentative case or an atmosphere of panic. It is tempting for dedicated campaigners to seize the opportunity. They might wish to prevail through reason but emotion is often a more powerful motivator for those with the power to change things.

8. What Is the Current Status of Moral Panics in Social Science?

The study of moral panics has always been peripheral in sociology as a whole. It belongs somewhere on the edge of the sociological universe: in the impenetrable mountains of cultural and media studies, where the wandering traveller will be starved of oxygen; or near the clinging swamp of criminology ready to suck down its next unwary victim. Moral panic analysis is also ostensibly stuck in a time warp. It belongs to the late 1960s and early 1970s, when there were lots of British youth subcultures to fuss about, or at the very latest to the American drug scares of the 1980s.

With the admittedly influential exception of the mugging study (Hall et al. 1978), little work was published on moral panics in the 1970s in the UK. At this time the social constructionist approach to social problems was finding its clearest articulation in the USA (Spector and Kitsuse 1977). Substantial studies of specific moral panics remained comparatively rare until the 1980s.

Two issues stand out as reawakening interest in moral panic analysis in both countries: (physical) child abuse (Nelson 1984; Parton 1985) and AIDS (Weeks 1985; Altman 1986). Studies published in the 1990s about the 1980s drugs problem focussed on rather different forms – crack cocaine in the USA (Reeves and Campbell 1994) and softer recreational drugs in the UK (Parker et al. 1998). Both provided further impetus to moral panic analysis. Such work was consolidated in reviews (Goode and Ben-Yehuda 1994; Thompson 1998; Critcher 2003). Meanwhile, Cohen added new introductions to *Folk Devils and Moral Panics*, as the second edition appeared in 1987 and the third in 2002, 15 and 30 years respectively after original publication. In three decades moral panic analysis had left its mark on three areas of social scientific enquiry: social policy, criminology and media studies.

The most pressing current questions about moral panic analysis are how it connects with two comparatively new concepts: discourse in cultural studies and risk in sociology. In *Moral Panics and the Media* I used two accessible and reliable guides – Lupton on risk (1999a) and Mills on discourse (1997) – to explore how these two highly influential perspectives might relate to the concept of moral panics. The potential remains unrealized. Risk theory has struggled to release itself from its two original formulations: global environmental risk and individual biographical risk. Issues about food safety seem more easily encompassed within its scope than perceived threats to the moral order. In a collection edited by Lupton (1999a), for example, one essay on childhood and risk (Jackson and Scott

1999) is entirely compatible with a feminist version of the moral panic framework. Another, however, on fear of crime (Tulloch 1999) adopts a strongly poststructuralist position which denies moral panic any legitimacy.

As for discourse, even those who follow Foucault's fascination with discourses about deviance seem remarkably reluctant to apply them to contemporary examples. On the rare occasion they do (Ashenden 1996; Bell 2002), moral panic frameworks are ignored or derided. This is not perhaps so surprising. If you believe that power is dispersed and govern-mentality a strategy for self-management, you are hardly likely to appreciate an approach which emphasizes the centralization of power and governmentality as imposed from above. We may have to forsake Foucault and opt for analyses of discourse which carry less theoretical baggage, such as that within discursive psychology (Potter and Wetherell 1987). At any rate, it has become clear that risk theorists and discourse analysts are not going to come to moral panics so moral panics may have to go to them. The challenge awaits.

The Structure of This Book

The organization of this Reader mirrors my own habitual approach to moral panics. First, we must establish what basic moral panic models are, the task of extracts from classic statements in Part I. Second, we must test out the models against a wide range of cases. Part II provides extracts on eight potential moral panics. All come from the past 20 years but are otherwise varied in their geographical location and the issues they focus on. Third and as a result of examining cases, we should be able to identify some recurrent themes which merit separate examination. Part III has extracts on four themes emerging from the case studies: rhetoric, key events, media audiences and fear. Finally, at the end of all this activity, we should be in a position to re-evaluate the models. Part IV contains five influential critiques of moral panic models. Some question their detail; others advocate wholesale reform or even abandonment. Each Part has its own introduc-tion, outlining its focus, indicating the concerns of each extract and, where relevant, referring to other similar work.

Selecting the extracts was not easy. Even with help from anonymous reviewers, it became evident that there were quite different ideas about what the ideal 'Moral Panics Reader' should look like or contain. The final selection had to balance such considerations. Three-quarters of the extracts come from Britain or the USA. Not the same three-quarters are authored by men. Such biases of geography and gender are regrettable. To reflect them is to help perpetuate them. But the selection at least varies in the issues around which panics are constructed. Within each Part extracts are presented in date order which seemed the neatest way to index the development of the idea and application of moral panic models.

Moral panic analysis is currently undergoing a resurgence, as it is rediscovered by a new generation of scholars and students. I hope this volume will help stimulate their interest.

References

Acton, T. (1994) Modernisation, moral panics and gypsies, *Sociology Review*, 4(1): 24–8.

Adam, B.D. (2003) The Defense of Marriage Act and American exceptionalism: the 'gay marriage' panic in the United States, *Journal of the History of Sexuality*, 12(2): 259–76.

Altman, D. (1986) *AIDS and the New Puritanism*. London: Pluto Press.

Ashenden, S. (1996) Reflexive governance and child sexual abuse: liberal welfare rationality and the Cleveland Inquiry, *Economy and Society*, 25(1): 64–88.

Atmore, C. (1997) Rethinking moral panic and child abuse for 2000, in J. Besant and R. Hil (eds) *Youth, Crime and the Media*. Melbourne: National Clearing House for Youth Studies.

Atmore, C. (1999) Towards rethinking moral panic: child sexual abuse conflicts and social constructionist responses, in C. Bagley and K. Mallick (eds) *Child Sexual Abuse and Adult Offenders: New Theory and Research*. Aldershot: Ashgate Publishing.

Baerveldt, C., Bunkers, H. D., Winter, M. and Kooistra, J. (1998) Assessing a moral panic relating to crime and drugs policy in the Netherlands: towards a testable theory, *Crime, Law and Social Change*, 29: 31–47.

Bell, V. (2002) The vigilante parent and the paedophile: the *News of the World* campaign 2000 and the contemporary governmentality of child abuse, *Feminist Theory*, 3: 83–102.

Bennett, T. and Holloway, K. (2004) Gang membership, drugs and crime in the UK, *British Journal of Criminology*, 44(3): 305–23.

Bonnet, F. (2004) The aftermath of France's last moral panic and its sociology, *International Journal of Urban and Social Research*, 28(4): 948–51.

Burns, R. and Crawford, C. (1999) School shootings, the media and public fear: ingredients for a moral panic, *Crime, Law and Social Change*, 32: 147–68.

Campbell, C. and Clark, E. (2000) 'Gypsy invasion': a critical analysis of newspaper reaction to Czech and Slovak Romani asylum seekers in Britain, 1997, *Romani Studies*, 5(10): 23–47.

Chapman, S. (1998) *Over Our Dead Bodies: Port Arthur and Australia's Fight for Gun Control*. New South Wales: Pluto Press.

Cohen, S. (2002) Introduction to the third edition, *Folk Devils and Moral Panics*. London: Routledge.

Critcher, C. (2003) *Moral Panics and the Media*. Milton Keynes: Open University Press.

de Young, M. (2004) *The Day Care Ritual Abuse Moral Panic*. Jefferson, NC: McFarland and Company Inc.

Erikson, K. (1966) *Wayward Puritans: A Study in the Sociology of Deviance*. New York: John Wiley.

Goode, E. (2000) No need to panic? A bumper crop of books on moral panics, *Sociological Forum*, 15(3): 543–52.

Goode, E. and Ben-Yehuda, N. (1994) *Moral Panic: The Social Construction of Deviance*. Oxford: Blackwell.

Hall, S., Critcher, C., Jefferson, T., Clarke, J. and Roberts, B. (1978) *Policing The Crisis: Mugging, the State and Law and Order*. London: Macmillan.

Jackson, S. and Scott, S. (1999) Risk anxiety and the social construction of childhood, in D. Lupton (ed.) *Risk and Sociocultural Theory*. Cambridge: Cambridge University Press.

Jenkins, P. (2001) *Beyond Tolerance: Child Pornography on the Internet*. New York: New York University Press.

Killingbeck, D. (2001) The role of television news in the construction of school violence as a 'moral panic', *Journal of Criminal Justice and Popular Culture*, 8(3): 186–202.

Kitzinger, D. (2000) The theory of moral panic, *Replika*, 40: 23–48.

Kitzinger, J. (2004) *Framing Abuse*. London: Pluto Press.

Kohn, M. ([1992] 2001) *Dope Girls: The Birth of the British Underground*. London: Granta Books.

Lauderdale, P. (1976) Deviance and moral boundaries, *American Sociological Review*, 41: 660–76.

Lupton, D. (1999a) *Risk*. London: Routledge.

Lupton, D. (ed.) (1999b) *Risk and Sociocultural Theory*. Cambridge: Cambridge University Press.

McGlagan, G. (2005) *Guns and Gangs: Inside Black Gun Crime*. London: Allison and Busby.

Mills, S. (1997) *Discourse*. London: Routledge.

Nelson, B. (1984) *Making an Issue of Child Abuse*. Chicago: University of Chicago Press.

Parker, H., Aldridge, J. and Measham, F. (1998) *Illegal Leisure: The Normalization of Recreational Drug Use*. London: Routledge.

Parton, N. (1985) *The Politics of Child Abuse*. London: Macmillan.

Pearson, G. (1983) *Hooligan: A History of Respectable Fears*. London: Macmillan.

Peelo, M., Francis, B., Soothill, K., Pearson, J. and Ackerley, E. (2004) Newspaper reporting and the public construction of homicide, *British Journal of Criminology*, 44: 256–75.

Potter, J. and Wetherell, M. (1987) *Discourse and Social Psychology*. London: Sage.

Pritchard, C. and Stroud, J. (1999) Men and women who kill, and men who abuse children: a study of the psychiatric-child abuse interface, in C. Bagley and K. Mallick (eds) *Child Sexual Abuse and Adult Offenders: New Theory and Research*. Aldershot: Ashgate Publishing.

Reeves, J.L. and Campbell, R. (1994) *Cracked Coverage: Television News, the Anti-Cocaine Crusade and the Reagan legacy*. Durham, NC: Duke University Press.

Richardson, J. (1997) The social construction of satanism: understanding an international social problem, *Australian Journal of Social Issues*, 32(1): 61–85.

Spector, M. and Kitsuse, J.L. (1977) *Constructing Social Problems*. Menlo Park, CA: Cummings.

Springhall, J. (1999) Violent media, guns and moral panics: the Columbine High School massacre, *Pedagogica Historica*, 35(3): 621–41.

Sutherland, E. (1950) The diffusion of the sex psychopath laws, *American Journal of Sociology*, 56: 142–8.

Thompson, K. (1998) *Moral Panics*. London: Routledge.

Tulloch, J. (1999) Fear of crime and the media: sociocultural theories of risk, in D. Lupton (ed.) *Risk and Sociocultural Theory*. Cambridge: Cambridge University Press.

Victor, J.S. (1998) Moral panics and the social construction of deviant behavior: a theory and application to the case of ritual child abuse, *Sociological Perspectives*, 41(3): 541–65.

Watson, J. and Hill, A. (2003) *Dictionary of Media and Communication Studies*. London: Arnold.

Weeks, J. (1985) *Sexuality and its Discontents*. London: Routledge.

Wood, B. (1999) Panic, what panic? The moral deficit of new right politics in Aotearoa New Zealand, *New Zealand Sociology*, 14(1): 85–110.

MODELS

Overview

This part contains extracts from four books which in their own way and time helped to establish the moral panic framework.

Reading 2 is where it all began. Though it is now accepted that the first use of the term moral panic was by Jock Young (1971), its development belonged to Stan Cohen. First published in 1972, *Folk Devils and Moral Panics* must have the most often quoted opening paragraph in British sociology. But there was and is much more to Cohen's work which is captured in some of the extracts from Chapter 1 presented here.

Cohen inherited a transactional approach which stressed that deviance was not a property of acts or persons but a label constructed in the course of interaction. Central to this process is the role of the mass media, in modern society the single most important source of information about who or what is deviant. Whether actively involved themselves or merely reporting the activities of others, the media have tangible effects upon what we call a deviant group or behaviour. Less tangible, but by no means less important, are their effects on a generalized sense of anxiety, that things are slipping out of control. All of this is central to understanding the basic role of the media in society, much of which is taken up with identifying, naming and assessing deviance of all kinds. This obsession with deviance follows a pattern, rooted in collective behaviour. It has been revealed by disaster research, from which Cohen derives a structure (warning, impact, inventory and reaction) which will shape the book as a whole. Cohen remains from first to last interested in not only how reaction is constructed but also its impact on both labellers and labelled.

In *Reading 3*, Hall et al. (1978) take the model developed by Cohen and give it a radical twist. The media remain central but their role is now conceived in terms of ideological power. Moral panics are forms through which a political crisis and its resolution are signified. The media reproduce and thus validate the versions of primary definers drawn from authoritative institutions. Hall et al. admit that a framework dominated by the state and hegemony is not a natural habitat for the moral panic concept but they are prepared to transplant it. For them it has the function of revealing how the population is persuaded to allow the state to assume additional powers to deal with a problem it has itself constructed.

They see moral panics as having escalated and become politicized from the late 1960s, immediately after the Mods and Rockers panic analysed by Cohen. As the targets widen, the moral panic sequence is speeded up. Once, dramatic events or moral entrepreneurs provoked moral panics as a reaction; now, the state actively seeks out folk devils in order to validate a general crackdown to preserve law and order. This process they call a 'signification spiral': once set in motion, the moral panic will amplify itself.

They introduce two further concepts to validate their claim that moral panics have been appropriated to the cause of state hegemony. One is 'convergence' where otherwise unrelated groups of deviants are given labels to articulate a spurious similarity, so that student protestors become hooligans. The second is the idea of 'thresholds' of concern against which deviants are mapped. These start at the level of permissiveness and move through illegality to outright violence. At this last point, the state claims it is entitled to adopt extreme measures. One justification, as relevant now as then, is the threat of terrorism.

Reading 4 comes from the alternative to Cohen: Goode and Ben-Yehuda (1994). They reprise the emergence of a moral panic with the perceived threat of nominated folk devils, against whom decisive action needs to be taken. They then outline the five crucial elements which define any moral panic proper. There must first be a measurable level of 'concern' about the group and its behaviour. Second, 'hostility' is directed against identifiable folk devils. Third is the existence of sufficient 'consensus' among the relevant public, which may be national or local. Significant dissent, especially if organized, may contest the moral panic. Fourth is what they see as the most crucial characteristic of the moral panic: 'disproportionality'. The concern over the deviant group is in excess of what can be justified by any objective measure of the threat. This judgement can almost always be made, even if sometimes tentatively. It is the key judgement; without it, we cannot identify the existence of a moral panic. Finally, all moral panics are 'volatile'; whether their effects are long or short term, the panic itself is sustainable only for a brief period.

For Goode and Ben-Yehuda, identifying and analysing moral panics is a scientific and not a political enterprise. Any issue can be subjected to scrutiny, whether or not the analyst is sympathetic to its cause. In that effort different measures of disproportionality remain crucial. Four indicators are provided: the exaggeration of statistics, their fabrication, ignoring other harmful conditions and disregarding fluctuations over time. A barrage of questions about the nature and origins of moral panics is outlined, with a final note on the function of moral panics as reinforcing moral boundaries, especially during times of unsettling social change.

Reading 5 presents a rare effort by Thompson (1998) to carefully compare Goode and Ben-Yehuda with Cohen. The American perspective stresses the role of collective behaviour and claims makers while the British version stresses the role of politicians and the mass media. The work of Hall et al. is taken to be an example of what Goode and Ben-Yehuda call the 'elite engineered' explanation of moral panics but Thompson suggests this may be an over-simplification of their work. Goode and Ben-Yehuda's own preference for explanation at the level of interest groups has some merit but it cannot account for the multiplicity and overlap of moral panics as convincingly as the concepts of signification spiral and convergence. Despite these differences the two models have a lot in common, not least the tendency identified by Philip Jenkins (1992) to find in moral panics expressions of anxiety over the pace and direction of rapid social change. Both would also benefit from integrating insights from risk theory and discourse analysis.

The original authors seem to regard their models as mutually compatible. They are certainly respectful of each other's work. Goode and Ben-Yehuda's book is dedicated to Cohen. They see him as responsible for the 'launch' of the concept which they are seeking to further develop. Cohen has described Goode and Ben-Yehuda's work as an attempt to provide 'a rather clearer definition of the concept' which has 'distinguished the separate elements in the original definition' (Cohen 2002: xxii). He goes on to make a particularly strong endorsement of the criterion of disproportionality. I have suggested (Critcher 2003) that Cohen's model can be termed processual and Goode and Ben-Yehuda's attributional. There are, no doubt, different views about which is the superior or how far they might be amalgamated.

References

Cohen, S. (2002) Introduction to the third edition, *Folk Devils and Moral Panics*. London: Routledge.

Critcher, C. (2003) *Moral Panics and the Mass Media*. Milton Keynes: Open University Press.

Jenkins, P. (1992) *Intimate Enemies: Moral Panics in Contemporary Great Britain*. New York: Aldine de Gruyter.

Young, J. (1971) The role of the police as amplifiers of deviancy, negotiators of reality and translators of fantasy: some aspects of our present system of drug control as seen in Notting Hill, in S. Cohen (ed.) *Images of Deviance*. Harmondsworth: Penguin Books.

Further Reading

Cohen, S. ([1972] 2002) *Folk Devils and Moral Panics*. 3rd edn. London: Routledge.

Goode, E. and Ben-Yehuda, N. (1994) *Moral Panics: The Social Construction of Deviance*. Oxford: Blackwell.

Hall, S., Critcher, C., Jefferson, T., Clarke, J. and Roberts, B. (1978) *Policing The Crisis: Mugging, the State and Law and Order*. London: Macmillan.

Thompson, K. (1998) *Moral Panics*. London: Routledge.

DEVIANCE AND PANICS

Stan Cohen (1973)

Societies appear to be subject, every now and then, to periods of moral panic. A condition, episode, person or group of persons emerges to become defined as a threat to societal values and interests; its nature is presented in a stylized and stereotypical fashion by the mass media; the moral barricades are manned by editors, bishops, politicians and other right-thinking people; socially accredited experts pronounce their diagnoses and solutions; ways of coping are evolved or (more often) resorted to; the condition then disappears, submerges or deteriorates and becomes more visible. Sometimes the object of the panic is quite novel and at other times it is something which has been in existence long enough, but suddenly appears in the limelight. Sometimes the panic passes over and is forgotten, except in folklore and collective memory; at other times it has more serious and long-lasting repercussions and might produce such changes as those in legal and social policy or even in the way the society conceives itself.

One of the most recurrent types of moral panic in Britain since the war has been associated with the emergence of various forms of youth culture (originally almost exclusively working class, but often recently middle class or student based) whose behaviour is deviant or delinquent. To a greater or lesser degree, these cultures have been associated with violence. The Teddy Boys, the Mods and Rockers, the Hells Angels, the skinheads and the hippies have all been phenomena of this kind. There have been parallel reactions to the drug problem, student militancy, political demonstrations, football hooliganism, vandalism of various kinds and crime and violence in general. But groups such as the Teddy Boys and the Mods and Rockers have been distinctive in being identified not just in terms of particular events (such as demonstrations) or particular disapproved forms of behaviour (such as drug-taking or violence) but as distinguishable social types. In the gallery of types that society erects to show its members which roles should be avoided and which should be emulated, these groups have occupied a constant position as folk devils: visible reminders of what we should not be. The identities of such social types are public property and these particular adolescent groups have symbolized – both in what they were and how they were reacted to – much of the social change which has taken place in Britain over the last twenty years.

In this book, I want to use a detailed case study of the Mods and Rockers phenomenon – which covered most of the 1960s – to illustrate some of the more intrinsic features in the emergence of such collective episodes of juvenile deviance and the moral panics they both generate and rely upon for their growth. . . .

At the beginning of the decade, the term 'Modernist' referred simply to a style of dress; the term 'Rocker' was hardly known outside the small groups which identified themselves this way. Five years later, a newspaper editor was to refer to the Mods and Rockers incidents as 'without parallel in English history' and troop reinforcements were rumoured to have been sent to quell possible widespread disturbances. Now, another five years later, these groups have all but disappeared from the public consciousness, remaining only in collective memory as folk devils of the past, to whom current horrors can be compared. The rise and fall of the Mods and Rockers contained all the elements from which one might generalize about folk devils and moral panics. And unlike the previous decade which had only produced the Teddy Boys, these years witnessed rapid oscillation from one such devil to another: the Mod, the Rocker, the Greaser, the student militant, the drug fiend, the vandal, the soccer hooligan, the hippy, the skinhead.

Neither moral panics nor social types have received much systematic attention in sociology. In the case of moral panics, the two most relevant frameworks come from the sociology of law and social problems and the sociology of collective behaviour. Sociologists such as Becker (1963) and Gusfield (1963) have taken the cases of the Marijuana Tax Act and the Prohibition laws respectively to show how public concern about a particular condition is generated, a 'symbolic crusade' mounted, which with publicity and the actions of certain interest groups, results in what Becker calls *moral enterprise*: '. . . the creation of a new fragment of the moral constitution of society' (1963:145). Elsewhere Becker (1966) uses the same analysis to deal with the evolution of social problems as a whole. The field of collective behaviour provides another relevant orientation to the study of moral panics. There are detailed accounts of cases of mass hysteria, delusion and panics, and also a body of studies on how societies cope with the sudden threat or disorder caused by physical disasters.

[...]

The major contribution to the study of the social typing process itself comes from the interactionist or transactional approach to deviance. The focus here is on how society labels rule-breakers as belonging to certain deviant groups and how, once the person is thus type cast, his acts are interpreted in terms of the status to which he has been assigned. It is to this body of theory that we must turn for our major orientation to the study of both moral panics and social types.

The Transactional Approach to Deviance

The sociological study of crime, delinquency, drug-taking, mental illness and other forms of socially deviant or problematic behaviour has, in the last decade, undergone a radical reorientation. This reorientation is part of what might be called the *sceptical* revolution in criminology and the sociology of deviance. The older tradition was *canonical* in the sense that it saw the concepts it worked with as authoritative, standard, accepted, given and unquestionable. The new tradition is sceptical in the sense that when it sees terms like 'deviant', it asks 'deviant to whom?' or 'deviant from what?'; when told that something is a social problem, it asks 'problematic to whom?'; when certain conditions or behaviour are described as dysfunctional, embarrassing, threatening or dangerous, it asks 'says who?' and 'why?'. In other words, these concepts and descriptions are not assumed to have a taken-for-granted status.

The empirical existence of forms of behaviour labelled as deviant and the fact that persons might consciously and intentionally decide to be deviant, should not lead us to assume that deviance is the intrinsic property of an act nor a quality possessed by an actor. Becker's formulation on the transactional nature of deviance has now been quoted verbatim so often that it has virtually acquired its own canonical status:

> ... deviance is created by society. I do not mean this in the way that it is ordinarily understood, in which the causes of deviance are located in the social situation of the deviant or in 'social factors' which prompt his action. I mean, rather, that *social groups create deviance by making the rules whose infraction constitutes deviance* and by applying those rules to particular persons and labelling them as outsiders. From this

point of view, deviance is *not* a quality of the act the person commits, but rather a consequence of the application by others of rules and sanctions to an 'offender'. The deviant is one to whom the label has successfully been applied; deviant behaviour is behaviour that people so label. (1963: 9)

What this means is that the student of deviance must question and not take for granted the labelling by society or certain powerful groups in society of certain behaviour as deviant or problematic. The transactionalists' importance has been not simply to restate the sociological truism that the judgement of deviance is ultimately one that is relative to a particular group, but in trying to spell out the implication of this for research and theory. They have suggested that in addition to the stock set of *behavioural* questions which the public asks about deviance and which the researcher obligingly tries to answer (why did they do it? what sort of people are they? how do we stop them doing it again?) there are at least three *definitional* questions: why does a particular rule, the infraction of which constitutes deviance, exist at all? What are the processes and procedures involved in identifying someone as a deviant and applying the rule to him? What are the effects and consequences of this application, both for society and the individual?

Sceptical theorists have been misinterpreted as going only so far as putting these definitional questions and moreover as implying that the behavioural questions are unimportant. While it is true that they have pointed to the dead ends which the behavioural questions have reached (do we really know what distinguishes a deviant from a non-deviant?), what they say has positive implications for studying these questions as well. Thus, they see deviance in terms of a process of becoming – movements of doubt, commitment, sidetracking, guilt – rather than the possession of fixed traits and characteristics. ... The meaning and interpretation which the deviant gives to his own acts are seen as crucial and so is the fact that these actions are often similar to socially approved forms of behaviour (Cohen 1971; Rubington and Weinberg 1968).

The transactional perspective does not imply that innocent persons are arbitrarily selected to play deviant roles or that harmless conditions are wilfully inflated into social problems. Nor does it imply that a person labelled as deviant has to accept this identity: being caught and publicly labelled is just one crucial contingency which *may* stabilize a deviant career and sustain it over time. Much of the work of these writers has been concerned with the problematic nature of societal response to deviance and the way such responses affect the behaviour. This may be studied at a face-to-face level (for example, what effect does it have on a pupil to be told by his teacher that he is a 'yob who should never be at a decent school like this'?) or at a broader societal level (for example, how is the 'drug problem' actually created and shaped by particular social and legal policies?).

The most unequivocal attempt to understand the nature and effect of the societal reaction to deviance is to be found in the writings of Lemert. (1951; 1967) He makes an important distinction, for example, between primary and secondary deviation. Primary deviation – which may arise from a variety of causes – refers to behaviour which, although it may be troublesome to the individual, does not produce symbolic reorganization at the level of self-conception. Secondary deviation occurs when the individual employs his deviance, or a role based upon it, as a means of defence, attack or adjustment to the problems created by the societal reaction to it. The societal reaction is thus conceived as the 'effective' rather than 'original' cause of deviance: deviance becomes significant when it is subjectively shaped into an active role which becomes the basis for assigning social status. Primary deviation has only marginal implications for social status and self-conception as long as it remains symptomatic, situational, rationalized or in some way 'normalized' as an acceptable and normal variation.

Lemert was very much aware that the transition from primary to secondary deviation was a complicated process. Why the societal reaction occurs and what form it takes are dependent on factors such as the amount and visibility of the deviance, while the effect of the reaction is dependent on numerous contingencies and is itself only one contingency in the development of a deviant career. Thus the link between the reaction and the individual's incorporation of this into his self-identity is by no means inevitable; the deviant label, in other words, does not always 'take'. The individual might be able to ignore or rationalize the label or only pretend to comply. This type of face-to-face sequence, though, is just one part of the picture: more important are the symbolic and unintended consequences of social control as a whole. Deviance in a sense emerges and is stabilized as an artefact of social control; because of this, Lemert can state that '... older sociology tended to rest heavily upon the idea that deviance leads to social control. I have come to believe that the reverse idea, i.e. social control leads to deviance, is equally tenable and the potentially richer premise for studying deviance in modern society.'

It is partly towards showing the tenability and richness of this premise that this book is directed. My emphasis though, is more on the logically prior task of analysing the nature of a particular set of reactions rather than demonstrating conclusively what their effects might have been. How were the Mods and Rockers identified, labelled and controlled? What stages or processes did this reaction go through? Why did the reaction take its particular forms? What – to use Lemert's words again – were the 'mythologies, stigma, stereotypes, patterns of exploitation, accommodation, segregation and methods of control (which) spring up and crystallize in the interaction between the deviants and the rest of society' (1951:55)?

There are many strategies – not mutually incompatible – for studying such reactions. One might take a sample of public opinion and survey its attitudes to the particular form of deviance in question. One might record reactions in a face-to-face context; for example, how persons respond to what they see as homosexual advances (Kitsuse 1962). One might study the operations and beliefs of particular control agencies such as the police or the courts. Or, drawing on all these sources, one might construct an ethnography and history of reactions to a particular condition or form of behaviour. This is particularly suitable for forms of deviance or problems seen as new, sensational or in some other way particularly threatening. Thus 'crime waves' in seventeenth-century Massachusetts, (Erikson 1966) marijuana smoking in America during the 1930s, (Becker 1963), the Teddy Boy phenomenon in Britain during the 1950s (Rock and Cohen 1970) and drug-taking in the Notting Hill area of London during the 1960s (Young 1971a) have all been studied in this way. These reactions were all associated with some form of moral panic and it is in the tradition of studies such as these that the Mods and Rockers will be considered. Before introducing this particular case, however, I want to justify concentrating on one especially important carrier and producer of moral panics, namely, the mass media.

Deviance and the Mass Media

A crucial dimension for understanding the reaction to deviance both by the public as a whole and by agents of social control, is the nature of the information that is received about the behaviour in question. Each society possesses a set of ideas about what causes deviation – is it due, say, to sickness or to wilful perversity? – and a set of images of who constitutes the typical deviant – is he an innocent lad being led astray, or is he a psychopathic thug? – and these conceptions shape what is done about the behaviour. In industrial societies, the body of information from which such ideas are built, is invariably received at second hand. That is, it arrives already processed by the mass media and this means that the information has been subject to alternative definitions of what constitutes 'news' and how it should be gathered and presented. The information is further structured by the various commercial and political constraints in which newspapers, radio and television operate.

The student of moral enterprise cannot but pay particular attention to the role of the mass media in defining and shaping social problems. The media have long operated as agents of moral indignation in their own right: even if they are not self-consciously engaged in crusading or muck-raking, their very reporting of certain 'facts' can be sufficient to generate concern, anxiety, indignation or panic. When such feelings coincide with a perception that particular values need to be protected, the preconditions for new rule creation or social problem definition are present. Of course, the outcome might not be as definite as the actual creation of new rules or the more rigid enforcement of existing ones. What might result is the sort of symbolic process which Gusfield (1967) describes in his conception of 'moral passage': there is a change in the public designation of deviance. In his example, the problem drinker changes from 'repentant' to 'enemy' to 'sick'. Something like the opposite might be happening in the public designation of producers and consumers of pornography: they have changed from isolated, pathetic – if not sick – creatures in grubby macks to groups of ruthless exploiters out to undermine the nation's morals.

Less concretely, the media might leave behind a diffuse feeling of anxiety about the situation: 'something should be done about it', 'where will it end?' or 'this sort of thing can't go on for ever'. Such vague feelings are crucial in laying the ground for further enterprise, and Young has shown how, in the case of drug-taking, the media play on the normative concerns of the public and by thrusting certain moral directives into the universe of discourse, can create social problems suddenly and dramatically (1971b). This potential is consciously exploited by those whom Becker calls 'moral entrepreneurs' to aid them in their attempt to win public support.

The mass media, in fact, devote a great deal of space to deviance: sensational crimes, scandals, bizarre happenings and strange goings on. The more dramatic confrontations between deviance and control in manhunts, trials and punishments are recurring objects of attention. As Erikson notes, 'a considerable portion of what we call "news" is devoted to reports about deviant behaviour and its consequences' (1966:12). This is not just for entertainment or to fulfil some psychological need for either identification or vicarious punishment. Such 'news' as Erikson and others have argued, is a main source of information about the normative contours of a society. It informs us about right and wrong, about the boundaries beyond which one should not venture and about the shapes that the devil can assume. The gallery of folk types – heroes and saints, as well as fools, villains and devils

– is publicized not just in oral-tradition and face-to-face contact but to much larger audiences and with much greater dramatic resources.

Much of this study will be devoted to understanding the role of the mass media in creating moral panics and folk devils. A potentially useful link between these two notions – and one that places central stress on the mass media – is the process of deviation amplification as described by Wilkins (1964). The key variable in this attempt to understand how the societal reaction may in fact *increase* rather than decrease or keep in check the amount of deviance, is the nature of the information about deviance. As I pointed out earlier, this information characteristically is not received at first hand, it tends to be processed in such a form that the action or actors concerned are pictured in a highly stereotypical way. We react to an episode of, say, sexual deviance, drug-taking or violence in terms of our information about that particular class of phenomenon (how typical is it), our tolerance level for that type of behaviour and our direct experience – which in a segregated urban society is often nil. Wilkins describes – in highly mechanistic language derived from cybernetic theory – a typical reaction sequence which might take place at this point, one which has a spiralling or snowballing effect.

An initial act of deviance, or normative diversity (for example, in dress) is defined as being worthy of attention and is responded to punitively. The deviant or group of deviants is segregated or isolated and this operates to alienate them from conventional society. They perceive themselves as more deviant, group themselves with others in a similar position, and this leads to more deviance. This, in turn, exposes the group to further punitive sanctions and other forceful action by the conformists – and the system starts going round again. There is no assumption in this model that amplification *has* to occur: in the same way – as I pointed out earlier – that there is no automatic transition from primary to secondary deviation or to the incorporation of deviant labels. The system or the actor can and does react in quite opposite directions. What one is merely drawing attention to is a set of sequential typifications: under X conditions, A will be followed by A1, A2, etc. All these links have to be explained – as Wilkins does not do – in terms of other generalizations. For example, it is more likely that if the deviant group is vulnerable and its actions highly visible, it will be forced to take on its identities from structurally and ideologically more powerful groups. Such generalizations and an attempt to specify various specialized modes of amplification or alternatives to the process have been spelt out by Young (1971a; 1971b). In the case of drug-taking. I intend using this model here simply as one viable way in which the 'social control leads to deviation' chain can be conceptualized and also because of its particular emphasis upon the 'information about deviance' variable and its dependence on the mass media.

The Case of the Mods and Rockers

I have already given some indication of the general framework which I think suitable for the study of moral panics and folk devils. Further perspectives suggest themselves because of the special characteristics of the Mods and Rockers phenomenon, as compared with, say, the rise of student militancy or the appearance of underground newspaper editors on obscenity charges. The first and most obvious one derives from the literature on subcultural delinquency. This would provide the structural setting for explaining the Mods and Rockers phenomenon as a form of adolescent deviance among working-class youth in Britain. ... At various points in these chapters, the relevance of subcultural theory will be commented on, although my stress on the definitional rather than behavioural questions precludes an extended analysis along these lines.

Another less obvious orientation derives from the field of collective behaviour. I have already suggested that social types can be seen as the products of the same processes that go into the creation of symbolic collective styles in fashion, dress and public identities. The Mods and Rockers, though, were initially registered in the public consciousness not just as the appearance of new social types, but as actors in a particular episode of collective behaviour. The phenomenon took its subsequent shape in terms of these episodes: the regular series of disturbances which took place at English seaside resorts between 1964 and 1966. The public image of these folk devils was invariably tied up to a number of highly visual scenarios associated with their appearance: youths chasing across the beach, brandishing deckchairs over their heads, running along the pavements, riding on scooters or bikes down the streets, sleeping on the beaches and so on.

Each of these episodes – as I will describe – contained all the elements of the classic crowd situation which has long been the prototype for the study of collective behaviour. Crowds, riots, mobs and disturbances on occasions ranging from pop concerts to political demonstrations have all been seen in a similar way to *The Crowd* described by Le Bon in 1896. Later formulations by Tarde, Freud, McDougall and F.H. Allport made little lasting contribution and often just elaborated on Le Bon's contagion hypothesis. A more useful recent theory – for all its deficiencies from a sociological viewpoint – is Smelser's (1962) 'value added schema'. In the sequence he suggests, each of the following determinants of collective behaviour must appear: (i) structural conduciveness; (ii) structural strain; (iii) growth and spread of a generalized belief; (iv) precipitating factors; (v) mobilization of the participants for action; (vi) operation of social control.

[. . .]

A special – and at first sight somewhat esoteric – area of collective behaviour which is of peculiar relevance, is the field known as 'disaster research'. This consists of a body of findings about the social and psychological impact of disasters, particularly physical disasters such as hurricanes, tornadoes and floods but also man-made disasters such as bombing attacks. Theoretical models have also been produced, and Merton argues that the study of disasters can extend sociological theory beyond the confines of the immediate subject-matter. Disaster situations can be looked at as strategic research sites for theory-building: 'Conditions of collective stress bring out in bold relief aspects of social systems that are not as readily visible in the stressful conditions of everyday life (Merton 1963). The value of disaster studies is that by compressing social processes into a brief time span, a disaster makes usually private behaviour, public and immediate and therefore more amenable to study. (Fritz 1963).

[. . .]

The work of disaster researchers that struck me as most useful when I got to the stage of writing up my own material on the Mods and Rockers was the sequential model that they have developed to describe the phases of a typical disaster. The following is the sort of sequence that has been distinguished:

1. *Warning*: during which arises, mistakenly or not, some apprehensions based on conditions out of which danger may arise. The warning must be coded to be understood and impressive enough to overcome resistance to the belief that current tranquillity can be upset.
2. *Threat*: during which people are exposed to communication from others, or to signs from the approaching disaster itself indicating specific imminent danger. This phase begins with the perception of some change, but as with the first phase, may be absent or truncated in the case of sudden disaster.
3. *Impact*: during which the disaster strikes and the immediate unorganized response to the death, injury or destruction takes place.
4. *Inventory*: during which those exposed to the disaster begin to form a preliminary picture of what has happened and of their own condition.
5. *Rescue*: during which the activities are geared to immediate help for the survivors. As well as people in the impact area helping each other, the suprasystem begins to send aid.

6. *Remedy*: during which more deliberate and formal activities are undertaken towards relieving the affected. The suprasystem takes over the functions the emergency system cannot perform.
7. *Recovery*: during which, for an extended period, the community either recovers its former equilibrium or achieves a stable adaptation to the changes which the disaster may have brought about.

Some of these stages have no exact parallels in the Mods and Rockers case, but a condensed version of this sequence (*Warning* to cover phases 1 and 2; then *Impact*; then *Inventory*; and *Reaction* to cover phases 5, 6 and 7) provides a useful analogue....

My focus is on the genesis and development of the moral panic and social typing associated with the Mods and Rockers phenomenon. In transactional terminology: what was the nature and effect of the societal reaction to this particular form of deviance? This entails looking at the ways in which the behaviour was perceived and conceptualized, whether there was a unitary or a divergent set of images, the modes through which these images were transmitted and the ways in which agents of social control reacted. The behavioural questions (how did the Mods and Rockers styles emerge? Why did some young people more or less identified with these groups behave in the way they did?) will be considered, but they are the background questions. The variable of societal reaction is the focus of attention.

References

Becker, H.S. (1963) *Outsiders: Studies in the Sociology of Deviance*. New York: Free Press.

Becker, H.S. (ed.) (1966) *Social Problems: A Modern Approach*. New York: John Wiley.

Cohen, S. (ed.) (1971) *Images of Deviance*. Harmondsworth: Penguin Books.

Erikson, K.T. (1966) *Wayward Puritans: A Study in the Sociology of Deviance*. New York: John Wiley.

Fritz, C.F. (1963) Disaster, in R.K. Merton and R.A. Nisbet (eds) *Contemporary Social Problems*. London: Rupert Hart-Davis.

Gusfield, J. (1963) *Symbolic Crusade: Status Politics and the American Temperance Movement*. Urbana, IL: University of Illinois Press.

Gusfield, J. (1967) Moral passage: the symbolic process in public designations of deviance, *Social Problems*, 15(3): 175–88.

Kitsuse, J.I. (1962) Societal reaction to deviant behaviour: problems of theory and method, *Social Problems*, 9(4): 247–56.

Lemert, E.M. (1951) *Social Pathology: A Systematic Approach to the Study of Sociopathic Behaviour*. New York: McGraw-Hill.

Lemert, E.M. (1967) *Human Deviance, Social Problems and Social Control*. Englewood Cliffs, NJ: Prentice Hall.

Merton, R. (1963) Introduction, in A.H. Barton *Social Organisation Under Stress: A Sociological Review of Disaster Studies*. Washington, DC: National Academy of Sciences.

Rock, P. and Cohen, S. (1970) The Teddy Boy, in V. Bogdanor and R. Skidelsky (eds) *The Age of Affluence: 1951–1964*. London: Macmillan.

Rubington, E. and Weinberg, M.S. (eds) (1968) *The Interactionist Perspective*. New York: Collier-Macmillan.

Smelser, N.J. (1962) *Theory of Collective Behaviour*. London: Routledge & Kegan Paul.

Wilkins, L.T. (1964) *Social Deviance: Social Policy, Action and Research*. London: Tavistock.

Young, J. (1971a) The role of the police as amplifiers of deviancy, negotiators of reality and translators of fantasy: some aspects of our present system of drug control as seen in Notting Hill, in S. Cohen (ed.) *Images of Deviance*. Harmondsworth: Penguin Books.

Young, J. (1971b) *The Drug Takers: The Social Meaning of Drug-Taking*. London: Paladin.

3 | THE CHANGING SHAPE OF 'PANICS'

Stuart Hall, Chas Critcher, Tony Jefferson, John Clarke and Bryan Roberts (1978)

The mass media are not the only, but they *are* among the most powerful, forces in the shaping of public consciousness about topical and con- troversial issues. The signification of events in the media thus provides one key terrain where 'consent' is won or lost. Again, as we have argued earlier, the media are formally and institutionally independent of direct state interference or intervention in Britain. The signification of events, in ways which reproduce the interpretations of them favoured by those in power, therefore takes place – as in other branches of the state and its general spheres of operation – through the formal 'separation of powers'; in the communications field, it is mediated by the protocols of balance, objectivity and impartiality. This means both that the state cannot directly command, even if it wished, precisely how public consciousness will be attuned on any particular matter, and that other points of view do, of necessity, gain access and have some right to be heard. Although this is a process which is heavily structured and constrained ... its result is to make the 'reproduction of the dominant ideologies' a problematic and contradictory process, and thus to recreate the arena of signification as a field of ideological struggle. In analysing the way the post-war crisis came to be signified, then, we shall not expect to find a set of monolithic interpretations, systematically generated by the ruling classes for the explicit purpose of fooling the public. The ideological instance cannot be conceived in this way. ... There is of course no simple consensus, even here, as to the nature, causes and extent of the crisis. But the overall tendency is for the way the crisis has been ideologi- cally constructed by the dominant ideologies to win consent in the media, and thus to constitute the substantive basis in 'reality' to which public opinion continually refers. In this way, by 'consenting' to the view of the crisis which has won credibility in the echelons of power, popular consciousness is also won to support to the measures of control and containment which this version of social reality entails.

Statements by key spokesmen – what we have called 'primary definers' – and their representation through the media therefore form a central part of our reconstruction. But in order to understand how these played a part in the shifts in the nature of hegemony within the state and the political apparatus over the relevant period, a number of intermediary concepts need to be introduced. The problem concerns the relation to our analysis – which is pitched at the level of the state apparatuses and the maintenance of forms of hegemonic domination – of the phenomenon described earlier as the *moral panic*. The concepts of 'state' and 'hegemony' appear, at first sight, to belong to different conceptual territory from that of the 'moral panic'. And part of our intention is certainly to situate the 'moral panic' as one of the forms of appearance of a more deepseated historical crisis, and thereby to give it greater historical and theoretical specificity. This relocation of the concept on a different and deeper level of analysis does not, however, lead us to abandon it altogether as useless. Rather, it helps us to identify the 'moral panic' as one of the principal surface manifestations of the crisis, and in part to explain how and why the crisis came to be *experienced* in that form of consciousness, and what the displacement of a conjunctural crisis into the popular form of a 'moral panic' accomplishes, in terms of the way the crisis is managed and contained. We have therefore retained the notion of the 'moral panic' as a necessary part of our analysis: attempting to redefine it as one of the key ideological forms in which a historical crisis is 'experienced and fought out'. One of the effects of retaining the notion of 'moral panic' is the penetration it provides into the otherwise extremely obscure means by which the working classes are drawn in to processes which are occurring in large measure 'behind their backs', and led to experience and respond to contradictory developments in ways which make the operation of state power legitimate, credible and consensual. To put it crudely, the 'moral panic' appears to us to be one of the principal forms of ideological consciousness by means of which a 'silent majority' is won over to the support of increasingly coercive measures on the part of the state, and lends its legitimacy to a 'more than usual' exercise of control.

There is a tendency, in the early years of our period, for there to develop a succession of 'moral panics' around certain key topics of controversial public concern. In this early period, the panics tend to be centred on social and moral rather than political issues (youth, permissiveness, crime). Their typical form is that of a dramatic event which focuses and triggers a local response and public disquiet. Often as a result of local organising and moral entrepreneurship, the wider powers of the control culture are both alerted (the media play a crucial role here) and mobilised (the police, the courts). The issue is then seen as 'symptomatic' of wider, more troubling but less concrete themes. It escalates up the hierarchy of responsibility and control, perhaps provoking an official enquiry or statement, which temporarily appeases the moral campaigners and dissipates the sense of panic. In what we think of as the middle period, in the later 1960s, these panics follow faster on the heels of one another than earlier: and an increasingly amplified general 'threat to society' is imputed to them (drugs, hippies, the underground, pornography, long-haired students, layabouts, vandalism, football hooliganism). In many instances the sequence is so speeded up that it bypasses the moment of *local* impact; there was no upsurge of grass-roots pressure required to bring the drugs squad crunching in on cannabis smokers. Both the media and the 'control culture' seem more alerted to their occurrence – the media quickly pick up the symptomatic event and the police and courts react quickly without considerable moral pressure from below. This speeded-up sequence tends to suggest a heightened sensitivity to troubling social themes.

There is indeed in the later stages a 'mapping together' of moral panics into a *general panic* about social order; and such a spiral has tended, not only in Britain, to culminate in what we call a 'law-and-order' campaign, of the kind which the Heath Shadow Cabinet constructed on the eve of the 1970 election, and which powered Nixon and Agnew into the White House in 1968. This coalescence into a concerted campaign marks a significant shift in the panic process, for the tendency to panic is now lodged at the heart of the state's political complex itself; and from that vantage-point, all dissensual breaks in the society can be more effectively designated as a 'general threat to law and order itself', and thus as subverting the general interest (which the state represents and protects). Panics now tend to operate from top to bottom. Post-1970, the law-and-order campaigners seem to have effectively sensitised the social-control apparatuses and the media to the possibility of a general threat to the stability of the state. Minor forms of dissent seem to provide the basis of 'scapegoat' events for a jumpy and alerted control culture; and this progressively pushes the state apparatuses into a more or less permanent 'control' posture. Schematically, the changing sequence in moral panics can be represented as follows:

1   *Discrete moral panics* (early 1960s, e.g. 'mods' and 'rockers')
    Dramatic event → public disquiet, moral entrepreneurs (sensitisation)
    → control culture action

2   'Crusading' – *mapping together discrete moral panics to produce a speeded-up' sequence* (late 1960s, e.g. pornography and drugs)
    Sensitisation (moral entrepreneurship) → dramatic event → control culture action

3   *Post-'law-and-order' campaign: an altered sequence* (post-1970 e.g. mugging)
    Sensitisation → control culture organisation and action (invisible) → dramatic event → control culture intensified action (visible)

But what are the signifying mechanisms – in the media and the sources on which they depend – which sustain these shifts in the sequence? What 'signification spirals' sustain the generation of the moral panic?

Signification Spirals

The *signification spiral* is a way of signifying events which also intrinsically escalates their threat. The notion of a signification spiral is similar to that of an 'amplification spiral' as developed by certain sociologists of deviance (Wilkins 1964, Young 1971). An 'amplification spiral' suggests that reaction has the effect, under certain conditions, not of lessening but of increasing deviance. The signification spiral is a *self-amplifying sequence within the area of signification*: the activity or event with which the signification deals is *escalated* – made to seem more threatening – within the course of the signification itself.

A signification spiral seems always to contain at least some of the following elements:

1   the identification of a specific issue of concern;
2   the identification of a subversive minority;
3   'convergence', or the linking, by labelling, of this specific issue to other problems;
4   the notion of 'thresholds' which, once crossed, can lead to an escalating threat;
5   the prophesy of more troubling times to come if no action is taken (often, in our case, by way of references to the United States, the paradigm example); and
6   the call for 'firm steps'.

There are two key notions – 'convergence' and 'thresholds' – which are the escalating mechanisms of the spiral.

Convergence: In our usage 'convergence' occurs when two or more activities are linked in the process of signification so as to implicitly or explicitly draw parallels between them. Thus the image of 'student hooliganism' links 'student' protest to the separate problem of 'hooliganism' – whose stereotypical characteristics are already part of socially available knowledge. This indicates the manner in which *new* problems can apparently be meaningfully described and explained by setting them in the context of an old problem with which the public is already familiar. In using the imagery of hooliganism, this signification equates two distinct activities on the basis of their *imputed* common denominator – both involve 'mindless violence' or 'vandalism'. Another, connected, form of convergence is listing a whole series of social problems and speaking of them as 'part of a deeper, underlying problem' – the 'tip of an iceberg', especially when such a link is also forged on the basis of implied common denominators. In both cases the net effect is *amplification*, not in the real events being described, but in their 'threat-potential' for society. Do such convergences *only* occur in the eye of the signifying beholder? Are they entirely fictional? In fact, of course, significant convergences do and have indeed taken place in some areas of what might be described by the dominant culture as 'political deviance'. Horowitz and Liebowitz (1968) have pointed out that the distinction between political marginality and social deviance is 'increasingly obsolete' in the United States of the late 1960s. Similarly, Hall has argued that in respect of certain areas of British protest politics in the late 1960s and 1970s: 'the crisp distinction between socially and politically deviant behaviour is increasingly difficult to sustain' (1974: 263).

Convergences, for example, take place when political groups adopt deviant life-styles or when deviants become politicised. They occur when people, thought of in passive and individual terms, take collective action (for example, claimants), or when supporters of single-issue campaigns enter into a wider agitation or make common cause. There can be real convergences (between workers and students in May 1968) as well as ideological or imaginary ones. However, signification spirals do not depend on a necessary correspondence with real historical developments. They may represent such real connections accurately, or they may mystify by exaggerating the nature or degree of the convergence, or they may produce altogether spurious identities. For example, in the 1970s some homosexuals involved in the Gay Liberation movements *did* belong to the radical or marxist left. A signification which, however, assumed that all homosexual reformers were 'marxist revolutionaries' would be one which inflected a real convergence in an ideological direction – an exaggeration whose credibility would nevertheless no doubt depend on its kernel of truth. Such an inflection would also be a misrepresentation – misrepresenting both the many reformers who were without overt political commitment, and the critique which even those who were marxists regularly made of traditional 'left' attitudes towards sexual issues. Such an inflection would be 'ideological' exactly because it signified a complex phenomenon in terms of its problematic part only. It would also entail 'escalation', since it exaggerates out of all proportion the one element most troubling and threatening to the established political order. The earlier example of 'student hooliganism' works in much the same way. this time connecting and identifying two almost wholly discrepant phenomena. But this example also shifts the political terms of the issue – that posed by the emergent student movement – by resignifying it in terms of a more familiar and traditional, non-political (hooliganism) problem; that is, by translating a *political* issue into a *criminal* one (the link with violence and vandalism) – thereby making easier a legal or control, rather than a political, response from the authorities. This transposition of frameworks not only depoliticises an issue by *criminalising* it, but it also singles out from a complex of different strands the most worrying element – the violent one. The resignification process thus also simplifies complex issues – for example, by 'making plain' through elision what would otherwise have to be substantiated by hard argument (e.g. that all student protest is mindlessly violent). Thus the movement's 'essential hooliganism' comes to pass for substantiated truth. Such significations also carry, embedded within them, concealed premises and understandings (for example, those referring to the exceedingly complex relation between politics and violence). Finally, by signifying a political issue through its most extreme and violent form, signification helps to produce a 'control' response – and makes that response legitimate. The public might be reluctant to see the strong arm of the law arbitrarily exercised against legitimate political protesters. But who will stand between the law and a 'bunch of hooligans'? Imaginary convergences therefore serve an ideological function – and that ideological function has real consequences, especially in terms of provoking and legitimating a coercive reaction by both the public and the state.

Thresholds: In the public signification of troubling events, there seem to be certain thresholds which mark out symbolically the limits of societal tolerance. The higher an event can be placed in the hierarchy of thresholds, the greater is its threat to the social order, and the tougher and more automatic is the coercive response. *Permissiveness*, for example, is a low threshold. Events which break this threshold contravene traditional moral norms (e.g. taboos on premarital sex). They therefore mobilise moral sanctions and social disapproval – but not necessarily legal control. But the struggles which take place, and the moral crusades which are mounted to defend the shifting boundary of 'permissiveness', can be resolved if some aspect of a 'permissive' act *also* infringes the law, if it breaks the *legal threshold*. The law clarifies the blurred area of moral disapproval, and marks out the legally impermissible from the morally disapproved of. New legislation, of either a progressive or restrictive character, is thus a sensitive barometer of the rise and fall of traditional moral sentiment, e.g. the shifts around the question of abortion. The transgression of the legal threshold raises the potential threat of any action; impermissible acts contravene the moral consensus, but illegal acts are a challenge to the legal order and the social legitimacy which it enshrines. However, acts which pose a challenge to the fundamental basis of the social order itself, or its essential structures, almost always involve, or at least are signified as leading inexorably across, the *violence threshold*. This is the highest of the limits of societal tolerance, since violent acts can be seen as constituting a threat to the future existence of the whole state itself (which holds the monopoly of legitimate violence). Certain acts are of course violence by any definition: armed terrorism, assassination, insurrection. Much more problematic are the whole range of political acts which do not necessarily espouse or lead to violence, but which are thought of as 'violent' because of the fundamental nature of the challenge they make to the state. Such acts are almost always signified in terms of their *potential for social violence* (violent here being almost a synonymn for 'extremism'). Robert Moss has recently argued that 'The conquest of violence is the signal achievement of modern democratic societies' (1976). By 'conquest of violence' here he must mean not its disappearance but its confinement to the state, which exerts a monopoly of *legitimate* 'violence'. Therefore every threat which can be signified as 'violent' must be an index of widespread social anarchy and disorder – perhaps the visible tip of a planned conspiracy. Any form of protest thus signified immediately becomes a law-and-order issue:

> When the state is not seen to be fulfilling this basic function, in the face of a serious and sustained upsurge of violence – either criminal or political – we can be sure of one thing: that sooner or later, ordinary citizens will take the law into their own hands or will be disposed to support a new form of government better equipped to deal with the threat.

We may represent some of the thresholds employed in signification spirals diagrammatically, as in Figure 3.1. The use of convergences and thresholds together in the ideological signification of societal conflict has

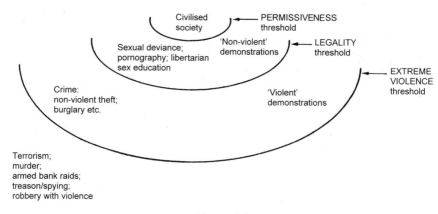

Figure 3.1

the intrinsic function of *escalation*. One kind of threat or challenge to society seems larger, more menacing, if it can be mapped together with other, apparently similar, phenomena – especially if, by connecting one relatively harmless activity with a more threatening one, the scale of the danger implicit is made to appear more widespread and diffused. Similarly, the threat to society can be escalated if a challenge occurring at the 'permissive' boundary can be resignified, or presented as leading inevitably to a challenge at a 'higher' threshold. By treating an event or group of actors not only in terms of its/their intrinsic characteristics, aims and programmes, but by projecting the 'anti-social potential' across the thresholds to what it *may* cause (or, less deterministically, lead to), it is possible to treat the initial event or group as 'the thin edge of a larger wedge'. The 'permissiveness' of the counter-culture appears far more menacing when 'long hair' and 'free sex' are seen as the inevitable forerunners of drug-taking, or where every pot-smoker is signified as a potential heroin addict, or where every cannabis buyer is an incipient dealer (i.e. involved in illegal acts). In turn, the threat to illegality is immeasurably escalated, if drug-taking inevitably makes every user 'prone to violence' (either because drugs lower his reason, or provoke him to rob to sustain the habit). Similarly, peaceful demonstrations become more threatening if always described as potential scenarios for violent confrontations. The important point is that, as issues and groups are projected across the thresholds, it becomes easier to mount legitimate campaigns of control against them. When this process becomes a regular and routine part of the way in which conflict is signified in society, it does indeed create its own momentum for measures of 'more than usual control'.

References

Hall, S. (1974) Deviancy, politics and the media, in P. Rock and M. McIntosh (eds) *Deviance and Social Control*. London: Tavistock.

Horowitz, I.L. and Liebowitz, M. (1968) Social deviance and political marginality, *Social Problems*, 15(3).

Moss, R. (1976) *The Collapse of Democracy*. London: Temple-Smith.

Wilkins, L. (1964) *Social Deviance: Social Policy, Action and Research*. London: Tavistock.

Young J. (1971) *The Drugtakers*. London: Paladin.

MORAL PANICS:
AN INTRODUCTION
Erich Goode and Nachman Ben-Yehuda
(1994)

At times, then, societies are gripped by moral panics. During the moral panic, the behavior of some of the members of a society is thought to be so problematic to others, the evil they do, or are thought to do, is felt to be so wounding to the substance and fabric of the body social, that serious steps must be taken to control the behavior, punish the perpetrators, and repair the damage. The threat this evil presumably poses is felt to represent a crisis for that society: something must be done about it, and that something must be done now; if steps are not taken immediately, or soon, we will suffer even graver consequences. The sentiment generated or stirred up by this threat can be referred to as a kind of fever; it can be characterized by heightened emotion, fear, dread, anxiety, hostility, and a strong feeling of righteousness. In a moral panic, a group or category engages, or is said to engage, in unacceptable, immoral behavior, presumably causes or is responsible for serious harmful consequences, and is therefore seen as a threat to the well-being, basic values, and interests of the society presumably threatened by them. These perpetrators or supposed perpetrators come to be regarded as the enemy – or an enemy – of society, 'folk devils' (Cohen, 1972), deviants, outsiders, legitimate and deserving targets of self-righteous anger, hostility, and punishment.

The moral panic, then, is characterized by the feeling, held by a substantial number of the members of a given society, that evildoers pose a threat to the society and to the moral order as a consequence of their behavior and, therefore, 'something should be done' about them and their behavior. A major focus of that 'something' typically entails strengthening the social control apparatus of the society – tougher or renewed rules, more intense public hostility and condemnation, more laws, longer sentences, more police, more arrests, and more prison cells. If society has become morally lax, a revival of traditional values may be necessary; if innocent people are victimized by crime, a crack-down on offenders will do the trick; if the young and the morally weak, wavering, and questionable are dabbling (or might dabble) in evil, harmful deeds, they should be made aware of what they are doing and its consequences. A major cause of the problem is, some will say, society's weak and insufficient efforts to control the wrongdoing; a major solution is to strengthen those efforts. Not everyone gripped by the moral panic sees legislation and law enforcement as the solution to the problem, however. Even when there is widespread agreement that the problem exists, the proper solution will be argued about, fought over, and negotiated; eventually, some legal outcome, one way or the other, will be reached – that is, to legislate or not to legislate – as a result of interaction between and among contending parties. Nonetheless, the question of the appropriate social and legal control of the responsible parties *almost inevitably* accompanies the moral panic. And legislation and its enforcement are usually seen as only one step; for those for whom the behavior in question is seen as a threat, measures such as education, socialization, normative changes, prevention, 'treatment,' and 'cures' will be suggested and debated.

[...]

Indicators of the Moral Panic

What characterizes the moral panic? How do we know when a moral panic takes hold in a given society? The concept of the moral panic is defined by at least five crucial elements or criteria.

Concern

First, there must be a heightened level of *concern* over the behavior of a certain group or category and the consequences that that behavior presumably causes for the rest of the society. This concern should be manifested or measureable in concrete ways, through, for example, public opinion polls, public commentary in the form of media attention, proposed legislation, social movement activity, and so on. Best (1990, p. 160) distinguishes *concern* from *fear*. We agree. The concern felt by the public need not manifest itself in the form of fear, although both have at least one element in common: both are seen by those who feel them to be a reasonable response to what is regarded as a very real and palpable threat.

Hostility

Second, there must be an increased level of *hostility* toward the group or category regarded as engaging in the behavior in question. Members of this category are collectively designated as the enemy, or an enemy, of respectable society; their behavior is seen as harmful or threatening to the values, the interests, possibly the very existence, of the society, or at least a sizeable segment of that society. That is, not only must the condition, phenomenon, or behavior be seen as threatening, but a clearly identifiable group in or segment of the society must be seen as *responsible* for the threat. Thus, a division is made between 'us' – good, decent, respectable folk – and 'them' – deviants, bad guys, undesirables, outsiders, criminals, the underworld, disreputable folk – between 'we' and 'they'. This dichotomization includes *stereotyping*: generating 'folk devils' or villains and folk heroes in this morality play of evil versus good (Cohen, 1972, pp. 11–12). In a slightly less dramatic fashion, we can see a parallel between the stereotyping process in moral panics and the routine processing of criminal suspects: the suspicion of the police that a crime has been committed or is in progress is aroused in part on the basis of stereotypical characteristics possessed by a suspect, such as age, race, presumed socio-economic characteristics, physical appearance, location, and so on (Barlow, 1993, pp. 358–61).

Consensus

Third, there must be substantial or widespread *agreement* or *consensus* – that is, at least a certain minimal measure of consensus in the society as a whole or in designated segments of the society – that the threat is real, serious, and caused by the wrongdoing group members and their behavior. This sentiment must be fairly widespread, although the proportion of the population who feels this way need not be universal or, indeed, even make up a literal majority. To put it another way: moral panics come in different sizes – some gripping the vast majority of the members of a given society at a given time, others creating concern only among certain of its groups or categories. At no exact point are we able to say that a panic exists; however, if the number is insubstantial, clearly, one does not. It should be stated that we will focus on some society-wide moral panics, but others we look at will be subcultural, local, or regional. Consensus that a problem exists and should be dealt with can grip the residents of a given group or community, but may be lacking in the society as a whole; this does not mean that a moral panic does not exist, only that there is group or regional variation in the eruption of moral panics. Some discussions (for instance, Zatz, 1987) do not even posit widespread public concern as an essential defining element of the moral panic, while others (Hall et al., 1978) assume that public concern is little more than an expression of elite interests.

Is it possible to have a moral panic *in the absence of* strong public concern? The elitist conception of moral panics regards public concern as irrelevant, either ignoring it altogether or regarding it as epiphemenonal, virtually an automatic byproduct of a conspiracy 'engineered' or 'orchestrated' by the powers that be. The problem with this approach is that many campaigns motivated by elite interests and engineered by elite efforts fail to materialize or simply fizzle out. . . .

In addition, the general public, or segments of the public, have interests of their own, and often become intensely concerned with issues that elites would just as soon be ignored – as we shall see, nuclear contamination and fears of satanism offer examples here. To sweep public concern under the rug as an irrelevant criterion of the moral panic is either to fail to recognize a key ingredient in this crucial process or to make a seriously mistaken assumption about its dynamics.

Still, it is important to remind ourselves that definitions of threat or crisis are rarely unopposed in a large, complex society. The question of whether or not a society is seriously threatened at a given time by a given agent or problem is typically debated, argued about, negotiated. To put the matter a bit differently, in some moral panics, the opposing voice is weak and unorganized, while in others, it is strong and united.

[. . .]

Disproportionality

Fourth, there is the implicit assumption in the use of the term moral panic that there is a sense on the part of many members of the society that a more sizeable number of individuals are engaged in the behavior in question than actually are, and the threat, danger, or damage said to be caused by the behavior is far more substantial than, is incommensurate with and in fact is 'above and beyond that which a realistic appraisal could sustain' (Davis and Stasz, 1990, p. 129). ... The degree of public concern over the behavior itself, the problem it poses, or condition it creates is far greater than is true for comparable, even more damaging, actions. In short, the term moral panic conveys the implication that public concern is in excess of what is appropriate if concern were directly proportional to objective harm. In moral panics, the generation and dissemination of figures or numbers is extremely important – addicts, deaths, dollars, crimes, victims, injuries, illnesses – and most of the figures cited by moral panic 'claims-makers' are wildly exaggerated. Clearly, in locating the moral panic, some measure of objective harm must be taken.

[...]

We acknowledge that determining and assessing the objective dimension is often a tricky propostion. Scientists frequently draw conclusions from incomplete information. Many scientific studies are poorly conducted; the conclusions of many scientists which have been accepted as true by the scientific community have been shown to be, upon closer inspection, erroneous and invalid. Contrarily, all too often, conclusions eventually accepted as true were regarded as false for years because of factors completely or largely extraneous to the nature of the evidence. (See Ben-Yehuda, 1985, pp. 106–67, Ben-Yehuda, 1990, pp. 181–219, for a discussion of some of these issues.) Occasionally, scientific fraud – 'fudging,' 'cooking,' or fabricating data, or plagiarizing the work of others – is revealed (Ben-Yehuda, 1985, pp. 168–207; Kilbourne and Kilbourne, 1983). All of this is quite true and worth reiterating. Moreover, all of these statements apply with equal force to medicine, the social sciences, and allied fields. In short, the same frailties to which ordinary men and women are subject also befall the expert; no statement by any scientist, expert, or knowledgeable figure should be regarded as definitive or final. All statements based on evidence are tentative; we can never know anything with absolute certainty. All statements, including those made by scientists, are constructions from a particular vantage point.

However, admitting that there are flaws in what is taken as some expert or scientific wisdom should not be stretched and twisted to reach the conclusion that what scientists and other experts say about the nature of the material and social world is untrue, or no more likely to be true than those made by the man and woman on the street. ... Even those who argue for the relativity of scientific, medical, and other expert truth in theory, *in practice* accept the fact that experts know more than the rest of us. ... The fact is, we place varying degrees of confidence in different statements. We can be almost completely confident that some propositions, accepted by all or almost all practicing natural or social scientists, medical figures or other experts, are true: the earth is round, not flat; species were generated over a period of billions of years through a process of evolution, and not in a single week through divine creation; the existence of the Holocaust – the systematic murder of millions of Jews and other ethnic groups by the Nazis during the 1930s and 1940s – is a verified historical fact, and is not a false claim hoked up by evil Zionists and their agents and dupes; and so on. Likewise, and more to the point of moral panics, we can have a great deal of confidence, given the nature of the evidence, that: LSD does not seriously damage chromosomes or cause birth defects; satanists are not kidnapping, abusing, torturing, and murdering tens of thousands of children every year in the United States and England; legal drug use is responsible for far more deaths than the abuse of illegal drugs; in 1982, not even close to half of Israeli high school students abused illegal drugs, nor do they do so now; in Renaissance Europe, hundreds of thousands of men and women did not literally consort with an actual, concrete devil; and so on.

In short, though we must be cautious, modest, and tentative about making statements concerning what is real and true about events in the material world, we nonethless can be fairly confident that some statements are true and others are false....

It is only by knowing the empirical nature of a given threat that we are able to determine the degree of disproportionality. The concept of the moral panic *rests* on disproportionality. If we cannot determine disproportionality, we cannot conclude that a given episode of fear or concern represents a case of a moral panic. Again: we can only know disproportionality by assessing threat from existing empirical information. But, once again, to repeat: our knowledge of the material world is never definitive, never absolutely certain. We are permitted only *degrees* of confidence. Still, that may be enough, for some issues, to feel fairly certain that what we say is correct.

Volatility

And fifth, by their very nature, moral panics are *volatile*; they erupt fairly suddenly (although they may lie dormant or latent for long periods of time, and may reappear from time to time) and, nearly as suddenly, subside. Some moral panics may become *routinized* or *institutionalized*, that is, the moral concern about the target behavior results in, or remains in place in the form of, social movement organizations, legislation, enforcement practices, informal interpersonal norms or practices for punishing transgressors, after it has run its course. Others merely vanish, almost without trace; the legal, cultural, moral, and social fabric of the society after the panic is essentially no different from the way it was before; no new social control mechanisms are instituted as a consequence of its eruption. But, whether it has a long-term impact or not, the degree of hostility generated during a moral panic tends to be fairly limited temporally; the fever pitch that characterizes a society during the moral panic during its course is not typically sustainable over a long stretch of time. In that respect, it is similar to fashion, the fad, and the craze; the moral panic is, therefore, as we saw, a form of collective behavior.

[...]

We believe that these criteria spell out a more or less definable, measurable social phenomenon.

[...]

In short, the concept, moral panic, does *not* define a concern over a given issue or putative threat about which a given cynical observer is unsympathetic, or feels is morally or ideologically inappropriate. ... The moral panic is a phenomenon – given its broad and sprawling nature – that can be located and measured in a farily unbiased fashion. It does not matter whether we sympathize with the concern or not. What is important is that the concern locates a 'folk devil,' is shared, is out of synch with the measureable seriousness of the condition that generates it, and varies in intensity over time. As we shall see, if that concern is focused exclusively on moral or symbolic issues as ends in themselves, it cannot be regarded as a moral panic. The point that the moral panics concept is scientifically defensible, and not an invidious, ideologically motivated term of debunking, needs to be stressed in the strongest possible fashion.

Criteria of Disproportionality

... How do we know that the attention accorded a given issue, problem, or phenomenon is disproportional to the threat it poses? Is referring to a certain issue as a 'moral panic' nothing more than a 'value judgment,' an arbitrary claim that it does not deserve to receive as much attention as it has? While we agree with Ungar (1992, p. 497) that, with *some* conditions, 'it is impossible to determine the nature of the objective threat' – and therefore, for that condition, to measure the dimension of disproportionality – this is most decidedly not true for many, possibly most, conditions. ... Here are four indicators of disproportionality.

Figures exaggerated

First, if the figures that are cited to measure the scope of the problem are grossly exaggerated, we may say that the criterion of disproportionality has been met....

Figures fabricated

Second, if the concrete threat that is feared is, by all available evidence, nonexistent, we may say that the criterion of disproportionality has been met....

Other harmful conditions

Third, if the attention that is paid to a specific condition is vastly greater than that paid to another, and the concrete threat or damage caused by the first is no greater than, or is less than, the second, the criterion of disproportionality may be said to have been met. . . .

Changes over time

Fourth, if the attention paid to a given condition at one point in time is vastly greater than that paid to it during a previous or later time without any corresponding increase in objective seriousness, then, once again, the criterion of disproportionality may be said to have been met. . . .

[. . .]

Disproportionality: A Recapitulation

Thus, each of the concrete indicators mentioned above – figures on the objective seriousness of the problem are exaggerated, the existence of a materially nonexistent problem, gross differences in concern among various conditions, and radical fluctuations in concern over time without corresponding material changes in seriousness – provides a criterion for disproportionality, the fourth element in our definition of the moral panic. . . . The concept has objective validity; it is not a value judgment, but a phenomenon in the material world that can be located, measured, and analyzed. If we define the concept out of existence, we will fail to notice major social processes that have had an impact on human societies, possibly, for the duration of human history. Given the ubiquity and influence of the moral panic, it demands attention.

[. . .]

Moral Panics: An Overview

Societies everywhere have at times been gripped by moral panics and yet, as Cohen says (1972, p. 11), they have received insufficient systematic attention. More research has been devoted to the moral panic in the past decade than was true of the decade following Cohen's introduction of the concept. Still, we need to know far more about them than we do. Focusing on moral panics raises a number of questions. Who is it, exactly, whose expression of concern defines the moral panic? How much concern in how many individuals constitutes a genuine case of moral panic? Why do some panics occur among certain segments among the public but not others – that is, why are some panics socially and subculturally localized, while others grip a people society-wide? How do they get started? What, exactly, is the active agent responsible for their genesis? Do they arise as a result of enterprise – that is, the conscious efforts of the few – or do they emerge on a more widespread, grassroots, populist basis? If it is the former, is there any such thing as a moral panic without popular support? If it is the latter, are specific agents necessary at all, or can moral panics erupt without specific agents, leaders, or entrepreneurs? How do the efforts of the few effect concern among the many? Is it possible for certain incipient moral panics to fail to take hold? Why do panics over a particular issue burst forth at one time but not another – that is, why are they patterned according to a specific *timing*? Are certain individuals, types of individuals, or segments of society more likely to initiate the moral panic? If certain individuals, types of individuals, or social categories attempt to launch a moral panic, is it more likely to be successful – that is, to take hold – in comparison with the outcome of the efforts of other individuals, types of individuals, or social categories? Once started, do moral panics take on a life of their own, or do they require sustained nurturance? Why do panics over certain issues grip specific groups or categories in a society but leave others indifferent? Whose values are being expressed by the panic? Whose interests does the moral panic serve? Are certain behaviors more intrinsically frightening than others – and more likely to generate moral panics? What is the role of the media in reporting and sustaining a moral panic? What is the role of the state or the government in the generation and maintenance of the moral panic? Why do moral panics die out? What is their long-term legacy or impact? What characterizes those that have a long-term impact versus those that do not?

Moral panics frequently erupt in modernizing and modern society, a fact that should cause us to question their sophisticated, tolerant, *laissez-faire* stance toward nonconformity. In fact, it is entirely likely that moral panics serve as a mechanism for simultaneously strengthening and redrawing society's moral boundaries – that line between morality and immorality, just where one leaves the territory of good and enters that of evil. When a society's moral boundaries are sharp, clear, and secure, and the central norms and values are strongly held by nearly everyone, moral panics rarely grip its members – nor do they need to. However, when the moral boundaries are fuzzy and shifting and often seem to be contested, moral panics are far more likely to seize the members of a society (Ben-Yehuda, 1985).

References

Barlow, H.D. (1993) *Introduction to Criminology.* 6th edn. New York: Harper/Collins.

Ben-Yehuda, N. (1985) *Deviance and Moral Boundaries: Witchcraft, the Occult, Science Fiction, Deviant Sciences and Scientists.* Chicago: University of Chicago Press.

Ben-Yehuda, N. (1990) *The Politics and Morality of Deviance: Moral Panics, Drug Abuse, and Reversed Stigmatization.* Albany, NY: State University of New York Press.

Best, J. (1990) *Threatened Children: Rhetoric and Concern about Child-Victims.* Chicago: University of Chicago Press.

Cohen, S. (1972) *Folk Devils and Moral Panics: The Creation of the Mods and Rockers.* London: MacGibbon & Kee.

Davis, N. and Stasz, C. (1990) *Social Control of Deviance: A Critical Perspective.* New York: McGraw-Hill.

Hall, S., Critcher, C., Jefferson, T., Clarke, J. and Roberts, B. (1978) *Policing the Crisis: Mugging, the State, and Law and Order.* London: Macmillan.

Kilbourne, B.K. and Kilbourne, M.T. (1983) *The Dark Side of Science.* San Francisco: Pacific Division, American Association for the Advancement of Science.

Ungar, S. (1992) The rise and (relative) decline of global warming as a social problem, *The Sociological Quarterly*, 33(4): 483–501.

Zatz, M. (1987) Chicago youth gangs and crime: the creation of a moral panic, *Contemporary Crises*, 11(2): 129–58.

5

THE HISTORY AND MEANING OF THE CONCEPT

Kenneth Thompson (1998)

In our discussion of various case studies we will draw on a range of theories, but the main emphasis will be on the role of the mass media in relation to cultural politics and the politics of anxiety in the 'risk society'. It is this aspect that has been least developed in the literature on moral panics, and it is also the factor that seems most likely to explain the frequency and spread of moral panics in Britain. American sociologists have tended to emphasize social psychological factors, such as anxiety and stress, portraying moral panics as just another form of collective behaviour, or in terms of interest groups and social movements; whilst, for a period beginning in the mid-1970s, British studies such as Stuart Hall et al. portrayed moral panics mainly in terms of a crisis of capitalism and a consequent increase in state authoritarianism. However, it can be argued that some of the most useful contributions of each of these approaches have yet to be fully combined into an explanatory framework. The American studies have been particularly insightful in their analyses of the role of moral entrepreneurs and claims-makers. But the influence of these opinion leaders depends on publicity through the mass media. And it could be argued that the originality of the work of Hall and his colleagues at the Birmingham Centre for Contemporary Cultural Studies lay not so much in their use of Marxist concepts and theories concerning capitalism and the state, but rather in their pioneering and imaginative approach to cultural studies as symbolic politics, particularly their analyses of subcultures and the 'signification spiral' – a way of publicly signifying issues and problems which is intrinsically escalating, i.e. 'it increases the perceived potential threat of an issue through the way it becomes signified' (Hall and Jefferson 1976:77).

Although sociologists aspire to develop a universalistic science and to avoid theoretical ethnocentrism, there can be no doubt that different national conditions lead to differences of theoretical emphasis. Whilst it is true that American sociologists took up the concept of moral panics with some enthusiasm after it originated in Britain, there are clear differences of emphasis. For example, Goode and Ben-Yehuda incorporate the concept into the fields of social movements and collective behaviour studies, which have a prominent place in American sociology, whereas Cohen made only passing references to social movements and collective behaviour (Cohen 1972: 120). Social movements are defined as organized efforts by a substantial number of people to change or resist change in some important aspect of society, and their principal aim is to establish the legitimacy of a specific claim about a social condition (Goode and Ben-Yehuda 1994: 116). Social movements are distinguished from *established pressure groups* or *lobbies*, on the grounds that they are mainly composed of outsiders without direct access to policy-makers and legislators, and their statements do not receive automatic attention in the media. In order to further their claims they have to gain the media's attention and attempt to secure legitimation for their definition of the reality of the condition being addressed. They do this by painting their issue in terms of good versus evil, and the language of moral indignation. The focus is on the worst aspects of the condition they are denouncing as if these are typical and representative. For example, a moral panic about pornography may be generated by focusing exclusively on pornography involving children or violence, even though these constitute a small proportion of pornography (Goode and Ben-Yehuda 1994: 120).

Goode and Ben-Yehuda distinguish between a *'middle level' outsider interest groups (or social movements) model* of moral panics, a *grassroots model* and an *elite-engineered model*. On the whole, they themselves favour the 'middle level' approach, although they accept that some attention should be paid to the other two levels.

The grassroots model sees moral panics as a direct and spontaneous expression of a widespread concern and anxiety about a perceived evil threat. . . .

Proponents of an elite-engineered model are said to be critical of such a grassroots model explanation, arguing that crime and the repression of crime are important in 'enabling the ruling stratum to maintain its privileged position' (Chambliss and Mankoff 1976: 15–16). However, Goode and Ben-Yehuda tend to confuse an 'elite model' with a 'class model'. The former refers to a social group whose main concern is to maintain their privileged social status, whereas a class model is concerned with the reproduction of a structure of socio-economic relations (i.e. capitalist social relations). In the latter model the tendency has been to look at the ways in which the state, through institutions such as the media, social workers, the police and the courts, maintains and reproduces the social order. The portrayal of the muggings panic in 1970s Britain by Stuart Hall et al. is cited by Goode and Ben-Yehuda as an illustration of an elite-engineered theory of moral panics. This is because it specifically focused on questions such as 'What forces stand to benefit from it? What role has the state played in its construction? What real fears is it mobilising?' (Hall et al. 1978: viii). However, Stuart Hall et al. insisted that they were not presenting a 'conspiratorial' interpretation in which an elite consciously plotted to maintain their power and privileges. It is true that at times their language did seem to be arguing that the ruling elite orchestrates hegemony, and as a result manages to convince the rest of society – the press, the general public, the courts, law enforcement – that the real enemy is not the crisis in British capitalism but the criminal and the lax way he has been dealt with. However, this suggestion of a conscious strategy on the part of a group of people, the 'elite', is not typical of their analysis. On the whole their emphasis is on structural tendencies, the ways in which institutions tend to favour certain interpretations of events that have the effect of maintaining social order, because they are 'structured in dominance'. In other words, the media tend to 'reproduce the definitions of the powerful' (Hall et al. 1978: 57); they 'faithfully and impartially ... reproduce symbolically the existing structure of power in society's institutional order' (ibid.: 58). The media, especially, do not necessarily consciously set out to generate a moral panic with the intention of diverting attention from economic problems, but economic problems create strains and the media respond by amplifying the symptoms of strain, such as fears about a breakdown in law and order.

American sociologists have been less inclined than their British counterparts to look for society-wide cultural and social structural explanations such as crises of capitalism and cultural hegemony (although there are exceptions, as in the case of Chambliss and Mankoff 1976). Goode and Ben-Yehuda are more typical in preferring an interest-group theory of moral panics, arguing that moral panics are more likely to emanate from the middle rungs of the power and status hierarchy. In the interest-group perspective, 'professional associations, police departments, the media, religious groups, educational organizations, may have an independent stake in bringing an issue to the fore – focusing media attention on it or transforming the slant of news stories covering it, alerting legislators, demanding stricter law enforcement, instituting new educational curricula, and so on' (Goode and Ben-Yehuda 1994: 139). And it is true that these middle-range theories are extremely serviceable for explaining the immediate causes of individual moral panics, particularly the role of moral entrepreneurs who launch crusades that may become panics. What they do not explain is the multiplicity or rapid succession of moral panics in a particular period. Furthermore, because they define the media as simply another middle-range interest group they do not explain the convergence or the linking by labelling of the specific issue to other problems, which is an element in the 'signification spiral' discussed by Hall and Jefferson (1978).

[...]

A signification spiral does not exist in a vacuum. It can only work if the connecting links are easily established by drawing on pre-existing ideological complexes or discursive formations. Philip Jenkins, in his study of contemporary British moral panics, whilst insisting that there was insufficient evidence to support the political processes suggested in the 'Marxist' account of Stuart Hall et al., did agree that it provides strong confirmation for viewing panics as interdependent and he regretted that the issue of interdependence was not frequently discussed (Jenkins 1992: 12). However, although Jenkins admits that moral panics tend to appear in groups rather than singly, and that they are related to wider anxieties and social contextual factors, he tends to focus most of his explanation on claims-makers and interest groups. He believes that this is now justified for explaining even British moral panics because Britain has become more like America:

> Like many European countries, British society in the last two decades has become more oriented to the politics of interest groups than to traditional notions of class, and issues of race, ethnicity, and gender have become pivotal. British politics in the 1960s and 1970s were dominated by issues with a powerful and overt class content: union power, regulation of strikes and industrial conflict, nationalization of industry. In the 1980s, the emphasis shifted to interest group politics and social issues such as censorship, feminism, gay rights, education, and public morality (which is not to say that a class agenda may not underlie many or most of these issues). In all of these areas, debate would be conditioned by moral panics, by stereotypes of sexual violence and threatening sexual predators. (Jenkins 1992: 46)

Jenkins is right to point out the growth of interest groups and claims-makers, and their pursuit of *'symbolic politics* and the *'politics of substitution'*, through which they drew attention to a specific problem in part because it symbolized another issue, which they could not address directly. For example, the decriminalization of homosexuality meant that those who wished to denounce such practices as immoral had to do this in an indirect way by raising fears about the threat to children and the supposed upsurge of paedophilia. He also refers to some of the fundamental cultural and social changes making for a politics of anxiety underlying the symbolic politics represented in moral panics, such as those over child sexual abuse within the family (1985–7), paedophile sex rings (1987–9), the alleged wave of child murder cases (1986–90) and similar cases. Many of these factors combined to unsettle traditional gender relations and ideas about sexuality, particularly with regard to women's roles, the family and the care of children. The economic changes included a worldwide slump, increased competition between western and eastern capitalist economies, a shift from manufacturing to service industries, an increase in the female workforce (including working mothers), and a decline of economic activity in old industrial and inner city areas. The corresponding political changes included a return to neo-liberal, free-market policies and pressures to cut welfare state benefits that had provided a safety net for the victims of economic change, which in turn increased insecurity for many groups. Many of the moral panics that accompanied these profound social changes could well be interpreted in terms of the politics of anxiety, symbolic politics or the politics of substitution.

Two theoretical streams that have not yet been incorporated into the explanation of moral panics are those emanating from Ulrich Beck's concept of *risk society* (Beck 1992) and Michel Foucault's work on *discursive formations* (Foucault 1971). The concept of risk society is relevant to developing the politics of anxiety explanation of moral panics. Whilst Foucault's work on discursive formations could help in developing the ideas about the signification spiral and the process of convergence, discussed by Hall and his colleagues.

References

Beck, U. (1992) *Risk Society*. trans. M. Ritter, London: Sage.

Chambliss, W. and Mankoff, M. (eds) (1976) *Whose Law? What Order?* New York: Wiley.

Cohen, S. ([1972]/1980) *Folk Devils and Moral Panics: The Creation of the Mods and Rockers.* London: MacGibbon & Kee; new edition with introduction, Oxford: Martin Robertson.

Foucault, M. ([1971]/1981) *L'Ordre du discours,* Paris: Gallimard: trans. by R. Young as The order of discourse, in R. Young (ed.) *Untying the Text: A Poststructuralist Reader.* London: Routledge.

Goode, E. and Ben-Yehuda (1994) *Moral Panics: The Social Construction of Deviance*. Oxford: Blackwell.

Hall, S. and Jefferson, T. (1976) *Resistance Through Rituals: Youth Subcultures in Post-War Britain*. London: Hutchinson.

Hall, S., Critcher, C., Jefferson, T., Clarke, J. and Roberts, B. (1978) *Policing the Crisis: Mugging, the State, and Law and Order*. London: Macmillan.

Jenkins, P. (1992) *Intimate Enemies: Moral Panics in Contemporary Great Britain*. New York: Aldine de Gruyter.

Overview

In his latest introduction to *Folk Devils and Moral Panics*, Cohen (2002: viii) suggests that 'the objects of moral panics belong to seven familiar clusters of social identity'. These are: (1) young working-class violent males; (2) school violence: bullying and shoot-outs; (3) wrong drugs used by wrong people in wrong places; (4) child abuse, including satanism and paedophilia; (5) sex and/or violence in the media; (6) welfare cheats and single mothers; (7) refugees and asylum seekers. The selection of cases in this section does not quite match Cohen's profile. School violence and welfare cheats or single mothers are absent (though on the latter as moral panic, see Evans and Swift 2000). Instead, there are three varieties of child abuse, with the important case study of AIDS which is absent from Cohen's list, in addition to those he does recognize: media violence, drugs, immigration/asylum seekers and street crime. Each reading at least mentions the moral panic concept, though there is considerable variation in the precise way it is applied.

In *Reading 6*, Jeffrey Weeks (1989) discusses AIDS in the UK as a moral panic. Weeks divides the development of the AIDS crisis into three phases. The middle phase (1983–85) is that of moral panic, preceded by the phase of 'dawning crisis' (1981–82) and followed (1985 onwards) by one of 'crisis management'. In the moral panic phase a media-based hysteria over the 'gay plague' was countered by the mobilization of the gay movement in a context where the HIV virus had been identified but there was no effective treatment. However, this potential for a recognizable moral panic was never realized. The medical establishment and gay organizations, in a sometimes uneasy alliance, became the primary definers of the issue. As the crisis deepened, governments took heed of expert advice and launched campaigns aimed at prevention through safe sex. By the end of the 1980s there were signs that the calmer and more reasoned approach to this public health crisis had prevailed and Weeks could anticipate the time when AIDS would become routinized as a sexually transmitted disease.

Weeks' own explanation of reaction to AIDS stresses its role as 'the bearer of a number of political, social and moral anxieties' only indirectly related to AIDS, including concerns over promiscuity, permissiveness and drugs. A primarily gay disease caught through sexual adventuring symbolized a much wider range of shifts in personal morality and behaviour.

Weeks' use of the term moral panic was subsequently criticized in conceptual terms by Watney (*Reading 18* in this volume) and in empirical terms by Berridge (1992). However, Fordham (2001) argued that in the cultural context of Thailand, AIDS was used to construct a moral panic about prostitution. In a later more general analysis of AIDS, Weeks (1993: 25) defended the use of moral panic: 'we can, I still believe, use this concept, with caution, as a helpful heuristic device to explore the deeper currents which shaped the developing HIV / AIDS crisis'. He remains alert to the limitations of the model: its inability to account for the complexities of AIDS and the general shortcoming that it is a template rather than an explanation.

In *Reading 7* Jenkins and Maier-Katkin (1992) analyse the 'satanic panic' in the USA at the end of the 1980s. This claimed that organized groups of Satanists (literally devil worshippers) were engaged in a nationwide conspiracy to abduct, sexually exploit and even murder children. The whole panic was based on the repetition of 'facts' and 'cases' from very small number of so-called experts, either religious fundamentalists or serving police officers. The lack of any hard evidence to support these claims did not prevent their spread which peaked in 1988. It proved sufficient to remind people of a few notorious cult killings and to appeal to a general belief that the Devil or at least evil was among us.

Jenkins and Maier-Katkin suggest that this was a classic moral panic fuelled by three specific factors. First, there was and is a general predisposition amongst the American public to believe in conspiracy theories. Second, at this time there occurred increasingly fierce competition among news media, producing a greater susceptibility to sensational stories. Third, there existed a highly organized and well-resourced network of the Religious Right who sought to exploit the issue for their own ends.

The panic has been documented in some detail in Richardson et al.

(1991) for the USA and Jenkins (1992) for the UK. It had little lasting effect, except on the detail of some child protection laws. Its significance lies elsewhere. It is rare for a moral panic to be almost entirely a fabrication but, along with the UK's dangerous dogs scare of 1990–91 (Podberscek 1994), this appears to be one. It also reveals in particularly stark form a belief in the Devil or at least in evil. Very obvious in this instance, such an underlying belief may also be a factor in other moral panics with an apparently more secular agenda. It is finally the religiosity of the whole affair which to the British eye especially seems so bizarre. We are briefly back, it would seem, in the world of seventeenth-century Massachusetts, on the trail of Satanists as the twentieth-century equivalent of witches.

Chiricos (1996) in *Reading 8* analyses a 1993–94 panic about violent crime in the USA and so interrelates themes which now resonate in other countries: race, class, crime and social control. Chiricos's position is stark. Scares about violent crime are used to justify punitive action against the underclass and to divert attention away from economic problems and the nature of deviant behaviour. This is achieved by an ideological distortion of real problems and results in repressive measures which are counter-productive since they increase the alienation of the underclass.

Chiricos identifies clear resemblances between the violent crime panic of 1993–94 and that of crack cocaine in 1986. In both there was a sudden explosion of media interest though statistically the problem was on the wane; what was a long-standing problem was made to seem new by emphasizing the extreme youth of the perpetrators and the spread beyond the confines of the ghetto; the clear emphasis was on the need for punitive measures which increased prison sentences and incarcerated even more young black males.

Chiricos argues that this moral panic was a deliberate ideological ploy to draw attention away from the deteriorating economic situation of the underclass. It involved misrepresenting figures about crime rates and ignoring figures about unemployment rates. The main long-term consequence was to place even more young black men in prison. It seems to have been driven largely by a (white) mass media concerned to identify a (black) menace from the ghetto. This apparently quintessential US scenario is now being played out in many European cities where a fateful combination of deprivation, frustrated masculinity, drugs and guns may produce more noticeable violent crime. The media system's response is to eschew understanding or remedying ghetto conditions in favour of striking fear into readers or viewers.

A similar perspective on 'race' and crime in the USA can be found in Chambliss (1995). McCorkle and Miethe (1999) studied a local moral panic on the same issue while Schissel (1997) examined the construction of youth crime in Canada. I have cited 'gun culture' as an example of failed moral panic in Britain (Critcher 2005). *Reading 9* from Stockwell (1997) is a case study of the mass shooting in the town of Port Arthur in the Australian state of Tasmania in 1996. Martin Bryant shot dead 35 people in an apparently random attack. Stockwell applies to it Cohen's model, especially the disaster-derived warning, impact, inventory and reaction phases. Two issues were constructed around Port Arthur. The first was gun control where, as we saw in the Introduction to this volume, federal laws were immediately passed heavily restricting gun ownership. Stockwell asks pointedly if this is to be regarded as a moral panic, 'when the devil is real?'

Much easier to spot as a mythical construction was the attempt to blame the tragedy on violent videos. Despite the lack of any evidence that Bryant was interested in any sort of videos, the pull of the issue proved too strong. The murder of James Bulger in Britain in 1993, blamed on video nasties, provided the Australian media with a handy template. The *Child's Play* movie series was again implicated on the flimsiest of evidence. New censorship moves were proposed to tighten film classification, restrict times of movies on television and have all new sets fitted with a V chip.

Stockwell explicitly draws out lessons of the case study for moral panic models as a whole. Here there were no independent moral entrepreneurs; the issue was driven solely by a combination of government and media. There were no folk devils, since in both cases (guns and videos) objects were the focus of attention. A key event like this also throws up several possibilities for moral campaigns or panics. The murderer Bryant had a history of mental illness and relations with far-right groups, either of which might have become a focus but did not. Stockwell argues that moral panics are not automatic reflexes but active choices from a field of possibilities. As a result, journalists can and should challenge the grounds and nature of such choices made by media organizations. As noted in the Introduction to this book, the Bryant episode has also been discussed in terms of the campaign for gun control laws (Chapman 1998). It can also be compared with reaction to the 1999 Columbine school shooting (Burns and Crawford 1999; Killingbeck 2001; Springhall 1999).

In *Reading 10* Kitzinger (1999) analyses local and national media coverage of controversies over access to the Register of Sex Offenders introduced in the UK in 1997. Access was restricted to professionals, thus preventing ordinary people knowing if a convicted sex offender was living in or near their neighbourhood. Local newspapers were very active in revealing their presence. On some public housing estates there were protests when it became known that sex offenders had been allocated accommodation.

Kitzinger recounts how media and professional opinion frequently denounced the lynch mob mentality of such protests or condemned the whole furore as a moral panic but she demurs from such simplistic disavowal. There were real issues behind the headlines. Strategically placed professionals had no agreed roles in monitoring offenders. Policies over community notification were inconsistent. Where local residents failed to trust professionals or feared for their own children's safety, these were not unreasonable concerns. They resorted to direct action because other channels were not open to them. Restoring normality here meant that professionals resumed their secret and unaccountable jurisdiction over convicted sex offenders, whilst others remained ignorant of where such offenders were or how they were being monitored. Nevertheless, Kitzinger finds unhelpful the discourse about paedophilia which dominated public discussion of the whole issue. This presents sexual abusers as abnormal outsiders whereas sexual abuse is more likely to be perpetrated on children by men whom they trust.

The paedophilia issue generally, as in this example, is exceptional in the UK because of the level and type of public concern it evokes, which Kitzinger suggests has its own validity. In offering their support, the local media were much more sympathetic than the dismissive national media. All this complexity tends to resist any straightforward application of the moral panic model, about which Kitzinger is generally sceptical. Yet her critique of the 'paedophile' label is an account of how constructing a folk devil can have such a damaging effect upon realizing what the actual problem is and who are its most likely perpetrators.

Other writers to have used the moral panic model to analyse paedophilia in the UK include Critcher (2002). Its emergence in the USA is traced by Jenkins (1998). More recently, in a detailed study of local newspaper coverage of sex offenders, Cheit (2003) agrees that stranger danger is overplayed but observes the level of coverage to be quite low and the distortions involved to be those typical of routine news reporting.

In *Reading 11* Ost (2002) delivers a legal perspective on a possible moral panic. She sets out to consider whether in the UK there has been a moral panic about the possession of child pornography. Even if there has, this does not invalidate concerns about its circulation and use. The article stresses the need to understand the complexities of the law, why possession was originally made a criminal offence at all and how punishments for it were incrementally increased. These resulted from what Ost sees as a moral panic among the media, police, judiciary and politicians. It was based on two assumptions: either possessing child pornography was inherently immoral, so should be made illegal; and/or such material would inevitably have harmful effects on the behaviour of the possessor.

Ost scrutinizes these and other claims about child pornography with forensic precision. Evidence for the claim that possession of pornography encourages men to abuse children transpires to be uneven and contradictory. This kind of unsubstantiated claim is characteristic of a moral panic. However, there are other grounds for objecting to child pornography: that children are often abused to produce it and that it has the undesirable effect of encouraging children to be viewed as objects of sexual deᵤire. It is not quite that those supporting the moral panic are right for the wrong reasons; it is more that only part of their case stands up but it is enough to support current legislation.

The complexity of the law and its interpretation should perhaps be more important in moral panic analysis, along the lines pursued here. Ost's account confirms the importance of the five Ps in the moral panic (press, pressure groups, politicians, police, public opinion). In the original, much of which has had to be edited out here, there is especially strong emphasis on the importance of what judges think about child pornography. It also reminds us that a moral panic may contain a kernel of truth. Though the laws passed may be based on a distorted view of the issue, they nevertheless capture in their net those who do constitute a danger to children, however indirect. We know independently (Greek and Thompson 1992) that originally the pornography issue was driven by religious fundamentalist claims makers (the National Viewers and Listeners Association), as well as more secular campaigners (the National Society for the Prevention of Cruelty to Children). Both organizations have encouraged moral panics for their own agendas (Critcher 2003). But despite all that, and the fragility of the evidence adduced to support their claims, Ost argues that the measures taken were appropriate to address some real dangers posed by the mere possession of child pornography.

In *Reading 12* Welch and Schuster (2005) tackle two parallel issues, foreign terrorists in the USA and asylum seekers in the UK, over roughly the same period of 2001–3. They seek to heed Cohen's (2002) call for more comparative studies and his suggestion that there may be 'quiet' as well as 'noisy' moral panics. In the UK the issue of asylum seekers is a noisy one, conducted openly in the pages of the mass press where stories about 'bogus' asylum seeker stories appeared regularly from 2001. Amidst such controversy, the UK government substantially increased its powers of detention and expulsion. A few organizations sought to defend the rights of asylum seekers and criticized the terms of the debate. Though their voices were drowned out, the whole process did at least take place in public arenas.

Not so with terrorists in the USA post-9/11. The powers of government agencies to detain without trial and expel without tribunal were extended and applied, with little public debate and less legal scrutiny. The level of secrecy made it difficult to discover, much less openly criticize, what was going on. Few wanted to appear to be defending terrorists. Unlike the UK, all this was conducted quietly without public debate, at least in the mainstream media.

In the UK the government pandered to 'public' – that is, press – opinion with a series of highly publicized or noisy administrative and legal measures. In the USA the 'war on terror' was pursued almost in secret, more quietly. Normally, openness in government is characteristic of the USA and secrecy of the UK. In this instance the roles were reversed. Both, however, utilize what Welch and Schuster identify as strategies of denial where governments deny either that any of this is happening or that it means what it seems to.

This study adds to our comparative knowledge by looking at similar, if not precisely the same, issues in different nations. There are, of course, differences. If nothing else, the USA is a nation of immigrants while the UK is a nation against immigrants. But in both countries there is revealed a state apparatus ruthlessly pursuing its own ends in the cause of its own survival at the expense of established constitutional principles. The construction of the stranger as a danger in the context of heightened international tension has an extraordinary effect on the imagination of the public and the actions of politicians.

Analysts of the construction of the asylum seeker issue in Britain have tended to use models of 'othering' derived from work on images of ethnic outsiders (Bailey and Harindranath 2005) but there is every reason to suppose that moral panic models could be used equally well. The asylum seeker threat to the UK receded, only to be replaced by that of immigration from Eastern Europe. The terrorist threat is likely to persist on both sides of the Atlantic for decades to come. A broad approach to how all forms of terrorism have been constructed in the USA is available in Jenkins (2003). This serial moral panic will not go away but is destined to become a permanent feature of the political landscape in these two countries.

Reading 13 (Meylakhs 2005) looks at the drugs issue as a moral panic in the setting of contemporary Russia. Meylakhs analyses the reporting of drugs problem in four St Petersburg newspapers as compared with national papers. National coverage grew rapidly in 1998, peaked during 1999–2001 and fell away throughout 2002–3. In the St Petersburg press, expanded coverage of the problem was restricted to the first six months of 2002. The key event locally was the murder of an academic, allegedly by drug addicts.

Meylakhs establishes that on all available measures drug usage in Russia is slightly below the norm for Western Europe. This did not prevent massive exaggeration of the nature of the problem. Four discursive strategies are identified: a 'signification spiral' employing images of calamity or disaster; 'automatic problematization' with drug use inherently connected to crime and to AIDS; 'categorization work' which permits all users of any kind of drugs to be indiscriminately classed as addicts; and 'selective typification' which assumes all drug users to graduate to criminal activity. The press mobilizes concern by a rhetoric of calamity and calls for citizens to form action committees. Drug users as folk devils are constructed as insiders who have transgressed. During the brief moral panic a discourse of criminalization prevailed, only to be displaced by the originally dominant discourse of medicalization.

Meylakhs shows us some remarkable consistencies in the discourse about drugs between contemporary Russia and Europe, North America and Australasia over the years (see, for example, Reinarman and Levine 1989). Opinion veers between the need to help victims rehabilitate themselves and wanting to imprison those who wilfully continue to use drugs and support their habit through criminal enterprise. The rise and fall of press interest is not related to changes in the actual incidence of the problem, though it may be triggered by a key event. However, press coverage was locally much less extreme than nationally.

Legal changes were more symbolic than real and were in any case later reversed. This was a moral panic which did not quite happen. Many of the ingredients were there but, as might be expected in a country emerging from years of communist dictatorship, there is striking absence of pressure group activity, either for or against the moral panic. Once these emerge, then the profile of players and the discourse they employ may closely resemble those already evident in mature democracies.

References

Bailey, O.G. and Harindranath, R. (2005) Racialized 'othering': the representation of asylum seekers in the news media, in S. Allan (ed.) *Journalism: Critical Issues*. Maidenhead: Open University Press.

Berridge, V. (1992) AIDS, the media and health policy, in P. Aggleton, P. Davies and G. Hart (eds) *AIDS: Rights, Risk and Reason*. Bristol: The Falmer Press.

Burns, R. and Crawford, C. (1999) School shootings, the media and public fear: ingredients for a moral panic, *Crime, Law and Social Change*, 32: 147–68.

Chambliss, W.J. (1995) Crime control and ethnic minorities: legitimising racial oppression by creating moral panics, in D.F. Hawkins (ed.) *Ethnicity, Race and Crime*. Albany, NY: State University of New York Press.

Chapman, S. (1998) *Over Our Dead Bodies: Port Arthur and Australia's Fight for Gun Control*. New South Wales: Pluto Press.

Cheit, R.E. (2003) What hysteria? A systematic study of newspaper coverage of accused child molesters, *Child Abuse and Neglect*, 27: 607–23.

Cohen, S. (2002) Introduction to the third edition, *Folk Devils and Moral Panics*. London: Routledge.

Critcher, C. (2002) Media, government and moral panic: the politics of paedophilia in Britain 2000–1, *Journalism Studies* 3(4): 520–34.

Critcher, C. (2003) *Moral Panics and the Media*. Milton Keynes: Open University Press.

Critcher, C. (2005) Mighty dread: journalism and moral panics, in S. Allan (ed.) *Journalism: Critical Issues*. Maidenhead: Open University Press.

Evans, P.M. and Swift, K.J. (2000) Single mothers and the press: rising tides, moral panic and restructuring discourses, in S.M. Neysmith (ed.) *Restructuring Caring Labour*. Oxford: Oxford University Press.

Fordham, G. (2001) Moral panic and the construction of national order: HIV/AIDS risk groups and moral boundaries in the creation of modern Thailand, *Critique of Anthropology*, 21(3): 259–316.

Greek, C.E. and Thompson, W. (1992) Anti-pornography campaigns: saving the family in America and England, *International Journal of Politics, Culture and Society*, 5(4): 601–15.

Jenkins, P. (1992) *Intimate Enemies: Moral Panics in Contemporary Great Britain*. New York: Aldine de Gruyter.

Jenkins, P. (1998) *Moral Panic: Changing Concepts of the Child Molester in Modern America*. New Haven, CT: Yale University Press.

Jenkins, P. (2003) *Images of Terror*. New York: Aldine de Gruyter.

Killingbeck, D. (2001) The role of television news in the construction of school violence as a 'moral panic', *Journal of Criminal Justice and Popular Culture*, 8(3): 186–202.

McCorkle, R.C. and Miethe, T.C. (1999) The political and organizational response to gangs: an examination of a 'moral panic' in Nevada, *Justice Quarterly* 15(1): 41–64.

Podberscek, A.L. (1994) Dog on a tightrope: the position of the dog in British society as influenced by press reports on dog attacks (1988 to 1992), *Anthrozoos*, VII(4): 232–41.

Reinarman, C. and Levine, H.G. (1989) The crack attack: politics and media in America's latest drug scare, in J. Best (ed.) *Images of Issues: Typifying Contemporary Social Problems*. New York: Aldine de Gruyter.

Richardson, J., Best, J. and Bromley, D. (eds) (1991) *The Satanism Scare*. New York: Aldine de Gruyter.

Schissel, B. (1997) Youth crime, moral panics, and the news: the conspiracy against the marginalized in Canada, *Social Justice*, 24(2): 165–84.

Springhall, J. (1999) Violent media, guns and moral panics: the Columbine High School massacre, *Pedagogica Historica*, 35(3): 621–41.

Weeks, J. (1993) AIDS and the regulation of sexuality, in V. Berridge and P. Strong (eds) *AIDS and Contemporary History*. Cambridge: Cambridge University Press.

Further Reading

Barker, M. and Petley, J. (eds) (1997) *Ill Effects: the Media/Violence Debate*. London: Routledge.

Berridge, V. (1996) *AIDS in the UK: The Making of Policy 1981–1991*. Oxford: Oxford University Press.

Hall, S., Critcher, C., Jefferson, T., Clarke, J. and Roberts, B. (1978) *Policing The Crisis: Mugging, the State and Law and Order*. London: Macmillan.

Jenkins, P. (2001) *Beyond Tolerance: Child Pornography on the Internet*. New York: New York University Press.

Reeves, J.L. and Campbell, R. (1994) *Cracked Coverage: Television News, the Anti-Cocaine Crusade and the Reagan Legacy*. Durham, NC: Duke University Press.

6

AIDS:
THE INTELLECTUAL AGENDA
Jeffrey Weeks (1989)

All diseases have social, ethical and political dimensions. Diseases affect individuals, not abstract entities or collectivities, and affects them in variable ways, according to their general social condition and bodily health. What makes disease culturally and historically important, however, is the way in which meanings are attached to illness and death, meanings and interpretations which are refracted through a host of differing, and often conflicting and contradictory social possibilties. These shape the ways we interpret illness, and therefore organize the ways in which we respond.

There is a long tradition of connecting disease with moral issues: 'sickness' and 'sin' are terms which have long been linked, and often interchangeably, especially in periods of heightened social anxiety. So there is nothing intrinsically new in the ways in which AIDS has been culturally interpreted, signified and given strong moral meaning.

[...]

In one sense then the social response to AIDS has been governed by the same tendency to moral inflation that has characterized a number of other life-threatening diseases in the past. But there are also important differences, differences which reveal much about the times we are living in. In the first place we are living through *this* disease, and the ways in which it is affecting us, and people we know and love, and the communities we inhabit. Second, we are living in a culture which at one time seemed to promise the triumph of technology over the uncontrollable whims of nature, and yet here is a new virus that has apparently confounded science....

Third, and perhaps most important, AIDS has become the symbolic bearer of a host of meanings about our contemporary culture: about its social composition, its racial boundaries, its attitudes to social marginality; and above all, its moral configurations and its sexual mores. A number of different histories intersect in and are condensed by AIDS discourse. What gives AIDS a particular power is its ability to represent a host of fears, anxieties and problems in our current, post-permissive society.

My aim in this chapter is not so much to provide an exhaustive explanation of why this is the case as to offer an intellectual framework within which we can identify the main forces at work. I shall begin by identifying the main phases of the social reaction to AIDS this far in its history. Through this it will be possible to characterize the present. Put briefly, my argument will be that AIDS already has a complex history which irrevocably shadows the way we think and the way we act. I will then discuss some of the key issues that need to be addressed in responding to the AIDS crisis. These provide the outlines of an agenda for historical and social science research, and for the political and social approaches needed to live with AIDS.

Responses to AIDS

Looking back over the years since 1981, when AIDS first emerged as a new and devastating illness, there is a potential danger that we will see the period as a monolithic whole, characterized by a deepening crisis and geometric spread of the disease....

There have, in fact, been at least three distinct phases in the social responses to AIDS so far. The boundaries between these are neither clear cut, nor absolute. Many features recur throughout, though with different weightings and emphases. Nevertheless, each period has its own distinct characteristics. Each needs looking at in turn.

The Dawning Crisis (1981–82)

There is of course a pre-history to AIDS stretching back to the mid-1970s, and by 1980 the dimensions of the potential crisis were already beginning to appear in statistics recording health problems amongst gay men (Shilts, 1988). It was not until the summer of 1981, however, that these developments became an embryonic public issue. It was then that the first stories began to appear in medical journals and in the gay press reporting the emergence of mysterious new illnesses among gay men in the USA. There were three major features of this first phase.

First, there was an awakening sense of anxiety amongst those most immediately affected, mainly gay men in the American cities with large gay populations. (New York, San Francisco and Los Angeles), but also members of the Haitian community in America, and haemophiliacs. At the same time, this was accompanied by a certain moral and sexual complacency which suggested that this new illness was either a scare story or a minority problem. This was the period when gay men began debating whether they needed to change their sexual habits, when fears began to emerge about the possible effects of AIDS on the achievements of gay liberation, and when those who advocated sexual abstinence or safer sex (for example, Berkowitz and Callen, 1983) were denounced for delivering the lesbian and gay community back into the embrace of the medical discourse from which it had all too recently escaped (Weeks, 1985). Because the cause, or causes, of the syndrome of illnesses were unknown, so the responses were contested and confused.

Second, there were exploratory medical and scientific attempts to define the nature, epidemiology and significance of this new phenomenon. These can be traced in the evolution of the terminology used to describe the syndrome – from 'the gay cancer' to GRID (Gay-Related Immune Deficiency), to the eventual acceptance in 1982 of the acronym AIDS – a shift, at least in the scientific world, from the initial identification of the disease with the community that first experienced it to a recognition of a more general danger. The four Hs were rapidly identified as 'risk categories': homosexuals, heroin users, haemophiliacs and, most controversially of all, Haitians. Allied to this shift were certain problems. Too narrow a definition of AIDS, relating it only to its terminal stages, threatened to encourage the view that the illness was invariably fatal, and resistance to it hopeless. But too broad a definition, to cover all of what became known as AIDS related conditions and the presence of sero-positivity, threatened equally to obscure important distinctions....

Third, this period saw the development of the characteristic style of governmental response that was to dominate the next phase: widespread indifference. There were many factors influencing this, including the coincidence that in the USA, and to a lesser extent elsewhere, the onset of AIDS occurred at the very moment that the Federal Administration was intent on cutting public expenditure. But over and above this, there was the overwhelming fact that AIDS was a disease that seemed to be confined to marginal, and (with the possible exceptions of haemophiliacs) politically and morally embarrassing, communities. More particularly, it was seen as a gay disease at a time when the view was being sedulously cultivated that the gay revolution had already gone too far (Weeks, 1986 and 1989).

Moral Panic (1982–85)

The marginality of people with AIDS, and its identification as a 'gay plague', were central to the second phase which occurred between 1982–85, that of moral panic. Moral panics occur in complex societies when deep-rooted and difficult to resolve social anxieties become focused on symbolic agents which can be easily targetted. Over the past century sexuality has been a potent focus of such moral panics – prostitutes have been blamed for syphilis, homosexuals for the cold war and pornography for child abuse and violence. Whilst the concept of a moral panic does not explain why transfers of anxiety like these occur – this has to be a matter for a historical analysis – it nevertheless offers a valuable framework for describing the course of events (Weeks, 1985; and for a critique of moral panic theory see Watney, 1987 and 1988).

From about 1982, AIDS (now identified as a distinctive set of diseases with definable, if as yet not precisely known, causative factors), became the bearer of a number of political, social and moral anxieties, whose origins lay elsewhere, but which were condensed into a crisis over AIDS. These included issues such as 'promiscuity', permissive lifestyles and drug taking. . . .

This period of moral panic was characterized by a number of features. First, it saw the rapid escalation of media and popular hysteria. This was the golden period of the New Right and Moral Majority onslaught in the USA, with leading lights claiming to see in AIDS God's or nature's judgment on moral decay. This was the period also when the term 'gay plague' became the favourite term of tabloid headline-writers (Wellings, 1988). This was the time when people with the disease were blamed for it. These were the years which witnessed the widespread appearance of 'rituals of decontamination': lesbians and gay men were refused service in restaurants, theatre personnel refused to work with gay actors, the trash cans of people suspected of having AIDS were not emptied, children with the virus were banned from schools, and the dead were left unburied. 'AIDS' as a symbolic phenomenon thereby grew out of, and fed into, potent streams of homophobia and racism.

Second, during 1983 and 1984, despite rather than because of the frantic international rivalry, the Human Immunodeficiency Virus (HIV) was at last identified and given its agreed name. This opened new opportunities for responding to the disease; but it also, inevitably, signalled the formidable difficulties in producing a vaccine against it, or a cure for it.

Third, this period saw the emergence of a massive self-help response from the communities most affected, and particularly from the lesbian and gay community. Organizations such as Gay Men's Health Crisis in New York or the Terrence Higgins Trust in London emerged as much more than special interest pressure groups. They became, in the absence of a coherent national strategy, the main vehicles of health education and social support. As Robert Padgug (1986) has suggested, one of the most striking features of AIDS has been the unusual, perhaps unique degree to which the group that was most affected by it took part in all aspects of its management. This included the provision of social aid and health care to people with AIDS, whether gay or not, the conduct of research, lobbying for funds and other government intervention, the creation of educational programmes, and negotiation with legislators and health insurers.

While governments throughout the West remained largely silent, these self-help groupings achieved remarkable results in safer-sex education. The identification of the virus, and its likely modes of transmission, made it clear that it was wrong to talk of risk categories; there were instead *risk activities*. And risk itself could be reduced by relatively simple measures – by using condoms, by cutting out certain unprotected sexual activities, and by not sharing needles if you were an injecting drug user. What was needed above all was education on prevention. Whilst national governments were as yet reluctant to undertake this, others by necessity picked up the candle, and with notable success too. . . .

Crisis Management (1985 to the present)

1985 was the turning point. Partly this was a result of chance factors, the most important of which was the well-publicized illness and death of Rock Hudson which dramatized the impact of the disease, and the inadequacy of American facilities: Hudson went to Paris, where in fact the virus had first been isolated, for treatment. The major reason, however, was the increasing evidence that AIDS was not just a disease of execrated minorities but a health threat on a global scale, and one which in world terms, largely affected heterosexuals. This initiated the period in which we now live, one in which the dominant response has been crisis management.

There are a number of key characteristics of this period. First, governments began to respond on a scale that approximated a little more to the magnitude of the crisis. . . . From 1985, . . . we can trace a new urgency in governmental response. In Britain there had been virtually no government response until 1984. Only then was there intervention to prevent the further contamination of the blood supply (and by implication, prevent the spread of AIDS to 'the innocent'). In 1985, the government took powers compulsorily to detain in hospital people who were perceived as likely to ignore medical advice and were at risk of spreading the disease. Both these measures were dictated by a fear that AIDS might infiltrate the so-called general population. But in 1985 only £135,000 was set aside by the government for education and prevention. By the end of 1986, with the dramatic adoption of a new policy in November of that year, this had leapt a hundredfold (Weeks, 1986).

This change of heart was not the result of a sudden excess of altruism. The key factor was the generalization of risk, and the key precipitating event came with the publication of the US Surgeon-General's report on AIDS in October 1986. This allowed AIDS to achieve the 'critical mass' to become a major issue on the official social agenda (Shilts, 1988).

The new policy was organized around a sustained public campaign aimed at preventing the spread of the virus – this is the second major characteristic of the period. There was a certain historical irony therefore in the fact that the shift in policy was inspired by an arch-conservative Reaganite appointee in the USA (the Surgeon-General, Dr. C.E. Koop), and led by the Thatcher government in Britain at a time when its moral agenda reasserting traditional family values, rolling back the tide of 'permissiveness', and sharply defining the limits of sex education in schools, was unfolding. For a policy of prevention aimed not only to warn the general population about the risks, but to work with, and to take advantage of experience generated within the very lesbian and gay community it elsewhere sought to challenge (Weeks, 1988).

A third characteristic flowed from this shift in policy, accentuating trends already in existence: the period witnessed a significant 'professionalization' of organized responses to AIDS. In part, this involved a professionalization of the self-help groupings themselves, as public funds flowed into them, and demands upon their services increased. A new alliance, not without its problems, between the medical profession and the communities at risk began to be forged. At the same time, a different sort of professionalism began to emerge which actively distanced itself from the lesbian and gay community as AIDS became seen as a universal problem. Moreover, . . . as a consequence of HIV, genito-urinary medicine and allied medical practice moved from being cinderella specialisms to well-funded, high status work.

As if by a necessary reflex, this period also saw the rapid growth of alternative health care and therapies, as people with AIDS and HIV infection have sought to retain responsibility for the condition of their own bodies (Spence, 1986; Tatchell, 1986).

Finally, the period has seen a deepening of the health crisis itself, as the dimensions of AIDS and HIV infection have become clearer and its costs to individuals and society more widely understood. Today we live in a situation where there is widespread understanding of the nature of AIDS and its mode of transmission; where some of the early fear and loathing has perhaps diminished; but where prejudice and discrimination against people with AIDS and HIV is widespread; where the disease has been defined as a major public issue deserving of public funding, though still not to the degree necessary; and where the very term AIDS still carries with it a symbolic weight it should not have to bear.

[...]

Historical and Social Science Issues

The key problem here is: why did *this* disease, at this particular time, become the symbolic carrier of such a weight of meaning. Other new diseases have emerged in the recent past – Legionnaire's Disease is the best known – and there have been epidemics of others. Some, such as genital herpes and hepatitis B, have caused major bouts of anxiety and much social philosophizing, in ways that prefigure the reaction to AIDS. But it was AIDS that became the disease of the 1980s, and it was AIDS that came to public consciousness as the twentieth-century plague.

One of the most important factors behind this was the association of AIDS with marginal populations. As a disease that appeared to affect disproportionately black people and gay men, anxiety about AIDS was thereby able to draw on pre-existing tensions concerning race and sexual diversity, ones which were already coming to the fore in the early 1980s in the contemporary political discourse of the New Right (Hammonds, 1987). But this only pushes the question a little way back. These factors themselves clearly relate to wider anxieties. At the heart of these, I would argue, are deeply rooted fears about the unprecedented rate of change in sexual behaviour and social mores in the past two generations.

It is now quite well established that sexuality has been at the heart of public discourse since at least the early nineteenth century as a barometer of social anxiety and a conductor of social tensions. Sexuality has become both central to personal identity and a key element in social policy (Foucault, 1979).

The response to AIDS was able to draw on a variety of beliefs and concepts which often reach back into the mists of time, or at least the sexual debates of the last century. The definition of AIDS as a medico-moral problem echoes the debates in the 1830s and 1840s in England about the environmental factors associated with the spread of cholera and typhoid

(Mort, 1987). The categorization of gay men as a risk category replays the definition of prostitutes as the reservoir of venereal disease in the mid-nineteenth century. Even the suggestion that those at risk should be seg-regated and quarantined has a precedent in the Contagious Diseases Acts of the 1860s which sought compulsorily to test women suspected of being prostitutes in various English garrison towns (Weeks, 1989). There is little new, it seems, in the field of sexual regulation.

But what is new, however, is the fluidity of sexual identities and the emergence of new sexual communities since the 1960s. These have pro-vided opportunities for many, but anxiety for others whose own sense of self, and perception of the normal order of things, has been severely threatened by the speed of social change. Such change has provided a fertile recruitment ground for the moral politics of the New Right and has helped to create those constituencies most frightened by the emergence of AIDS (Weeks, 1985). For such people, AIDS comes to represent all the changes that have occurred over recent decades, as well as their fearful con-sequences. Culturally, the ground for the social reaction of AIDS was prepared before any one noticed the range of illnesses afflicting gay men and others. In a sense therefore there was already an immanent problem awaiting a symbolic resolution. To this extent, AIDS was a crisis waiting to happen.

Political Issues

AIDS is a cultural phenomenon, but in an age when culture and politics are more inextricably mingled than ever before, and when the politicization of everyday life continuously expands, it is inevitable that it should also become a political issue. AIDS first appeared in a period of profound political re-formation in most Western countries, represented most clearly by the rise of the New Right-inflected administrations of Reagan in the USA and Thatcher in Britain.

The significance of this political shift for AIDS was two-fold. First, these governments were ideologically committed to cutting government expen-diture at a time when the emergence of a major health crisis clearly demanded a substantial increase in governmental spending on health ser-vices. After 1985, resources were indeed put into AIDS support services and AIDS-related research, but more often than not the sums involved were much less than was demanded by those in the front line. They were also often provided as part of a redistribution of resources within an already determined budget (Shilts, 1988; Small, 1988).

[...]

Governments always have to prioritize expenditure decisions, and no-one could realistically expect that in a world of finite resources all that is demanded can be readily provided. But clearly also decisions about AIDS funding have been shaped by wider political considerations. ... It was politically difficult for a government committed to a moral crusade against drugs to simultaneously fund syringe exchange schemes – an action likely to be seen by its more avid supporters as condoning drug abuse. From the beginning of the crisis, there has therefore been an ultimately irresolvable contradiction between the needs of people with AIDS and the political imperatives of New Right regimes.

This brings me to the second political factor relevant to AIDS, the importance of symbolic issues in New Right politics in the 1980s. In both the USA and Britain, high priority has been given to restoring national pride and economic strength. This has produced material effects (strengthened defence, a more nationalistic foreign policy, economic well-being), but also a number of less tangible outcomes: a desire to 'walk tall' in the world, a desire to restore old values and so on.

At the centre of New Right discourse has been a symbolic crusade against what were seen as the moral excesses of the 1960s and 1970s, what in Britain has been called 'permissiveness', and an effort to reaffirm traditional family and sexual values. In practical terms, the effects have been limited. President Reagan found it virtually impossible to carry through any of his family policy, and Mrs Thatcher's direct ventures into moral politics were on the whole (with some important exceptions) rhetorical rather than legislative. But New Right propagandists have been more successful in setting the terms of the debate on sexuality, and AIDS has provided a convenient marker for their case.

[...]

[Such] arguments ... help create an environment in which it becomes permissable for people to be openly hostile towards non-traditional sexual life-styles. The effects of this may be incalculable. It has been argued (Shilts, 1988) that in fact the anti-gay backlash stimulated by AIDS has been much exaggerated, and certainly there has as yet been no wholesale abrogation of gay rights in the wake of AIDS. On the other hand, there are signs of a substantial drop of support for lesbian and gay rights in Britain. ... It is difficult to find any other reason for this shift, in a climate that still remained relatively liberal on sexual matters, except for anxiety over AIDS.

[...]

It would be wrong, however, to believe that this political agenda has been easily accepted, or uncontested. One of the interesting features of the political response to AIDS has been the divisions it has revealed within the dominant political movements and agencies of government. In recent years both America and Britain have witnessed sharp, if often covert, conflicts within government about how to respond to AIDS: conflicts of priorities and of interest between politicians and civil servants, medical and scientific advisors and pressure groups (Shilts, 1988; Weeks, 1988). As a sensitive political issue, not susceptible to easy solution, AIDS has therefore provided important insights into the complexities of policy formation in pluralist societies.

[. . .]

Conclusion

It will not have escaped anyone's attention that none of the issues discussed above are peculiar to AIDS. This echoes my conviction that the only way to understand the political and ethical implications of AIDS is to see it in a wider social context: of rapid social change and the anxieties attendant upon this, especially those changes which have affected sexual behaviour and values, race and social non-conformity; of political and moral struggles in which old certainties have collapsed and new and competing ones emerged; of new personal identities, many of them now fashioned in the furnace of personal suffering.

I began by describing three phases within the AIDS crisis so far, and suggested that we are currently living through a period of crisis management. This by definition means that we are addressing symptoms rather than fundamental causes. The subsequent discussion of key issues suggests that latent in the current situation is a more developed and rational response based on a realistic assessment of risk, a balanced understanding of the nature of AIDS and HIV infection, an awareness of the resources needed to deal with this, and the political and moral will necessary to find and use those resources. The challenge to society and governments in the next few years lies in harnessing this potential in order to move toward a more rational and progressive solution.

In many ways AIDS is like many other illnesses which devastate individual lives. What is remarkable about AIDS, however, is not simply its virulence, but the weight of symbolic meaning that it carries. Because of this, it throws into sharp focus the murkier preoccupations of our age. It carries a burden which those who experience it most personally should not have to bear. Perhaps the real signal that a new period is upon us will come when AIDS does become just another disease demanding the same care, attention and social resources as any other.

References

Berkowitz, R. and Callen, M. (1983) *How to Have Sex in an Epidemic*. New York: News from the Front.
Foucault, M. (1979) *The History of Sexuality, vol. 1, An Introduction*. London: Allen Lane.
Hammonds, E. (1987) Race, sex, AIDS: the construction of the other, *Radical America*, 20: 6.
Mort, F. (1987) *Dangerous Sexualities*. London: Routledge and Kegan Paul.
Padgug, R. (1986) AIDS in historical perspective, paper presented at the American Historical Association, 28 December.
Shilts, R. (1988) *And the Band Played On: Politics, People and the AIDS Epidemic*. Harmondsworth: Penguin Books.
Small, N.J. (1988) AIDS and social policy, *Critical Social Policy*, 21: 9–29.
Spence, C. (1986) *AIDS, Time to Reclaim our Power*. London: Lifestory.
Tatchell, P. (1986) *AIDS, A Guide to Survival*. London: Gay Men's Press.
Watney, S. (1987) *Policing Desire*. London: Comedia/Methuen.
Watney, S. (1988) AIDS, 'Moral Panic Theory' and homophobia, in P. Aggleton and H. Homans (eds) *Social Aspects of AIDS*. Lewes: Falmer Press.
Weeks, J. (1985) *Sexuality and its Discontents*. London: Routledge and Kegan Paul.
Weeks, J. (1986) *Sexuality*. London: Tavistock.
Weeks, J. (1988) Love in a cold climate, in P. Aggleton and H. Homans (eds) *Social Aspects of AIDS*. Lewes: Falmer Press.
Weeks, J. (1989) *Sex, Politics and Society*. 2nd edn. Harlow: Longman.
Wellings, K. (1988) Perceptions of risk – media treatment of AIDS, in P. Aggleton and H. Homans (eds) *Social Aspects of AIDS*. Lewes: Falmer Press.

SATANISM:

MYTH AND REALITY IN A CONTEMPORARY MORAL PANIC

Philip Jenkins and Daniel Maier-Katkin
(1992)

Proofs of a Conspiracy

In the 1960s, Richard Hofstadter identified the 'paranoid style' as a dominant theme in American history. For two centuries, successive political and social movements have been galvanized by fears of dangerous 'outsiders' and their conspiratorial assaults on the American polity. The alleged culprits have included a kaleidoscopic array of social, religious and ethnic groups, from the Illuminati in the 1790s through Catholics, Freemasons and slaveholders in the nineteenth century, to Communists in more recent times. ... Often, such a movement should be understood not as a response to a genuine problem, but as a symbolic campaign reflecting the interests of particular movements and pressure groups, regardless of the objective basis of the alleged danger. Frequently, the issue provides a vehicle which permits these groups to impose their views on law or social policy (Gusfield 1966; 1981).

Since the 1970s, sociologists have often applied the term 'moral panic' to such generalized fears, and there have been several impressive case-studies. Apart from the intrinsic interest of such an account, it also illuminates the values, fears and conflicts of the age which apparently needs to imagine such an external threat. Observing the construction of such 'conspiracies' and problems therefore provides a powerful tool for social analysis. If in fact a society can be understood in terms of its fears, then America in the last decade offers a rich mine for social scientists. There have been wildly exaggerated claims about threats as diverse as child abuse and abduction, serial murder, drug abuse and even satanism or devil worship. We wish to se the last of these to understand some of the forces which are producing uch far reaching claims about current threats and conspiracies.

In the late 1980s, it was increasingly alleged that the United States was acing a serious crime-wave associated with the occult or satanism. Charges of devil-worship have occurred sporadically throughout American history, but the origin of the current concern can be dated to 1983–1984, and the cult' allegations associated with the McMartin preschool case in southern California. Dozens of similar cases of 'ritual abuse' followed, the most celebrated perhaps being that in the small Minnesota community of Jordan. This was also the time at which memoirs purported to tell of recalling ritual abuse suffered during childhood or adolescence; and serious attention was paid to accounts of human sacrifice and cannibalism (Smith and Pazder 1980; Spencer 1989).

From mid-1985, the various allegations were publicized on network television programs, especially ABC's *20/20*. Journalistic and popular studies naturally followed, and there was an explosion of books on the subject from 1988 onwards. By no means all the accounts were uncritical, but most agreed that there was a serious problem. Satanic or occult crime (the terms were used with little distinction) was apparently associated with numerous acts of vandalism and juvenile delinquency, but also with heinous offenses like serial murder and mass child abuse. The victims might run into many thousands each year, with children especially likely to be mutilated and sacrificed. ... The corollary was that urgent action needed to be taken to deal with the problem, and that police and prosecutorial agencies would have to play the leading role in the proposed reforms.

By contrast, the present paper contends that 'occult crime' and satanism are fringe activities that the vast majority of agencies will never encounter. The alleged problem is a classic moral panic, with political roots that can be easily traced to the fundamentalist religious Right. The whole issue was devised and defined in such a way that reflected the concerns and ambitions of Christian fundamentalists at a time when this movement was undergoing rapid expansion, especially in the early 1980s. The sensationalistic charges were explored enthusiastically by mass media then experiencing economic challenges and rivalries which encouraged a 'tabloid' presentation of events. This uncritical acceptance of the problem by the media led to widespread dissemination of the charges, without recognition of the wider social and political connotations.

The Scale of Occult Crime

Recent accounts have suggested that the threat of occult crime is all the more serious because it is linked to many other contemporary dangers. Some of the more extreme charges derive from *The American Focus on Satanic Crime*, a compilation from the works of several leading claims makers. Satanists are said to be connected with:

> the murders of unbaptized infants, child sexual abuse in daycare, rape, ritual abuse of children, drug trafficking, arson, pornography, kidnapping, vandalism, church desecration, corpse theft, sexual trafficking of children and the heinous mutilation, dismemberment and sacrifices of humans and animals. [they are] responsible for the deaths of more than 60,000 Americans each year, including missing and runaway youth. (Peterson 1988:i)

The following remarks are from [a TV interview with] Ted Gunderson, formerly a senior member of the Los Angeles office of the FBI, and a contributor to the *American Focus*:

> I can say that there is a network of these people across the country who are very active, they have their own rest and relaxation farm, they are in contact with each other, it ties in loosely to the drug operation, it ties into motorcycle gangs and it goes on and on. They have their own people who specialize in surveillances and photography, and in assassinations.

Gunderson wrote:

> I have been told it is a common occurrence for these groups to kidnap their victims (usually infants and young children) from hospitals, orphanages, shopping centers and off the streets. I have been informed that satanists have been successful in their attempts to influence the Boy Scouts and, in recent years, have concentrated their efforts in recruiting Little League baseball players by infiltrating the coaching staffs and establishing pre-schools throughout the US.

> A Boise, ID police officer believes that fifty thousand to sixty thousand Americans disappear each year and are victims of human sacrifices of satanic cults ... Most of the victims are cremated, thus there is no body and no evidence. I know of an occult supply store in Los Angeles, California that sells portable crematories. (Peterson 1988:3)

The practice of satanism could draw literally millions into deviant and hazardous practices, with the young especially at risk. [on television] Geraldo Rivera claimed that:

> It is teenagers who are most likely to fall under the spell of this jungle of dark violent emotions called satanism, and in some cases to be driven to committing terrible deeds ... There is no doubt that teenage satanic activity in this country is increasing dramatically

The commonplace view is that occult 'dabbling' will lead to serious cult involvement: young people will become 'self-styled satanists', or even 'Religious satanists' and 'Cult satanists'. This last category – who are seen as the most dangerous and most inclined to criminality – are seen as part of a sinister clandestine network, possibly of national proportions. Journalist Maury Terry (1987) has suggested that 'There is compelling evidence of the existence of a nationwide network of satanic cults, some branched into child pornography and violent sadomasochistic crime, including murder'. (Terry, incidentally, has worked closely with Gunderson.) This national cult is linked not only to major incidents of child sexual abuse, but to celebrated serial murder cases, including the Manson 'family' murders and the 'Son of Sam' affair in New York City.

All the accounts of occult crime draw a connection with serial murder, generally focussing on the same four or five celebrated cases. Undoubtedly, some of these offenders were strongly influenced by occult ideas, most dramatically in the cases of Leonard Lake and Charles Manson....

In the face of this danger, police agencies and prosecutors are 'uninformed' or naive, and fail to follow leads that would lead them to the conspiratorial networks behind certain outrageous crimes. In the words of Geraldo Rivera, 'Many satanic crimes are not recognized as such. ... These ritualistic crimes are everywhere, and yet in most communities they are either overlooked or under-reported.'

Police scepticism in these matters is natural; but other writers have suggested that satanic cults may have infiltrated police agencies and local government authorities.

[...]

In particular, their role as coroners may explain why so many satanic murders remained undetected.

These charges may appear to be outrageous hyperbole, but it is worth stressing how commonplace they are in the contemporary media. The most controversial account was probably a Geraldo Rivera special at Halloween 1988, entitled *Devil Worship: Exposing Satan's Underground*, which might be disregarded as mere sensationalism or 'trash television'. But Geraldo and Oprah Winfrey were by no means isolated in promoting this hysteria.

Satanism was exposed in equally lurid terms on network programs like *20/20* (for example, 'The Devil Worshippers', May 16, 1985) and NBC's *1986* (as on August 19, 1986). Such views also earned the respectful attention of more sober news programs, even on National Public Radio's *Morning Edition*. In March, 1988, this program presented a lengthy and sympathetic account of an Indiana detective and his unsuccessful efforts to make his superiors appreciate the real dangers of local satanic cults, who supposedly undertook sacrifice and grave-robbery.

Many police officers took the danger seriously. Charges concerning 'occult crime' were publicized in a number of celebrated trials; and there were cases where murders did appear to be connected with the practice of satanism. The apparent 'wave' of occult crime was discussed in the specialized press directed at the law enforcement community, in journals like *Police, Police Chief* and *Law Enforcement News*. The topic was covered in numerous training seminars directed at police officers and supervisors. 'Satanic' and cult crime has become a specialization of a number of police experts ('occult cops'), who are widely quoted in the media as urging public recognition of the new threat. Even more remarkable, the danger of satanism was cited by a growing number of therapists, who accepted the reality of ritual abuse, and who cited this type of crime as a causal factor in multiple personality disorder.

[...]

The Claims-makers

As with any social problem, it is essential to identify the 'claims-makers' who introduce the themes and define the shape of the ensuing controversy; and to observe the means by which they present their particular issue to a wider public (Best 1989; Spector and Kitsuse 1987). In the case of a sensational panic like satanism, it is especially interesting to see the rhetorical devices used to dispel incredulity about these remarkable charges. A writer will commonly introduce a theme, and suggest that the occult might play 'some' role in this particular problem. An example might then be given to support this idea. Other quotes then gradually build up the scale of the occult role until the reader is convinced that the whole problem is in fact little more than a facet of the immense satanic menace.

These quotes are judiciously chosen, and few can be described as untrue in specifics. Larson, for example, quite rightly notes that 'Some cult watchers and police agree that a large number of missing children are victims of human sacrifice cults' (1989: 125). Of course, these 'experts' may be utterly wrong in their belief, but his actual sentence is quite true: they do indeed agree on this. He then develops his argument as if the initial opinion is established as factual. 'According to the few survivors, children are abducted and subjected to the terrible intimidation of drugs and brainwashing before being sacrificed.' (We might note here that brainwashing a person one intends to kill anyway seems a massive waste of time and energy.) 'Innocent children and guiltless babies are perfect victims.' As a clincher, he then produces the remark of a police officer in Beaumont, CA., to the effect that '95 percent of all missing children are victims of occult-related abductions' (sic: italics in original). The unwary reader may well leave the page with the impression that this is the opinion of a well-known or widely respected police authority, instead of one individual in a specific department.

These 'law enforcement sources' are repeatedly used, and a small number of 'experts' are quoted time and again, as are a handful of therapists and medical writers. Obviously, the initial writers are not to blame for the ways in which their legitimately expressed opinions are later used or quoted; but the limited number of sources is worthy of note. Even when other sources are cited, it often turns out that these are in fact basing their statements on one of the major claims-makers. One of the most influential of the group is the FBI's Ted Gunderson. Another is Lieutenant Larry Jones of Boise, Idaho, who runs a 'Cult Crime Impact Newsletter' to track the progress of occult-related offenses. Jones believes firmly in the reality and seriousness of the danger, and deserves praise for his attempts to quantify the scale of the problem. However, he remains one isolated claims-maker, a 'moral entrepreneur', who appears to work from a perspective that is strongly Christian and evangelical.

Equally widely quoted is Kenneth Wooden, who investigated 'cult crimes' for the Rivera special on devil worship, and who appears in the video documentary *America's Best Kept Secret*. Wooden was a real pioneer in forming the contemporary view of 'devil-cults'. In the aftermath of the Jonestown massacre in Guyana, Wooden's investigations placed particular emphasis on the link between the Jim Jones movement and formalized or 'ritualized' child abuse, a striking and influential innovation at this time (*c.* 1980–81). Without mentioning satanic groups, Wooden argued that cults engaged in deviant sexual practices to undermine family links and cement group loyalty. Moreover, 'Babies, born into cults, their births unregistered, are reported to have died of unnatural causes and to have been buried in secrecy, like pets' (1981: 205). The groups themselves deliberately undertook gross and excessive acts in order to reduce the credibility of anyone who attempted to expose them. There was an urgent need for intensive investigation of 'cults', here identified as movements like the 'Moonies', the Children of God, and Scientologists. All these charges would shortly recur in the context of satanism.

Wooden was well-placed to ensure that his concerns were presented to a wider audience. As an investigator for *20/20*, he was involved in 1983–84 in producing a number of reports on topics like the disappearance and murder of children. These had titles like 'The lures of death' and 'They are murdering our kids'. Wooden is the founder of a 'National Coalition for Children's Justice' and he testified to a Congressional subcommittee in 1984 on the alleged problems of mass child appearances and the serial murders of young people. From about 1984, his deeply-felt concerns came to focus on the menace of 'satanic' cults, which appeared to unify the previous threats; and the shift in interest can be discerned in the content of *20/20*. It was Wooden who encouraged the controversial 'occult' survivor Lauren Stratford to publish her influential memoirs of satanic abuse. Like the Rivera program, Stratford's account also incorporates in its title the ominous phrase 'Satan's' underground'. Other major activists include the 'Cult Awareness Network', based in Chicago; and groups concerned with child abuse issues, like 'Believe the Children' or 'ACT-affirming Children's Truth'. Accounts of satanic and occult crime thus rely on a handful of sources, often with a strong political agenda in a particular locality. Believe the Children is based in Manhattan Beach, CA., where it originated in direct response to the McMartin farrago.

Tracking sources is essential if we are to understand some of the most remarkable aspects of the current panic, especially the view that the number of sacrificial victims might run to fifty thousand or so each year in the United States alone. This statement appears grotesque, especially when we recall that the *total* number of homicide victims annually is around twenty thousand. On the other hand, 'fifty thousand' was also the figure widely quoted in the equally disreputable claims made about missing children in the mid-eighties, so it was in the public consciousness. It is uncertain who first applied the number to sacrifical victims. Gunderson cites Jones as his source, but others attribute the figure to Al Carlisle, a consulting psychologist at the Utah State prison. Whatever the source, the statistic had entered the literature by 1986 at the latest, and the story began a life of its own.

The Nature of Satanism

This paper will not directly address the reality of human sacrifice charges, as these have been thoroughly rebutted in many other sources (Lanning 1989; Lyons 1988). 'Ritual abuse' remains equally unsubstantiated, and wholly improbable. (Jenkins and Maier-Katkin 1987; 1991; Eberle and Eberle 1986). But if such events did occur, then who are the cultists who would be responsible? Most of the believers in occult crime stress the role of a network of satanic groups, possibly many thousands strong. However, a curious distinction is drawn between 'public' or Religious satanists, and the more sinister 'Cult' satanists who actually undertake the crimes.

Among the religious satanists, we find well-established national groups like the Church of Satan, the Temple of Set and the Church of the Process, as well as a dozen or so local churches and sects (Lyons 1988). The theorists rarely accuse these groups of criminal acts, for a number of reasons that include fear of libel: in the 1970s, the Process successfully rebutted charges that it had been linked to the Manson family murders. It has also been pointed out that satanist leaders like Anton LaVey and Michael Aquino are too much in the public eye to undertake any serious crime, even if they wished to. In other words, there is a paradox that virtually any publicly admitted or active satanist must be regarded as a 'Religious' believer, and hence not active in the serious actions such as ritual abuse and child sacrifice.

Who then are these 'Cult satanists'? As so often, the evidence for such a clandestine network in any particular community is thin to the point of non-existence. Whenever a particular offender is arrested in a 'satanic' crime, then he is almost invariably a self-taught teenage dabbler like Pete Roland, Ricky Kasso or Sean Sellers, whose notion of the occult derived from horror films or the game 'Dungeons and Dragons'. Moreover, these crimes often seem closely related to the activities of teenage gangs and petty drug dealing. There is no suggestion that these youths had been drawn into any more sophisticated cult; and the evidence of wider or national links is, if possible, even weaker.

Even if there was such a cult, the accounts of their supposed practices, beliefs and rituals have many problems and inconsistencies. We may initially be troubled by the impressive continuity of the charges made against such groups from the accusations against out-groups throughout history, from ancient Christians and Gnostics through medieval Jews and heretics. ... This would tend to suggest that the alleged behaviors are imaginary, perhaps based on archetypal fears. On the other hand, this would not in itself prove that the actions have not occurred. However, the theorists of occult crime have described as 'characteristic' of this type of offense such a wide range of acts and symbols that almost any activity could be seen as fitting.

Particularly outrageous here is the 'satanic calendar' included in many sources, the list of specially significant days on which sinister rituals might occur. Police officers would thus be alerted to the true significance of peculiar acts occurring on such a day. There are indeed such special days, such as April 30 or All Hallow's Eve; but some recent calendars include forty or more dates, most with no known connection to any occult tradition. If we further include acts occurring 'near' a special day, then it would be almost impossible to avoid suggesting some ritual significance to a routine crime. Alleged occult graffiti are equally spurious. Among a vast and proliferating number of examples, it is especially startling to see the familiar 1960s 'peace' symbol co-opted as the satanic 'Cross of Nero'! Some sources include the Star of David as a symbol of what is anti-Christian, and thus satanic.

Christian Fundamentalism

In summary, the evidence presented for a satanic crime-wave in the United States seems wholly unconvincing, a tissue of improbable charges based largely on the assertions of questionable witnesses. Also dubious is the vocabulary employed by the various authors, and the lack of precision they so often demonstrate in their definitions. Other writers have discussed the problems in using terms such as *ritual, ritualistic, sacrifice,* and so on; but other words are even more troubling, and the most hazardous of all is probably *occult*. However, the misuse of the term is highly revealing because it suggests a great deal about the political and religious agendas of those most active in creating and exaggerating the 'satanic threat'. *Occult* and *satanic* are confounded in a way that reflects the views of the narrowest Christian sects, for whom all religious experience outside mainstream evangelical Christianity is suspect; and anything beyond Judaeo-Christian monotheism is quite literally of the devil. And it is these fundamentalist groups whose interests and concerns are reflected throughout the whole satanism panic.

The term 'occult' is very flexible. Literally, it implies the study of what is hidden, usually esoteric religious or mystical doctrines, and there is the suggestion that such studies would not be suitable for the great mass of people. The word might cover long-established activities such as palmistry, spiritualism, tarot card reading, fortune telling, and divining, to say nothing of ritual magic and unorthodox religious sects. All have certainly increased since the 1960s with the emergence of a New Age movement interested in astrology, reincarnation, astral projection and unconventional medicine. For some recent critics, however, these diverse practices are part of a spectrum which extends into serious criminality and devil-worship. 'Channeling', for example, is seen not as a harmless fad but as a modern form of shamanism, where literal demons are permitted to take possession of the human mind.

The *American Focus* comments indiscriminately that 'There are over five thousand occult groups in the US and Canada who have a general interest or active practice of pagan religious lore, witchcraft and satanism.' The theme of the New Age as the gateway to satanism is frequently represented in the books on sale in a typical 'Christian bookshop'. In the last decade, it has often been disturbing to witness these religious concerns and prejudices spilling over into the 'secular' mass media. Network television programs have illustrated reports on the growth of satanism and satanic crime by depicting flourishing occult and New Age bookstores, and implying a link between the phenomena. It has also been common for police sources to cite the presence of occult books in a suspect's home to buttress claims of 'ritual' criminality in a particular case.

But the strong religious agenda of the critics of 'diabolism' is easily discerned. Again and again, the same protagonists appear. The most quoted authority is probably Sean Sellers a teenage parricide who blamed his crimes on his experimentation with diabolism; and who has become a media personality as one of America's youngest death-row inmates. He now asserts that full acceptance of Christianity is the only way to rescue youths from the occult, and who practises a 'ministry' with this goal. He is closely advised by Tom Wedge, a fundamentalist minister termed 'the Satan Hunter', who is a contributor to the *American Focus*. The editor of this work began his list of dedications with an acknowledgement to Jesus Christ, while other contributing authors include Jerry Oglesby, of the 'National Council Against the Antichrist Movement'; and 'Citizens Against Ritual Abuse'. Another is the Rev. Mike Warnke, who claims to be a former satanic priest. Also influential is 'occult researcher' Peter Michas, yet another 'pastor', who has produced some of the more gruesome and far-reaching allegations.

One of the most quoted authorities is John Frattarola of *Passport* magazine, another source for claims about satanic activity, whose views are expressed in the video *America's Best Kept Secret*. Frattarola has attacked 'the gradual but consistent displacement of Christianity by a hodgepodge of occultic, mystic, Eastern pagan, New Age spirituality' It was *Passport* which published the widely quoted 'WICCA' document, allegedly the blueprint of a satanic plan to subvert Christian America by 1999. Jerry Johnston drew the obvious parallels between this piece and the *Protocols of the Elders of Zion*, and described the document as 'genuine as a three dollar bill'. Another of the widely sold books is by Bob Larson, who advocates Christianity as the solution to 'satanic' activities, and who is the author of books like *Straight Answers on the New Age* and *Larson's Book of Cults*. His *Edge of Evil* is a 'crossover', sold both in religious as well as 'mainstream' bookstores.

All the initial claims in the satanism panic can be found in the commonplaces of the religious Right in the 1970s. At that time, it was common to attack both the religious and political liberalism of mainstream American Christianity, and the theological tendency to deny the existence of a personal devil. Also to be condemned was the opening to other religions – the ecumenical *apertura* towards Rome, and the increased sympathy for Oriental and mystical religions. For the fundamentalists of the last two decades, New Age and mystical movements have been the Devil's Trojan Horse in the subversion of America, a means to introduce the gullible young to anti-Christian concepts and practices. . . .

At the end of the 1970s, these conservative ideas grew stronger and also gained some wider social acceptance. Increased reporting about cults and deprogramming led to public concern, while the People's Temple affair in Jonestown suggested the real and objective dangers of cult activity. An influential 'occult cop' like Sandi Gallant describes this incident as a real turning point in her own attitude towards cults as a law enforcement issue. Ken Wooden was a prominent investigator of the case; while Ted Gunderson dated his interest in cult crime to 1980. In addition, the religious Right was at the zenith of its political power in the early 1980s, and fundamentalist churches were rapidly gaining new adherents, to surpass the strength of established liberal denominations like the Episcopalians.

Networks of religious bookstores and electronic media ensured a public voice for the movement's concerns and prejudices. Evangelical and fundamentalist bookstores have long distributed works of religious controversy, with Catholics, Mormons and Jehovah's Witnesses the usual targets. In the last decade, however, 'cults', 'satanism' and even 'demonology' have acquired their own sections, often with literally dozens of recent titles on what are clearly felt to be topics of urgent concern. The figures would be even larger if we include 'occult' interpretations of the dangers posed by moral threats like abortion or rock music.

There exists a whole flourishing fundamentalist culture that is quite unknown to those who never frequent such bookstores. Several religious publishers have made minor industries out of attacking contemporary cults, satanism and unbelief. Huntington House is based in Louisiana; Crossways in Illinois; Harvest House in Oregon; Chick in California. Occasionally, their titles achieve sales in the hundreds of thousands, almost entirely through these religious outlets. . . .

Central to fundamentalist rhetoric is the real power of the Devil in the world as the source of all evil. By the 1970s, there were indeed real satanists in America, and these theories may have had a particular appeal to some who became active in notorious crimes. Once a few cases were publicized, it was natural for the fundamentalists to incorporate them into their wider world-view, and to construct a major national or worldwide conspiracy, suitably buttressed by impressive statistics. This provided preachers and ministers with a series of powerful arguments. If the conspiracy view were accepted, then religious liberalism had failed and the churches must come to a more basic acceptance of the reality of the force of evil. Also, an upsurge of diabolism was believed to support the fundamentalist belief in the imminence of the Second Coming of Christ, which would be preceded by the triumph of Antichrist.

Satanism was thus intimately linked to the fundamentalist diagnosis of the secular ills of society:

> The outbreak of satanic crimes and worship; an epidemic of killer diseases; the slaughter of over 22 million unborn children; the collapse of once solid financial institutions; the bankruptcy of American farmers; harsher and more unpredictable weather patterns; an increase of drug abuse, child abuse and pornography; the corruption and dis-integration of morals, values, ethics and integrity ... and the powerful rise of false religions right under our drooping eyes. (*Passport* Magazine March – April 1988))

The proposed remedies were as profoundly political as the analysis. A campaign against 'satanism' would in reality be a sweeping endeavor to remold American social life on the lines advocated by fundamentalists and extreme conservatives. 'Cult' and New Age activities were not only to be stigmatized, but might even be restricted or banned as leading to overt criminality. Censorship would be far ranging, extending to 'occultic' (*sic*) influences in films and the media, even (or especially) in children's cartoons. The thought and education of the young must be regulated, and the clergy could justify religious intervention in the schools by the need to drive out 'satanic' influences. It might appear trivial to most observers, but the mere existence of Halloween and its customs remains a source of deep scandal to religious fundamentalists, who would ideally prohibit it as a sinister initiation into devil-worship.

Repeatedly, the critics of satanic crime attribute its prevalence to the lax parental discipline of the generation that came of age in the 1960s; this problem could only be solved by a return to 'traditional moral values'. One speaker who emphasizes this as the antidote to the occult is Samantha Smith, of the highly conservative 'Colorado Eagle Forum'. The assault closely reflected ultra-Conservative political opinions, as New Age ideas are often associated in fundamentalist critiques with 'one-worldism', emphasis on international cooperation to the detriment of patriotism. Attacks on Oriental religions shade imperceptibly into critiques of Asian immigration into the United States.

More generally, 'normal' criminal acts such as drug dealing were to be seen as loosely connected with the objective evil that was satanism, thus discouraging liberal tendencies towards lenient or rehabilitative efforts towards offenders. In fact, 'devil-worship' became an all-embracing label with which to stigmatize any aspect of modern society with which the conservative religious leadership did not agree, especially in matters of the media. Pornography and explicit art or literature could be associated with child exploitation and ritual abuse; while rock music was blatantly connected with evil forces. Those who might once have denounced rock as 'jungle music' could now achieve wider social acceptance by stressing its satanic character, at the same time avoiding the taint of racism.

It is also possible to suggest more speculative aspects of the religious agenda. For example, the religious Right strongly opposed any change in women's traditional role as home-maker, and denounced the trend towards two-career families where children remained in day care. By emphasizing the widespread character of 'ritual abuse', the claims-makers were attempting to depict day-care centers as an extremely dangerous place for the young. They enjoyed enormous success in this, as witnessed by a rash of prosecutions, scandals and school-closures across the nation. It is possible that the widespread credulity reflected genuine ambiguity about the surrender of traditional family concepts, and the abandonment of children to others. The ensuing parental guilt found expression in the urgent need to condemn an outsider preying on one's children. This may also explain the belief that children given up to adoption agencies might find their way onto the altars of sacrifical cults.

Another (admittedly speculative) explanation might also account for one of the most mystifying aspects of the current panic, the emphasis on 'breeders'. These are women who claim to have bred children explicitly for the purpose of sacrificing them in a cult setting. The charge apparently originated with 'survivor' Lauren Stratford, but there are now hundreds of individuals claiming to be breeders, and the idea has been widely publicized

(Jenkins and Maier-Katkin 1987). In the context of the fundamentalist world-view, the focus on the breeders and their guilt reflects outrage at the prevalence of abortion. Here too, women are seen to have bred children for slaughter and butchery, and the religious groups offer counseling and therapy for mothers who are 'survivors' of this perceived crime. In the fundamentalist view, this post-Christian society expresses its hatred of God through many forms of child-murder; and abortion or euthanasia are concessions to the Devil little less overt than an actual ritual sacrifice. This may seem far-fetched, but the analogy is explicitly drawn in recent accounts of these 'unholy sacrifices of the New Age'.

[...]

Conclusion: the Implications for Policy

Those who attempt to warn society of the dangers of satanism have also been swift to propose solutions. The *American Focus*, for example, suggests the formation of powerful 'Ritual Crime Task Forces', made up of local state and federal agencies; while groups like the Cult Awareness Network should provide 'experts' for the extensive training of law enforcement officers. In addition, the full resources of the FBI should be used in profiling 'ritual' offenders. By contrast, we have argued that 'occult crime' is very different from the menace that is sometimes portrayed, and most of the serious charges are mythical. Whenever a police department has been tempted to credit the allegations, it has usually been embarrassed by the utter failure to produce results. There have been numerous local examples of 'wild-goose chases' after alleged satanic altars and cults; and attempts to dig for the bodies of satanic victims have been humiliating failures. The most notorious was the Lucas County affair in Ohio in 1985, when an expensive search for sixty or more bodies produced nothing.

In conclusion, satanism is neither 'the seduction of America's youth' nor 'America's best kept secret', and it is not 'terrorizing our communities'. It is a tiny fringe movement worthy only of treatment in the least responsible and most sensationalistic media. It should have no place in the agendas of contemporary police agencies, or in the files of responsible therapists. The satanism panic is of value chiefly for what it reveals about the enduring power of both conspiracy politics and fundamentalist religion in American life.

References

Best, J. (ed.) (1989) *Images of Issues*. New York: Aldine de Gruyter.

Eberle, P. and Eberle, S. (1986) *The Politics of Child Abuse*. Secaucus, NJ: Lyle Stuart.

Gusfield, J. (1966) *Symbolic Crusade*. Urbana, IL: University of Illinois Press.

Gusfield, J. (1981) *The Culture of Public Problems*. Chicago: University of Chicago Press.

Jenkins, P. and Maier-Katkin, D. (1987) Occult survivors, *Village Voice*, September 29.

Jenkins, P. and Maier-Katkin, D. (1991) Occult survivors: the origins of a myth, in J.T. Richardson, J. Best and D. Bromley (eds), *The Satanism Scare*. New York: Aldine de Gruyter.

Lanning, K. (1989) Satanic, occult and ritualistic crime: a law enforcement perspective, *Police Chief*, October: 62–85.

Larson, B. (1989) *Satanism: The Seduction of America's Youth*. Nashville, IN: Thomas Nelson Press.

Lyons, A. (1988) *Satan Wants You*. New York: Mysterious Press.

Peterson, A. (1988) *The American Focus on Satanic Crime, vol. 1*. South Orange NJ: American Focus Publishing Co.

Peterson, A. (1990) *The American Focus on Satanic Crime, vol. 2*. South Orange NJ: American Focus Publishing Co.

Smith, M. and Pazder, J. (1980) *Michelle Remembers*. New York: Congdon and Lattes.

Spector, M. and Kitsuse, J. (1987) *Constructing Social Problems*. New York: Aldine de Gruyter.

Spencer, J. (1989) *Suffer the Child*. New York: Pocket.

Terry, M. (1987) *The Ultimate Evil*. New York: Doubleday.

Wooden, K. (1981) *The Children of Jonestown*. New York: McGraw Hill.

MORAL PANIC AS IDEOLOGY: DRUGS, VIOLENCE, RACE AND PUNISHMENT IN AMERICA

8

Theodore Chiricos (1996)

In the summer and fall of 1993, violent crime captured the popular consciousness of America with a speed and intensity seldom seen. Searing images of 'random' violence directed at tourists in Florida, a truck driver in Los Angeles, passengers on a train, etc., competed with natural disasters to hold a nation in awe.

By January 1994, television networks had run week-long series on 'Kids and Crime' (CNN) and 'America the Violent' (NBC), or had featured specials on 'Florida, the State of Fear' (ABC) and 'Monster' Kody Scott (CBS) the notorious gangbanger from Los Angeles. Newsmagazines cover stories featured titles such as 'Growing Up Scared' (*Newsweek*), 'Lock 'Em Up and Throw Away the Key' (*Time*) and 'Florida: The State of Rage' (*U.S. News and World Report;* hereafter, U.S. News).

In the wake of the media feeding frenzy, Americans ranking crime/violence as the nation's foremost problem jumped from 9 percent to 49 percent between January 1993 and January 1994 (Gallup, 1994: 6). Not surprising, politicians and moral entrepreneurs swam furiously to stay atop the wave of public anxiety. Proposals to deal with the 'epidemic' of violence escalated demands for 'getting tough' – more police, more prison beds, longer mandatory sentences, 'hard time' for kids, more and faster executions, and 'three strikes, you're out!'

I will argue that the hysteria over violent crime is a classic example of 'moral panic' (Hall, et al., 1978; Jenkins, 1992). As Cohen emphasizes, the point of moral panic is 'not that there's nothing there' but that societal responses are 'fundamentally inappropriate' (1972: 204). Moreover, the panic over violence reinforces an ideological pattern recently established in the response to crack cocaine – an important consequence of which has been to greatly amplify the flow of African American men into our nation's prisons.

Specifically, the moral panic over violence, like its predecessor involving crack cocaine, is used to justify expanding the punitive apparatus of the state – even as crime rates are falling ... In addition, the panic diverts attention from contradictions of the nation's political economy that have promoted an extraordinary growth of economic inequality and expansion of the urban underclass (Kasarda, 1994; Ricketts and Sawhill, 1988). It is precisely this underclass that has become an increasingly 'privileged target group' for incarceration in the United States (Lynch and Sabol, 1992; Melossi, 1989).

In short, these moral panics not only provide the 'vocabularies of punitive motive' (Melossi, 1985) to justify an explosive growth of prison populations, but they obscure the declining condition of those most victimized by a changing political economy and by crime (urban, lower class, African-Americans, etc.) – even as they are incarcerated in unprecedented numbers. In doing so, moral panics perform both the 'positive' (Gouldner, 1976) and 'negative' functions (Larrain, 1983) commonly attributed to ideology.

[...]

A Working Concept of Ideology

Moral panics are ideological in two senses of the term. The first regards ideology as *partisan* discourse in the pursuit of interests and the second regards it as *distorting reality* in that pursuit ... Moral panics are ideological first, because they generate reports to justify 'doing something' of a public, partisan and generally punitive nature. But they are ideological as well, because of their capacity to blur and conceal. I argue that recent moral panics are an important part of an ideological discourse which: (1) *misunderstands* the dimensions and bases of the problem behaviors (drugs and violence); and (2) *displaces* attention from the role that coercive investment decisions have played in promoting conditions that encourage those very behaviors.

Contradiction Obscured by Moral Panics

Though workers in general have ... lost considerable ground in the past twenty years, those in the central cities of major metropolitan areas have lost the most. Wilson (1987) and Ricketts and Sawhill (1988) are among those who have documented the costs to urban Americans of decisions to move manufacturing jobs out of the cities. Those costs have been shown to be more than economic and include costs to family and community that help produce an underclass whose poverty is unprecedented in its concentration and isolation (Massey, 1990).

Even more harmful to central city residents has been the loss of low pay, entry level jobs – the kind of work that expanded substantially for much of the rest of the country....

A clear consequence of investment decisions that have moved manufacturing and entry level jobs out of central cities is a critical mismatch between available jobs and the skills of many people living there. So it is of little surprise that the numbers of 'surplus people' in central cities have soared in this period of disinvestment and deskilling....

The average increase in the rate of surplus males in central cities between the two time periods in 123 percent for whites and 185 percent for blacks. The increase for whites is greatest in the Midwest and for blacks in the south.

It would not be a serious overstatement to suggest that primarily, these are the people filling up our nation's prisons and jails. It may be coincidence, but in 1972 – about the time wages and circumstances of workers in the U.S. reached an all-time high – the number of prisoners and rate of incarceration reached a forty-four year low. Since then, as the conditions of workers have deteriorated, especially in central cities, the rates of incarceration have more than tripled. Ironically, the crime rate has increased only one-fourth as fast as imprisonment. In fact, since 1980, the crime rate has actually fallen, while prison populations have increased 138 percent.

So over the past fifteen years, the United States has had an expanding underclass, a declining crime rate and an exploding prison population. An expanding underclass hasn't led to an increase in crime, but members of that underclass are being incarcerated in unprecedented numbers. Something is missing in the chain linking political economy and punishment. Melossi (1985) has suggested that an important link in this chain may be provided by discourse that justifies repression.

The central point of this paper is that moral panics provide one part of that discursive link. They provide a 'vocabulary of punitive motive' (Melossi, 1985) that justifies a massive increase in prison population – even in the face of declining crime rates. At the same time, they divert attention from the consequences of investment decisions that include a rapid expansion in the number of people who either have nothing to lose from crime, or may actually derive value from the use of drugs or involvement in violence.

[...]

Moral Panics and Ideology

With few exceptions, the ideological significance of moral panics has received limited attention. At one level, it is apparent that all moral panics perform the 'positive' function of ideology. That is, they involve a partisan attempt to mobilize public action, and do so by using reports to justify commands to act. Almost any moral panic could be understood in such terms.

The role of ideology in promoting the misunderstanding or exaggeration of phenomena – a key dimension of 'negative' ideology – is also fairly common in accounts of moral panic (Jenkins, 1992). Indeed, misunderstanding is a basic premise of responses that are 'fundamentally inappropriate' – a central defining characteristic of moral panics (Cohen, 1972: 204). But the displacement of attention from one issue to another is a 'negative' function of ideology that has been less often attributed to moral panics. . . .

Recent Panics: Drugs and Violence

The U.S has experienced two major moral panics in the past eight years. The first, involving crack cocaine, began in the summer and peaked in the fall of 1986; the second, involving violent crime, began in the summer of 1993 and peaked early in 1994.

The two panics share several key features that underscore their common ideological substance and significance. The first was an explosion in the *volume* of media *reports* – which increased more than 400 percent during a six month period in each case. Moreover, these panics had several common *thematic emphases*. Both reported that: (1) behaviors thought characteristic of urban ghettos were spreading to previously 'safe' places; and, (2) 'carriers' of the spreading menace were increasingly children. In both instances the panics promoted a critical *misunderstanding* of the underlying behaviors which helped to justify *commands* for a radical expansion of *punitive controls*. At the same time, these panics *displaced* attention from the coercive consequences of investment decisions that diminished the value of work for so many and devastated the circumstances of America's urban ghettos.

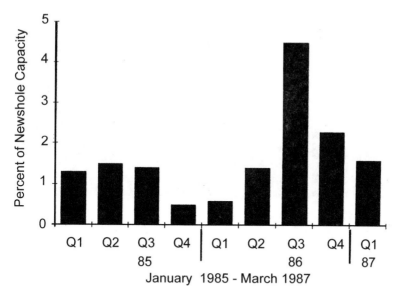

Figure 8.1 Media coverage of drug issues

Volume of Media Reports: Crack Cocaine and Violent Crime

Figure 8.1 adapted from Merriam (1989), shows media coverage of drug issues from January 1985 through March 1987. In the early 1980s, drugs accounted for about 1 percent of total news coverage tracked by The Conference on Issues & Media (CIM). At the beginning of 1986 the CIM index was still below 1 percent after a brief surge in 1985 (Merriam, 1989: 22–4).

Spurred by the death of basketball star Len Bias (June 19) media coverage of drugs shot up to 6 percent of all news in the two weeks ending August 10th. Ironically, when the White House declared a renewed 'war' on drugs in August, coverage began to fall. By the first quarter of 1987 the CIM index was back down to 1.1 percent (Merriam, 1989: 24–5).

The explosion of media *coverage* was punctuated by key reports in both print and television media. The *New York Times* assigned a full-time reporter to cover illegal drugs in November, 1985, and ran its first front-page story on crack during that month (Kerr, 1986: B6). On March 17, 1986 a *Newsweek* cover story reported on the 'Coke Plague' and the 'almost instant addiction' of 'crack' that moved a Los Angeles detective to conclude 'we have lost the cocaine battle' (1986a: 60). By May 23, NBC News anchor Tom Brokaw declared that 'crack' was 'flooding America'

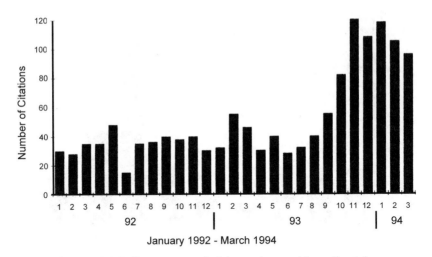

Figure 8.2 Media coverage of violent crime and juvenile violence

and had become the nation's 'drug of choice.' In June, *Newsweek* proclaimed crack the biggest story since Vietnam and Watergate (1986b: 15). On September 2, Dan Rather of CBS News hosted '48 Hours on Crack Street' – the most widely watched documentary in five years (Diamond et al., 1987: 10). NBC followed three days later with a prime-time special: 'Cocaine Country.' This was just one of *four hundred* crack or cocaine stories – 15 hours of air time – that NBC ran between April and November of 1986 (Reinarman and Levine, 1989: 118). By September, *Time* had recognized crack as 'the issue of the year' (1986: 25). Between March 30 and December 31, 1986 the *New York Times* carried 139 cocaine stories and the *Washington Post* carried 60 more (Danielian and Reese, 1989: 49).

The pattern of media coverage for violent crime was remarkably similar. Figure 8.2 shows the combined frequency of television and newspaper stories involving violent crime and juvenile violence between January 1992 and March 1994. By these measures, media attention varied within narrow parameters until the middle of 1993. Monthly newspaper citations rose from a low of *eighteen* in June to a high of *ninety-five* in November, dropping only slightly thereafter. Network television stories rose from a low of *four* in April to a high of *thirty-four* in January, 1994.

Noting that Los Angeles 'has the equivalent of a St. Valentine's Day massacre every day,' a May 31 editorial in *U.S. News* ascribed a mood of 'panic' to the citizens of that city (1993a: 82). That mood seemed to escalate nationally after the July rape and murder of two teenaged girls by six Houston gang members to whom 'life means nothing' (*Newsweek*

1993a: 16). Two weeks later (August 2) each of the national news-magazines ran cover stories on violent crime and the panic was on.

The images of violence escalated further with the murder of a German tourist in Miami (September 11), and a British tourist at a highway rest stop in North Florida. *Newsweek* headlined a 'State of Terror' and noted the incident 'sends shock waves overseas and reminds Americans of the epidemic violence in our streets' (1993b:40). Two weeks later, *U.S. News* headlined 'Florida: The State of Rage' where 'nine foreign visitors have been murdered since last October' (1993b: 40), and *Time's* report on 'Taming the Killers' asked if young murderers can be reformed or if 'they are fated to repeat their crimes' (1993a:58). On October 1, year-old Polly Klass was kidnapped from her California home – a story that galvanized all media outlets until her body was found two months later.

The media blitz continued through the end of the year with a major *U.S. News* report (November 8) on 'Violence in Schools' (1993c), followed the next week with 'The Voters Cry For Help' in dealing with 'the wave of crime fear gripping Americans' (1993d: 26). *Newsweek* headlined 'Death at an Early Age' on November 8 (1993c), and three weeks later ran an eight page cover story on 'Gangsta Rap and the Culture of Violence' (1993d). On December 8, CBS aired a one hour special on Florida – 'State of Fear.'

The mid-December 'Massacre on the Long Island Railroad' (*Newsweek* 1993e) that left five dead and nineteen wounded, pushed the panic to its greatest heights. Most major media outlets gave the story front page and lead coverage. *U.S. News* headlined 'Violence and its Terrifying Randomness' and asked 'Is no place in America safe from violence?' (1993e: 6). Shortly thereafter NBC News and CNN ran week long series on 'America the Violent' and 'Kids and Crime' respectively.

Reports: Qualitatively Different Dangers

In addition to the escalating volume of media attention, the moral panics over crack and violence were characterized by reports emphasizing new and greater dangers. Both drugs and violence were common to the American experience and the warrant for panic included, in both cases, reports of a menace that was qualitatively different and more terrifying.

Out of the ghetto – out of control

A key element in both panics was a presumption that dangerous behaviors thought common to inner-city neighborhoods were suddenly spreading out of the ghetto into middle America. By the early 1980s, freebasing – the precursor to 'crack' – was common to inner-city after-hours clubs (base houses) in Los Angeles and New York (Hamid, 1988). Cocaine freebase, packaged in retail form as 'crack' or 'rock' appeared in 1984. Its low price encouraged widespread use in poor neighborhoods of many cities by 1986 (Johnson et al., 1990: 16).

The March 17 *Newsweek* – which some consider pivotal for the emerging 'panic' – sounded the alarm on its cover: 'An Epidemic Strikes Middle America' (1986a). The seven page story included these descriptions of crack's expanding menace:

> Crack . . . is already creating social havoc in the ghettos of Los Angeles, New York and other large cities, and it is rapidly spreading into the suburbs on both coasts. (1986a: 59)

> And in Camden County NJ . . . prosecutor Samuel Asbell is convinced that the city's contagion has already spread to suburbia (1986a: 60)

> There is simply no question that cocaine in all its forms is seeping into the nation's schools. (1986a: 63)

Subsequent summer issues of *Newsweek* repeated the message of a spreading contagion.:

> Crack has captured the ghetto and is inching its way into the suburbs. . . (1986b: 16)

> There are ominous signs that crack and rock dealers are expanding well beyond the inner city. (1986b: 20)

> In part, the change in the public mood has a racist tinge: drugs simply have moved from the black and Hispanic underclass to the middle-class mainstream and are being felt as a problem there. (1986b: 15)

One analysis of television reporting on the 'crack epidemic' compared it with coverage given to 'Black Tar' – an especially potent form of heroin – that NBC News (March 28, 1986) identified as responsible '. . . for a growing number of addicts and corpses.' Why did crack become a major story in 1986 when Black Tar did not? Writing in *T.V. Guide*, Diamond et al. suggest:

> One reason has to do with those who are being affected and where those victims live. Black Tar stays in the ghetto, while crack is depicted as moving into 'our' – that is the comfortable TV viewers – neighborhoods. (1987: 7)

[...]

For more than twenty-years, drive-by shootings, gang-banging and narco-warfare have plagued many inner-city neighborhoods – terrifying their residents, and shortening their lives. Yet through all of this, from July, 1980 to January, 1993 no more than *nine percent* of Americans considered crime to be the nation's most important problem (U.S. Justice Department 1993a: 162). Suddenly in January of 1994 this measure jumped to *forty-nine percent* (Gallup, 1994: 6).

A central issue in the moral panic of 1993 was the presumption that violence was spreading from the inner-city into places once considered safe. *Time* was especially active in developing this theme. First, a carjacking feature – 'Hell on Wheels' – noted that 'the generation that fled the cities to escape violent crime finds that crime commutes too' (1993b: 45). A week later *Time* featured 'Danger in the Safety Zone' which chronicled violence 'in virtually all public places once regarded as safe havens' such as schools, hospitals, libraries and homes (1993c: 29). Then in the wake of the Long Island Railroad murders, *Time* observed:

> The slaughter produced a national shudder, the kind that follows any awful crime that bleeds into unexpected corners – the toddler caught, in a cross fire during a trip to the Denver zoo, eight people gunned down in a swanky San Francisco law firm, and now five dead and 18 wounded by the gunman on the commuter train. (1993d:20)

Reports about the spread of violence to places like Omaha, Nebraska (*Time*, 1993e) and Kenosha, Wisconsin (*Time*, 1993c) or Tomball, Texas – 'the sort of safe town where many residents leave their front doors unlocked at night' (*Time*, 1993c: 31) – established the premise that no place is safe. Quoting a Texas sociologist, *Newsweek* observed that 'We can be followed home from the supermarket, followed when we rent a car' – possibilities that 'reinforce the sense that there is no protection, there is nothing you can do' (1993b: 40).

The presumed *randomness* of violence elevates its threat to people who had learned to avoid 'dangerous' places. After the Long Island Railroad murders, *U.S. News* decried 'Violence and its Terrifying Randomness' (1993f: 6) and *Newsweek* reported that Americans are 'sick at heart about the recurrent episodes of random violence which mock our pretensions to order and civility' (1993g: 27). *U.S. News* concluded that 'it's the randomness and viciousness of crime in the 1990s, not just its extent, that elevates it as an issue' (1993c: 49), and *Time* noted 'the fear is getting worse because there is no pattern ... it is random, spontaneous and episodic' (1993c: 29).

Reports: It's Spreading to Our Children

The panics over crack cocaine and violent crime both drew heavily from reports emphasizing the escalating involvement of young people in drugs and violence. Menace, both to and from youth is a common theme in the anxiety of moral panics (Ben-Yehuda, 1986; Best, 1990; Cohen, 1972; Hall et al., 1978; Jenkins, 1992). Among the reasons may be that youngsters are presumably: (1) more vulnerable; (2) less predictable; (3) less remorseful and (4) physically closer to the rest of us, because they still live in our homes. Moreover, as Hall et al. observed, fears and panics about youth center on the 'indiscipline' of the young (1978: 145) – an episodic if not perennial threat to social order. Spread of the 'ghetto pathologies' of crack and violence to and through children clearly escalated the moral purchase for urgent punitive *commands* to deal with the behavior.

As noted above, the crack 'epidemic' was touched off by a *Newsweek* cover story – 'Kids and Cocaine' – that emphasized the availability of crack to young people due to its low cost. The story offered the following observations:

> An epidemic of cheap, deadly 'crack' exposes a generation of American children to the nightmare of cocaine addiction. (1986a: 58)

> In New York, eager buyers queue up outside crack houses ... and the lines according to one drug agent 'are loaded with kids.' There are white kids, black kids, Hispanic kids – kids from the ghetto and kids from the suburbs. (1986a: 59–60)

> 'There are two trends in cocaine use' says Frank LaVecchia, a former high-school guidance counselor who runs a drug-treatment center in suburban Miami: '*Younger and younger and more and more.*' (1986a: 58)

Television too, reported that cocaine was claiming younger and younger victims as it spread from college campuses to maternity wards. Tom Brokaw, on NBC *Nightly News* (July 7) reported that cocaine 'is becoming the college drug of the 80s,' and ABC's *World News Tonight* (July 11) reported on babies born with a cocaine addiction '... the newest victims of the American cocaine epidemic' (Diamond et al., 1987: 8).

[...]

The involvement of youth in violence – as both assailant and victim – is a major theme of the recent panic. In April of 1993, the *New York Times* ran a ten-part series entitled 'Children of the Shadows' that chronicled the violence filled world of ten kids from New York, Memphis, and Oakland.

On November 1, *The Washington Post* presented a front page story titled: 'Getting Ready to Die Young: Children in Violent D.C. Neighborhoods Plan Their Own Funerals' (1993). On November 7, 'Monster' Kody Scott – who began gangbanging at age 11 – was featured on *60 Minutes*.

In the six months between July 19, 1993 and January 10, 1994 the three major weekly newsmagazines ran the following headlines either on stories or covers:

Life Means Nothing: In Houston six teenagers are accused of mindlessly killing two young girls and seem not to care. Is adolescent brutality on the rise? (*Newsweek*, 1993a: 16)

Teen Violence: Wild in the Streets (*Newsweek*, 1993f: Cover)

Murder and mayhem, guns and gangs: a teenage generation grows up dangerous and scared (*Newsweek*, 1993f: 40)

A Boy And His Gun: Even in a town like Omaha, Nebraska, the young are packing weapons in a deadly battle against fear and boredom (*Time*, 1993e: 20–1)

Brutality as a Teen Fashion Statement (*Newsweek*, 1993g: 61)

Taming the Killers: Can young murderers be reformed? (*Time*, 1993a: 58)

Death at an Early Age (*Newsweek*, 1993c: 69)

Violence in the Schools: When Killers Come to Class (*U.S. News*, 1993c: Cover)

Growing Up Fast and Frightened (*Newsweek*, 1993h: 52).

When is Rap 2 Violent? (*Newsweek*, 1993d: Cover)

Growing Up Scared (*Newsweek*, 1993a: Cover)

U.S. News called attention to a 'chilling shift in adolescent attitudes: a sharp drop in respect for life' (1993c: 31) and *Time* led a story with this:

The names of the teenagers in this story aren't real, but the kids are – and they are all killers. They have murdered, some more than once, and are serving time. And they will still be young when they come up for parole. (1993a: 58)

A 16 year-old was quoted as saying: 'If you have a gun you have power ... Guns are just a part of growing up these days' (*Time*: 1993b: 21). In the same article Attorney General Janet Reno noted that violence is devastating this generation as surely as polio cut down young people 40 years ago, and concluded that youth violence is 'the single greatest crime problem in America today' (*Time*, 1993b: 43).

The Recent Panics: Misunderstanding Drugs and Violence

Like other moral panics, those concerning crack cocaine and violence involved key ideological distortions ... with important consequence for the commands developed to deal with them. In particular, while drug abuse and violence have been *substantial* and *enduring* problems in many inner-city neighbourhoods for decades, moral panic created the impression of a *sudden* and *escalating* firestorm spreading through society. The result is a political response that is – in Cohen's (1972) terms – *fundamentally inappropriate*.

In fact, in the United States, cocaine use *declined* during 1986 and violent crime rates *declined* during 1993 – the years of spreading moral panic. What did *not* decline in those years of panic were the dissolution, despair and nihilism (West, 1994) increasingly characteristic of inner-city neighborhoods, where the choice of drugs or violence has become for many, as reasonable and available as the choice of work. The consequence of treating the substantial and enduring problems of drugs and violence as if they are a sudden and escalating firestorm is that commands to deal with them seek *sudden* solutions that are *fundamentally inappropriate*. In an atmosphere of panic, building walls and stacking people behind them is faster and easier than doing the difficult work of restoring work and community to neighborhoods devastated by disinvestment and deskilling.

In showing how moral panic has misunderstood drug abuse and violence, I am *not* suggesting that these are somehow inconsequential problems. Rather, I argue that panic disguises the fact that drugs and violence have been *extraordinary* problems for several decades – problems borne disproportionately by the residents of inner-city neighborhoods. Indeed, these inner-city residents have been doubly victimized – first, by the profound changes in the political economy of cities and then by the drugs and violence that long ago began taking the place of work and community in many of those neighborhoods.

The principal misunderstanding helping to fuel the panic about cocaine in 1986 was that its use was increasing and spreading – especially among youth outside of the urban underclass. The spread was presumably a function of the low unit cost of the 'rock' or crack form of the drug. Various dimensions of this misunderstanding have been well documented elsewhere

(Diamond, et al. 1987; Goode, 1989; Jensen, et al. 1991; Orcutt and Turner, 1993: Reinerman and Levine, 1989), and require only brief note here.

Most important, whatever was happening to the *forms* of cocaine, there is little evidence that cocaine use *per se* was increasing – particularly in the general population. In fact, the annual survey of high school seniors conducted by the University of Michigan showed that reported use of cocaine *dropped* during 1986 – and has continued to drop – after reaching a ten year high in 1985 (U.S. Justice Department, 1993a: 329) Among college students, reported use of cocaine was also *lower* in 1986 than in 1985 (U.S. Justice Department, 1993a: 330–1). And with regard to the general population, the Justice Department reports that:

> Trend data from the national Household Survey on Drug Abuse indicates that current use of most drugs [including cocaine] rose from the early to late 1970s, peaked between 1979 and 1982 and has since declined. The increase in cocaine use was especially sharp in the late 1970s (U.S. Justice Department, 1992: 30)

The limits of survey data as a measure of behavior are well known, but there is little reason to conclude that reports of declining drug use after 1985 (or increasing drug use before 1985) reflect variation in the validity of self-reports more than variation in drug using behavior. And while there *is* evidence from hospital data that 'emergency room mentions' of cocaine and 'drug related deaths' increased between 1985 and 1986, the Drug Enforcement Administration issued a report at the height of the 'crack' panic which concluded that crack was a 'secondary, not a primary drug problem in most cities' and that 'its prevalence has been exaggerated by heavy news media attention' (*Washington Post*, 1986: A18).

[...]

The recent moral panic over violence has involved a similar pattern of exaggeration, distortion or 'misunderstanding.' Specifically, during 1993, when media coverage of violent crime increased by more than 400 percent and Americans ranking crime/violence as the nation's foremost problem also increased by more than 400 percent, the rate of violent crime, as measured by the *Uniform Crime Reports* showed a *decrease* of 1.5 percent from the previous year (See Figure 8.3). Forcible rapes declined 3.9 percent and robberies 1.9 percent. In contrast, aggravated assaults were up 0.7 percent and murders were up 3.2 percent. Even the slight increase in homicides, left the total (24,530) *lower* than the total and the rate for 1991 (U.S. Justice Department, 1994a: 58).

The National Crime Victimization Survey showed similar though not identical patterns for 1993. Overall, the rate of violent victimizations –

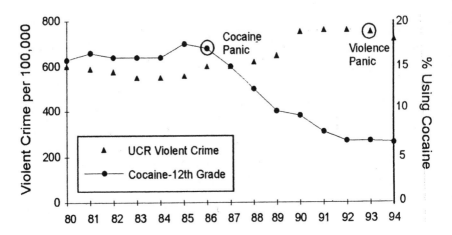

Figure 8.3 Violent crime and cocaine use trends (1980–94)

Sources: U.S. Justice Dept., 1994a; U.S. Justice Dept., 1995; and Johnston, 1994: High School Survey.

including attempts – increased slightly (5.6 percent) from the previous year. However, rates of *completed* violence actually *decreased* (3.2 percent). Reported rates for sexual assault were down (20.7 percent) and for robbery, were unchanged. The only violent crime to show an increase (6.9 percent) was assault (U.S. Justice Department, 1995:2).

If moral panic has 'misunderstood' or distorted the overall trends in violent crime, the emphasis on increasing *juvenile* violence – though exaggerated – has *some* basis in actual trends. Specifically, the *number of arrests* of persons under 18 years of age for violent Index crimes increased 5.6 percent between 1992 and 1993; for homicide, the increase was 13.7 percent. However, for several reasons, the number of arrests may not be the most appropriate measure of juvenile involvement in crime. A somewhat better indicator is suggested by the *Uniform Crime Report* which notes that 'involvement of juveniles in crime can be measured by the number of crimes in which they have been identified as the offenders' which may or may not involve an actual arrest of a juvenile (U.S. Justice Department, 1994a: 206)....

So if crime and violence were declining in 1993 and if juvenile involvement in violent crime was increasing only marginally, what accounts for the 400 percent increase in media coverage for these issues in the last six months of 1993 and the more than 400 percent increase in concern about crime and violence in the twelve months ending in January, 1994? One possibility is that there was little competing news and, as Sabato has noted, media 'feeding frenzies are more likely to develop in slow news periods such as the doldrums of summer ...' (1991: 79). The 'dull news alternative' was also raised by Cohen's (1972) account of a British moral panic and by Fishman's (1978) account of a New York City 'crime wave'.

It is also possible that in the summer of 1993, several highly publicized violent attacks so captured public consciousness that they came to define for many the essence of the crime problem. Because of saturation news coverage, there are few Americans who could not recount at least some details of the Reginald Denny beating in South Central Los Angeles, or the Monticello Florida rest area murder, or the Fort Lauderdale tourist murders, or the Long Island Railroad killings where a gunman walked the aisles of a speeding train and emptied his gun several times. And as noted above, all three national news magazines did lengthy features on violence two weeks after the gang-rape and murder of two teenaged girls who took a short-cut through the woods to their homes in Houston.

One common theme to these crimes is that each involved *white* victims and allegedly *black male* assailants who were unknown to the victims. Except for the Houston murders, each involved *adult* victims and except for the Long Island Railroad 'massacre' each of the assailants was *young*. Yet far from typical criminal violence these are tragic exceptions to the norm of victimization that occurs overwhelmingly *within* age and race bounds. Departures from the norm are often considered newsworthy. They may become more so when they resonate criminal stereotypes and tap into deeply held racial anxieties.

It is almost as if the recent panic emerged precisely when the violence that has devastated inner-city neighbourhoods for decades threatened – even if by stunning exception – to leap the boundaries and defy the norms of violent victimization. And as we have noted above, this is precisely what the reports of the moral panic tried to convey.

Recent Panics: Commands

The bottom line of all ideological discourse is the use of reports – whether they distort reality or not – to mobilize popular support to *do* something in the public arena. Because moral panics have such relentless energy and because they employ rhetoric like 'epidemic,' 'firestorm,' 'rising tide' and 'plague' the *urgency* of swift and serious action is explicitly justified....

Indeed, the command implications of moral panic over drugs and violence have been decisive, if nothing else. The response to the crack cocaine panic has been well documented elsewhere (Belenko et al., 1991; Kerr,

1986; Reinarman & Levine, 1989; Tonry & Wilson, 1990) and is briefly summarized here. In Washington, drug politics were rapidly transformed in the summer of 1986 by several factors, none more significant than the explosion of media reports. According to members of Congress and their aides 'when the media started talking about it, it lit a fire' (Kerr, 1986: B6).

On July 23, House Speaker 'Tip' O'Neill announced plans for comprehensive drug legislation to be voted on by September. The extraordinary pace of action was justified by House Democratic leader Jim Wright who commented that 'his most pressing concern was that Congress act before television lost interest in the drug story.' And Republican leader Robert Michel expressed fears that 'unless House Republicans joined in quickly, the Democrats could grab the issue as their own in time for the [November] election' (Kerr, 1986: B6). In September, President and Nancy Reagan went on television to call for a new 'crusade' against drugs and on October 17, 1986 Congress passed the Anti-Drug Abuse Act of 1986 – called by some 'the most far-reaching drug law ever passed' (Kerr, 1986: B6).

Even as the panic quickly subsided in Washington (Kerr, 1986) enthusiasm for getting tough on drugs – particularly crack cocaine offenders – mushroomed in the states. The 'no lose' proposition of moving swiftly and severely against marginalized segments of the urban underclass, who were seen as responsible for the spreading menace of crack – among other things – became a centerpiece of state and local social policy in the last half of the 1980s.

Nationwide, drug arrests increased more than 65 percent between 1986 and 1989 (U.S. Justice Department, 1993b: 9) and state prison admissions for drug crimes mushroomed 214 percent (33,100 to 103,800) between 1986 and 1990 (U.S. Justice Department, 1994b: 10). As a proportion of all state prison admissions in the U.S., those for drug offenses increased 372 percent during the 1980s – rising from 6.8 percent in 1980 to 32.1 percent in 1990 (U.S. Justice Department, 1994b: 10).

The most celebrated feature of this newest 'war on drugs' was the extraordinary set of penalties applied to the possession, sale or trafficking of *crack* as opposed to powder cocaine. Under federal law, 1 gram of crack counts as much as 100 grams of powder. Possession of 50 grams of crack brings a ten-year sentence; to get ten years for powder cocaine one would need 5,000 grams. Though patterns vary among the states, at least eight have adopted sentences for crack cocaine that are much more severe than for other drugs. Moreover, in federal law, only crack has mandatory minimum sentences for simple possession. All other drugs require possession with intent to sell (Cauchon, 1993: 2A).

A direct consequence of this panic inspired legislation has been a substantial increase in the flow of African Americans into prison. Specifically, because almost 92 percent of federal crack defendants are black (as opposed to 27 percent for powder cocaine) harsher penalties for crack weigh most heavily against African-American drug users. As a result, the rate of incarceration (per 100,000) increased 48 percent for blacks between 1986 and 1991 as compared to 34 percent for whites (U.S. Justice Department, 1994b: 9). Looked at another way, African Americans accounted for 38.2 percent of those in state prisons for drugs in 1986 and 53.2 percent by 1991. More remarkably, blacks incarcerated for drugs made up 3.3 percent of all state prisoners in 1986 and 11.3 percent in 1991 – a 242 percent increase (U.S. Justice Department, 1993b:623). By 1992, the rate of incarceration for African American males (2,678 per 100,000) was almost eight times as great as for the total population (344) (U.S. Justice Department, 1994b: 9). If those in jail, on probation or on parole are included, almost *one of every ten* adult black males in America was in the punitive custody of the state by 1991 (U.S. Justice Department, 1993b; 1994b).

Commands 'justified' by the panic over violent crime in late 1993 are still being realized and their full consequence can only be known in years to come....

At the federal level, the 'Violent Crime Control and Law Enforcement Act of 1994' was passed in August of that year. Touted by the Justice Department as 'the largest crime bill in the history of the country,' it 'will provide for 100,000 new police officers, $9.7 billion in funding for prisons and $6.1 billion in funding for prevention programs' (U.S. Justice Department, 1994c: 1). Beyond that, it expands the death penalty to cover sixty additional federal offenses; authorizes adult prosecution for 13-year-olds charged with serious violent crimes; provides 'stiffer penalties for violent and drug trafficking crimes committed by gang members'; has its own 'three strikes' provision; doubles the maximum term for repeat Federal sex offenders and among many other things:

> Creates new crimes or enhances penalties for: drive-by-shootings, use of semi-automatic weapons, sex offenses, crimes against the elderly, interstate firearms trafficking, firearms theft and smuggling, arson, hate crimes and interstate domestic violence. (U.S. Justice Department, 1994c: 1–2)

Several states, including California, have implemented 'three strikes' provisions mandating sentences between twenty-five years and life for persons convicted of a third felony. Many states have extended the reach of mandatory minimum sentencing, and many are greatly expanding their prison capacities. In state after state, during the 1994 political campaigns candidates fired competing 'get tough' salvos in efforts to cash in on the wave of crime fear sweeping the nation.

Conclusion: Moral Panic as Ideological Displacement

And so it's off to war again – if not the metaphorical 'war on drugs', then the literal war in the streets. And prisoners *will* be taken. The 'success' of moral panic as an ideological phenomenon could be no more aptly demonstrated. It not only mobilizes a massive expansion of the state's repressive apparatus – even as drug use and crime *decline* – but it diverts attention from the consequences of a one-sided class war that has involved not only disinvestment and deskilling, but regressive taxation, the pillaging of pension funds and the social safety net and assaults on the well-being of both the workplace and the environment (Bartlett and Steele, 1992; Lind, 1995).

These actions, which have made American capital more competitive in the 'global marketplace,' have also assisted in the dismantling of the middle class, the growth of an isolated underclass and a more unequal distribution of wealth and opportunity than at any time since the onset of the last Great Depression (Batra, 1987; Lind, 1995). The same conditions that have made enormous fortunes for a handful of investors, have made most Americans work harder for less and have consigned so many others – particularly in the urban underclass – to a superfluous present and a hopeless future.

But instead of waging war on the inhuman conditions fostered by policies of disinvestment and deskilling, that have hollowed our inner-city neighborhoods, we wage war on those individuals dehumanized by the lack of reasonable choices. Instead of waging war on unemployment, inadequate schools and the loss of hope we wage war on individuals destroyed by those very conditions. Instead of waging war on the factors contributing to an increasingly isolated underclass – for whom life has less and less meaning – we wage war against individuals who seek meaning in drugs and violence.

[...]

As noted above, the real danger of the recent moral panics is that they treat problems that have been *substantial* and *enduring* for several decades in many inner-city neighborhoods as if they are a *sudden* firestorm. An atmosphere of panic mobilizes demands for immediate repression and causes us to ignore the root problems of urban America that have grown and festered for decades. The same media frenzy that raises *decisiveness* to the cardinal virtue of public policy, lowers the chance that meaningful response to enduring problems will be undertaken.

Put behind walls another 100,000 or 500,000 or a million young men for whom drugs and violence have become meaningful choices – and what will happen? If nothing is done to restore work family and community to our central city neighborhoods, then successive waves of children will have and will make those same choices.

The triumph of moral panic as ideology is realized in the promotion of 'solutions' to the contradictions of capitalism that literally misrepresent and conceal their existence while mobilizing support to repress their most disadvantaged and visible victims. At the same time, and perhaps most important, moral panic keeps the vast majority of Americans – who are 'doing with less so that big business can have more' – focused on ostensible dangers from the underclass instead of the policies and profits of the investors of capital, who are responsible not only for the growth of that underclass but the frustrations and anxieties plaguing so many Americans.

References

Bartlett, D.L. and Steele, J.B. (1992) *America: What Went Wrong?* Kansas City: Andrews & McMeel.

Batra, R. (1987) *The Great Depression of 1990.* New York: Simon & Schuster.

Belenko, S., Fagan, J. and Chin, K.L. (1991) Criminal justice responses to crack, *Journal of Research in Crime and Delinquency*, 28: 55–74.

Ben-Yehuda, N. (1986) The sociology of moral panics: toward a new synthesis, *The Sociological Quarterly*, 27: 495–513.

Best, J. (1990) *Threatened Children.* Chicago: University of Chicago Press.

Cauchon, D. (1993) Sentences for crack called racist, *USA Today*, 23 May: 1A–2A.

Cohen, S. (1972). *Folk Devils and Moral Panics.* St Albans: Paladin.

Danielian, L.H. and Reese, S.D. (1989) A closer look at intermedia influences on agenda setting: the cocaine issue of 1986, in P. J. Shoemaker (ed.) *Communication Campaigns about Drugs: Government, Media and the Public.* Hillsdale. NJ: Lawrence Erlbaum Associates.

Diamond, E., Acosta, F. and Thornton, L.J. (1987) Is TV news hyping America's cocaine problem?, *T.V. Guide*, 7 February: 4–10.

Fishman, M. (1978) Crime Waves as Ideology, *Social Problems*, 25: 531–43

Gallup, G. (1994) *The Gallup Poll, No. 341*, (February), Wilmington, DL: Scholarly Resources, Inc.

Goode, E. (1989) *Drugs in American Society.* 3rd edn. New York: McGraw-Hill, Inc.

Gouldner, A. (1976) *The Dialectic of Ideology and Technology.* New York: Oxford University Press.

Hall. S., Critcher, C., Jefferson, T., Clarke, J. and Roberts, B. (1978) *Policing the Crisis: Mugging, the State and Law and Order*. London: Macmillan.

Hamid, A. (1988) From ganja to crack: establishment of the cocaine (and crack) economy, in A. Hamid (ed.) *Drugs and Drug Abuse: A Reader*. Littleton, MA: Copley.

Jenkins, P. (1992) *Intimate Enemies: Moral Panics in Contemporary Great Britain*. New York: Aldine de Gruyter.

Jensen, E.L., Gerber, J. and Babcock, G.M. (1991) The new war on drugs: grass root movement or political construction, *Journal of Drug Issues*, 21: 651–67.

Johnson, B.D., Williams, T., Dei, K. and Sanabria, H. (1990) Drug abuse in the inner city: impact on hard-drug users and the community, in M. Tonry and J. Q. Wilson (eds) *Drugs and Crime*. Chicago: The University of Chicago Press.

Kasarda, J.D. (1994) Industrial restructuring and the consequences of changing job locations. Unpublished, NC: Kenan Institute of Private Enterprise.

Kerr, P. (1986) Anatomy of the drug issue: how, after years, it erupted, *New York Times*, 17 November: A1, B6.

Larrain, J. (1983) *Marxism and Ideology*. London: The Macmillan Press.

Lind, M. (1995) To have and to have not: notes on the progress of the American class war, *Harpers Magazine*, June: 35–47.

Lynch, J.P. and Sabol, W.J. (1992) Macro-social changes and their implications for prison reform: the underclass and the composition of prison populations. Paper presented at the meetings of the American Society of Criminology, November.

Massey, D. (1990) American apartheid: Segregation and the making of an underclass, *American Journal of Sociology*, 96: 329–57.

Melossi, D. (1985) Punishment and social action: changing vocabularies of punitive motive with a political business cycle, *Current Perspectives in Social Theory*, 6: 169–97.

Melossi, D. (1989) An introduction: fifty-years later, 'Punishment and Social Structure' in comparative analysis, *Contemporary Crises*, 13: 311–26.

Merriam, J.E. (1989) National media coverage of drug issues, 1983–1987, in P.J. Shoemaker (ed.) *Communication Campaigns About Drugs: Government, Media and the Public*. Hillsdale, NJ: Lawrence Erlbaum.

Newsweek (1986a) Kids and cocaine, 17 March: 58–65.

Newsweek (1986b) Crack and crime, 16 June: 15–22.

Newsweek (1993a) Life means nothing, 19 July: 16–27.

Newsweek (1993b) In a state of terror, 27 September: 40–1.

Newsweek (1993c) Death at an early age, 8 November: 69.

Newsweek (1993d) Criminal records: gangsta rap and the culture of violence, 29 November: 60–4.

Newsweek (1993e) Death ride: massacre on the LIRR, 20 December: 26–31.

Newsweek (1993f) Wild in the streets, 2 August: 40–7.

Newsweek (1993g) Brutality as a teen fashion Statement, 23 August: 61.

Newsweek (1993h) Growing up fast and frightened, 22 November: 52.

Newsweek (1994a) Kids growing up scared, 10 January: 43–50.

Orcutt, J.D. and Turner, J.B. (1993) Shocking numbers and graphic accounts: quantified images of drug problems in the print media, *Social Problems*, 40: 190–206.

Reinarman, C. and Levine, H. (1989) The crack attack: politics and media in America's latest drug scare, in J. Best (ed.) *Images of Issues: Typifying Contemporary Social Problems*. New York: Aldine de Gruyter.

Ricketts. E.R. and Sawhill, I.V. (1988) Defining and measuring the underclass, *Journal of Policy Analysis and Management*, 7: 316–25.

Time (1986) Bringing out the big guns: the first couple and congress press the attack on drugs, 22 September: 25–6.

Time (1993a) Taming the killers, 11 October: 58–9.

Time (1993b) Hell on wheels, 16 August: 44–8

Time (1993c) Danger in the safety zone, 23 August: 29–32.

Time (1993d) Up in arms, 20 December: 18–26.

Time (1993e) A boy and his gun, 2 August: 20–7.

Tonry, M. and Wilson, J.Q. (eds) (1990) *Drugs and Crime*. Chicago: The University of Chicago Press.

U.S. Department of Justice (1992) *Drugs, Crime and the Justice System*. Washington, DC: U.S. Government Printing Office.

U.S. Department of Justice (1993a) *Sourcebook of Criminal Justice Statistics – 1992*. Washington, DC: U.S. Government Printing Office.

U.S. Department of Justice (1993b) *Drugs and Crime Facts, 1992*. Washington, DC: Bureau of Justice Statistics.

U.S. Department of Justice (1994a) *Crime in the United States – 1993*. Washington, DC: U.S. Government Printing Office.

U.S. Department of Justice (1994b) *Prisoners in 1993*. Washington, DC: Bureau of Justice Statistics.

U.S. Department of Justice (1994c) *Fact Sheet: Violent Crime Control and Law Enforcement Act of 1994*. Washington, DC, 24 October.

U.S. Department of Justice (1995) *Criminal Victimization 1993*. Washington, DC: Bureau of Justice Statistics.

U.S. News & World Report (1993a) Los Angeles under the gun, 31 May: 82

U.S. News & World Report (1993b) Florida: The state of rage, 11 October: 44–44.

U.S. News & World Report (1993c) Violence in schools, 8 November: 31–6.

U.S. News & World Report (1993d) The voters cry for help, 15 November: 26–30.

U.S. News & World Report (1993e) Violence and its terrifying randomness, 20 December: 6.

U.S. News & World Report (1993f) A new attack on crime, 18 October: 49.

West, C. (1994) *Race Matters*. New York: Vintage.

Wilson, W.J. (1987) *The Truly Disadvantaged: The Inner City, the Underclass, and Public Policy*. Chicago: University of Chicago Press.

9 PANIC AT THE PORT

Stephen Stockwell (1997)

Introduction

... On Sunday 28 April 1996, Martin Bryant murdered 35 people at Port
Arthur, Tasmania, and in surrounding districts. The Port Arthur murders
sit at the intersection of numerous media themes and this paper begins by
disentangling those themes against Cohen's (1973: 23) model of moral
panic: warning, impact, inventory and reaction (see Figure 9.1). This provides an opportunity to clarify the mechanics of moral panic thirty years
after the now-seemingly innocent frolics of the Mods and Rockers, the 'folk
devils' whom Cohen studied.

Of particular interest is the way in which some thematic elements were
pursued and transformed into fully-fledged moral panics with resultant
changes in government policy while others petered out into what, on
reflection, might be seen as an embarrassing silence.

Looking back at the media prior to the incident, we can now discern the
warning phase which, as Cohen explains, involves: 'some apprehensions
based on conditions out of which danger may arise' (1973: 22). The intense
media coverage of the Dunblane massacre in the weeks before the incident
and earlier stories about the easy availability of high-powered guns in
Tasmania are two obvious examples. A less obvious example, the relevance
of which will be discussed below, is the media attention afforded to the
racist statements of Pauline Hanson and other conservative politicians
during the March 1996 Federal election campaign.

Media coverage of the incident itself fits easily into Cohen's description
of impact: 'during which the disaster strikes and the immediate unorganised

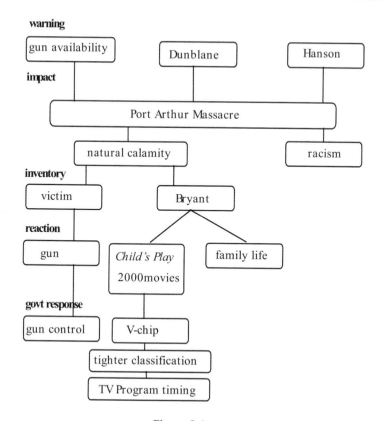

Figure 9.1

response to the death, injury and destruction takes place' (1973: 22). In situations like this, journalists are acting by instinct, struggling to comprehend and clarify events for a string of tight deadlines. For want of analysis, they find themselves drawing parallels to natural disasters or inexplicable calamities and resorting to ghoulish compilations of previous similar events and international coverage of this particular instance. While this instinctual, unorganised response has been criticised (*Mediawatch*, ABC-TV, 6 May 1996), it is very difficult to prescribe the correct manner of dealing with such a large, complex and emotive event except to proscribe clear criminal or ethical breaches, for example unauthorised entry to the perpetrator's home (*Mediawatch*, ABC-TV, 6 May 1996). It was in the confusion of the impact phase that the few brief references to a possible racist motive were made (*Daybreak*, Nine Network, 29 April 1996). The end of the impact phase was marked by the normalising pieces to camera by *Current Affair's* Ray Martin from Port Arthur on the evening of 29 April.

Over the following two days the inventory phase unwound with front page lists of the victims, the survivors recounting their close shaves and the exploration of the minutiae of Bryant's circumstances.

Real Devils

As the media environment settled after the murders, the shift from inventory to reaction was skillfully managed by the newly elected Howard Liberal Federal Government which used the opportunity to pursue two particular policy initiatives.

The first was to limit the availability of some semi-automatic weapons. It is interesting to consider whether this initiative was the result of a moral panic about guns or whether the murders merely prompted the government to take action which had widespread popular support before the Port Arthur incident. Certainly the Prime Minister announced his position after *A Current Affair* replayed a story which had previously displayed the ease of acquiring such weapons in Tasmania (Nine Network, 29 April 1996) but he acted so quickly that there was no opportunity for a fully-fledged panic to develop.

In this context an interesting issue arises for Cohen's account of moral panic generally. Given that the clear link between the availability of firearms and high rates of murder, suicide and fatal accidents in domestic situations had already been established (Gabor 1994), it is relevant to ask: is it possible to have a moral panic when the devils (guns) are real?

Opponents of gun control certainly attempted to generate a moral panic about the government's plans to limit gun availability. At a meeting in Gympie, vice-president of the Firearms Association, Ian McNiven, labelled the Prime Minister 'Jackboot Johnny' and described his position as a 'brutal, totalitarian' attack on the freedom of citizens. McNiven went on: 'Let me tell you something about freedom. You can only buy it back with the most expensive currency in the world. Once given up, freedom can only be bought back with blood' (Agence France Presse, May 16 1996).

In contrast to the close focus on the issue of gun control in the reaction phase, Bryant's history of social development received only passing mention in the press despite the weight of criminological literature which suggests that it is interpersonal trauma during childhood development which predisposes a person to violence and murder (Klapper 1960; Yarvis 1991; also 'Predators', *Four Corners*, 14 April 1997). See also Eisenberg (1980) on the role of adult sanction in predisposing children to violent responses.

Given that the conservative Federal and State Governments were involved in cutbacks to health and social services, a moral panic about the declining quality and availability of psychological services would appear justified. But the media ignored this path as too difficult and instead concentrated on Bryant's video viewing habits.

2000 Violent Videos

The second major government initiative prompted by the Port Arthur murders was another in the long series of inquiries into violence in the media (Stockbridge and Dwyer 1997). This initiative encouraged a moral panic about violent TV and videos to develop. The genesis of this moral panic is of particular interest. It began with Jana Wendt asking the ubiquitous American expert about the contribution of the perpetrator's family background to the murders (*Witness*, Seven Network, 30 April 1996). In a neat piece of spin control, the American responded by avoiding the question and raising the issue of violent videos.

The Australian media were quick to pick up the theme. A few quotes from the print media eloquently sketch the course of the moral panic about video violence from that point on:

> Bryant was also known for his love of movies, a passion he indulged with visits to Hobart video outlet Movie Madness... (*Daily Telegraph*, May 1 1996)

> Bryant's favourite video *Child's Play 2* – featured an evil doll called Chucky. 'He loved Chucky,' Jenetta (his former girlfriend) said. 'He used to go on about it all the time ... There was a phrase out of that movie he used to say: "Don't fuck with the Chuck. He used to get excited when he said that."' (*Daily Telegraph*, May 3 1996)

> Bryant's days consisted mainly of watching movies. His deserted house this week was littered by more than 20 videos. They were mostly violent American films, which local video stores said were his favourites. (*Courier-Mail*, May 4 1996)

> More than 2,000 violent and pornographic videos have been found at the home of Martin Bryant, the man accused of the Port Arthur massacre. The tapes, lining shelves in two rooms, were discovered when work began to empty his house in the Hobart suburb of New Town. (*Daily Telegraph*, May 15 1996)

This final claim was later refuted by the head of the Film Classification Board, John Dickie whose investigations revealed that the 2,000 videos were predominantly 'musicals and classics ... that belonged to the woman who owned the house previously [and] the only four videos that were not in that period of romance and dramas were two of Rowan Atkinson's *Blackadder*, one of *Nightmare on Elm Street* and one of *Taxi Driver*' (*Sydney Morning Herald*, June 29 1996: 2). But by then the panic had spread like a virus from hard news into the editorials and features (for example 'The message of violent media', *Australian*, May 11 1996: 23) and was making opportunistic adaptations within other stories (for example, 'Designer Deaths', *Courier-Mail*, June 3 1996, criticises 'ghoulish' photography in fashion magazines).

Child's Play

'Blaming' movies, and in particular the *Child's Play* series (*Child's Play* 1988, *Child's Play 2* 1990, *Child's Play 3* 1992), fitted easily into the media's scheme of things. The unfinished nature of the media effects debate, the popular view that violent movies can't be good for other people (while having no effect on me) and the right-wing tenor of the censorship case (which balanced the 'left-wing' gun control lobby) all combined to make violent videos a far easier issue to 'debate' than more difficult questions such as personal development and the shrinking social safety net.

Further, the *Child's Play* series already had a criminal record. *Child's Play 3* had been implicated in two murder cases in Great Britain. Eleven-year-old boys, Jon Venables and Robert Thompson had murdered toddler Jamie Bulger in February 1993 shortly after one of their fathers had rented *Child's Play 3*. While the father claimed the boys never had the opportunity to view the tape, there were some similarities between the murder of the child and activities in the movie and while the police did not seek to make a connection between the movies and the murder, in sentencing the boys, the judge attacked the availability of violent videos (*Press Association Newsfile*, May 4 1996).

There was also: 'the torture and murder of 16-year-old Suzanne Capper by five women in December 1992 ... [one of whom] Bernadette McNeilly, 27, had allegedly watched *Child's Play 3* and said "I'm Chucky. Wanna play?" before injecting her victim with amphetamines' (*Sun-Herald* May 5 1996). Also 'Police believe a cassette of the doll's chilling and robotic "I'm Chucky. Wanna play?" catchphrase was repeatedly played to [Capper] through headphones while she was tied to a bed for days on end' (*Sunday Age*, December 19 1993).

Analysis of the thematic content of the *Child's Play* series goes some way to suggest why this series was such an easy target for demonisation. The three movies feature Chucky, an orange-haired 'Good Guy' doll possessed by the soul of a dying mass murderer using voodoo and black magic. The doll then murders people in increasingly inventive ways as it attempts to shift its soul back into a human form.

A slasher movie centred on a doll who practises black magic is an open invitation to censorship advocates. As one critic said: 'This is certainly not Pinocchio or Babes in Toyland' (Harrington, *Washington Post*, November 10 1988). While the *Child's Play* series never strays far from the conventions of the slasher movie (for more on those conventions, see McCarty 1984; Scott and Stockwell 1987) and may be read as a camp homage to the genre (Parker 1988), the counter-intuitive malevolence of a doll terrorising a child produces a problematic space – Alice in the Twilight Zone – and its own bent dynamic.

Corporate Interests

Aside from its thematic content, there were other issues in its production history and corporate position that made *Child's Play 2* an acceptable target for a moral panic. The series was the product of young writers and directors with little studio support. The first instalments in the series were made relatively cheaply and produced strong box office returns. The third was a more extravagant production that barely covered its cost. There were no big stars, each movie had a different distributor and the critics agreed that Chucky had mined about as much as he could from the horror genre. There was little chance of *Child's Play 4* going into production and the series did not have the studio support or media connections to defend itself.

By picking out *Child's Play 2*, the news media avoided any stigma for their own coverage of the mass murder at Dunblane which friends of Bryant suggested may have been a trigger and also undercut criticism of violent product from the mainstream studios with which the Australian news media share close ownership and distribution links.

The result of the moral panic over video violence has been government action to produce more stringent classification of movies, further limiting timeslots in which adult material might be broadcast on television and requiring all new TVs to contain a V-chip that allows parents to limit their children's viewing (Stockbridge and Dwyer 1997). Meanwhile the *Child's Play* series is still on the video shop shelves and one is left with the concern that the combined effect of the V-chip and the review of classification ratings is that the baby could go out with the bath water: these changes can just as easily be used to censor Shakespeare or graphic war footage as Chucky's bizarre activities.

Racism

By concentrating on the availability of guns and media violence, the media, and the government, avoided probing a key motive apparent in Bryant's statements and behaviour: racism. This is not to suggest that racism was the only motive Bryant had for the massacre. He killed 33 Australians and only two Asian tourists and he appears to have harboured an assortment of grudges and obsessions against all manner of people and institutions but it is significant that his last recorded words before the massacre began were 'There a lot of WASPs around today, there aren't many Japs, are there? . . . I live here, and I can never get a park, with all the Jap buses' (*Herald Sun*, April 29; *The Age*, April 30). Just as revealing as Bryant's comments before the massacre are his actions in the Broad Arrow restaurant where the murders at Port Arthur began. From a close re-reading of the most thorough summaries of his actions ('The Carnage Cafe', *Sydney Morning Herald*, May 4 1996; 'Slaughter of Innocence' *Sun Herald*, 5 May 1996), it is apparent that from the moment Bryant took out his gun, he was moving towards the only Asian tourists in the restaurant. They were his third and fourth victims there. None of the summaries made this point explicitly and some even failed to include mention of the Asians among his victims (see for example 'In Cold Blood', *The Age*, May 3 1996). Also, while his comments prior to the massacre were reported during the confusion of the impact phase and some media outlets even pointed to their racist implications, that particular story ended there and did not even feature significantly in the inventory phase.

That the media failed to pursue racism as a motive and their subsequent concentration on guns and violent videos as prime causes of the murders raises some interesting questions. Why was a moral panic on racism deemed un-newsworthy? Do media managers see racism as so popular that it would not successfully demonise Bryant? Might the charge of racism increase sympathy for him? Did they judge that the issue might raise too many questions about Australia's attitude to race at a time when it was under international scrutiny? Or do they share, perhaps unconsciously, a certain complicity with the high level of racism in Australia, a complicity that was veiled by their readiness to instigate moral panics about other, carefully delineated, issues but not this one? It is beyond the scope of this paper to answer these questions in a thorough-going fashion though it is instructive to consider the AGB-McNair opinion poll taken in June 1996 (*Sydney Morning Herald*, June 19 1996: 6) which showed that 51% of those interviewed think that Australia's composition of migrant intake features 'too many from particular regions' which suggests that over half of Australians are willing to discriminate against migrants on the grounds of geographical, and therefore, racial origin.

Some Implications for Moral Panic Theory

The media coverage of the Port Arthur massacre raises some interesting insights into moral panics in the contemporary media environment. One point worthy of note is how the role of 'the moral entrepreneur' (Cohen 1973: 111–32) has shifted. No longer does a moral panic require 'massed Basil Fawltys' to identify the folk devils and initiate an 'Informal Social Control Culture' (Jones 1997). While the media rounded up the usual suspects (like Senator Brian Harridine) to play the role of moral entrepreneur in initial news coverage about video violence, it is apparent from the orchestrated nature of the video violence panic that its real entrepreneurs were the government and the media themselves. Close analysis of the interchanges that accelerated the video violence issue out of the spiral of silence shows the work that went into fuelling the panic. From the spin applied by the American expert discussed above there was subsequent close media attention to Bryant's viewing habits that led to the Prime Minister's statement announcing the inquiry. That statement was reported in similarly packaged news stories on various TV networks before being formalised by editorials and features and expanded into barely related issues (fashion photography) and outright fantasy (the 2000 violent videos).

Another point to note is that moral panics no longer need the focus of 'deviant' lower-class males as folk devils: Mods and Rockers in Cohen (1973), muggers in Hall et al. (1978), larrikins in Morgan (1997). Guns and videos, though perhaps most feared in the hands of 'deviant' lower-class males, are nevertheless objects, not people. This reflects the shift of moral panic theory out of sociology and into media theory. While Cohen set a precedent for this shift in his original work when he pointed to the media's 'ideological exploitation of deviance' (Cohen 1973: 166) in the production of moral panic around the Mods and Rockers imbroglio, that analysis is clearly rooted in the sociology of deviance rather than in any sociology of the media. Later Cohen himself acknowledges the influence of Stuart Hall and others who delineated 'the active social processes by which news is selected and created' (Cohen and Young 1981: 10), processes by which the media, as Hall et al. (1981: 365) say: 'albeit unwittingly and through their own autonomous routes – have become effectively an apparatus of the control process itself'.

This leads to the third point of note: the selectivity of the media in promoting some moral panics while others are allowed to fall by the wayside. It is important to question why government-sanctioned moral panics about gun availability and media violence received so much media coverage (while carefully deflecting blame away from the media corporations themselves), while equally germane issues such as the perpetrator's personal development and racism were ignored. The inability of the media to inquire about their own motives was brought home to me while doing the media rounds prior to this Moral Panic conference earlier this year. While journalists had no problem with exploring the issue of moral panics and, in fact, could not hide their glee at the prospect of generating a moral panic about moral panic, there was a hesitancy in accepting that moral panics always serve some interest. This came to a head on Phillip Adams' *Late Night Live* (ABC Radio, 3 April 1997) when it was suggested that among those interests served by moral panic might be the interests of media corporations themselves. Adams, an employee of Rupert Murdoch's News Corporation, was quick to dismiss such 'conspiracy theories'. But in light of the concentration of media ownership, the convergence of media capital and its integration with other forms of capital, it would hardly be surprising if the main interest served in the production of moral panics was the media's own corporate interest. In this environment, journalists may be their own worst enemies as they remain happily ensconced in a web of reflexive criticality and uncritical reflexivity – ready to promote a moral panic about moral panics but unwilling to probe why it might be necessary.

Using Moral Panic

These three points are a natural progression from the moral panic/media manipulation scenarios of Cohen, Hall et al. but to avoid the paranoiac dead end inherent in this position and alluded to by Phillip Adams, it is useful to approach moral panic from the audience's perspective. As an audience, we apprehend the moral panic discontinuously, as a cluster of disconnected elements strung out along the spectrum of news and current affairs reporting, from the sober activism of investigative journalism to the gutter press hackery of the blatantly misleading beat-up. We use the stories to stoke our moral indignation or, perversely, to side with the devil or we may just apprehend them as just a disparate collection of information passing us by. As the audience experiences it, the moral panic is just another meta-tool for organising the news, a meta-tool like beats or rounds or thematic campaigns that are used by editorial staff and public relations workers to create form from information.

Once this function of the moral panic becomes clear, then two corollaries are apparent. The first is the potential, indeed the responsibility, for working journalists to take on their traditional foes in editorial and PR in order to make each moral panic transparent, even as they are engaged in producing it. Journalists can and should clarify in whose interests the moral panic works as they create it. Their challenge is finding the space to confront the very power that empowers them, particularly when their material is being vetted by the same people (editors, corporate managers) who are fomenting the panic. But working journalists have long since learnt to subvert the system, to use the text they create to imply the full story, to position themselves as the dissenting voice or, when all else fails, to leak the story to a competitor.

The second corollary of moral panic as an editorial/PR tool is the possibility that forces marginalised by the media can employ the very same tool to pursue moral panics about the devils they judge to be real. The shift in the site of moral panic from sociology of deviance to media theory reflects 'the shift of emphasis from the real to communication [which] brings with it a shift from a technology of control to a technology of interactive semiotic participation where citizens of the media use TV news as their forum' (Hartley 1996: 43). As was pointed out above, there seems to be plenty of scope for moral panics about racism and the declining social safety net and they are topics that lend themselves to indignation by appropriate citizen-entrepreneurs.

References

Cohen, S. (1973) *Folk Devils and Moral Panics*. St Albans: Paladin.

Cohen, S. and Young, J. (eds) (1981) *The Manufacture of News*. London: Constable.

Eisenberg, G. (1980) Children and aggression after observed film aggression with sanctioning adults, in F. Wright et al. (eds) *Forensic Psychology and Psychiatry*. New York: Annals of the New York Academy of Sciences.

Gabor, T. (1994) *Impact of Availability of Firearms on Violent Crime, Suicide and Accidental Death*. Ottawa: Dept of Justice.

Hall, S. et al. (1978) *Policing the Crisis*. London: Macmillan.

Hall, S. et al. (1981) The social production of news: mugging in the media, in S. Cohen and J. Young (eds) *The Manufacture of News*. London: Constable.

Hartley, J. (1996) *Popular Reality*. London: Arnold.

Jones, P. (1997) The role of 'moral panic' in the work of Stuart Hall, *Media International Australia*, 85 (November): 6–16.

Klapper, J.T. (1960) *The Effects of Mass Communication*. New York: Free Press.

McCarty, J. (1984) *Splatter Movies*. Bromley: Columbus Books.

Morgan, G. (1997) The *Bulletin*, street crime and the larrikin moral panic in the late 19th century, *Media International Australia*, 85 (November): 17–23.

Parker, R. (1988) *Child's Play*: a film review at www.shoestring.org

Scott, P. and Stockwell, S. (1987) If it doesn't splatter, it doesn't matter, *Cane Toad Times*, January: 31–2.

Stockbridge, S. and Dwyer, T. (1997) Recurring moral panics and new methods of regulation, *Media International Australia*, 85.

Yarvis, R.M. (1991) *Homicide: Causative Factors and Roots*. Lexington, VA: Lexington Books.

THE ULTIMATE NEIGHBOUR FROM HELL?

STRANGER DANGER AND THE MEDIA FRAMING OF PAEDOPHILIA

Jennifer Kitzinger (1999)

What happens once convicted sex abusers are released from prison? Where do they live? How are they monitored? Do neighbours have a right to know who is living in their street? These questions gained a dramatic media prominence and public profile during the second half of the 1990s. In 1996 the [British] government unveiled plans to establish an official register of sex offenders which triggered media and public demands for community notification. People began to agitate for 'the right to know' when convicted sex abusers were housed in their communities: the government and 'the professionals' rapidly lost control of the news agenda and information distribution. The names and photographs of offenders were publicised in the press and passed on to neighbours. In some cases direct action was taken to drive these men out of their homes. Monitoring, supervision, 'treatment' and housing of offenders was disrupted and policy makers had to reconsider legislation, policy and practice.

This chapter examines the role of the media in shaping and responding to this crisis. It illustrates how particular events, combined with coverage in the local and national media, fuel debate and examines how media coverage tapped into existing community fears and frustrations. The chapter concludes by exploring how the 'paedophile crisis' built on pre-existing discourses about 'the paedophile' as a particular type of threat. The concept of 'the paedophile', I argue, locates dangerousness in a few aberrant individuals who can be metaphorically (if not literally) excluded from society and it focuses attention on stranger danger in ways which ignore the scale and nature of sexual violence throughout society and, especially, within families.

In addition to providing a substantive case study of the media's role in relation to social policy I also point to different strands which might usefully be examined in any such enquiry. This chapter argues against casual and inappropriate use of terms such as 'moral panic' or 'media hysteria' and suggests ways of moving beyond a media-centric analysis towards an understanding of the motives of media sources such as, in this case, neighbourhood pressure groups. I also argue for the importance of historical context. Analysis confined to the peak of media concern with a particular problem, is inadequate since it is important to interrogate the historical framework and 'common sense' assumptions which inform public discourse.

The Rise of the Paedophile Problem

Child sexual abuse was 'discovered' by the modern media in the mid-1980s. In the UK, this 'discovery' began in 1986 when Esther Rantzen devoted an entire programme called *Childwatch* to the issue and launched the children's helpline 'Childline'. This was quickly followed by a dramatic increase in attention to the issue of child abuse in the rest of the media. Analysis of *The Times*, for example, shows a four-fold increase in coverage of sexual abuse between 1985 and 1987 (Kitzinger 1996) and it became a regular topic for documentaries such as *Everyman* (BBC1, 8 May 1988), *Horizon* (BBC2, 19 June 1989), *World in Action* (ITV, 20 May 1991), and *Panorama* (BBC1, 7 December 1992). By the early 1990s, the issue began to appear in chat shows and drama programmes too. Sexual abuse storylines were incorporated into regular series such as *The Bill* (ITV, 29 January 1993) and *Casualty* (BBC1, 6 February 1993) as well as soap operas such as *EastEnders* and *Brookside* (see Henderson 1998).

Throughout this media attention a constant (but often shadowy) figure lurked in the background: the figure of 'the paedophile'. . . .

It was not until the second half of the 1990s, however, that public debate began to focus on the dilemmas posed by convicted sex offenders released back into the community. Although sporadic concern, especially around particular individuals, was evident earlier (see Soothill and Walby 1991), it was only in 1996 that media and public outrage focused on these men (and some women) who might invisibly slip back into society free to abuse again.

The origins of this particular focus can be located in 1996. Initial media attention to the 'paedophiles-in-the-community' problem was generated by central government policy initiatives. In March 1996 Michael Howard (then Home Secretary) proposed legislation to monitor sex offenders, details of which were published in June. This led to headlines such as: 'National paedophile register to be set up' (*The Times*, 23 March 1996), 'Paedophiles to be "marked men" on national register' (*The Times*, 18 May 1996) and Howard plans paedophile curbs' (*Guardian*, 13 June 1996). The legislation was introduced in December of that year prompting further headlines including: 'Paedophile lists for police' (*The Times*, 19 December 1996) and 'Crackdown on sex offenders unveiled' (*Guardian*, 19 December 1996).

Such reporting followed routine media practice whereby media agendas are traditionally set by high-status official sources (such as government bodies) (Tuchman 1978). But media coverage and public debate shifted rapidly as particular communities and sections of the media began to agitate for public access to the register and demand that communities be notified when dangerous individuals moved into their neighbourhood. Journalists and pressure groups picked up on similar community notification legislation in the USA known as 'Megan's Law'. Introduced in 1996 this legislation was named after a seven-year-old New Jersey girl, Megan Kanka, who was raped and murdered by a twice-convicted sex offender who lived across the street. Towards the end of 1996, and early 1997, the 'big story' for the media, but the major headache for policy makers, became not government initiatives, but public fear and anger. Headlines in the national press included: 'Parents in dark as paedophiles stalk schools' (*Guardian*, 24 November 1996), 'Paedophile out of prison "fearful for life and limb"' (*Observer*, 15 December 1996), 'Jeering mothers drive paedophile off council estate' (*The Times*, 11 January 1997), 'Stop hiding perverts say protest mums' (*Daily Mail*, 3 February 1997) and 'Town not told of paedophiles' stay' (*The Times*, 12 October 1997).

Protest rapidly spread from one area to another, and concern quickly escalated: the role of the local press in voicing these concerns was crucial. Although often ignored when thinking about the media, the local press can play a key role. ... The theme of 'paedophiles-within-the-community' received extensive regional media coverage across the UK from Aberdeen to Brighton, from Leicester to Belfast, from Teesside to Lancashire. Indeed, many of the national stories about paedophiles began life on the front page of local papers and some neighbourhood protests were sparked by local press reports rather than vice versa. Headlines from local papers announced: 'Angus mums on alert over local sex offender' (*Press and Journal* (Aberdeen), 17 June 1998), 'Parents besiege abuser's house' (*Press and Journal*, 17 July 1997), 'Residents pledge to continue campaign' (*Leicester Mercury*, 4 July 1998), 'Give us the right to know' (*Torquay Herald Express*, 2 September 1997), 'Parents' paedophile poster campaign' (*Evening Gazette*, (Teesside), 26 January 1998), 'Panic hits town over perverts' (*Belfast Telegraph News*, 22 March 1997) and 'Sex offender's home torched' (*Belfast Telegraph News*, 6 October 1997).

Such articles often included quotes from the host of local residents' groups which formed in response to the 'paedophile' threat: organisations such as 'Freedom for Children', 'People's Power', 'Parents Opposed to Paedophiles' and 'The Unofficial Child Protection Unit'. Reports were also often accompanied by photographs of local people marching with banners declaring 'Perverts out', (*Press and Journal*, 9 June 1997) or children carrying placards reading: 'Make me safe' (*Torquay Herald Express*, 2 September 1997). The *Manchester Evening News* published a front-page spread about a local sex offender alongside a photograph of him in his car behind a smashed windscreen after 'a vigilante mob had vented their anger' (cited in Thomas 1997: 68). The tone of some of this reporting was overtly provocative and clearly 'fed the flames' of protest.

Many newspapers adopted a more proactive role rather than merely reporting local unrest with whatever degree of approval or urgings of restraint. Some papers assumed the role of guardians of public safety, especially in relation to particular dangerous individuals. Robert Oliver, involved in the brutal sexual assault and killing of Jason Swift, was repeatedly pursued by journalists. The *Sun* asked readers to phone an emergency number if Oliver was spotted (*Guardian*, 18 October 1997) and, when he moved to Brighton the local paper, the *Evening Argus*, published his picture on their front page with the headline 'Beware this evil pervert' (*Evening Argus*, 14 October 1997).

In other cases, newspapers alerted people to the presence of 'paedophiles', either through knocking on the doors of neighbours and asking how they felt about living near a sex offender or through 'outing' them on the front page. The *Sunday Express* printed photographs and details of offenders with their last-known address under the headline 'Could these evil men be living next door to you?' (cited in Thomas 1997). The Scottish *Daily Record* produced a similar campaign, devoting the bulk of one issue to asserting a 'Charter for our children' and demanding 'The legal right for communities to be told when a pervert moves into the area' (*Daily Record*, 25 February 1997). Alongside articles headed 'End the suffering', 'Pervert's playground' and 'Monster freed to kill', they published a double-page 'Gallery of shame' with thirty-eight photographs and names of convicted offenders and details of their offences. Four of these were described as 'people power' success stories. One man was 'hounded out of Drumchapel housing scheme because of his sick background' and another 'forced into hiding' while 'people power drove sick child molester, Christie, 50 out of Stirling' (*Daily Record*, 25 February 1997).

'Moral Panics' and 'Lynch Mobs'?

Such media coverage and the public reactions it reflected, triggered and amplified, presented a major problem for those involved in monitoring and housing convicted sex offenders. The media were accused of whipping up 'hysteria', creating a 'moral panic' and encouraging a 'lynch mob mentality'. Routine community notification and the automatic right of public access to the sex offenders' register is opposed by chief constables, chief probation officers and the NSPCC (*Guardian*, 19 February 1997). The main reason for their opposition is the belief that it will not protect children. Instead it may result in vigilante action and drive offenders underground making it less possible to monitor or 'treat' them. Indeed, the Association of Chief Officers of Probation (ACOP) documented ten cases where the press had given editorial authority to campaigns to identify and expel offenders, leading to disruption of supervision and, even, to acts of violence (ACOP 1998). Convicted abusers were beaten up and driven from their homes, leaving behind arrangements put in place to monitor them (such as electronic tagging and video surveillance) and often absenting themselves from any treatment programmes. . . .

In addition, other people are often caught up in the violence and harassment aimed at 'paedophiles'. Hostels have been attacked (whether or not convicted sex offenders are in residence). The wife and child of one offender were named and driven from their home after it was set on fire. In an earlier case a young girl died after a house in which she had been staying was burnt down (*Guardian*, 10 June 1997). In Birmingham, the 81-year-old mother of a convicted sex offender was forced to move and her home was wrecked when the *Birmingham Evening Mail* twice publicised the address where she lived with her son. In Manchester, a man was badly beaten by a gang who mistook him for a paedophile named by the *Manchester Evening News*.

The panic about paedophiles has also been used to victimise individuals with no known official record of sex offences (and with no connection to convicted offenders). Sometimes it seemed little more than a convenient way of harassing unpopular or minority members of the community. . . . The *Sunday Times* documented '30 cases where men wrongly suspected of abusing children have been beaten and humiliated by gangs bent on driving them out of their homes' (*Sunday Times*, 2 November 1997). . . .

Clearly the media contributed to the spiral of unrest across the country and some coverage was at the very least counterproductive if not blatantly irresponsible. The media, however, did not create community protests out of thin air and it is fundamentally unhelpful to dismiss media and community reactions as a 'moral panic'. This concept implies that the panic is totally unjustified and that it is state-sanctified; neither could be asserted in this case without qualification. More fundamentally the theory fails to pay attention to the processes through which a 'moral panic' is engendered and therefore offers a way of glossing over rather than truly investigating public reactions (Miller et al. 1998). To accuse the media of whipping up 'hysteria' and creating 'lynch mob' violence is equally inadequate and ignores key sites through which community reactions evolve. . . .

Instead of dismissing public and media reactions as proof of their failure to match the rationality and objectivity of the policy makers, it is crucial to give detailed attention to the questions raised by 'the public' and to examine the processes which led to the policy makers and 'the professionals' losing control of the agenda. This is essential if we are to understand the many complex levels on which the media can play a role in social policy issues.

Theorising Community and Media Protest

The 'paedophile-in-the-community' coverage was driven by factors operating on three levels: the first concerns policy and practice initiatives; the second relates to local community responses and the role of local media; the third involves the underlying construction of 'the paedophile' which underpinned the whole debate.

Policy and practice: initiatives, developments and unanswered questions

The initial decision to establish a register placed the issue of 'paedophiles-in-the-community' on the public agenda: it begged more questions than it answered. How should these offenders be monitored and who should have access to this information? Policy and practice on this issue were clearly underdeveloped and often inconsistent. Legal rulings and professional disputes received extensive media coverage. There were, for example, several cases exposing uncertainty about sex offenders' housing rights. . . . Confusion also surrounded probation officers' responsibilities to pass on information about their clients to prospective employers. The Home Office originally advised probation officers not to notify employers of sex crime convictions in case employees were sacked leading to court actions for damages. This advice was quickly withdrawn . . .

Policy on notification to the general public seemed to develop in a similar ad hoc fashion. Particularly high-profile cases raised the following questions. If a housing officer takes it upon himself to inform tenants about a released sex offender on their estate should he be disciplined? Should schools be told, but not pass on the information to parents, or did this place headteachers in an untenable position? Should the police inform the public, but only under very special circumstances? One couple in North Wales, for example, was granted legal aid to sue police for publicising details about their sexual offences (*Manchester Evening News*, 9 June 1997). In some cases public warnings were released: 'Police warn of threat to young males: town on paedophile alert' (*Guardian*, 15 October 1997). In other cases communities were not informed, or only provided with information after media exposure. In a graphic illustration of direct interaction between the media and policy decisions one London Council decided to warn parents about a 'very dangerous' convicted abuser who had moved into their area, but only after learning that a television documentary was to name the man (*Guardian*, 27 March 1997). It was not until September 1997 that guidelines came into force clarifying procedures. Police were given the power to warn headteachers, youth group and play-group leaders and local child protection agencies that a convicted sex offender had moved into their area. But these guidelines did not empower the police to broadcast the names of paedophiles generally unless a professional risk assessment said this was necessary....

Consequently, in the second half of the 1990s there was a confluence of events (such as the release of particular notorious individuals) and the development of policy and procedures which heightened public awareness of this threat. The original highly newsworthy government initiatives set the news agenda, but that agenda was rapidly revised by the questions it posed about obvious areas of uncertainty.

To suggest that events drove the news agenda would be mere tautology. Some events became 'newsworthy' because of existing news hooks (the court case concerning the eviction of a 'paedophile', for example, would not have received so much media coverage outside this time). Minor events quickly become newsworthy because they are 'topical'. Thus 'satellite' reporting included escorted visits of convicted sex offenders to play-parks and fun-fairs and plans for a commercial UK 'paedophile directory'.

In addition, some of the events which generated peak news coverage around this time were also, of course, not official events (such as court cases, government announcements or inquiries); much of the coverage focused on the surrounding community action. In order to understand the extent of local neighbourhood and media protest it is also necessary to look more closely at these responses.

Neighbourhood reactions: democracy, trust and local information exchange and representation

The local media clearly fed into neighbourhood responses and helped to identify targets for popular anger. Concern about children's safety, however, was certainly not a new phenomenon. 'The paedophile' had already been established as 'public enemy number one' and, long before 1996, fear of the predatory paedophile was etched into the bedrock of parents' anxieties. In focus groups I conducted in the early 1990s, it was clear that fears of child abduction were woven into the fabric of parental experience....

People spoke about predatory men coming on to the housing estates and, in almost every group, parents described incidents where 'shady' individuals had been seen behaving suspiciously around playgrounds or children had been approached by strangers. Such events inevitably become the topic of conversation (e.g. outside the school gate) and parents felt they had a duty to seek out and share such information. By contrast assaults on children by men within the family were rarely shared with the community (Kitzinger 1998).

Given this background it is hardly surprising that the idea that known sex offenders were to be secretly housed in their neighbourhoods triggered grave concern. The very names of some of the community protest groups express their anger at the restrictions placed upon their lives (e.g. 'Freedom for Children') and their desire to assert their rights (e.g. 'People's Power'). Some protest groups also chose names which encapsulated their disillusionment with official protection and monitoring procedures (e.g. 'The Unofficial Child Protection Unit')....

Official incompetence was a recurring theme both in local discussion and in national coverage. Internationally high-profile cases of multiple sex abusers (from Dutroux in Belgium to Fred and Rosemary West in Cromwell Street) suggested that 'the professionals' could not be trusted to monitor and investigate properly....

If such cases inspired little faith in 'the authorities', then housing inequalities further exacerbated the crisis. Released prisoners, including convicted sex offenders, tend to be placed in hostels or offered housing in working-class areas and often on council estates. Where offenders were offered social housing, rather than returning to private accommodation, this also raised particular questions about policy. Many protesters expressed anger and frustration at the fact that their fate was to be decided by faceless bureaucrars who rarely lived in such areas themselves. The question often asked in public meetings called to reassure people was: 'How would *you* feel if he was living next door to you and your kids?' Residents often seemed to feel that council renants were expected to put up with living next to an incinerator, playgrounds built on polluted sites, damp housing or a failing local school. Now they were also expected to tolerate the country's most dangerous predators dumped on their doorsteps. . . .

For some protesters it was clear that direct action (ranging from seeking media publicity to vigilante activities) represented the only way of having their voices heard. The local media, for their part, were usually happy to cooperate and have a special remit to respond to local pressure groups and address community reactions. Local newspaper editorials demanding (or in effect providing) community notification presented the papers as standing up for their constituents, asserting a strong neighbourhood identity and fulfilling their functions as representative of 'the people'. While local media have problems representing some local concerns (such as pollution from a factory which is key to providing local jobs), the sex offender presented an apparently clear-cut 'enemy' and 'outsider'. . . .

In understanding media and public reactions, therefore, it is important not to be dismissive when 'the public' come into conflict with 'the experts' or when local 'NIMBYISM' seems to come into conflict with the 'wider public good'. Community concern and the conditions under which people are forced to live should not be underestimated. . . .

The issue of former neighbours returning from prison to live near their victims has certainly enjoyed considerable media prominence. A housing worker faced with press coverage of such a situation expresses some ambivalence about the media's role. The press focus was unhelpful and resulted in a defensive reaction from parts of the housing authority and generated unnecessary fear on the estate. But media coverage did trigger an official acknowledgement of the problem. Indeed:

> The media were useful in that the tenants had tried telling their housing officer and had not succeeded in persuading her to listen. It is a shame that the council obviously felt inaccessible so that they had to go to the press. There are lessons to be learned from that. But the press made sure that the council reacted. (Housing Officer, interview with author)

[. . .]

The media then should not be seen as merely 'interfering' in an area best left to 'the experts'. Public debate and involvement in social policy issues is a democratic and practical imperative. Questions from the media and 'the public' (as neighbours, tenants, and citizens) can disrupt important policy initiatives, but they can also be effective in pushing issues onto the policy agenda and refining procedures. There were far more fundamental problems, however, with the way in which the debate about paedophiles was framed in public discourse, including media coverage and policy making. . . .

Framing paedophiles: public, media and policy gaps in addressing child sexual abuse

Throughout this chapter the word 'paedophile' has appeared in inverted commas: the intention has been to signal the constructed nature of the term. 'The paedophile' has become the dominant way through which sexual threats to children are conceptualised and articulated, but the concept is laden with ideas and assumptions which confine thinking about this issue to a very narrow focus.

'The paedophile' is a concept enmeshed in a series of crass stereotypes which place the child sexual abuser 'outside' society. In the tabloid press abusers are 'animals', 'monsters' 'sex maniacs', 'beasts' and 'perverts' who are routinely described as 'loners' and 'weirdos'. Right across the media it is also implied that paedophiles, far from being 'ordinary family men', are more likely to be gay (for systematic analysis of this see Kitzinger and Skidmore 1995). Such conceptualisations were amply illustrated in the press reporting about 'paedophiles-in-the-community'. The *Daily Record*'s 'Gallery of shame', for example, perpetuated all the old stereotypes, highlighting particular words in bold block capitals. Struggling for variety of negative epithets to describe their gallery of thirty-eight sex offenders the paper ran through the usual list warning readers of: 'TWISTED Dickons [who] got eight years for raping two young sisters'; 'WEIRDO Sean Regan who was dubbed "The Beast"', and 'DEPRAVED paedophile Harley' who 'preyed on terrified children as young as six.' Other convicted offenders were variously described as: 'EVIL Herriot'; 'PERVERT teacher', 'SEXUAL predator', and 'SEX BEAST'. In among these highlighted adjectives one man was simply described as 'BACHELOR Paritt' (with its gay implications) and three of the descriptions highlighted a disability (e.g. 'DEAF Duff posed as a priest as he prowled the street' and 'DEAF MUTE Eaglesham, 66, carried out a series of sex attacks on a 10-year-old girl') (*Daily Record*, 25 February 1997).

Portraits of 'paedophiles' do more than simply stereotype and reinforce prejudice against particular minority groups. They also imply that paedophiles are a separate species, subhuman or 'a breed apart' (Hebenton and Thomas 1996). The term also singles out the sexual abuse of children, as if there were no connection between the acts of sexual abuse and exploitation perpetrated against children and those perpetrated against adult women. One interesting piece of information released by the Home Office during the height of the paedophile crisis was the fact that, by the time they are forty, one man in 90 has been convicted of a serious sex offence, such as rape, incest or gross indecency with a child (Marshall 1997). This fact, combined with evidence that most perpetrators of sexual assault are never convicted, suggests that every community is likely to have its share of sex offenders. The release of the Home Office statistic received some media attention, but was quickly forgotten and rarely integrated into the narrative of stories about 'paedophiles-in-the-community'. The fact that most 'paedophiles-in-the-community' were undetected and probably well integrated into their neighbourhood was rarely raised. The fact that most people would already know a sex offender was ignored.

To acknowledge that sexual violence was quite so endemic would have undermined the narrative thrust of most 'paedophile-in-the-community' stories. By confining their attention to a minority of convicted multiple abusers and defining those who sexually abuse children as a certain type of person, 'a paedophile', the media were able to focus not on society but on a few dangerous individuals within it. The problem of sexual violence was represented by the newspaper image of the man with staring eyes or the evil smirk, the 'beast' and 'fiend' who could be singled out, electronically tagged, exposed and expelled. If paedophiles are literally 'evil personified', then such evil can be exorcised by exclusion of these individuals from society. This individualised approach fits in with certain strands in criminological discourse (see Hebenton and Thomas 1996); it also fits in with the whole media shift towards 'dumbed down' personalised stories whereby, for example, journalists focus on the noisy and antisocial 'neighbour from hell' rather than examining the problem of 'sink estates' through analysis of employment, recreation facilities and housing condition (Franklin 1997). Paedophiles are, of course, in this sense the ultimate neighbour from hell.

The concept of 'the paedophile' is flawed. It locates the threat of abuse within the individual (rather than in social, cultural or bureaucratic institutions). In the context of abuse in children's homes, for example, attention can be focused on the cunning infiltrator while ignoring the nature of care system, funding and resourcing. In the case of other sites of abuse attention is confined to 'the outsider' and 'the loner' leaving the role of fathers, and the institution of the family unquestioned. The paedophile is presented as a danger which 'prowls our streets' and is used to reinforce the media's and policy makers' disproportionate focus on 'stranger danger' (Kitzinger and Skidmore 1995). Indeed, 'the paedophile' is a creature that embodies stranger danger. He reflects and sustains a focus on abusers as outcast from society rather than part of it....

If we adopt the word 'paedophile' and see it as synonymous with 'child sexual abuse' then we narrow the policy agenda. The fact that most children are assaulted by someone that they know virtually disappears from the debate and policies which would be deemed unacceptable if applied to 'ordinary men' become allowable. Commenting on government initiatives in relation to 'paedophiles' Kelly draws attention to the fact that 'paedophiles' may be denied the right to work with children or even to approach playgrounds, yet such proposals would cause outrage if applied to fathers (Kelly 1996: 46). Indeed, women are often forced by the courts to allow violent and abusive partners access to their children, even where those children have also been sexually abused by him.

The fundamental critique here is that the notion of the paedophile restricts definitions of 'the problem' and thus limits how we can envisage solutions. The term helps to obscure important aspects of sexual violence and shifts attention 'away from political solutions addressing male power and the construction of masculinity toward a range of "problem-management" solutions'. [Such as] ... 'long term incarceration' (*Mail*), 'risk assessment tribunals for dangerous men' (*Guardian* and *The Times*) and 'individual therapy (*Guardian*)' (McCollum 1998: 37).

Conclusion

This chapter has explored the role of the media, particularly the local media, in the 'paedophile crisis'. It has attempted to highlight the positive as well as the negative impact of coverage and to identify those factors which shaped and maintained the momentum of media attention. In presenting this case study I have tried to demonstrate the intertwined levels of analysis which can contribute towards theorising the relationship between the media and social policy. It is not sufficient simply to focus on media coverage. It is important to consider the motives of source organisations who seek out media publicity. It is also unhelpful to dismiss the media as 'interfering' or 'sensationalist' or to blame the press for 'media hype'. Instead, it is necessary to recognise their role as a forum for public debate. At the same time, however, it is vital never to accept the terms of that debate as cast in stone and always to question what is left out of the policy agenda as well as what is addressed. In this way one can combine detailed analysis of crisis coverage with critical reflection on the underlying assumptions which frame public discourse and limit visions for social policy.

References

Association of Chief Officers of Probation (1998) *Recent Cases of Public Disorder around Sex Offenders which have Impeded Surveillance and Supervision*. London: ACOP.

Franklin, B. (1997) *Newzak and News Media*. London: Arnold.

Hebenton, B. and Thomas, T. (1996) Sexual offenders in the community: reflections on problems of law, community and risk management in the USA, England and Wales, *International Journal of the Sociology of Law*, 24: 427–43.

Henderson, L. (1998) Making serious soaps: public issue storylines in TV drama serials, in G. Philo (ed.), *Message Received*, London: Longman.

Kelly, L. (1996) Weasel words: paedophiles and the cycle of abuse, *Trouble and Strife*. 33:44–9.

Kitzinger, J. (1996) Media representations of sexual abuse risks, *Child Abuse Review*, 5: 319–33.

Kitzinger, J. (1998) The gender politics of news production: silenced voices and false memories, in C. Carter et al. (eds) *News, Gender and Power* London: Routledge.

Kitzinger, J. and Skidmore, P. (1995) Playing safe: media coverage of child sexual abuse prevention strategies, *Child Abuse Review*, 4(1): 47–56.

Marshall, P. (1997) *The Prevalence of Convictions for Sexual Offending Research Findings 55*: London: Home Office Research and Statistics Directorate.

Miller, D., Kitzinger, J., Williams, K. and Beharrell, P. (1998) *The Circuit of Mass Communication: Media Strategies, Representation and Audience Reception in the AIDS Crisis*. London: Sage.

Soothill, K. and Walby, S. (1991) *Sex Crimes in the News*. London: Routledge.

Thomas, T. (1997) How could this man go free: privacy, the press and the paedophile, in E. Lawson (ed.) *Child Exploitation and the Media Forum: Report and Recommendations*. Dover: Smallwood Publishing Group, pp. 67–9.

Tuchman, G. (1978) *Making News: A Study of the Construction of Reality*. New York: Free Press.

CHILDREN AT RISK:

11

LEGAL AND SOCIETAL PERCEPTIONS OF THE POTENTIAL THREAT THAT THE POSSESSION OF CHILD PORNOGRAPHY POSES TO SOCIETY

Suzanne Ost (2002)

Introduction

The current law surrounding child pornography would seem to be a direct consequence both of the categorization of children as a vulnerable societal group in need of state protection from certain threats to their physical and psychological bodies, and of the perception of child pornography as material which may be morally harmful to society. In social and legal discourses and actual extra-linguistic institutional policies and practices, the phenomenon of child pornography appears to be identified as harmful for a number of reasons. First, it is recognized that child pornography poses a clear danger to children who are involved in the production of child pornography, whose physical and sexual abuse is often the very subject matter of the material created. Secondly, in recent years, a near consensus has emerged that children are at placed at risk simply as a consequence of an individual being in possession of child pornography. Finally, there appears to be an acceptance of the possibility that the availability of child pornography is harmful to society because it has a corrupting effect upon the general morality.

   This article analyses the social and legal response to the phenomenon of child pornography with a particular focus upon the act of possessing such material. Firstly, the statutory and case law surrounding child pornography is elucidated in section one. Section two investigates the question of whether the threat posed by child pornography may have been blown out of proportion due to the existence of a 'moral panic' about this phenomenon in our society. The discussion in the first part of section three focuses upon the question of whether there remain *real* grounds to suggest that the possession of child pornography poses a threat to society because consumers/possessors are – by the very fact of consumption/possession – actual sexual abusers of children. This issue is addressed through a discussion and analysis of existing literature and research which focuses upon both the occurrence of and the perpetrators of this type of abuse. The latter part of section three examines a further legitimating force behind the law, the argument that the market for child pornography encourages those who create such material to further abuse children in order to satisfy 'consumer' demand for harder core and more explicit material. This section also includes a discussion of the possibility that child pornography serves to promote the reification of children as sexual objects.

Additionally, this article addresses constructions of the child and the possessor of child pornography found in social, legal, and academic discourses. Thus, in section four, it is submitted that whilst the construction of the child as innocent in such discourses may promote society's compulsion to protect children from sexual abuse, children may actually be placed at *greater* risk of sexual abuse as a result of the effects of this construction. Furthermore, interpretations of the individual who possesses child pornography as being an actual child abuser could become problematized. This is particularly the case if the possession of child pornography in itself is not always an automatic signifier of actual child abuse. The focus, then, is upon the way in which constructions of the child and the possessor of child pornography in societal, legal, and academic discourses frame the debate regarding child pornography and create certain realities.

Whilst social construction theories often tend to be applied to phenomena perceived as 'safe', this article applies social construction theory to a phenomenon which society continues to find disturbing to discuss. As Higonnet comments with reference to American child pornography laws, 'It is frightening to question any provisions of child pornography law because they are so closely bound to the emotionally explosive issue of actual child abuse' (1998: 160). There is undoubtedly a very real risk that children are sexually abused through the production of child pornography. Thus, any academic analysis that retains its distance from populist/tabloid reactions by engaging in a critique of the value-judgements and assumptions upon which legal and social reactions are constructed through a series of selective interpretations is much more controversial. However, there may be greater dangers posed by the academic endorsement of an emotional over-reaction in this area, particularly if such endorsement can support draconian and/or counter-productive reactions. Consequently, I believe it is even more important to consider the way in which children and the individuals who possess child pornography are socially and legally constructed ...

The subject of child pornography requires examination in its own right. This is primarily because this phenomenon raises specific issues of its own due to the reality of the content of such material and the child status of some of those involved in its production. As Akdeniz comments, 'There can be no understanding of the special problem of child pornography until there is understanding of the special way in which child pornography is child abuse' (1997: 2).

Defining and Regulating Child Pornography: the Current Law upon the Creation, Distribution, and Possession of Indecent Photographs of Children

Whilst there may be no single universally accepted definition of child pornography, there is some general consensus as to what actually constitutes child pornography. The format child pornography takes is most usually visual, in the form of photographic images or video. The content of less hardcore pornographic photographs or videos of children can include images of children in provocative poses, images of naked children, and images of children's genitalia. Child pornography can then progress from images of the child's body alone to images of the child performing sexual acts upon adults or other children and adults having sexual intercourse with the child. Extreme hardcore child pornography may include images of the infliction of sadistic, physical harm to the child and occasionally, may even end in a child's death (Pierce 1984).

Under United Kingdom law, all such material is potentially capable of falling under the definition of 'an indecent photograph of a child' and various statutory offences relating primarily to the creation and distribution of child pornography are to be found within the Protection of Children Act 1978 (PCA). Under section 1(1)(a) and (b) of the PCA, an individual commits an offence if he or she takes or makes an indecent photograph of a child, distributes or shows such a photograph or has such a photograph in his or her possession for the purpose of showing or distributing it. A defence is available to a person charged with an offence under section 1 of the PCA if he or she had a legitimate reason for distributing or showing the photograph in question, or if he or she had not seen the photograph and did not know or have cause to suspect it was indecent.

[...]

The PCA defines a 'child' as an individual under the age of sixteen and a photograph as 'an indecent film, a copy of an indecent photograph or film, and an indecent photograph comprised in a film'. An individual convicted on indictment of one of these offences can face a prison sentence of up to ten years. Significantly, until January 2001, the maximum sentence that could be imposed upon an individual who was convicted on indictment under section 1 was three years. Increasing pressure from child protection lobby groups ensured that Parliament increased this maximum sentence through an amendment made to the PCA by the Criminal Justice and Court Services Act 2000 (CJCSA).

In order to address the exploitation of an expanding loophole in the law by producers of internet child pornography, the Criminal Justice and Public Order Act 1994 (CJPOA) amended section 7 of the PCA. Thus, the definition of a photograph was extended to include 'the negative as well as the positive version and data stored on a computer disc or by other electronic means which is capable of conversion into a photograph' (PCA, section 7(4)). Furthermore, the CJPOA ensured that pseudo-photographs (depictions of, for example, scenes of sexual abuse between adults, in which children's heads are superimposed upon adults' bodies), whether computerized or created through other means also come within the scope of the PCA. Provided that the predominant impression conveyed by the pseudo-photograph is that the person depicted is a child, then it will be construed to be an indecent photograph of a child 'notwithstanding that some of the physical characteristics shown are those of an adult'.

The PCA, as originally enacted, did not criminalize the act of possessing indecent photographs of a child *unless* such possession was with a view to showing or distributing such photographs. That the possession of indecent photographs of children was only one possible element of these offences is an indication that the simple possession of such photographs was not considered to pose a significant enough threat to children to warrant legal prohibition of such activity when carried out in isolation from acts of producing and distributing child pornography.

It is, therefore, significant that in 1988, further legislation criminalized the mere possession of child pornography. Section 160 of the Criminal Justice Act 1988 (CJA) states that 'It is an offence for a person to have any indecent photograph of a child in his possession' and this mere possession offence has been extended by the CJPOA to cover pseudo-photographs. Furthermore, the CJCSA has increased the maximum sentence for a person convicted of the possession offence on indictment to five years ...

In the space of sixteen years between the original enactment of the PCA and the creation of the additional child pornography offence under the CJA, the legal position upon the perceived dangers of possessing child pornography has gradually altered. The legislature now appears to have adopted the stance that even the mere possession of child pornography poses a threat to society.

The question which arises, then, is *why* the law considers society to be at threat from the possession of child pornography? I will now proceed to consider whether there are grounds to suggest that the current legal and societal response to the possession of child pornography may have been influenced by the emergence of a moral panic within our society as to the extent of the threat posed by this phenomenon.

Moral Panics and the Question of Whether There is a Danger of *Real* Harm to Children

In this section, I will consider whether there are indications to suggest there has been a moral panic about child pornography through an examination of the way in which the media, the public, the police, the judiciary and politicians have responded to this and related phenomena.

According to Devlin (1965), the law should be used as a tool to regulate private immoral behaviour if the behaviour in question poses a threat to the moral fibre of society and consequently, society itself. As applied to the act of possessing child pornography then, Devlin's argument would suggest that such behaviour could threaten moral values which affirm the sacred status of the child and the rights that our society has ascribed to children.

If the possession of child pornography is deemed to be an immoral act, then the next question that must be addressed is whether our society has an undistorted perception of the threat that this activity poses, both to the public morality *and* to children themselves. If there is evidence to suggest that societal views upon the dangers posed by possessing child pornography have become distorted, leading to an undue exaggeration of a perceived threat, then there may be grounds to argue that there is a currently a moral panic about this phenomenon in our society . . .

In order to consider whether a moral panic does in fact exist with regards to child pornography, it is necessary to consider the reaction to the threat that child pornography poses by the media, the public, law enforcement agencies, and politicians, and to consider whether these reactions have had any impact upon the current legal and societal stance taken towards the phenomenon.

In considering how our society responds to the danger posed to children by child pornography, the media's coverage of child pornography undoubtedly plays a significant role in influencing the level of concern that is attached to this phenomenon. When reporting upon cases involving child pornography, newspapers tend to use headlines which include emotive, sensationalist language such as 'Tide of Computer Porn No One can Stop' and 'Internet Child Sex Perverts Escape Justice'. Such language emphasizes the possible dangers posed by child pornography and is undoubtedly capable of provoking and – over time – reinforcing strong public reaction. Indeed, the media's extensive coverage of paedophilia *generally* has clearly evoked a powerful public reaction ...

This hard-line reaction to suspected paedophiles, including those individuals found to be in possession of child pornography is taken further by the police, who made demands for the extension to the sentences imposed upon those convicted of the offence of possession and called for the wider powers to track down child pornography offences on the internet which they now have under the Regulation of Investigatory Powers Act 2000. Furthermore, the fact that the police consider taking action against those who possess child pornography as a priority is evidenced through the existence of a specialist Paedophilia Unit within the Organized Crime Group of the Specialist Operations Department, a unit which tracks down those who possess and distribute child pornography ...

The current strong moralistic societal reaction to child pornography permeates through to the judiciary also. The moral character of the judiciary's chosen language when providing judgements in child pornography cases can hardly go unnoticed, nor can the courts' perpetuation of common-sense assumptions about the immoral characters of possessors of child pornography ... The judiciary may be seen to be responding to those found in possession of child pornography in a way which indicates the existence of judicial opinion that this activity constitutes immoral behaviour which poses a clear, significant threat to our society. In order to avoid defining such a perception as a panic, it would have to be proven that it is based upon an accurate estimation of the risk that the possession of child pornography poses.

The possible dangers posed by child pornography have further been brought to the forefront of public consciousness by the recent political focus upon tackling the phenomenon. In its 2001 Manifesto, the Labour Party pledged to 'take measures to tackle the problem of child pornography on the internet' and in a later speech, Jack Straw highlighted the powers that have been given to the police to tackle child pornography under the Regulation of Investigatory Powers Act. By promoting the need to address the availability of child pornography as a significant political issue, the Labour Party may have increased public concern about the threat that child pornography poses to society.

What I have sought to argue here is that an examination of the responses of the media, the public, law enforcement agencies, the judiciary, and politicians to child pornography may indicate that a moral panic currently exists concerning child pornography and the possession of such material in our society ... [T]he possible existence of a moral panic could colour our perceptions of the actual threat posed by the phenomenon of child pornography. Certainly, the possession of child pornography may well cause real actual and possible harms; however, these need to be coolly identified as such and supported by empirical evidence. It is necessary to stand back and objectively assess the real dangers of child pornography in order to *avoid* moral panic-induced counter-productive reactions. Thus, in the following section, I will consider the actual and possible harms caused by the possession of child pornography, both to children and society as a whole.

Identifying the Dangers Posed to Children by the Possession of Child Pornography

[...]

1. Constructions in academic and legal discourses of the possessor of child pornography as the actual sexual abuser of children

According to many academic authors, the major threat posed by the possession of child pornography can be found in the purposes which lie behind the possession of such material (Tate 1990; Renvoize 1993; Edwards 2000) ...

Some authors have argued that child abusers use child pornography as a method of seducing children (Akdeniz 1997). Potentially, then, the fact that child pornography is possessed and distributed is considered to be harmful to children due to the *possibilities* of such pornography fuelling the fantasies of child abusers and being adopted as a both a seduction technique and a means of behaviour validation.

Proponents of the argument that the distribution and sharing of child pornography amongst actual child sexual abusers serves as a means of behaviour validation may find support from a well-publicized international police investigation into the Internet child pornography ring named 'Wonderland Club'. On 2 September 1998, this investigation uncovered 750,000 indecent photographs of children which were distributed by and to Wonderland Club members across the world. In a series of simultaneous raids, 107 members of the club were arrested. Significantly, a BBC *Panorama* programme which revealed certain aspects of the police investigation into the Wonderland Club focused upon the argument that the sharing of child pornography effectively served as a means of behaviour validation for members of the club. The evidence put forward by the police in the programme would seem to support the argument that child pornography can be used as a method of reassurance and confirmation that a paedophile's sexual fantasies are shared by others. However, does this also signify that those who possessed the pictures of children actually shared the lifestyle of the actual abusers rather than just sharing similar thoughts? Whilst it may be possible that members of the club shared the same sexual fantasies, they were not necessarily incited to go out and live the same lifestyle as that experienced by members who were actual abusers of children and to commit the same abuse.

Certain research findings may appear to validate the argument that a relationship exists between the possession and use of child pornography and child sexual abuse. For example, the findings from Marshall's (1988) research study involving fifty-one child sex abusers revealed that 67 per cent of the participants made use of 'hard core sexual stimuli'. However, although such studies could reveal a correlative relationship, in that some child abusers do use child pornography, they may fail to demonstrate a clear *causal* relationship between the use of child pornography and the occurrence of child sexual abuse. Certainly, it is possible that individuals use child pornography for sexual stimulation, yet have no inclination to actually go out and commit child abuse.

Other research studies have aimed to establish that beyond a correlative link between the possession of child pornography and the occurrence of child sexual abuse, there also exists a causal link. Perhaps, significantly, the findings of a study carried out by Elliott, Browne and Kilcoyne (1995) indicated that 21 per cent of child sex abusers interviewed used pornography as a disinhibition method prior to committing child abuse. Similarly, Marshall' s (1988) research indicates that just over one-third of the child sex abusers who participated in the study used 'hard core sexual stimuli' as an incitement to commit child sexual abuse. However, it is important to note that these studies did not limit the categories of 'pornography' or 'hard core sexual stimuli' to child pornography. Indeed, Marshall notes that the child sex abusers who took part in his study did not make any greater use of child pornography than did other sexual offenders, such as rapists who participated in the study. Moreover, Marshall himself comments that the focus upon whether child sex abusers use 'hard core sexual stimuli' could cause child sex abusers to make use of opportunity for blaming their offences upon external sources rather than their own internal selves. Therefore, in operating upon the assumption that a causal relationship exists between using child pornography and committing child sexual abuse, the academic discourses discussed above may inadvertently provide actual child sex abusers with a convenient excuse for their behaviour.

It could be argued, therefore, that whilst the existence of a causal relationship between the possession of child pornography and the occurrence of child abuse is frequently espoused in academic discourses, the existence of such a relationship is far from certain (Howitt 1995).

[...]

2. Criminalizing the possession of child pornography in order to discourage those who commit sexual abuse against children

Undoubtedly, there is a clear, synonymous link between the *production* of certain forms of child pornography and child sexual abuse; child sexual abuse often forms the content of child pornography, is the very substance of the photograph or video in question ... The very phenomenon of child pornography itself then, often ensures the occasioning of direct and actual harm to children involved in its production. Whilst the offence of possessing child pornography may not in itself cause *direct* harm to children, it may do so *indirectly* by encouraging the occurrence of child sexual abuse which forms the content of child pornography. Such an argument does seem to lend legitimation to the law which criminalizes the possession of child pornography...

The argument that criminalizing the possession of child pornography would reduce actual child sexual abuse could perhaps be challenged by reference to Higonnet's contention that there is no evidence of a large, commercially profitable market for child pornography. Thus, criminalizing the possession of such material is unlikely to have any real impact as child pornography is a 'marginal fringe phenomenon', most often 'home made and clandestinely circulated among a small group of people' (1998: 179). However, it is possible to respond to this contention by considering whether those who produce child pornography are *primarily* motivated by the desire to gain financially, or rather, are motivated by the knowledge that others want and are able to view the material they produce. If it is the latter as opposed to the former, then the 'market reduction' argument still holds true.

Whilst the 'market reduction' argument may prove convincing in terms of reducing the harm caused to children by discouraging the production of child pornography involving real children, one could argue that it loses force when the child pornography in question takes the form of a pseudo-photograph, generated on a computer without the involvement and abuse of a child. Does criminalizing the possession of such material really reduce the harm posed to children?... [E]ven if children are not at as great a risk of harm through the availability of this particular form of child pornography, the fact that children are harmed through the production and availability of *much* child pornography does still lend support to the 'market reduction' justification for criminalizing the possession of child pornography. Additionally, it could be argued that criminalizing the possession of such material reinforces the legal and societal stance that child sexual abuse will not be tolerated.

Linked to the 'market reduction' argument is the possibility that allowing individuals to possess child pornography encourages an acceptance of the representations of children that can be found in child pornography. Child pornography, in objectifying children as sexual objects or resources for unbridled exploitation, may promote the *reduction* of children to this status. If such objectification does become reification, then the reduction of children to objects in order to satisfy adult sexual desires can only encourage those who commit actual child sexual abuse.

[...]

If, as I have argued, the societal desire to protect children lies at the heart of the child pornography laws and the possession of child pornography encourages both the production of such material and the acceptance of representations of children that encourage child sexual abuse, then in striving to protect children from harm, we may have the greatest legitimating factor behind these laws. In the final section of this article, I wish to examine a popular construction of the child in society which further legitimates the law and to consider whether reliance upon this construction may, in fact, be placing children at greater risk of harm.

The Potential Damaging Effect of Constructions of Innocence

As the discussion thus far should demonstrate, a focus upon child protection and child welfare permeates throughout the law surrounding child pornography. That the law prioritizes children's welfare and safety is undoubtedly a consequence of legal and social constructs of the child which centre upon vulnerability and, significantly, innocence ...

The desire to protect children becomes even more compelling when their innocence is set against constructions of the possessor of child pornography as immoral and depraved. The characters of the child victim and the individual who possesses child pornography are thus presented in legal discourses as being at two polarized extremes. On the one hand, the child is pure and chaste, on the other, the possessor of child pornography is depraved, an individual whose '*perverted* tastes include collecting and viewing indecent photographs of children'. The breadth of the chasm between innocence and depravity serves to justify the legal prohibition upon any activity which draws the innocent child and the corrupt possessor of child pornography together, even if the child's presence is in the form of a visual representation only.

Reliance upon popular constructions of children as 'innocent' in legal and social discourses surrounding child pornography is, however, problematical. Although the focus upon childhood innocence may have ensured the enactment of legislation which aims to protect children, the very idea of childhood innocence could itself be arousing to child sex abusers. As Kitzinger comments:

> Innocence is a powerful and emotive symbol, but to use it to provoke public revulsion against sexual abuse is counterproductive. For a start the notion of childhood innocence is itself a source of titillation for abusers ... In a society where innocence is a fetish ... focusing on children's presumed innocence only reinforces men's desire for them as sexual objects. (1988: 79)

Kitzinger's argument receives reinforcement from the findings of Howitt's (1995) research study, involving a group of paedophiliac sex offenders. He questioned the participants regarding their use and experience of pornography. Perhaps the most significant finding which emerged from the study was that, whilst on the whole, child pornography did not play a part in the offenders' fantasies and sexual activities, some of the offenders were aroused by non-pornographic imagery of children. Material such as children's clothes catalogues, Walt Disney videos, and television advertisements showing naked babies or toddlers in nappies were some of the types of non-pornographic imagery referred to by offenders (Howitt 1995). In our focus upon childhood innocence, therefore, we may be promoting an ideology of childhood which *encourages* child sexual abuse (Higonnet 1998). Our objectification of children as innocent may cause us to *reduce* them simply to objects of innocence, the one aspect of childhood that may be of the greatest attraction to the child sexual abuser.

Certain attitudes to childhood innocence as represented by nonpornographic naked images of children may further encourage conceptions of children as sexually arousing (Adler 2001) ... Thus, a societal objectification of the child as innocent, and consequent interpretations of this symbol of childhood when represented through child nudity as being sexual, may serve to reinforce the idea of childhood innocence as both sexual and titillating. Furthermore, constructions of children's naked bodies as sexual could have a harmful effect on children themselves in terms of the way that they perceive their bodies. In analysing American laws on child pornography, Higonnet comments: 'Recent child pornography law casts shame on the child's body. When every photograph of a child's body becomes criminally suspect, how are we going to avoid children feeling guilt about any image of their bodies?' (1998: 180).

Our perception that images of naked children promote perverse fantasies and encourage the sexualization of children may therefore be infringing children's rights, particularly, their right not to be ashamed of their own bodies. What I have sought to argue in this section is that whilst law and society attempt to protect children through deference to notions of childhood innocence, constructions of innocence and purity may actually be those most attractive to the individuals whom society is trying to protect children from. Furthermore, current societal reactions to photographs depicting childhood nudity as sexual may effectively cater for paedophiles and harm children by affecting the way in which they view their own bodies.

Conclusion

It has not been my aim in this article to challenge the legitimating factors behind the law surrounding child pornography generally – particularly as the law which prohibits the creation of child pornography seeks to prevent the occurrence of child sexual abuse which often forms the content of such material. I have argued, however, that we may currently be witnessing a moral panic in terms of the threat which the possession of child pornography poses to our society. Constructions and representations of a person who is found to have such material in his or her possession provided by the media, the police and the judiciary give rise to the argument that if action is not taken to prohibit such behaviour, the moral status of the child as sacred in our society is at significant risk. As noted, this has given rise to a number of both positive and counter-productive effects.

In considering the reasons why, despite the possible existence of a moral panic, the current legal stance may still be both necessary and defensible, I have sought to argue that the social and legal desire to protect children from sexual abuse does focus to a large extent upon possibility that the possessor of child pornography will commit sexual abuse. The discussion in this article should indicate that any link between the possession of child pornography and child sexual abuse is contingent and variable rather than necessarily causal. Significantly, however, there do seem to be stronger arguments to suggest that the criminalization of the possession of child pornography may serve as a discouragement to those who produce child pornography, and sexually abuse children in the process, by limiting the market for their material. Furthermore, the fact that the possession of child pornography is an unlawful act may serve to deter the propagation of representations of children which objectify and reduce them to sexual objects. Thus, I would conclude that the strongest legitimating force behind the current law exists in the protection it may offer to children by discouraging individuals from committing child sexual abuse in order to create child pornography and in its reinforcement of the fact that our society will not tolerate child sexual abuse and the reification of children as sexual objects.

The legal prohibition upon the possession of child pornography certainly serves to reassure society that, as far as possible, the law protects innocent children. However, society's desire to shield children by upholding the dominant social construction of childhood innocence may effectively be placing children at greater risk of harm from those who find the idea of innocence attractive. Interpreting and constructing naked images of children as indecent and sexualized may also be damaging to children in terms of the way they perceive their bodies.

As society attempts to tackle the problem of child sexual abuse, tracking down possessors of child pornography may appear to be a more attainable goal than, for example, eradicating child sexual abuse which occurs in the home. In the former case, it is easier to obtain proof of the offence and there is no involvement of child witnesses. Whilst child pornography may not be an ever present feature of child sexual abuse, the law surrounding child pornography does enable the police to successfully tackle one aspect of child sexual abuse. This in itself is surely a further powerful justification behind the current legal position.

References

Adler, A. (2001) The perverse law of child pornography, *Columbia Law Review*, 101(2): 209.

Akdeniz, Y. (1997) The regulation of pornography and child pornography on the internet, *Journal of Information, Law and Technology*, 1.

Devlin, P. (1965) *The Enforcement of Morals*. Oxford: Oxford University Press.

Edwards, S. (2000) Prosecuting 'child pornography': possession and taking of indecent photographs, *Journal of Social Welfare and Family Law*, 22(1): 1–21.

Elliott, M., Browne, K. and Kilcoyne, J. (1995) Child sexual abuse prevention: what offenders tell us, *Child Abuse and Neglect*, 19(5): 579–94.

Higonnet, A. (1998) *Pictures of Innocence*. London: Thames and Hudson.

Howitt, D. (1995) Pornography and the paedophile: is it criminogenic? *British Journal of Medical Psychology*, 68(1): 15–27.

Kitzinger, J. (1988) Defending innocence: ideologies of childhood, *Feminist Review*, 28 (January): 77–87.

Marshall, W. (1988) The use of sexually explicit stimuli by rapists, child molestors, and nonoffenders, *Journal of Sex Research*, 25(2): 267–88.

Pierce, L. (1984) Child pornography: a hidden dimension of child abuse, *Child Abuse and Neglect* 8(4): 483–93.

Renvoize, J. (1993) *Innocence Destroyed: A Study of Child Sexual Abuse*. London: Routledge.

Tate, T. (1990) *Child Pornography: An Investigation*. London: Methuen.

12

DETENTION OF ASYLUM SEEKERS IN THE UK AND US
DECIPHERING NOISY AND QUIET CONSTRUCTIONS

Michael Welch and Liza Schuster (2005)

Introduction

Particularly for long periods of time, detention is among the gravest acts the state can take against people. The seriousness of detention is even greater under circumstances in which persons are held not on criminal or immigration charges but rather after fleeing persecution. The current practice of detaining asylum seekers in the UK and the US worries human rights organizations, especially since they clash with the United Nations Convention on Refugees. Still, the controversy has taken different forms in otherwise similar nations. While there is considerable public and political attention directed at asylum seeking in Britain, the putative problem in the US remains muted; nevertheless, the consequences are the same, subjecting asylum seekers to unnecessary detention in harsh conditions of confinement.

... This work examines the controversy over the detention of asylum seekers, sorting out differences between the UK, where voices on both sides of the debate are public and loud, and the US, where the issue is quietly concealed by government officials ... The detention of asylum seekers clearly demonstrates that certain facets of the war on terror manifest more as immigration and social control rather than as crime control. Supposedly operating under the umbrella of the war on terror, the Department of Homeland Security has gained greater authority over immigration and asylum matters. Human rights organizations are concerned over that shift in power since it can lead to abuse. The United Nations recently documented a pattern of mistreatment among US airport inspectors who detained, handcuffed and intimidated travellers fleeing persecution in an effort to discourage them from requesting political asylum and thereby deporting them. Some of those who were deported had even demonstrated a credible fear of persecution, the principal criterion for asylum (*New York Times*, August 13 2004: A11) ...

[A] blanket detention order [was] issued by Attorney-General John Ashcroft in 2003. The government claims that wholesale detention is necessary to protect the US from terrorist threat; however, the order is a response to the case of David Joseph, a Haitian asylum seeker. The Board of Immigration Appeals upheld the decision to release Joseph on bond but Ashcroft insists that his release would prompt a mass exodus from Haiti to the US. Moreover, the State Department went so far as to say that Haiti has become a staging point for terrorists from the Middle East (*Associated Press*, April 24 2003 EV: 1–2). Arabs and Muslims are also being detained and deported for minor offences.

Moral Panic as a Theoretical Grid

... [T]he moral panic paradigm has undergone considerable development since it entered the literature more than thirty years ago ... In its infancy, moral panic theory incorporated an emerging sociology of deviance and embryonic cultural studies, reflecting the changing social mood of the late 1960s ... When *Folk Devils and Moral Panics* was released in its third edition in 2002, Cohen looked back on how moral panic as a concept has been used – and misused – by academics and journalists ... Three extensions of moral panic theory are considered: social constructionism, media and cultural studies, and risk.

... Cohen confronts a significant problem facing moral panic analysis, namely its subjective nature. 'Why is reaction to Phenomenon A dismissed or downgraded by being described as "another moral panic" while the putatively more significant Phenomenon B is ignored, and not even made a candidate for moral signification?' (Cohen: 2002: xxi). As a partial remedy, Cohen calls for a comparative sociology of moral panic that provides researchers an opportunity to discern why a certain condition manifests as a pseudo-disaster in one nation but not in other. Moreover, comparative research invites critical analysis in determining the many forms and nuances of moral panic.

... Further refining the sociology of moral panic, Cohen (2002) distinguishes between noisy and quiet constructions. As the name suggests, noisy constructions manifest in moral panic accompanied by high levels of public, political, and media attention. By contrast, quiet constructions emerge as a more contained entity in which the 'claims makers are professionals, experts, or bureaucrats working in an organization with little or no public or media exposure' (2002: xxiii) . . . [W]e pursue this facet of moral panic theory in an attempt to decipher why reaction to asylum seekers has taken the form of noisy panic in Britain while remaining muted in the US. A comparative approach between two similar societies contributes to efforts to reveal the nuances of moral panic. . .

Previous research displays the utility of this paradigm in understanding the processes and consequences of moral panic over immigrants in the US during the 1990s (Welch 2002; 2003a). Exaggerated claims were used to justify an official crackdown on so-called illegal aliens, creating a greater reliance on detention. In the UK, a similar campaign has been directed against asylum seekers. According to Cohen, 'in media, public, and political discourse in Britain the distinctions between immigrants, refugees, and asylum seekers have become hopelessly blurred' (2002: xviii). Furthermore, asylum issues in the UK 'are subsumed under the immigration debate which in turn is framed by the general categories of race, race relations and ethnicity' (2002: xviii). Beginning in the 1990s, growing numbers of asylum seekers were met with hostility in the UK, producing such newspaper headlines as these: 'Warning over new influx of gypsies' (*Daily Mail*, October 23 1997); 'Handouts galore! Welcome to soft touch Britain's welfare paradise: Why life for them here is just like a lottery win' (*Daily Mail*, October 10 1997); 'Script for a scam: In letters back home asylum gypsies tell their friends how to get into Britain' (*Daily Mail*, October 24 1997). As Cohen explains:

> Governments and media start with a broad public consensus that *first*, we must keep out as many refugee-type of foreigners as possible; *second*, these people lie to get themselves accepted; *third*, that strict criteria of eligibility and therefore tests of credibility must be used. For two decades, the media and the political elites of all parties have focused attention on the notion of 'genuineness.' This *culture of disbelief* penetrates the whole system. So 'bogus' refugees and asylum seekers have not really been driven from their home countries because of persecution, but are merely 'economic' migrants, attracted to the 'Honey Pot' or 'Soft Touch Britain'. (2002: xix)

Researchers have tracked the formation of moral panic, particularly in the British media where so-called bogus asylum seekers are publicly vilified. The Runnymede Trust (1996) surveyed asylum coverage in the print media, finding a pattern of racist rhetoric that likened migration and asylum seeking to natural disasters. Those metaphors, such as 'tides', 'waves', 'floods', and 'swamps' serve to dehumanize migrants and refugees while exaggerating the size, scale and threat of the phenomenon. So-called 'bogus' asylum seekers are blamed for placing an undue burden on social welfare while taking jobs from British citizens. Kaye (1998) found that 58 per cent of articles in his British press sample contained labels characterizing asylum seekers as bogus rather than genuine.

... Bralo (1998) conducted a discourse analysis of news coverage in the UK... [A]sylum seeking was portrayed as a social problem for Britain rather than as an opportunity to provide safe haven for people fleeing persecution. Refugees were labelled as 'others' who should be met with suspicion (Angel-Ajani 2003; Young 2003). Natural disaster metaphors were used to describe strains on the welfare state. 'THE FLOOD of bogus asylum seekers into Dover has left the local council facing a potential 10 million [pounds] crisis that could see basic social services slashed, it emerged yesterday' (*Daily Mail*, October 21 1997: 1).

Other labels frequently attached to asylum seekers depicted them as 'benefit scroungers', 'cheats' and 'fraudulent'. Some were criminalized as 'hoodlums' and 'gangsters' or sweepingly demonized: 'Why are we a haven for evil foreigners?' (*Daily Mail*, December 20 1997:1). Modern forms of racism were common, particular in reference to Islamic fundamentalism, [such as]: 'Lying guerrilla wins thousands for a few weeks behind bars' (*Daily Mail*, December 18 1997:1). In that article, a detainee is described as 'an Islamic guerrilla fighter [who] is to be paid "substantial" damages by the Home Secretary despite lying about his asylum case ... A judge has ruled that he was "illegally detained" for nearly five weeks by suspicious immigration authorities.' Bralo concludes her discourse analysis thus:

> The exclusion and discrimination are produced by the media through the use of language, contextualization, prominence of voices and agenda setting and reproduced from the primary definers in our case official/government sources. Immigration discourse cuts deep into the issues of power and is therefore of great importance for dominant ideologues. (1998: 24)

Detaining Asylum Seekers in the UK

Analyzing the controversy over asylum seeking in the UK, Cohen refers to disproportionality as a key indicator of moral panic:

Assume we know, that over the last three years, (i) that X% of asylum seekers make false claims about their risk of being persecuted; (ii) that only a small proportion (say 20%) of this subgroup have their claims recognized and (iii) that the resultant numbers of fake asylum seekers are about 200 each year. Surely then the claim about 'the country being flooded with bogus asylum seekers' is out of proportion. (2002: xxviii)

... [T]he lack of proportion in societal reaction to asylum seeking in the UK... manifests in the detention and harsh treatment of asylum seekers. Let us turn specifically to the practice of detention in the UK.

Most European Union states are now bound by the European Convention on Human Rights. Article 5 of the Convention guarantees the right of liberty and the security of the person but does permit the detention of individuals to facilitate removal (Schuster 2000; 2002). Until the 1990s there were no permanent centres for detention in Britain, because it was an exceptional measure. When implemented for large groups of people, barracks or similar camps or buildings would usually be commandeered, as happened during the two world wars. Otherwise individuals would be detained in prisons.

New detention centre rules were introduced in 2001 covering conditions in the centres and the provision of reasons for detention... Variable operating standards produced significant differences between centres. People detained under the 1972 Immigration Act were usually over-stayers (people who had entered on a tourist, visitors or other visa and remained after their visa had expired), frequently brought to the attention of the immigration authorities through denunciations, traffic accidents or crimes (as victims or perpetrators). Prior to 1988, asylum seekers averaged approximately 5,000 per year and were rarely deported or detained. Those granted the status of refugee tended to come as part of a resettlement programme or came from the Soviet Bloc and were readily granted asylum. Occasionally people would be stopped on entry and detained awaiting removal, but at any one time there would usually be between 200–300 people in detention. This situation changed significantly in the 1990s. The numbers of people detained annually increased from around 250 people to over 2,000 (Schuster 2003a; 2003b).

... [Detention centres] expanded significantly under the present New Labour government. The 1999 Immigration and Asylum Act stepped up the practice of detention, massively increasing the number of places. Despite government promises to end the practice, asylum seekers continue to be housed in prisons, with removal from a detention centre to a prison sometimes used to punish detainees...

In the UK, unlike most other European countries, there is no legal limit to the time a person may be held. The longest known period is the detention of an Indian national – Karamjit Singh Chahal (6 years and 2 months). He was finally released on November 15th 1997 after the Strasbourg Court ruled it would be illegal to deport him. It was this decision that forced the Home Office to introduce the 2000 Terrorism Act. In 1999 the British government promised to introduce the right to automatic bail hearings, [but this was] never implemented and was withdrawn in the 2002 Nationality, Immigration and Asylum Act. Detainees now have to request a bail hearing and many are unaware of this possibility. For people detained on or shortly after arrival, it is difficult to find sureties (Jackson 2003).

The Home Office argues that only those believed to be likely to abscond are detained. Detention centres have been renamed 'removal' centres. However, the majority of detainees are eventually released, because of conditions in the country of origin, because travel documents cannot be issued, because they are allowed to appeal, because they are released on bail, because they are granted leave to remain on compassionate grounds or because their claim for asylum is eventually allowed...

Activists among groups supporting asylum seekers are fighting back by challenging distorted perceptions of asylum seekers that lead to scapegoating and detention. Whereas moral panics in the past have occurred more easily because crusaders exploited the media to advance their claims concerning a putative social problem, nowadays human rights activists rely on organized tactics that confront governmental and media claims about the threats of asylum seekers, attempting to create a more informed public consciousness. Moreover, taken together, claims making and fighting back contribute to the noisy nature of moral panic. Whereas noisy panic over asylum seekers – leading to controversial detention practices – is characteristic of the controversy in the UK, a different form of societal reaction is evident in the US, where detention of asylum seekers is a remarkably quiet form of social control.

Clampdown on Asylum Seekers in the US

The unnecessary detention of asylum seekers in a post-9/11 America is an extension of prevailing trends in imprisonment. 'Tough on crime policies' contributing to mass incarceration provide a template for the detention of undocumented immigrants (Simon 1998; Welch 2003a). The tragic events of September 11th clearly have served to intensify the government's commitment to detention, producing an array of civil and human rights violations (Welch 2003b). The crackdown on undocumented immigrants and foreigners also extends to asylum seekers (Welch 2004).

Between September 11th 2001 and December 2003, more than 15,300 asylum seekers were detained at US airports and borders. From the port of entry asylum seekers are transported to jail, often in handcuffs, and usually without any clear understanding of why they were being detained. In detention, once they pass a screening interview, asylum seekers are legally eligible to be paroled if they satisfy the DHS parole criteria (i.e. community ties, no risk to the community, and that identity can be established). However, in practice, even asylum seekers who meet those criteria remain in detention. Immigration officials too often ignore or selectively apply the parole criteria, which exist only in guideline form rather than formal regulations. Compounding matters, an asylum seeker whose parole request is denied by DHS officials has no legal recourse. Since the attacks of September 11th, stricter measures have been introduced, including Operation Liberty Shield and the Blanket Detention Order of 2003.

Operation liberty shield

A recent programme officially titled Operation Liberty Shield was initiated by the DHS on the eve of the war with Iraq. It required detention of asylum seekers from 33 countries where Al Qaeda has been known to operate. Even asylum seekers who did not raise any suspicions of security or flight risks were detained for the duration (six months or more) of their asylum proceedings.

[...]

Operation Liberty Shield – portrayed as a comprehensive national plan designed to protect citizens, secure infrastructure and, most importantly, deter terrorist attacks – was terminated after only one month of operation. The government apparently abandoned the programme in the face of intense pressure from human rights organizations. Still, arriving asylum seekers from the designated locations continue to be subject to mandatory detention upon their arrival in the US under the 1996 expedited removal law. Although asylum seekers from those nations are now technically eligible to apply for parole, it is unclear how many will actually be released.

Blanket detention order of 2003

Adding to the government's escalating war on terror, Attorney-General John Ashcroft issued a profoundly significant directive on April 17 2003.

Under it, illegal immigrants, including asylum seekers, can be held indefinitely without bond if their cases present national security concerns... Framed as necessary for maintaining national security, the actual trigger was the case of Haitian asylum-seeker, David Joseph. The DHS sought the opinion from the Attorney-General after the Board of Immigration Appeals upheld a judge's decision to release Joseph on $2,500 bond. Ashcroft argued that 'national security would be threatened if the release triggered a huge wave of immigrants to attempt to reach US shores' distracting the 'already-strained Coast Guard, Border Patrol and other agencies that are busy trying to thwart terror attacks' (*Associated Press*, April 4 2003 EV:1). The State Department claimed that Haiti has become a staging point for non-Haitians considered security threats (i.e. Pakistanis and Palestinians) to enter the US.

Whereas most of the immigration issues have been transferred to the DHS, the measure promises to centralize further the power of the Attorney-General in area of asylum seeking. Human rights groups opposed the blanket detention order. Amnesty International denounced Ashcroft's ruling to hold groups of asylum-seekers and other non-citizens in detention indefinitely, noting that the provision extends to those who pose no danger to the US... The blanket detention policy violates international standards specifying that the detention of asylum seekers be limited to exceptional cases under law. Furthermore, governments have the burden of demonstrating the need for detaining of asylum seekers in prompt and fair individualized hearings before a judicial or similar authority.

Prior to Aschroft's order, immigration judges have used two individualized criteria to determine whether to release asylum seekers, namely, flight risk and danger to the community. Afterwards, all non-citizens may be detained indefinitely even if they do not pose risk of flight or a threat to society...

In 2003, immigration lawyers learned that DHS and ICE quietly initiated a pilot detention programme in Connecticut to detain asylum seekers and other immigrants who were not already in custody; actually, the programme began one month earlier with no notification to the public. Among those detained under that programme are asylum seekers who are in removal proceedings after having voluntarily identified themselves to immigration authorities by applying for asylum... Contributing to the criminalization process, the government has set out to prosecute asylum seekers, at least in Florida, if they arrive with false documents. Although the use of false documents can be a felony punishable up to ten years in jail, until now US authorities had not generally charged asylum seekers with such offences...

Deciphering Divergence

The invention and dramatization of so-called bogus asylum seekers as a popular stereotype are much more of a British phenomenon than an American one. The perceived threat of asylum seekers in the US has been quietly contained within government agencies and not a publicly shared construction. Whereas there have been spikes of panic over foreigners (most recently those perceived as being Arab and Muslim) and undocumented workers (mostly Latino) in the US since September 11th, the putative problem of asylum seeking does not resonate in the public mind. Privately, however, American government officials have quietly embarked on their own detention campaign. Since 9/11, US government officials insist that policies requiring the detention of asylum seekers serve national security interests (Ratner 2003).

... [O]ther key distinctions between British and American societies help explain their different constructions of asylum seekers. Criminal justice systems in the US and UK are similar in their heavy-handed responses to crime but there remain important cultural distinctions that shape popular and political perceptions of asylum seekers. Among the most obvious cultural features of the US is its history – and identity – as an immigrant nation, alongside contemporary liberal movements toward multiculturalism. Although the US has experienced periods of anti-immigrant sentiment, even as recently as the 1990s, there has yet to be any large-scale public panic directed specifically at asylum seekers (Welch 2002; 2004). The US government may distinguish between various immigrant populations (e.g. asylum seekers, refugees, and undocumented workers) but in the eyes of Americans they are all lumped together as immigrants, regardless of the circumstances that brought them ashore.

In England, however, historical forces underpinning asylum reveal a unique set of priorities, deeply intertwined in colonial politics. Robin Cohen (1994) traces asylum provisions to the period of William the Conqueror when there was a formal strategy to exert control over newly colonized territories. By extension, immigration and asylum – as well as expulsions and deportations – symbolized and reproduced the power of the monarch. Eventually, the 'right to exclude' was legislated in Parliament in reaction to the wave of forced migration amid the French Revolution; in particular, the Aliens Act of 1793 granted the government authority to remove aliens. Conversely, awarding sanctuary served another key political function insofar as it demonstrated a seemingly benevolent side of British government, displaying a sense of moral superiority over other nations that are reluctant to provide safe haven for those fleeing persecution.

... [S]ome contemporary features of British culture remain relatively insignificant in the US, most notably the role of the tabloid media. Certainly, in the US, media sensationalism continues to influence popular and political views of crime and other social problems. By comparison, the degree to which British tabloid journalism penetrates politics, thereby shaping discourse over the putative threat of asylum seekers, is virtually unmatched by any American news outlet. Some headlines in Britain read: 'Thousands have already [come to the UK] bringing terror and violence to the streets of many English towns' (*Sunday People*, March 4 2001: 2); 'Fury as 20,000 Asylum cheats beat the System to Stay in Britain; Get them Out' (*Daily Express*, July 30 2001: 4); 'Kick Out All This Trash' (*Sunday People*, March 5 2000: 10). Negative reactions to migrants and asylum seekers have a long history in British political culture. Moreover, 'successive British governments have not only led and legitimated public hostility, but spoken with a voice indistinguishable from the tabloid press' (Cohen, 2002: xix).

Due to the interlocking of tabloid media, politics, and public opinion, the detention of asylum seekers in the UK conforms to a European-wide phenomenon of incarcerating foreigners, or 'suitable enemies' who symbolically represent an array of social anxieties:

This process is powerfully reinforced and amplified by the media and by politicians of all stripes, eager to surf the xenophobic wave that has been sweeping across Europe since the neoliberal turn of the 1980s. Sincerely or cynically, directly or indirectly, but with ever more banality, they have succeeded in forging an amalgam of immigration, illegality, and criminality. (Wacquant, 1999: 219)

In Britain, the detention of asylum seekers as a noisy construction – and state ritual – reaffirms legality to the witnessing public hungry for expressive punishments. That penal ceremony has reached a media theatre onto whose stage politicians pronounce their claim to clamp down on so-called bogus asylum seekers fraudulently in search of welfare benefits, education, health care, housing and jobs. In 2003 former Cabinet member Stephen Byers proposed that all asylum seekers who fail to register with the government be deprived of access to British schools and hospitals. Byers defended his proposal, saying: 'It is not racist to address the legitimate worries and concerns that people have about asylum and immigration, but it would be irresponsible not to do so' (*Guardian*, July 31 2003: 6).

By contrast, the quiet nature of detention of asylum seekers in the US is contoured along a different set of law enforcement priorities, namely the war on terror compounded by the Bush administration's commitment to government secrecy. Months following the investigation of the attacks on the WTC and the Pentagon, Attorney-General Ashcroft repeatedly denied access to basic information about many of those in detention, including their names and current location. Such secrecy has been denounced by human rights and civil liberties advocates, as well as by news organizations. Even some political leaders have complained that the Attorney-General has failed to explain adequately the need for those drastic measures... Similar degrees of secrecy surrounding detention are evident in other spheres of the American war on terror, including Abu Ghraib (Baghdad), Baghram (Afghanistan), and Guantanamo Bay (Cuba).

Conclusion

Despite their divergence on popular perceptions of asylum seekers, American and British governments have adopted similar strategies, namely detention... Cohen (2002) predicts that more anonymous, or 'nameless', folk devils will emerge. That forecast is especially pertinent to those fleeing persecution whose actual identity and biography are frequently obscured from public consciousness; instead they are commonly labelled as bogus and undeserving. As a result, 'social policies once regarded as abnormal – incarcerating hundreds of asylum seekers in detention centers run as punitive transit camps by private companies for profit – are seen as being normal, rational and conventional' (Cohen 2002: xxxiv; see Molenaar and Neufeld 2003).

These developments in the detention of asylum seekers, in both the UK and US, have strong implications for an emergent sociology of denial. Cohen (2001) concentrates on the content of denial manifesting in three forms: literal, interpretive, and implicatory. Literal denial is as blunt as it is blatant (e.g. officials insist 'that atrocity did not occur'), serving as a blanket defence against acknowledging the undisputed facts. Under interpretive denial, however, the facts are not refuted but are given a different spin, thus altering the meaning (e.g. officials argue 'what happened is not what you think it is'). In the third form, implicatory denial does not refute either the facts or their conventional meaning; rather, the psychological, political, or moral consequences are denied, minimized, or muted. By reducing the significance of the harm of human rights violations and other atrocities, officials evade their responsibility to intervene.

At a higher level of abstraction, denial can permeate entire governments, societies, and cultures. Indeed, denial becomes official when it is public, collective and highly organized. Unlike totalitarian regimes that go to great lengths to rewrite history and block out the present, denial in democratic societies is subtle, often taking the form of spin-doctoring and public agenda setting. But similar to totalitarianism, democratic nations also build denial into the ideological facade of the state. Denial becomes even more ubiquitous when whole societies slip into collective modes of denial. For citizens, cultural denial becomes a potent defence mechanism against acknowledging human rights abuses within their own nation (Cohen, 2001; Welch, 2003b, 2005).

Sociologists investigating social problems ought to confront both polarities of societal reaction. Moral panic, exaggeration, and prejudice represent one extreme, namely over-reaction. Still, we must not neglect under-reaction at the other end of the spectrum, including apathy, indifference, and denial. The unnecessary detention of asylum seekers in the UK is facilitated by over-reaction in the form of moral panic driven by politicians and tabloid journalists who characterize those fleeing persecution as bogus and threats to the welfare state. That over-reaction simultaneously produces under-reaction whereby human rights violations against those seeking refuge fail to reach a critical mass.

Similarly, in the US, quiet constructions of asylum seekers as threats to national security also serves to keep their unjust confinement from entering the collective conscience.

References

Angel-Ajani (2003) A question of races?, *Punishment and Society*, 5(4): 433–48.

Bralo, Z. (1998) (Un)cool Britannia: discourse analysis of construction of refugees in the UK press. Unpublished Master's thesis, Department of Social Psychology, London School of Economics and Political Science.

Cohen, R. (1994) *Frontiers of Identity: The British and the Others*. London: Longman.

Cohen, S. (2001) *States of Denial: Knowing about Atrocities and Suffering*. Cambridge: Polity.

Cohen, S. (2002) *Folk Devils and Moral Panics: The Creation of Mods and Rockers*, 3rd edn. London: Routledge.

Jackson, A. (2003) The detention of asylum seekers in the UK: bail for immigration detainees, *Feminist Review*, 73: 118–22.

Kaye, R. (1998) Redefining refugee: the UK media portrayal of asylum seekers, in K. Koser and H. Lutz (eds) *The New Migration in Europe: Social Constructions and Social Realities*. London: Macmillan.

Molenaar, B. and Neufeld, R. (2003) The use of privatized detention centers for asylum seekers in Australia and the UK, in A. Coyle, A. Campbell and R. Neufeld (eds) *Capitalist Punishment: Prison Privatization and Human Rights*. London: Zed Books.

Ratner, M. (2003) Making us less free: War on terrorism or war on liberty?, in S. Aronowitz and H. Gautney (eds) *Implicating Empire: Globalization and Resistance in the 21st Century World Order*. New York: Basic Books.

Runnymede Trust (1996) Survey of asylum coverage in the national daily press, *The Runnymede Bulletin*, December 1995 / January 1996. London: Runn, ede Trust.

Schuster, L. (2000) A comparison of asylum policy in seven European states, *Journal of Refugee Studies*, Special Issue 13(1): 118–32.

Schuster, L. (2002) Asylum and the lessons of history: an historical perspective, *Race and Class*, 44(2): 40–56.

Schuster, L. (2003a) The Use and Abuse of Political Asylum in Britain and Germany. London: Frank Cass.

Schuster, L. (2003b) Asylum seekers: Sangatte and the Channel tunnel, Parliamentary Affairs, Special Issue on Crisis Management: 56(3).

Simon, J. (1998) Refugees in a carceral age: the rebirth of immigration prisons in the United States, *Public Culture*, 10(3): 577–607.

Wacquant, L. (1999) Suitable enemies, foreigners and immigrants in the prisons of Europe, *Punishment and Society*, 1(2): 215–22.

Welch, M. (2002) *Detained: Immigration Laws and the Expanding I.N.S. Jail Complex*. Philadelphia, PA: Temple University Press.

Welch, M. (2003a) Ironies of social control and the criminalization of immigrants, *Crime, Law & Social Change: An International Journal*, 39: 319–37.

Welch, M. (2003b) Trampling of human rights in the war on terror: implications to the sociology of denial, *Critical Criminology: An International Journal*, 12(1): 1–20.

Welch, M. (2004) Quiet constructions in the war on terror: subjecting asylum seekers to unnecessary detention, *Social Justice: A Journal of Crime, Conflict & World Order*, 31(1–2): 113–29.

Welch, M. (2005) Immigration lockdown before and after 9/11: ethnic constructions and their consequences, in M. Bosworth and J. Flavin (eds) *Race, Gender and Punishment: Theorizing Differences*. New Brunswick, NJ: Rutgers University Press.

Young, J. (2003) To these wet and windy shores: recent immigration policy in the UK, *Punishment and Society*, 5(4): 449–62.

THE DISCOURSE OF THE PRESS AND THE PRESS OF DISCOURSE
CONSTRUCTING THE DRUG PROBLEM IN THE RUSSIAN MEDIA

Peter Meylakhs (2005)

Introduction

This article explores how the drug problem was constructed in the Russian press at the turn of the century. It contributes to shifting Russian sociology away from an exclusive attention to drug users and their 'problems' to those who construct and define the drug situation in order to problematize 'self-evident' and 'taken-for-granted' categories in dominant medical and criminological discourses.

In contemporary Russian sociology work on drug use adopts an objectivist paradigm; any negative (in the researcher's eyes) condition is automatically identified as a social problem. Thus, in case of drug use, the sociologist's task is reduced to description of the condition (as a rule in quantitative terms) by means of answering questions such as who uses what and how often, the public's attitude to it, and what can be done to stop it. Not long ago at a conference on the prevention of drug addiction, all medical professionals as one talked about necessity of cooperation between all specialists dealing with the problem, with sociologists assigned the role of statisticians who, as one doctor put it, 'measure the social constants', i.e. demographers that collect routine information but who do not have any authority for real sociological analysis of the situation. Unfortunately, exactly this scenario unfolds in Russian society where all too often sociologists are engaged in serving and confirming dominant medical and criminal theories, providing their statistical legitimation. In labelling theory's language, Russian sociologists are mainly occupied with studying those 'who are labelled' and much less often those 'who label'.

Though very scarce, works of constructionist orientation do exist in the Russian sociology of deviant behavior. Particularly noteworthy are articles written by Smirnova (2000), Bludina (2000), and Kosterina (2002), all devoted to analyzing the construction of moral panics around drugs in the Russian regional press. However, despite their considerable merits, these works have a number of shortcomings. First, in spite of their declared constructionist orientation, they have a strong objectivist bias. For instance, Kosterina writes that 'modern mass media have unlimited possibilities both in covering and constructing social problems' (2002: 200). One can conclude from this quote that 'covering' and 'constructing' are totally different things, that it is possible to cover a problem without taking part in its construction. It implicitly follows from this that covering is conferring on audience some objective, unitary, and peremptory 'truth', while constructing is something artificial, creating something ex nihilo. Such a point of view misinterprets the concept of social construction of reality, reducing it to the creation and dissemination of various myths and lies for economic or political gain. Any linguistic activity is a social (re)construction of reality, just as the social construction of reality is accompanied by the creation of linguistic categories. All social problems are socially constructed regardless of whether the sociologist-researcher considers them legitimate or not. Second, these works brilliantly analyze the Russian drug situation and its presentation by Russian media but pay insufficient attention to the *discursive* mechanisms in the construction of a drug moral panic. This article undertakes the tasks of filling gaps in the works of contemporary Russian sociologists of constructionist orientation, using a case study of the representation of drug use in the national and local Russian press.

Drug Use in the Media Public Sphere

Within the framework of this study an analysis was conducted of articles in leading regional Saint Petersburg newspapers on the subject of drugs and drug addiction for the period 1997 to 2003. The analyzed newspapers included: *Sankt Peterburgskie vedomosti, Nevskoe vremia, Chas Pik* and *Vecherniy Peterburg*. I have chosen for analysis those articles (news briefs, news items, columns, editorials, and features) that individually or in combination used the words 'drugs' and 'drug addiction'. These were identified by the search engine Integrum. Additionally, to compare portrayals of the drug situation in Saint Petersburg with those in Russia overall, parallel articles were analyzed in national newspapers. The latter included: *Rossiyskaya gazeta, Nezavisimaya gazeta, Izvestiya, Moskovskiy komsomolets,*

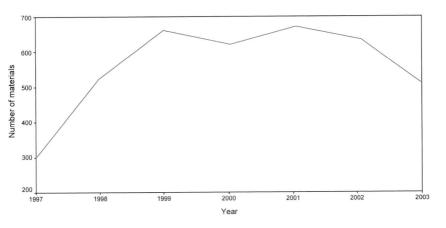

Figure 13.1 Drug-related articles in leading Russian newspapers, 1997–2003

Komsomolskaya Pravda, Kommersant, Sovetskaya Rossiya. Data analysis was both quantitative and qualitative.

The moral panic about drugs did not last long, according to the trends in the total numbers of drug-related stories in all the national and two local newspapers (*Sankt Peterburgskie vedomosti* and *Nevskoe vremia*). In all these papers the trend is very similar – a sharp growth in the number of articles in 1998 and 1999, and a gradual decline in 2002 and 2003. For instance, in *Nezavisimaya gazeta* the number of articles mentioning drug addiction in 1997 was 45, 93 in 1998, 113 in 1999, 128 in 2000, 130 in 2001 and 84 in 2002. By 2003 the decline was even more apparent with just 51 articles. Figure 13.1 presents these results diagrammatically.

As is evident from Figure 13.1 and Figure 13.2, the interest of the press in drug use waxes and wanes. This contradicts the view of the press as a mirror of public problems, reacting to the extent of the real danger. The drug situation did not change, or only changed slightly, while the rise and fall of press interest was dramatic. Also one can see a certain pattern, such as peaks in 1999 and 2001 for practically all outlets. This pattern identifies tendencies characteristic of the press as a whole which do not vary with editorial decisions in each newspaper. *Rossiyskaya gazeta* is as mainstream as you can get because it is the official newspaper of the Russian government, where official pronouncements were regularly made about the enforcement or revision of drug laws. Its interest in the drug problem peaked in 1999 and had faded by 2001. On March 24, 1999 an article appeared in the newspaper, which informed the readers that drug addiction worried the Russian citizens more than all other social problems combined.

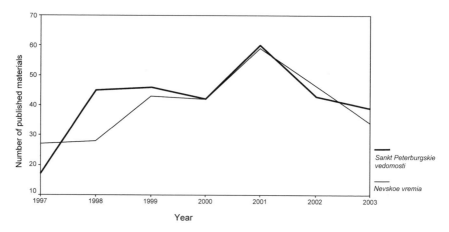

Figure 13.2 Drug-related articles in two leading Saint Petersburg newspapers, 1997–2003

In Saint Petersburg drug addiction was declared the most pressing problem two years later – in 2001 (*Nevskoe vremia*, 26.04. 2001).

Taking a broad brush, we can outline a picture of the overall Russian drug situation as consisting of three main phases. Phase 1 we call 'Before the tempest'. The media constantly publish apocalyptic forecasts. Phase 2 we call 'The Hurricane'. There is a deluge of articles on drugs. Their main subject: apocalypse has already come. There are demands to increase penalties for drug use and drug sale, including the death penalty. Similar measures are advocated by some regional governors. Harshening of drug legislation takes place consequently in 1997 and 1998. Phase 3 we call 'After the storm'. Interest in the problem gradually subsides. Repressive rhetoric used to advocate punishment by legal institutions gives way to rehabilitative rhetoric used to advocate treatment by medial institutions (though both are essentially social control mechanisms). This change finds expression in legal change with an amendment to the Criminal Code in the autumn of 2003 that partly liberalizes the extant drug laws. In parallel fashion the rhetoric shifts away from the right of the community to be protected from drug-related crime to the rights of the individual to be protected from state power.

In Saint Petersburg, however, the moral panic was short-lived. Analysis of coverage in the region's newspapers (*Sankt Peterburgskie vedomosti, Nevskoe vremia, Chas Pik,* and *Vecherniy Peterburg*) suggests that a classic moral panic only lasted from January to July 2002. In January the murder of a prominent Russian academic Glebov, allegedly by drug addicts, served

as a key event (Kepplinger and Habermeier 1995). It linked the drug pro-
blem with another social problem – mugging (especially of the elderly).
There then appeared signs of what could qualify as moral panic. Here is the
Sankt Peterburgskie vedomosti on February 12, 2002.

Almost half of the crime today is one way or another related to drugs.
Poor pensioners are attacked in the street not by 'tough guys' (who
have totally different 'objects') but by crazed Maries and Peters from
around the corner who have already sold everything from their houses
and now are ready to do any 'exploit' including murder to prevent the
upcoming 'cold turkey' and get a 'joint'. Not so long ago we felt sorry
for these Maries and Peters. Sick people, we thought, deserving not
punishment but medical treatment. Numerous international organizations and parties rose to defend these pathetic junkies, demands to
soften drug laws were uttered on various forums, conferences, and
demonstrations. We must admit: drug addiction is INCURABLE by
modern means. All that is sold to us as a result of the treatment is only
so called remission, that is, temporary retreat of the disease. The only
way of fighting drug addiction and crimes related to it is COMPLETE
ISOLATION of drug addicts from society. It is time to admit honestly
that the powers that be have been too humane.

Nevertheless, it should be emphasized that by and large such a reaction was
not typical of the local press. A more restrained and ambivalent position to
the drug user as both victimizer and victim was more characteristic. One of
the distinctive features of moral panics is demonization of groups that bear
responsibility for the situation (Goode and Ben-Yehuda 1994; Hier 2003).
Yet, such demonization of drug addicts took place in the Saint Petersburg
press for only a short period. Nevertheless, the discursive strategies of the
Saint Petersburg newspapers were very similar to those of their national
counterparts. Most obviously, both attempted to define the situation as a
'catastrophic' problem compromising national security.

We need to consider whether this claim was valid. A full assessment is
beyond the scope of this paper but available evidence attests to the contrary. According to the European Monitoring Centre for Drugs and Drug
Addiction (EMCDDA 2002) in 2002 lifetime experience of cannabis use
was reported to vary from 10 per cent (Finland) to 25 to 30 per cent
(Denmark and the United Kingdom) of the whole adult population, with a
substantial number of European countries reporting figures of around 20
per cent (Belgium, Germany, Spain, France, Ireland and the Netherlands).
The figures for those who tried other drugs are significantly lower. In
America, the country that implements one of the harshest drug policies in

the Western world, 34 per cent of adults reported lifetime experience of cannabis and 11 per cent of cocaine (SAMHSA 2000). By comparison, in 2000 in Saint Petersburg, according to Russian researchers Keselman and Matskevich (2001), 18.5 per cent of the residents reported their lifetime drug use. 6.5 per cent of the city population tried drugs once or couple of times, and 6.5 per cent used drugs previously on a relatively regular basis but later ceased using drugs. The remaining third described their current drug use. Most who tried drugs used cannabis. [Some] 13.1 per cent of Russian adolescents reported their recent drug use (Chepurnikh 2003) as compared to 5–15 per cent of young adults in Europe.

However, these figures are in stark contrast to those reported by the local and national media. For instance, it was reported that there were regions in Russia where virtually all young people aged from 18 to 23 were addicted to drugs (*Vecherniy Peterburg*, 3.11.2000); and that in Saint Petersburg the number of drug addicts amounted to 400,000 people, almost one in ten of the city's total population (*Vecherniy Peterburg*, 12.02.2003), or that more than 13 million drug addicts resided in Russia (*Nevskoe vremia*, 31.01.2003). Such a 'rhetoric of calamity' was a necessary discursive ritual for conveying almost any information about drugs.

The Construction of the Heightened Danger of Drug Use by the Media

Discursive strategies designed to foster a heightened sense of danger from drug use were common to both the national and local press. Four seemed particularly important.

1 Signification spiral (Hall and Jefferson 1976). In this process one or more social problems are presented as progressively more threatening. So a drug problem becomes an epidemic, then a 'plague' or 'national disaster'. A related process is convergence which occurs 'when two or more activities are linked in the process of signification as to implicitly or explicitly draw parallels between them ... In both cases, the net effect is amplification, not in the real events being described but in their potential threat for society' (Hall et al. 1978: 223). For instance, in the Russian press two lexemes have been especially popular: *narkoterrorism* (drug terrorism) that implies that those who sell drugs are tantamount to terrorists, and *narkointerventsia* (drug intervention), which emphasizes the 'non-Russian' and imported character of drug use, thereby linking drug use with invasion and occupation.

2 Automatic problematization. This occurs when the drug problem becomes connected to other social problems such as crime and AIDS. Automatic problematization differs from convergence in that the latter refers to a form of signification while the former links two conditions with each other, not semantically but causally. I call such problematization automatic because the magnitude of these satellite problems is automatically and self-evidently set in direct relation with number of drug users, whilst other possible causes are all but neglected. For instance, it is postulated that the number of HIV-positive persons grows *only* because the number of drug users is on the rise. 'Fighting AIDS and fighting drug use are essentially equal in all the world' (*Nevskoe vremia*, 13.07.2001). That HIV spreads mainly because drug users share syringes and other drug paraphernalia, and that the epidemic could be checked by organizing syringe exchange programs, was largely ignored at the height of the drug panic.

The same holds true for crime. All so-called 'drug crime' was reported to be dependent only on the number of drug users, even though much of such crime was a consequence of the *laws* regulating drug use rather than drug use itself. Highlighting the relation between drugs and AIDS was more typical of the Saint Petersburg press, whereas the national press placed more emphasis on automatic problematization. 'Relating the spread of drug use to the growth of juvenile crime is *self-evident*: one evil begets the other. It is known that a person, who gets addicted to drugs, is a person without future. But it would be more correct to say that such a person has a criminal future, which threatens the whole society' (*Rossiyskaya gazeta*, 20.3.1998, emphasis added). Also, in the period that immediately preceded the onset of the drugs moral panic, the Saint Petersburg media were much more in favour of syringe exchange programs than the national media.

However, as the moral panic developed, such ideas faded from the media discourse, despite continued growth in the prevalence and incidence of HIV. For example, in a feature article to commemorate AIDS victims in *Sankt Peterburgskie vedomosti* on May 16, 2002, (at the height of the moral panic), there was not a single reference to syringe exchange programs although the issue had appeared regularly two years earlier. It seems that the newspaper was unwilling even to mention measures so unpopular in that period. Yet, from the second half of 2002 when the moral panic began to decline, the issue started appearing again.

3 Categorization work. In this discursive strategy all people that use any drugs no matter how frequently are ascribed to one category – 'drug addicts'. This situation is analogous to one that exists in criminal and medical discourses, where a 'drug addict' and a person who has tried or uses any drug, no matter how rarely, are virtually the same. In criminal discourse it is because he/she committed or continues to commit such crimes as the acquisition and possession of drugs; and in medical discourse it is because, having tried drugs, this person has taken an irreversible step towards drug addiction with dependence just a question of time. Not to try drugs is the only way not to become a drug addict. Taking into account that the drug addict is allegedly prepared to do anything to get a fix ('drug addicts suffering from "cold turkey" readily commit murder to procure a "potion"', *Nevskoe vremia*, 28.11.2003), and that he/she 'infects' 7–10 people a year (*Chas Pik*, 06.10.2002), the situation really looks catastrophic. Indeed, in 2003 it is reported (*Sankt Peterburgskie vedomosti*, 10.09.2003) that there are 4 million drug addicts in Russia. Simple arithmetic shows that in 2004 there will be 40 million people ready for anything to get a fix. By 2005 the number would be 400 million, twice the total Russian population.

4 Selective typification. When presenting crimes related to drug use, the mass media cover mostly grave crimes such as murder and write about them extensively; in so doing, they try to present such crimes as typical of drug users while in reality the proportion of drug users who have committed such crimes is very small (Rusakova 2000).

Mobilization Strategies of Mass Media

The agents or moral entrepreneurs participating in the construction of a moral panic about drugs must not only demonstrate the various dangers of drug use but also attempt to mobilize society for a battle with the evil. Hence, the importation of mobilization strategies. Ibarra and Kitsuse define rhetorical idioms as complexes of definitions that utilize language in order to situate problematized condition-categories in moral universes (1993: 34). Thus, 'the rhetoric of calamity is distinguished by being composed of metaphors and reasoning practices that evoke unimaginability of utter disaster' (1993: 41). Such rhetoric is also supposed to unite all agents competing in the social problems market under one umbrella since all other problems turned out to be logically subordinate to the one that is pregnant with inevitable catastrophe. Those who employ such rhetoric for a war on drugs are pursuing the goal of mobilizing and closing the ranks of both the general public and official institutions.. Both the Saint Petersburg and the national media used such rhetoric extensively. 'Why pay so much attention now to the economy, if in twenty years Russia will turn into a colony of drug addicts?' (*Rossiyskaya gazeta*, 19.3.1999). 'I don't understand what the leaders of the country or the city think now. They build the Ice Palace, roads, monuments ... But in a little while we will need only one kind of construction sites – graveyards, if we don't attend to youth problems right away' (*Nevskoe vremia*, 30.05.2001).

The second mobilization strategy is direct mobilization – calls to organize 'committees of responsible citizens', and to ring various drug control agencies to report not only those who are suspected in drug selling but drug users as well. ('Call the police for your neighbour's sake', *Rossiyskaya gazeta*, 26.2.1999). The fact that such calls can be a means for settling personal scores is completely ignored in the heat of the battle. Such direct mobilization was advocated less often in Saint Petersburg than in Russia as a whole.

Personification of Evil

Social problem construction consists not only of constructing conditions but also of constructing putative people who are attributed a role of a causal agent of the condition's harm (Looseke 1993, 2003). Thus, along with society's mobilization for battle with the evil, personification of this evil is also necessary. Any moral panic is accompanied by the construction of 'folk devils', i.e. those who are personally responsible for the situation. Drug use is a complex phenomenon conditioned by a range of social, cultural, and political factors. Personification of evil serves simultaneously to dramatize and concretize the situation (making the evil look simple and clear). Hence, the construction of the drug addict as the embodiment of evil helps to divert attention from complex structural and institutional aspects of social reality and reduce the problem to simply one of extermination, isolation, or the resocialization of personality. Gusfield, discussing the construction of the drinking-driving problem, writes that 'to build excitement and narrative around such objects as safety belts, auto design, alcohol availability, and user friendly roads may be possible but seems to lack the possibilities of villainy that the drinking-driving drama contains' (1989: 434). Besides, on such 'folk devils' can be heaped the blame for other social problems (Reinarman and Levine 1995), for instance, the harsh economic situation or the shortage of conscripts in the Russian army.

The construction of the 'other' in the case of the drug problem has a number of peculiar traits, different from those that can be seen in other discourses of exclusion, e.g. ethnic discourse. In discourses of exclusion 'they' are strangers from the outside who have transgressed the physical boundaries of the community. In the media discourse on drugs 'they' are a transmuted 'we', who have slighted and infringed the community's moral boundaries. At any minute anyone of 'us' may become one of 'them' ('In fact, every family is in danger now', *Nevskoe vremia*, 8.4.2000). Sometimes, it allegedly happens against the will of the victim – a mutagenic substance (drug) is injected by force. Neither money nor 'good family' can prevent this misfortune. ('Americans have concluded that the probability that a child would become a drug addict was the same for the president's family and for the alcoholic's family', *Chas Pik*, 29.8.2001.) But the chance that one of 'them' can become one of 'us' again is negligible. ('Only one out of hundred drug addicts is cured. And even this lucky one may at any time relapse back to drug use', *Sankt Peterburgskie vedomosti*, 21.4. 2000.) Two main dangers 'they' represent are being prepared to do anything for a fix and 'infecting' others.

Despite this set of common features in constructing the image of the drug addict in the Saint Petersburg and the national press, there were also significant differences. Thus, when portraying the drug addict the national press used a much more emotional and sometimes hysterical tone and language, calling drug addicts 'genetic moral degenerates' (*Rossiyskaya gazeta*, 12.10.2000), or 'criminals or potential criminals' (*Rossiyskaya gazeta*, 31.10.1998) ready to betray or kill at any minute (*Rossiyskaya gazeta*, 30.10.1998). The local print media adopted a more moderate and ambivalent position towards drug users as victimizers and victims. Despite all the 'terrible deeds' that drug addicts commit, it was often emphasized that they are 'our sick children' (*Sankt Peterburgskie vedomost*, 26.06.2002). This was the biggest difference between the two.

Overall, the moral panic about drug use was very brief, in Saint Petersburg only the first few months of 2002. It was also incomplete. Although, as might be expected in a moral panic, the drug situation was often depicted as catastrophic, the systematic demonization of drug users was not apparent. Without such demonization, another key criterion for a moral panic, hostility towards the offending group, could not be realized.

Legitimation of the Definition of the Situation

Finally, the constructed definition of the situation must be legitimized, which was accomplished in two ways. The first legitimation strategy of mass media was an appeal to experts' opinions. Experts and the mass media are at each other's service (Thompson 1998; Hall et al. 1978). The mass media objectify experts' opinions and give them the legitimacy of public exposure. The reverse process takes place when the mass media claim to speak on the public's behalf, whereupon official agencies can refer to the media's views as legitimate and 'real' public opinion. As a result, the media reproduce the experts' positions and the experts reproduce those of the media. In the case of the drug problem, such experts for the most part were representatives of the Ministry of Interior and the Ministry of Public Health, who, as a rule, pointed to the catastrophic character of the situation and came out in favor of taking harsh, sometimes draconian measures.

One of the main points over which these two professional groups differed was the curability of drug addiction. To own a problem is to have the right to name it and to be able to suggest something that can be done about it (Gusfield 1989:433). Knowledge of such recipes is a profession's license to own the problem. For that reason, even at the height of the drug scare, representatives of the medical profession kept saying that drug addiction was not a hopeless business, though to explain the very modest results of state rehabilitation programs, they had to stress that treatment was a hard and complicated process, without guaranteed outcomes. The medical profession had to insist that drug addiction was curable in order to maintain their professional jurisdiction over the problem. Before and after the brief panic, that view was accepted. But during the panic itself an alternative view was accepted that, since drug addiction was incurable, it was justified to arrest and imprison those involved. This, of course, passes jurisdiction to a quite different group: repressive institutions of social control, such as the police and Federal Drug Control Agency. 'The best [drug use] prevention is to arrest drug users and drug dealers as almost one hundred percent of those who mug pensioners procure money for a fix by this way, says deputy chief of the city criminal police Andrey Kemenev' (*Nevskoe vremia*, 21.2.2002).

Also, the drug users themselves are often accredited with an expert role, albeit ambiguous and imperfect. If they say something which confirms dominant discourses, they are legitimized as a people 'from the street' who know the problem firsthand. But if they articulate anything contracting dominant discourses, their pronouncements are declared 'junky myths' or deliberate dissemination of the drug mafia's lies.

The second strategy employed to legitimate the press definition of the drug situation was attempted elimination of any definitions which challenged those of the media or primary definers (Hall et al. 1978), such as the police and medical professions. As a rule, media claims-makers utilized expressions such as 'everybody knows', 'in all countries', 'it is obvious', 'it is natural to assume' and the like, in this manner trying to neutralize discussion, to show the self-evident and indisputable character of their definition of reality, to monopolize the discourse and marginalize alternatives.

Everything that contravened media and primary definers' positions was declared mythical and discarded without further consideration. Statements were frequent that referred to some mysterious forces that tried to liberalize the extant legislature, albeit the 'forces' themselves were virtually absent in media discourse in the period of moral panic. Moreover, the opponents were often vilified as criminals who were engaged in propaganda in favor of drug use (which is against Russian law), and/or were on the drug mafia's payroll. Hence potential counter-discourses were delegitimized. Such counter-discourses might acknowledge that drug problems can be solved or alleviated not only by reduction of number of drug users but also by other measures (minimizing harm related to drug use). They might also focus attention on drug laws and their respective harm and renounce the 'war on drugs' policy. A primary motive for criminalization lies in the moral domain because those driving the moral panic wish to protect moral boundaries, not challenge them.

That is why, for instance, in an address by the Russian Parliament to the United Nations of October 30, 1999, the problem of legalization or decriminalization of drugs is equated with the problem of drug use and abuse. 'The problem of drug abuse, legalization of drugs is in the class of problems that threaten to annihilate the human civilization' (*Rossiyskaya gazeta*, 10.30.1999). In this respect the position of the Saint Petersburg media was different from the national press since it resisted branding counter-discourses as necessarily produced by drug barons.

Conclusion

Let us draw some conclusions. We can assert that the interest of the national and local press in the drug problem declined from 2001 onwards and by 2003 was at the level of 1998. Despite definitions of a 'catastrophic' drug problem in Saint Petersburg, concern did not generally assume the form of a moral panic, since one of its essential characteristics was absent or present insufficiently – the construction of 'folk devil' or demonization of drug users. Nevertheless, for a short period at the beginning of 2002 such demonization was evident, so that briefly media discourse resembled a moral panic.

In this study a number of media discursive strategies directed to the construction of the heightened danger of drug use were determined. These included: signification spiral, automatic problematization, categorization work, and selective typification. The mobilization strategies of the mass media were also established, such as a rhetoric of calamity intended to unite all agencies competing in the social problems market under a single umbrella, and the strategy of direct mobilization – invitations to ring various drug control agencies. Whereas for the national Russian press demonization of the drug user was typical, the Saint Petersburg press regarded the drug user more ambivalently, as both victimizer and victim.

Legitimation of the media's definition of the situation was accomplished by appeals to experts' opinions and attempts to eliminate competing definitions. An expert role was attributed to agents of drug control institutions, medical personnel, and drug users themselves. Additionally, in contrast to their national colleagues, the Saint Petersburg press did not make attempts to criminalize counter-discourses. More recently, as the medicalized view of drug addiction regained ground, the national press has reverted to a view closer to that of the Saint Petersburg press. But the field of discourse could easily be destabilized again in the future.

References

Bludina, U. (2000) Molodejnie Kulturi, mass media I fenomen 'moralnikh panic', in E. Omelchenko (ed.) *Drugoie Pole*. (in Russian) Ulianovsk: Srednevoljskiy nauchniy center.

Chepurnikh, E. (ed.) (2003) *Ozenka Narkosituatsii v Srede Detey, Podrostov i Molodeji*. (in Russian) http://www.narkotiki.ru/research_5663.html

European Monitoring Centre for Drugs and Drug Addiction (EMCDDA) (2002) *2002 Annual Report on the State of the Drugs Problem in the European Union and Norway*. Luxembourg: Office for Official Publications of the European Communities.

Goode, E. and Ben-Yehuda, N. (1994) *Moral Panics: The Social Construction of Deviance*. Oxford: Blackwell.

Gusfield, J. (1989) Constructing the ownership of social problems: fun and profit in the welfare state, *Social Problems*, 36: 431–41.

Hall, S., Critcher, C., Jefferson, T., Clarke J. and Roberts, B. (1978) *Policing the Crisis: Mugging, the State and Law and Order*. London: Macmillan.

Hall, S. and Jefferson, T. (eds) (1976) *Resistance Through Rituals: Youth Sub-cultures in Post-War Britain*. London: Hutchinson.

Hier, S. (2003) Risk and panic in late modernity: implications of converging sites of social anxiety, *British Journal of Sociology*, 54(1): 271–91.

Ibarra, P. and Kitsuse, J.L. (1993) Vernacular constituents of moral discourse: an interactionist proposal for the study of social problems, in J.A. Holstein and G. Miller (eds) *Reconsidering Social Constructionism: Debates in Social Problems Theory*. New York: Aldine de Gruyter.

Kepplinger, H.M. and Habermeier, J. (1995) The impact of key events upon the presentation of reality, *European Journal of Communication*, 10(3): 371–90.

Keselman, L. and Matskevich, M. (2001) *Socialnoe prostranstvo narkotisma* (in Russian). Saint Petersburg: Meditsinskaya Pressa.

Kosterina, I. (2002) Kriminal, skandali, reklama I propovedi: narkomaniya I nar-kotiki v prezentatsiyakh SMI, in E. Omelchenko (ed.) *Trinadzatiy Shag: Sociologiya Narkotizatsii* (in Russian). Ulianovsk: UlGU Publishing.

Looseke, D.R. (1993) Constructing conditions, people, morality, and emotion: expanding the agenda of constructionism, in G. Miller and J.A. Holstein (eds) *Constructionist Controversies: Issues in Social Problems Theory*. New York: Aldine de Gruyter.

Looseke, D.R. (2003) *Thinking About Social Problems*. New York: Aldine de Gruyter.

Reinarman, C. and Levine, H. (1995) The crack attack: America's latest drug scare, 1986–1992, in J. Best (ed.) *Images of Issues: Typifying Contemporary Social Problems*. New York: Aldine de Gruyter.

Rusakova, M. (2000) Narkotiki v Rossii, in Y. Gilinski (ed.) *Deviantnost I Socialniy Control v Rossii*. (in Russian). Saint Petersburg: Aleteya.

Smirnova, N. (2000) Panica ili Znanie? Konstruirovaniye problemi rosta potre-bleniya narkotikov sredi molodeji v mestnoy presse, in E. Omelchenko (ed.) *Geroinashegovremeni. Sociologicheskie Ocherki* (in Russian). Ulianovsk: Srednevoljskiy nauchniy center.

Substance Abuse and Mental Health Services Administration (SAMHSA), Office of Applied Studies (2000) *National Household Survey on Drug Abuse*, http://www.samhsa.gov/oas/oas.html

Thompson, K. (1998) *Moral Panics*. London: Routledge.

PART III

THEMES

Overview

Applying either or both moral panic models to series of case studies, as happened in Part II, will inevitably reveal themes recurrent in the context of quite different issues. There are many potential choices to be made here. In my earlier work (Critcher 2003), I identified the themes of comparative study, the role of the media and the salience of childhood. As I stressed in that work, the implications which emerge depend very much on the range of case studies examined. Since the case studies in this Reader are wider than in my earlier book, the common themes are more abstract. Four such themes were eventually selected, even though the articles exploring them do not necessarily use the term moral panic.

The first theme is the rhetoric of moral panics. In *Reading 14* Best's analysis of the missing children issue leads him to pay detailed attention to the rhetorical strategies used by claims makers. This provides a useful example of the centrality of language to moral panics. What the Americans call rhetoric is analogous to what the Europeans call discourse. Either way, the construction of a panic depends upon the establishment of particular ways of speaking about the issue. Best explains how key players set about this task. The other extracts do not directly use moral panic models or concepts. They have nevertheless been included because they provide access to problems which keep cropping up in moral panic analysis and deserve consideration in their own right.

Reading 15 by Williams and Dickinson does not mention moral panics by name but is about the highly salient theme of fear of crime. It sets out to investigate what is often assumed by moral panic analysis: how far frightening media messages actually make readers or viewers afraid. Both their methods and their findings would benefit from replication. *Reading 16* by Kepplinger and Habermeier is again not directed specifically at moral panics but does provide an influential account of a third central theme in them: the causes and consequences of 'key events' for the newsmaking process. Many moral panics have their key event, often a tragedy involving a recognizable victim. The authors explore how such an event comes to frame subsequent media coverage of the issue.

The final extract is of a different order altogether. It explores a fourth recurrent theme of moral panic analysis: why publics of various kinds seem predisposed to panic. The answer frequently given is that they are in a state of social anxiety, induced by rapid change in society as a whole or in their own circumstances. The focus of Altheide in *Reading 17* is on anxiety expressed as fear. He explores what he calls a discourse of fear which seems to have permeated American culture. Though as always we should be wary of generalizing from the exceptional case of the USA, fear and loathing do appear to be emotional mainsprings of any moral panic and we may need to do more to understand where they come from and how they are sustained. Having explained the logic behind the choice of themes and extracts, the rest of this introduction indicates the main thrust of each article.

In *Reading 14* Best (1990) approaches claims making as a rhetorical activity, using an established distinction between grounds, warrants and conclusions. The 'grounds' of the argument are the alleged facts about the issue: how it is defined, the cases used to exemplify it and the estimates of its prevalence. 'Warrants' are the constructed justifications for urgent action, often implicit so difficult to challenge. In the case of missing children, such warrants included some specific to the issue, such as the inherent value of children, their blamelessness as victims and the evils which would follow abduction. Other more generalized warrants stressed the inabilities of authorities to intervene, the desire to return to fundamental objectives and the need to override established rights to achieve the goal of protection. 'Conclusions' are the goals which grounds and warrants have been designed to support. Three typical goals are raising public awareness, advocating protective measures and extending strategies of social control. Thus rhetorical strategies are not merely tools for claims makers; they are fundamental to the whole enterprise.

Best's work interestingly returns us to some points originally made by Cohen but subsequently lost. For example, both talk about 'orientations', ways of interpreting a problem that privilege some interpretations and exclude others. The recognition that rhetorical practice structures what can be said about a problem is very close to the assumptions of discourse analysis. Language does not simply express the problem but actively constitutes it. The strategies Best describes are not confined to the missing children issues. The same warrants (labelling the problem, exemplary cases, statistical estimates), grounds (why the innocent suffer and the guilty should be published) and aims (to raise awareness, advocate action and alter the balance of rights) are easily found in more recent issues, such as terrorism or asylum seekers/immigration. The formation of an effective discourse is absolutely central for claims makers. Each discourse is different but all moral panics have one. Less clear may be what is distinctive about moral panic discourses. Any campaigning group on any issue, for example, environmentalism, might use very similar ploys. If there is something which renders moral panics discourses distinctive, it may be that they seek to mobilize fear. What on the surface may appear to be a rational argument is deep down viscerally emotional.

Reading 15 by Williams and Dickinson (1993) is an example of a comparatively rare effort in moral panic analysis: to trace how far media coverage, in this case readership of particular newspapers, has a discernible effect on how audiences view their social experience. A content analysis of a month's coverage in 10 national daily newspapers in the UK charted the number and type of violent, interpersonal crimes reported. A postal questionnaire to a representative sample of nearly 300 people in the south of Britain measured media exposure and fear of crime. Twenty of the survey respondents analysed the extent to which 50 stories could be judged as sensational and/or fearful.

As expected, tabloid newspapers reported more crime, concentrated unduly on personal violent crime and used photographs extensively. Readers recognized that exaggerated coverage might produce unjustified fear. The survey showed that knowledge of personal violent crime was very dependent on media sources. Fear of crime was higher amongst readers of downmarket compared with mid-market or up-market papers. This fear was reflected in such behaviour as willingness to venture out after dark. The findings are measured but clear-cut. While readers recognized that newspapers often sensationalized crime, such coverage nevertheless did affect their perceptions of the reality of the crime problem and thus sense of vulnerability. The more popular the newspaper, the more likely it is to produce a fearful response.

Personal violent crime is a regular theme of moral panics, with the recurrent motif that the streets are no longer safe. To ascertain if such rhetoric does affect public perceptions is important but rarely undertaken. More speculative ideas about the prevalence of fear in society here receive some empirical backing, with the popular press culpable of exploiting it. Whether intended or not, the habitual exaggeration and sensationalism of personal violent crime by newspapers may make readers more frightened than they should or need be. In a parallel American study, Chiricos et al. (1997) found middle-aged women to feel vulnerable as a result of television coverage of crime, which the researchers suggest is because television is more likely to cover crimes with women like them as the victims. The result both sides of the Atlantic is pressure for measures to be taken to allay fears produced by media coverage. This is one precondition for a moral panic.

It is common to find admissions that studies suffer from the lack of data about public reactions to media coverage, as in Welch et al.'s (2002) analysis of a panic about gang rapes in the New York press. Also frequent are exhortations to acknowledge that 'audiences must be seen and appreciated for their imaginative and active roles in moral panics' (de Young 1998: 275). Few studies manage this, one outstanding exception being the work of Kitzinger (2004) on British media coverage of child abuse and audience reactions to it, a model of methodological and conceptual clarity.

In *Reading 16*, Kepplinger and Habermeier (1995) examine the role of key events in triggering interest media interest in an issue. They analyse three examples taken from the German press in the mid-1980s: the death of Rock Hudson, a petrol tanker accident and an earthquake. The only one directly relevant to moral panics is Rock Hudson's death from AIDS which proved to be a turning point in the unfolding of that issue. The other two are disasters, one made by man and one by nature. But the underlying processes may well apply to the key events which so often seem central to moral panics.

Sometimes an event is of such magnitude that it is easy to see why it has immediate impact. But other events achieve prominence less because of their own characteristics than the sensitivities of the press at the moment of their occurrence. Key events are crucial because they focus the attention of key players: journalists and their readers, pressure groups and policy makers. The case studies largely validate the analysts' initial assumptions. The key event stimulates additional coverage of the topic or trend which the event is taken to embody. The bigger the key event, the more this will happen. The media scour past and present for more examples which are then reinterpreted as symptoms of the defined problem.

As Best points out, atrocity tales and typical cases are crucial to the rhetorical construction of a problem. Key events often furnish this; if there are none current, those from the past will do. Though Kepplinger and Habermeier do not use the phrase, agenda setting occurs as the media present key events and the underlying issue to the public, pressure groups, policy makers and politicians. The key event makes the problem visible to a wider audience and increases the pressure to ensure that this sort of thing does not happen again. All this, often telescoped in time, is quite typical of what happens in a moral panic. The framing of subsequent events in terms of the key event has been termed 'prototyping' by Brosius and Eps (1995) or 'media templates' by Kitzinger (2000). All trace how journalists are primed by a key event to find others resembling it which are then reported in ways which exaggerate the similarity.

Though not directly aimed at moral panics, Kepplinger and Habermeier's account of these processes remains the most influential to date and is invariably cited by those seeking to explain the effect of a key event on the course of a moral panic. Examples of such attempts include a negative case examined by Cromer (2004). He concluded that a murder in Israel by two teenage boys failed to become a key event because their middle-class backgrounds confused efforts to impose a single, unanimous interpretation. Soothill et al. (2004) tried to determine why some British murders attracted newspaper attention while others did not. Their symbolic meaning seemed crucial but could not be predicted from the characteristics of the victim or perpetrator. It was not clear why the media did or did not recognize a murder as symbolic.

Reading 17 by Altheide takes a much wider view of the factors which predispose media and their publics to panic. He argues that modern America is dominated by a discourse of fear, to be found not only in the news media but in the myths and fictions of popular culture as a whole. In a diverse and fragmented society, stable identities and common experiences become hard to find. What can be universally recognized is potential status as a victim. Such common status stimulates collective antagonism to those alien others who allegedly pose a threat. Altheide makes the comparison with religion explicit: no longer convinced by the Christian concepts of fear, damnation and salvation, we construct secular versions. We fear neither God nor the Devil but other humans who embody evil; we seek salvation not from the ministrations of the Church but from retribution by the state.

Altheide stresses that some foci for fear are recurrent, one being crime. But, as a pervasive state, fear can shift its orientation and expand its horizons. The feared other can be at one time a black mugger, at another an Islamic terrorist. To use Goode and Ben-Yehuda's (1994) terms, the target may alter but the content, of fear, remains constant.

Altheide's thesis, developed in the whole book from which the extract is taken and in various journal articles, is initially convincing and offers a coherent account of the collective psychological and cultural themes which are common to all moral panics, regardless of the topic of the moment. Yet there are difficulties. Can we convincingly identify motifs common to both fictional and factual media? Does the religious analogy imply that the experience of fear is a universal need? If the argument seems to insist that society as a whole has become more fearful, what evidence from the past and the present can be used to test out such an assumption?

Like the work of Glassner (1999) for the USA and Furedi (1997) for Britain, the persuasiveness of the thesis should not blind us to the remaining problems of theory and evidence. Hunt (1999), for example, casts a sceptical historian's eye over claims that some periods are more anxious or fearful than others; it is too easy to read evidence selectively or partially in order to support an overall thesis. Still, like the other extracts in this section, Altheide's work is provocative in the literal sense. As others respond, we may begin to get better insight into the recurrent themes of moral panics: claims makers' rhetoric, media audience reactions, symbolic events and a discourse of fear. One day we may fumble our way towards some understanding of how they all interrelate as the recurrent themes of moral panics, wherever and whenever they happen.

References

Brosius, H. and Eps, P. (1995) Prototyping through key events: news selection and the case of violence against aliens and asylum-seekers in Germany, *European Journal of Communication*, 10(3): 391–412.

Chiricos, T., Eschholz, S. and Gertz, M. (1997) Crime news and fear of crime: towards an identification of audience effects, *Social Problems*, 44(3): 342–57.

Critcher, C. (2003) *Moral Panics and the Media*. Milton Keynes: Open University Press.

Cromer, G. (2004) 'Children from good homes'; moral panics about middle-class delinquency, *British Journal of Criminology*, 44: 391–400.

Hunt, A. (1999) Anxiety and social explanation: some anxieties about anxiety, *Journal of Social History*, 32(3): 509–28.

Kitzinger, J. (2000) Media templates: patterns of association and the (re)construction of meaning over time, *Media, Culture and Society*, 22: 61–84.

Kitzinger, J. (2004) *Framing Abuse: Media Influence and Understanding of Sexual Violence Against Children*. London: Pluto Press.

Soothill, K., Peelo, M., Pearson, J. and Francis, B. (2004) The reporting trajectories of top homicide cases in the media: a case study of *The Times*, *The Howard Journal*, 43(1): 1–14.

Welch, M., Price, E.A. and Yankey, N. (2002) Moral panic over youth violence: wilding and the manufacture of menace in the media, *Youth and Society*, 34(2): 3–30.

Further Reading

Furedi, F. (1997) *Culture of Fear: Risk-taking and the Morality of Low Expectation.* London: Cassell.

Glassner, B. (1999) *The Culture of Fear: Why Americans Are Afraid of the Wrong Things.* New York: Basic Books.

Ibarra, P.R. and Kitsuse, J. (1993) Vernacular constituents of moral discourse: an interactionist proposal for the study of social problems, in J.A. Holstein and G. Miller (eds) *Reconsidering Social Constructionism.* New York: Aldine de Gruyter.

Lupton, D. (1999) *Risk.* London: Routledge.

Miller D., Kitzinger, J., Williams, K. and Beharrell, P. (1998) *The Circuit of Mass Communication: Media Strategies, Representation and Audience Reception in the AIDS Crisis.* London: Sage.

Mills, S. (1997) *Discourse.* London: Routledge.

14

RHETORIC IN CLAIMS ABOUT MISSING CHILDREN

Joel Best (1990)

By the mid-1980s, the missing-children problem had achieved extraordinary visibility. Americans saw photographs of missing children on milk cartons and grocery bags, billboards and televised public service messages. Toy stores and fast-food restaurants distributed abduction-prevention tips for both parents and children. Parents could have their children fingerprinted or videotaped to make identification easier; some dentists even proposed attaching identification disks to children's teeth. ... In short, ordinary citizens may have encountered explicit reminders of missing children more often than reminders of any other social problem.

This problem achieved prominence quickly; the term 'missing children' seems to have been coined in 1981. The term encompassed three familiar phenomena: runaways (children – most often adolescents – who chose to leave home and usually returned within a few days); child snatchings (noncustodial parents who illegally took their own children without the custodial parent's permission); and abductions by strangers (who might keep, sell, ransom, molest, or kill the child).

Between 1979 and 1981, several cases in which children presumably were abducted by strangers received national publicity. These included the 1979 revelations that John Wayne Gacy had murdered thirty-three youths, the 1979–81 series of twenty-eight murders of Atlanta youths, the 1981 murder of Adam Walsh (age six, who disappeared from a shopping mall and whose severed head was later recovered), the 1979 disappearance of Etan Patz (age six, who left for school one morning and was not seen again), and the 1980 return of Steven Stayner (age fourteen, who had lived with his kidnapper for seven years).

Assisting in some of these cases were existing child-search organizations, such as Child Find, which had been established primarily to help locate children taken during custody disputes. By 1981, child snatching had received a good deal of attention, but the response of the press, law enforcement, and the general public was ambiguous. Magazine articles and television programs sometimes portrayed the kidnapping parent favorably. ... Federal legislation – the 1980 Parental Kidnapping Prevention Act – had little effect, because the Justice Department refused to pursue cases without evidence that the child was in danger of abuse or neglect. ... Moreover, public opinion remained split; only 64 percent of the respondents to a 1981 CBS/*New York Times* poll fully agreed that federal kidnapping laws should apply to child snatching.

Organizations like Child Find clearly found it advantageous to link their cause to the widespread sympathy for parents whose children were abducted by strangers. The label 'missing children' made this link possible. The U.S. Senate held its first hearing on missing children in October 1981. Magazine and newspaper articles began to appear. On October 10, 1983, NBC broadcast 'Adam,' a docudrama about Adam Walsh that ended with a roll call of fifty-five missing children. The National Center for Missing and Exploited Children – funded by a federal grant – opened in 1984. By the year's end, pictures of missing children were being printed on milk cartons, shopping bags, and other paper products. The concept of missing children had become common currency.

Rhetoric and Claims-Making

Because constructionist interpretations usually emphasize the importance of social organization, most researchers pay far more attention to the process of claims-making and the people who make claims than to the claims themselves. This is intentional. Spector and Kitsuse (1977) acknowledge that claims may be grounded in values, but they warn against trying to explain claims-making by simply specifying claimants' values and motives. Instead, they argue that 'values are one of the resources members use in their efforts to define conditions as social problems' (1977: 96). However, they do not explore systematically how values become incorporated into claims. Similarly, most constructionist case studies seem to treat claims as a given.

Claims have received some critical examination (Aronson 1984; Gusfield 1981). In particular, Gusfield insists that scientific evidence used to support claims about the drinking-driving problem must not be viewed simply as objective evidence but should be seen in terms of rhetoric – part of the claims-makers' efforts to persuade. This chapter extends Gusfield's argument; it applies rhetorical analysis to claims made in the construction of the missing-children problem, then attempts to assess the broader role of rhetoric in social problems construction.

Claims-makers inevitably hope to persuade. Typically, they want to convince others that X is a problem, that Y offers a solution to that problem, or that a policy of Z should be adopted to bring that solution to bear. While the success of claims-making may well depend in part on the constellation of interests and resources held by various constituencies in the process, the way claims are articulated also affects whether they persuade and move the audiences to which they are addressed. Claims-making, then, is a rhetorical activity. Rhetoric – the study of persuasion – can be used to analyze claims.

In *The Uses of Argument*, Stephen Toulmin (1958) examined the structure of arguments. He began by drawing a distinction 'between the *claim* or conclusion whose merits we are seeking to establish (C) and the facts we appeal to as a foundation for the claim – what I shall refer to as our *data* (D)' (Toulmin 1958: 97 emphasis in original). The link between *D* and *C* can only be established by reference to a third kind of proposition – what he called warrants (W), 'which can act as bridges, and authorise the sort of step to which our particular argument commits us' (Toulmin 1958: 98). Thus Toulmin suggested that every argument has a basic structure:

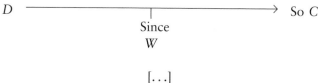

$$D \xrightarrow{\hspace{5cm}} \text{So } C$$
$$\text{Since}$$
$$W$$

[...]

Recent versions incorporate additional, minor types of statements and substitute the term 'grounds' for 'data.' Toulmin's principal categories of statements – grounds, warrants, and conclusions – can be used to analyze the rhetoric of the missing-children campaign. While these claims refer specifically to the missing-children problem, their rhetorical structure parallels claims-making for many social problems.

Grounds

In any argument, statements about grounds provide the basic facts that serve as the foundation for the discussion that follows. Obviously, facts are themselves socially constructed knowledge. Claims-makers and their audiences may agree to accept grounds statements without question, or one or both parties may have reservations about the statements' truth, their relevance, the methods used to establish them, and so on. Although the specific facts at issue depend upon the particular claims being made, some types of grounds statements recur in many claims-making campaigns. Three types of grounds statements consistently appeared in claims-making about missing children: definitions, typifying examples, and numeric estimates.

Definitions

Perhaps the most fundamental form of claims-making is to define a problem, to give it a name. Identifying the topic under discussion limits what can be said; a definition makes some issues relevant, while relegating others out of bounds (Gusfield 1981; Lake 1986). Definitions can both establish a topic's domain and offer an orientation toward that topic.

Domain Statements

A definition identifies a phenomenon, setting its boundaries or domain. Someone who understands a definition can examine phenomena and determine which do and which do not fall within the defined category's domain.

Domain statements are particularly important when claimants hope to call attention to a previously unacknowledged social problem. Following Pfohl (1977), we might speak of discovery movements – claims-makers who announce that they have discovered a new problem. They may argue that the problem is in fact new (e.g., modern technology is destroying the ozone layer), or they may describe the problem as something that presumably has existed for some time but has only now been recognized for what it is (e.g., child abuse). In either case, such domain statements have the power of novelty; they attract interest because they claim to identify a new phenomenon.

Claims-making about missing children involved the creation of a new domain. In this case, there were few efforts to offer precise, technical definitions; claims-makers usually did not specify the age at which one stops being a child, or the length of time a child must be gone to be considered missing. The term was intended to be broad, inclusive, to encompass several misadventures that might befall children. . . .

Most claims-makers preferred an inclusive definition of missing children. Some child-search organizations distributed photos of missing individuals who were in their twenties. Other crusaders argued that children who returned home after even a brief disappearance should be considered missing children. . . .

Orientation Statements
Typically, claims-makers' definitions give an orientation to the problem. That is, in addition to specifying a problem's domain, there is some assessment of the sort of problem it is. . . . Definitions, then, guide the way we interpret the problem, suggesting appropriate avenues for response.

Claims-making about missing children emphasized that 'missing' meant endangered, that even runaways and children taken in child snatchings faced terrible risks:

> Once they are on the street they are fair game for child molestation, prostitution, and other exploitation. To label them 'runaways' and disregard their safety is to suggest our own lack of compassion and real understanding for this difficult problem. (Senator Hawkins in U.S. Senate 1981: 2).

> Parental child abuse is a fact. Parents hurt, and kill, their children every day. . . . We must assume that a parent who breaks civil laws [by child snatching] will break the laws of responsible parenting. (Kristin C. Brown in U.S. Senate 1981: 76)

This theme of potential violence and exploitation received support by coupling definitions to horrific examples of missing children.

Typifying examples

Although definition might seem to be the logical first step in claims-making, it frequently follows an introductory example. Newspaper and magazine articles that called attention to the missing-children problem routinely began with one or more atrocity tales. Similarly, the initial U.S. Senate (1981) hearings on the problem began with the parents of Etan Patz, Adam Walsh, and Yusuf Bell (age nine, one of the murdered Atlanta school-children) describing their children's disappearance.

Opening with an emotionally riveting 'grabber' is a standard journalistic technique (Johnson 1989). By focusing on events in the lives of specific individuals, these stories make it easier to identify with the people affected by the problem. Horrific examples give a sense of the problem's frightening, harmful dimensions.

In addition to these obvious effects, atrocity tales perform another, less visible function. The atrocity – usually selected for its extreme nature –

typifies the issue; it becomes the referent for discussions of the problem in general. Crusaders routinely used stranger-abductions – which they acknowledged to be the least common cause of missing children – as referents. Between 1981 and 1985, congressional hearings featured testimony by parents of eleven missing children; eight of these children had been abducted by strangers. . . .

Estimating the problem's extent

Once examples establish a problem's human dimensions, claims-makers often try to assess its magnitude. The bigger the problem, the more attention it can be said to merit, so most claimants emphasize a problem's size. For missing-children crusaders, these estimates took three forms.

Incidence Estimates

Perhaps the most straightforward way to establish a social problem's dimensions is to estimate the number of cases, incidents, or people affected. Claims-makers argue that a widespread problem demands attention. Thus claims-making about the missing-children problem relied heavily on estimates of the number of children affected. These were necessarily inexact. Missing children need not come to official attention. Moreover, the various official agencies that might learn about missing children had no standard set of criteria for defining cases. Some police departments, for instance, required that twenty-four or seventy-two hours pass before a child could be deemed missing. And even if local agencies kept records, there was no national clearinghouse to compile statistics.

One commonly cited figure was 1.8 million cases per year – a total that included runaways (which claims-makers acknowledged constituted the vast majority of all cases), abductions by noncustodial parents (frequently estimated at one hundred thousand annually), and abductions by strangers. The latter category received most of the attention, although estimates generally declined over time.

Frequently these estimates were buttressed by claims about the number of missing children found murdered: 'There are about 4,000–8,000 of these children each year who are found dead and probably a majority have experienced some type of sexual exploitation' (Representative Simon in U.S. House 1981: 11).

Although the initial claims-making about the missing-children problem did distinguish among runaways, custodial kidnappings, and stranger-kidnappings, those who repeated the claims often lost sight of these distinctions. Thus a pamphlet, 'To Save a Child,' distributed by a Chicago television station, began: 'Nearly 2,000,000 children in this country disappear from their homes each year. Many end up raped, forced into prostitution and pronography. Many are never heard from again.' By including runaways to estimate the number of missing children and then focusing attention on atrocity tales about stranger-abduction, claims-makers led many people to infer that the most serious cases were commonplace. Public opinion surveys found that many people assumed stranger-abductions were common, accounting for a large share of missing children (Field Institute 1987; Fritz and Altheide 1987; Miller 1985).

During 1985, the larger estimates of the number of missing children came under attack. Led by the *Denver Post* (which earned a Pulitzer Prize for its coverage of the issue), the press used FBI and other criminal justice statistics to challenge the estimates' accuracy. ... The articles emphasized that stranger-kidnappings accounted for a very small proportion of missing children. These counterclaims were newsworthy, in part, because the originally acknowledged distinction among types of missing children had become lost in later claims-making.

Growth Estimates

A second claim that may be made about a social problem's dimensions is that things are getting worse – the problem is growing and, unless action is taken, there will be further deterioration. ... Claimants often describe problems as epidemic – a metaphor that suggests more people will be affected as the problem spreads (see U.S. Senate 1983a, 74).

Range Claims

The epidemic metaphor also suggests that people may be indiscriminately affected, that the problem extends throughout the social structure. Often, this claim is explicit: '[Missing] children come from small towns in rural America, and from our largest cities. They are from all races and ethnic backgrounds. They grow up in upper class neighborhoods, in the suburbs, and in the inner cities' (Senator Howard Metzenbaum in U.S. House 1985b, 9).

Claims that a social problem's range extends throughout society serve an important rhetorical function. By arguing that anyone might be affected by a problem, a claims-maker can make everyone in the audience feel that he or she has a vested interest in the problem's solution.

Warrants

Warrants have a special place in Toulmin's scheme; they are statements that justify drawing conclusions from the grounds. Disputes about grounds (e.g., whether stranger-abductions annually number in the hundreds or the tens of thousands) need not damage conclusions. A claims-maker might argue, for instance, that even a single child abducted by a stranger is one too many, and that, therefore, something must be done. But concluding that something must be done demands that one accept some warrant that the problem deserves attention:

> Unless, in any particular field of argument, we are prepared to work with warrants of *some* kind, it will become impossible in that field to subject arguments to rational assessment. The data we cite if a claim is challenged depend on the warrants we are prepared to operate with in that field, and the warrants to which we commit ourselves are implicit in the particular steps from data to claims we are prepared to take and to admit (Toulmin 1958: 100 – emphasis in original)

This passage refers to two important issues. First, it notes that there are fields of argument. Toulmin (1958: 14) originally defined fields in terms of types of arguments: geometric proofs, legal reasoning, and so on. More recent analyses ... suggest that fields must be understood sociologically; within specific social units (e.g., a dyad, an academic discipline), members hold particular lines of reasoning to be valid. Thus, for an argument to be persuasive, the individual to be persuaded must ordinarily belong to a field that deems the warrant valid.

The second point to which Toulmin alludes is that warrants often are implicit. Although an argument may advance in a thoroughly public fashion, with each step available for inspection, there are good reasons to gloss over warrants. It is in the warrant that values most often come into play. While it is relatively easy to debate the merits of grounds statements, it is more difficult to defend a warrant that one's audience refuses to validate. An implicit warrant may circumvent the discovery that the audience belongs to a different argument field.

Because references to warrants may be oblique or implicit, any list is necessarily selective. The following discussion considers six warrants that figured prominently in claims-making about missing children. While each warrant was tailored to some degree for discussions of missing children, each also represents a more general type of justification found in claims-making about various social problems.

The value of children

Zelizer (1985) argues that children have become defined as economically worthless but sentimentally priceless. Missing-children claims-makers often referred to the extraordinarily high sentimental value of children. Kenneth Wooden charged that priceless children

> are being treated like garbage. Raped and killed, their young bodies are discarded in plastic bags, on trash trucks, and left on dumps. ... Like litter, they are thrown into lakes, rivers, and streams – the tender drift wood of life. Some are found on roadsides like empty soda and beer cans, ... or cast aside like broken furniture in dirty, empty houses or stripped, abandoned cars in wooded or swamp areas. ... Poor little wilted flowers, plucked from the vases of home and safety of parents, are, in large part, left unburied and alone in the openness of fields – and now the closed minds of our thoughts (U.S. House 1984, 55).

Claimants argued that children were 'our most valuable resource' (U.S. House 1985b: 1), 'the leading endangered species of today' (U.S. Senate 1985b: 31), deserving 'the highest of all priorities' (U.S. House 1981: 124): 'One missing child is certainly too many. And one missing child should be the concern of the Government' (U.S. House 1985a: 8).

Claims-makers contrasted law enforcement's reluctance to respond when priceless children were reported missing with its reaction to reports of stolen property....

Because children were deemed priceless, the terrible uncertainty felt by parents of missing children became a prominent warrant. Parents' first-person testimony, as well as many journalistic accounts, focused on the parents' extraordinary sense of loss. The readiness with which crusaders referred to the value of children indicates that this warrant was uncontroversial – literally a motherhood issue.

Blameless victims

In addition to emphasizing the devastation felt by parents, claimants focused on the horrors experienced by missing children. John Walsh testified: 'Right now at this very moment there are little children out there in the hands of whatever, crying, pleading and are begging that mommy and daddy or Mr. Policeman or some one [sic] come to their aid or look for them to save them' (U.S. Senate 1981: 30). The understanding that children are powerless innocents, coupled with a definition of all missing children as facing terrible risks, presented a strong warrant.

Claims-makers described children as blameless, as well as priceless. Even runaways, who might be considered responsible for their situation, were not to be blamed: 'Many are running from abuse, both physical and sexual, or from intolerable home lives' (Senator Hawkins in U.S. Senate 1981: 2). Similarly, references to so-called throwaways – children who had been expelled from their homes – dealt only with the failings of the caretakers who rejected the children, never with the children's behavior.

Blameless victims offer rhetorical advantages to claims-makers. Public opinion and official policy often distinguish between 'innocent' victims and those who are thought to share some complicity for their fate. Christie (1986) argues that the 'ideal victim' – the one most likely to elicit sympathy – is weak, engaged in a respectable activity, and overcome by a more powerful stranger. Victims who do not fit this pattern may be stigmatized, rather than supported. ... Certainly, presenting victims as blameless makes it more likely that claims will be ratified.

Associated evils

Claims-makers argued that missing children often were stolen by or later became prey to child abusers, sex offenders, pimps, pornographers, drug dealers, organized criminals, and Satanists....

Charges implicating deviants or popular culture in the missing-children problem suggest possible alliances between the claims-makers and those concerned with other problems. But the choice of associated evils was selective. Claims-makers devoted remarkably little attention to exploring the causes of the missing-children problem. And when causes were mentioned, they usually involved individual pathology: runaways sought to escape abusive parents; child snatchers were motivated by hatred. Crusaders made little effort to locate causes in complex social conditions, preferring to assign responsibility to criminal or perverted individuals.

Deficient policies

Claims-makers insisted that existing policies and resources could not handle the missing-children problem. Assuming that most missing children were runaways who would return on their own, many local police departments delayed investigating until a child had been missing a day or more. But claims-makers warned that waiting even a few hours made it more difficult to locate a missing child who did not return, especially in cases of abduction....

Typically, claims-makers explained that local and federal law enforcement agencies delayed entering missing-children cases because most children returned without official intervention. But atrocity tales demonstrated that some reports involved serious crimes. The crusaders, then, sought to change official priorities, to have law enforcement respond to every missing-child report.

Claims-makers also attacked current policies toward runaways. They criticized the 'self-proclaimed "child advocates"' who had fought for the 1974 Juvenile Justice and Delinquency Prevention Act which 'labeled runaway children ... as "status offenders," and required them to be "deinstitutionalized," and not controlled, treated, or protected' (U.S. Attorney General 1986: 2). Because police no longer held runaways, parents might not be informed when their children were located. Claims-makers argued that the JJDP Act needed modification, so that officials could take runaways into custody. Insisting that current policies and resources could not locate all missing children, claimants presented a warrant for change.

Historical continuity

Claims-makers often expressed surprise at the FBI's failure to pursue reports of stranger-abductions. The bureau, they argued 'was primarily created to assist in the war on kidnaping' (John Walsh in U.S. Senate 1981, 56). Greater federal involvement in missing-children investigations, then, would be consistent with the history of federal law enforcement. Similarly, passing one federal law related to missing children provided a warrant for advocates of additional bills; relying solely on the original 'Missing Children's Act would be like treating major surgery with Band-Aids' (U.S. Senate 1984: 98).

Using historical continuity to justify future actions is usually a conservative warrant. Emphasizing consistency with past policies – or with founders' intent – may be especially useful when claimants address bureaucracies or institutions. Other crusaders adopt a very different approach, arguing that a problem calls for a revolutionary break from the past. Such a claim seems most likely to persuade those with little invested in past policies.

Rights and freedoms

In the United States, claims-making about government policy commonly involves warrants about rights and freedoms. Debates about abortion and illicit drugs feature detailed analyses of constitutional issues. In contrast, references to rights and freedoms served as little more than a touchstone for missing-children claims-makers; when they did raise the issue, it was to endorse the rights of victims. John Walsh testified: 'A country that can launch a space shuttle ... but does not have a centralized reporting system or a nationwide search system for missing children, certainly need [*sic*] to reaffirm the very principles that this country was founded on, namely, *personal freedoms*' (U.S. Senate 1981: 25 – emphasis in original). In later testimony, Walsh responded to concerns that centralized records systems threatened personal freedoms:

> Well, believe me, the women who are murdered by these people and the children, their privacy is invaded to the maximum. I think people have had it, I think that personal freedom now relates to the possibility and the ability to have personal freedom from crime and to be not afraid to go shopping or a woman to leave an office to go to her car in a parking lot. (U.S. Senate 1983b: 28)

Similarly, the Dee Scofield Awareness Program argued: 'Once it is determined that the slightest possibility of foul play exists, a child's constitutional rights are violated if that child is not considered a victim until it can be proven otherwise' (U.S. Senate 1981: 196). In short, missing-children claims-makers spoke of freedom from abduction and exploitation, of rights to protection by the authorities.

Conclusions

Like other forms of argument, claims-making presents conclusions – typically calls for action to alleviate or eradicate the social problem. Claims-makers may have an agenda with several goals. In the case of the missing-children problem, claims-makers hoped to affect the general public – in particular, parents – as well as official policy.

Awareness

Initially, missing-children crusaders sought to bring the problem to public attention. Their goal was not merely greater public awareness; they hoped to enlist the public in searching for children. Originally these efforts reached relatively few people. Reporters who covered the story were urged to accompany their articles with photos of missing children, while Child Find and other child-search organizations distributed directories filled with pictures of missing children. With the 1983 broadcast of 'Adam,' the problem became well established; commercial and government agencies began printing billions of images on milk cartons, utility bills, and so on. These efforts had some success; the advertising campaigns were credited with locating some children, and polls showed considerable public awareness of the missing-children problem (Field Institute 1987; Miller 1985).

Prevention

Claims-makers also emphasized the importance of prevention. They urged parents to assemble files of recent photographs, fingerprints, and other material that could be used by investigators if a child disappeared. Pamphlets gave lists of safety tips – ways to protect children from abduction – and parents could choose among many new books and videotapes designed to teach children to protect themselves.

Typifying the problem with atrocity tales about stranger-abductions shaped the construction of these preventive measures. Typically, both the safety tips and the materials intended for children focused on warnings about strangers. Prevention campaigns had such titles as 'Too Smart for Strangers' and 'Strangers and Dangers,' while one standard tip warned that having a child's name on clothing might let a stranger approach and call the child by name. However useful such advice might be in preventing stranger-abductions, it had limited relevance for child snatchings and runaways.

Social control policies

Dissatisfied with official efforts to locate missing children, claimants demanded new social control policies. The 1982 federal Missing Children's Act insured that parents could list a missing child with the National Crime Information Center's computers; if a local police department refused to enter the child's name, federal agents were required to do so. Claims-makers also campaigned for state laws to require police to begin searching immediately upon receiving a report of a missing child and to list all reported children with NCIC. ... Other recommended policies included requiring schools to notify parents whenever children were absent and to transfer school records and birth certificates whenever children changed school districts, modifying FBI practices so that all reported stranger-abductions would lead to federal investigations, and giving police greater authority to apprehend and hold runaways.

Two themes united these recommendations. First, believing that the thousands of local law enforcement agencies made it harder to coordinate searches, claims-makers sought to centralize police power....

Second, crusaders argued that children and adolescents should be subject to greater social control. The U.S. Attorney General's Advisory Board on Missing Children blamed the 1974 JJDP Act for limiting police powers to hold runaways and rejecting 'the historic notion that children have a right to be in the custody of their parents or legal guardians' (1986, 2). The Board recommended amending the act.…

Other objectives

In addition to advancing ways to prevent abductions and recover missing children, claims-makers promoted several other causes. Because everyone agreed that statistics on the number of missing children were little more than guesses, claims-makers sought a federal study to count missing children. … In fact, crusaders used missing children as a peg in attacking a wide range of evils. The U.S. Attorney General's Advisory Board on Missing Children's (1986: 22–30) recommendations included prosecuting the 'adult offender who abuses children, leads them into prostitution, victimizes them by pedophilic conduct or pornography, or pushes them into street crime'; extending the statute of limitations for 'child sexual abuse crimes'; 'careful screening of people who work with children'; and studying the relationship between popular culture and child exploitation. In these cases, 'missing children' apparently served as a rubric for addressing a range of other threats to children.

Rhetoric in Social Problems Construction

The example of the missing-children problem suggests that rhetoric plays a central role in claims-making about social problems. Atrocity tales typified the missing children problem; case histories of stranger-abduction, coupled with estimates that there were two million missing children per year, convinced many people that the problem could not be ignored. People responded empathically to the horrors experienced by parents and children. The claimants' warrants – the emphasis on the priceless, blameless nature of children, the association of missing children with other evils (especially exploitative sexual deviance), and the assertion that existing policies and resources could not cope with the problem – drew much of their power from the examples of atrocities. The campaign's conclusions about the need for increased public awareness, prevention, and social control also followed from the perception that atrocities were in some sense representative. Kidnapping, mutilation, and murder had few defenders; presented this way, the missing-children problem was uncontroversial.

Nor is the missing-children problem atypical. Claims-makers routinely use examples or case histories to typify social problems. ... Such images become a convenient shorthand for describing complex social conditions. By characterizing a problem in terms of an individual's experiences, the claims-maker helps the audience imagine how they might respond under the same circumstances. The portrait may invite sympathy and understanding, or it may encourage the audience to feel that they would never succumb to the same pressures or temptations; in either case, the problem becomes less abstract, the claims easier to comprehend.

If grounding claims in examples is commonplace, finding convincting warrants is essential. Warrants bridge the gap between grounds and conclusions. An audience might accept a claimant's version of a problem without adopting the recommended policies. Warrants, through references to values and interests, justify solutions. Viable claims (Schneider 1985) have compelling warrants.

Rhetoric is central, not peripheral, to claims-making. Claims-makers intend to persuade, and they try to make their claims as persuasive as possible. Claims-making inevitably involves selecting from available arguments, placing the arguments chosen in some sequence, and giving some arguments particular emphasis. These are rhetorical decisions. Moreover, as claims-makers assess the response to their claims, or as they address new audiences, claims may be revised and reconstructed in hopes of making them more effective. In such cases, even the most ingenuous claims-maker must become conscious of doing rhetorical work.

References

Aronson, N. (1984) Science as a claims-making activity, in J. W. Scheider and J. I. Kitsuse (eds) *Studies of the Sociology of Social Problems*. Norwood, NJ: Ablex.

Christie, N. (1986) The ideal victim, in E. A. Fattah (ed.) *From Crime Policy to Victim Policy*. London: Macmillan.

Field Institute (1987) Threats to children, *California Opinion Index 2*, March: 1–4.

Fritz, N.J. and Altheide, D. (1987) The mass media and the social construction of the missing children problem, *Sociological Quarterly*, 28: 473–92.

Gusfield, J.R. (1981) *The Culture of Public Problems: Drinking-Driving and the Symbolic Order*. Chicago: University of Chicago Press.

Johnson, J.M. (1989) Horror stories and the construction of child abuse, in J. Best (ed.) *Images of Issues*. New York: Aldine de Gruyter.

Lake, R.A. (1986) The metaethical framework of anti-abortion rhetoric, *Signs*, 11: 478–99.

Miller, C. (1985) Child-abduction worries excessive, area poll finds, *Denver Post*, 13 May: 1A.

Pfohl, S.J. (1977) The discovery of child abuse, *Social Problems*, 24: 310–23.

Schneider, J.W. (1985) Social problems theory: the constructionist view, *Annual Review of Sociology*, 11: 209–29.

Spector, M. and Kitsuse, J.I. (1977) *Constructing Social Problems*. Menlo Park, CA: Cummings.

Toulmin, S.E. (1958) *The Uses of Argument*. Cambridge: Cambridge University Press.

U.S. Attorney General's Advisory Board on Missing Children (1986) *America's Missing and Exploited Children*. Washington, DC: Office of Juvenile Justice and Delinquency Prevention.

U.S. House of Representatives (1981) *Implementation of the Parental Kidnapping Prevention Act of 1980*. Hearings held by the Subcommittee on Crime, Committee on the Judiciary. 97th Cong., 1st sess., 24 September.

U.S. House of Representatives (1984) *Title IV, Missing Children's Assistance Act*. Hearings held by the Subcommittee on Human Resources, Committee on Education and Labor. 98th Cong., 2nd sess., 9 April.

U.S. House of Representatives (1985a) *Oversight Hearing on the Missing Children's Assistance Act*. Hearings held by the Subcommittee on Human Resources, Committee on Education and Labor. 99th Cong., 1st sess., 21 May.

U.S. House of Representatives (1985b) *Photograph and Biography of Missing Child*. Hearings held by the Subcommittee on Postal Personnel and Modernization, Committee on Post Office and Civil Service. 99th Cong., 1st sess., 25 June.

U.S. Senate (1981) *Missing Children*. Hearings held by the Subcommittee on Investigations and General Oversight, Committee on Labor and Human Resources. 97th Cong., 1st sess., 6 October.

U.S. Senate (1983a) *Child Kidnapping*. Hearings held by the Subcommittee on Juvenile Justice, Committee on the Judiciary. 98th Cong., 1st sess., 2 February.

U.S. Senate (1983b) *Serial Murder*. Hearings held by the Subcommittee on Juvenile Justice, Committee on the Judiciary. 98th Cong., 1st sess., 12 July.

U.S. Senate (1984) *Missing Children's Assistance Act*. Hearings held by the Subcommittee on Juvenile Justice, Committee on the Judiciary. 98th Cong., 2nd sess., 7, 21, February; 8, 13, 21 March.

Zelizer, V.A. (1985) *Pricing the Priceless Child*. New York: Basic Books.

15

FEAR OF CRIME:

READ ALL ABOUT IT? THE RELATIONSHIP BETWEEN NEWSPAPER CRIME REPORTING AND FEAR OF CRIME

Paul Williams and Julie Dickinson (1993)

Fear of crime (FOC) has been identified as a problem in its own right. ... Moore and Trojanowicz (1988) argue that reasonable fears concerning crime can be harnessed to fight the threat of crime, but when these fears become unreasonable they amount to a counterproductive response and become a social problem.

Research has highlighted many sources of fear of crime, such as being a victim, environmental characteristics (e.g. living in a high crime rate area), and physical vulnerability ... but most people have been neither a victim nor a witness of crime. This suggests that the perception that individuals have of the 'crime problem' must be due largely to indirect sources. The purpose of this paper is to examine the links between FOC and one of those sources – newspapers.

Crime and the News

Crime reporting in the news media has been a focus of concern because of the assumption that the salience given to certain types of crime, notably those involving sex or violence, creates a distorted picture of reality which is reflected in the beliefs of news consumers. ... News is clearly vulnerable to distortion, for everyday events cannot simply be mirrored by news-papers. There are so many events that could be reported that journalists must be selective and it is this process of selection which is the first stage of 'creating news' (Tuchman 1978). Lester has argued that selection is determined by a 'template ... [of] ... official and unofficial values, norms and beliefs' (1980: 5), including beliefs about commercial viability (cf. Humphries 1981). Fishman (1978), for example, described how a 'crime wave' against the elderly of New York was 'created' by reporters who began to search for and highlight more cases of attacks on the elderly. . . .

The frame context in which the news is presented (e.g. reporting style, page format) can vary from one newspaper to another to such an extent that Quinney (1970) has suggested that an individual's conception of crime may depend upon the newspaper he or she reads. This relationship will be investigated in this study. However, it is important to note than the relationship between news reporting and public opinion is not necessarily that of a biased press shaping unresisting wills (cf. Smith 1984). The consumer is also actively involved in investing news with meaning and may, for example, choose which newspaper to buy on the basis of how accurate and truthful he or she believes the reporting to be.

[. . .]

The first part of the research project involved a detailed quantitative content analysis of the major national daily newspapers of Britain. Measurements of frequencies and areas of crime reports were taken to show how different newspapers vary in the attention they devote to crime, and highlighted particularly the disproportionate predominance given to personal violence crimes (PVCs). . . .

A questionnaire survey was then carried out to determine whether readers of newspapers which give more attention to crime (particularly PVC) and report it in a more salient way, rated higher on cognitive, affective, and behavioural measures of FOC. . . . A qualitative analysis was also undertaken to assess how *frightening* and *sensationalized* the reporting styles appeared.

The overall hypothesis was that readers of newspapers containing more salient crime reports would have greater FOC.

Stage 1: Quantitative Content Analysis

Every copy of the ten most popular British national daily newspapers *The Times, The Guardian, The Independent, The Daily Telegraph* (broadsheets); *Daily Express, Daily Mail, Today* (mid-market tabloids); *Daily Mirror, The Sun, Daily Star* (low-market tabloids) published during a four-week period commencing 19 June 1989 was subjected to a detailed quantitative content analysis to measure the following aspects of salience.

(a) proportion of each paper's newshole given over to crime,

(b) proportion of each paper's newshole given over to personal violence crimes (PVCs);
(c) proportion of crime news area given over to PVC reports;
(d) proportion of front page news area given over to PVC reports;
(e) salience of PVC reports on pages in general;
(f) salience of PVC reports on front pages;
(g) salience of PVC report headlines;
(h) number, size, and relative area of photographs accompanying PVC reports.

A quantitative measure of the salience of the PVC reports was created by comparing the proportionate page area devoted to PVC reports with the proportionate page area devoted to all other reports. . . .

Stage 2: Questionnaire Survey

Design

A questionnaire survey was carried out to measure the following variables:

(a) perceptions of risks to the population at large;
(b) anxiety about personal victimization and safety;
(c) avoidance strategies.

Age, sex, educational background, and socioeconomic status were also measured.

Subjects

Two hundred and ninety subjects completed the [postal] questionnaire. They were all from the Worthing/Littlehampton area of West Sussex, England. Sex ratios (160 female, 130 male), mean age (50.9 years), and a distinctive bimodal age distribution were all in keeping with the population sampled according to local census information.

[. . .]

Stage 3: Qualitative Analysis

Design

A qualitative analysis of PVC reports from each paper was conducted to measure two further independent variables: the fearfulness and the sensationalism of the reporting styles.

Subjects

Of 290 subjects who completed the questionnaire survey of FOC, 127 volunteered to take part in 'further research'. Twenty of these were selected to judge qualitative aspects of newspaper reporting styles....

Materials

Fifty PVC reports were randomly selected from the supply of newspapers used in the quantitative analysis. ... The headlines and opening sentences (to a maximum of eighty words) were transposed into the same typed format. Two short questions were placed under each report, requesting respondents to judge (on a 1–7 scale) the 'fearfulness' and 'sensationalism' of reporting style....

Procedure

Ten reports (one from each newspaper) were sent to each of the subjects, together with a letter explaining what was required of them – namely, the judging of the style of the reporting....

Results

Quantitative content analysis

(a) Proportion of newshole given to crime Table 15.1 shows the area of crime news calculated as a percentage of the total newshole for each newspaper. On average, 12.7 per cent of event-oriented news reports were about crime. Tabloids (particularly low-market ones) devoted most newshole space to crime.

(b) Proportion of newshole given to personal violence crime Overall, 8.2 per cent of event-oriented news stories reported PVCs. The percentages for each newspaper are shown in Table 15.2. Tabloid newspapers (particularly low-market ones) gave the highest priority to PVCs.

(c) PVC reports as proportion of crime news On average, newspapers devote 64.5 per cent (with little variation) of the space that they allocate to crime reporting to stories dealing with PVCs. This compares with official figures suggesting that only 6 per cent of crime involves personal violence (Mayhew 1989).

Table 15.1 Proportion of newspaper newsholes devoted to crime

Newspaper	Mean newshole area (cm²)	Mean crime area (cm²)	Crime area Newshole area (%)	Rank
Times	11,777	748	6.4	(3)
Independent	10,251	591	5.8	(2)
Guardian	10,583	543	5.1	(1)
Telegraph	10,392	942	9.1	(4)
Mail	5,286	1,024	19.4	(7)
Express	4,465	775	17.4	(6)
Today	5,725	803	14.0	(5)
Mirror	4,346	1,151	26.5	(8)
Sun	4,284	1,304	30.4	(10)
Star	4,015	1,129	28.1	(9)
			X = 12.7	

Table 15.2 Proportion of newspaper newsholes devoted to crimes involving personal violence

Newspaper	Mean newshole area (cm²)	Mean PVC area (cm²)	PVC area Newshole area (%)	Rank
Times	11,777	503	4.3	(3)
Independent	10,251	305	3.0	(1)
Guardian	10,583	348	3.3	(2)
Telegraph	10,392	627	6.0	(4)
Mail	5,286	733	13.9	(7)
Express	4,465	480	10.7	(6)
Today	5,725	489	8.5	(5)
Mirror	4,346	747	17.2	(8)
Sun	4,284	815	19.0	(9)
Star	4,015	768	19.1	(10)
			X = 8.2	

(d) Proportion of front-page news given to PVC The analysis showed that, on average, 13.9 per cent of front-page space is devoted to reporting PVCs....

(e) Salience of PVC news reports Table 15.3 shows the salience scores for each newspaper. Tabloids (particularly low-market ones) had the most

Table 15.3 Salience of PVC reports

Newspaper	Page area (cm²)	Area of each PVC report (cm²)	Area of each non-PVC report (cm²)	Salience scores	Rank
Times	1,924	112.8	147.5	−1.81	(2)
Independent	2,038	81.3	161.6	−3.94	(1)
Guardian	1,953	120.7	148.2	−1.41	(4)
Telegraph	1,957	91.2	124.1	−1.68	(3)
Mail	955	194.0	143.0	5.34	(5)
Express	913	240.0	149.9	9.87	(9)
Today	936	230.7	164.2	7.11	(7)
Mirror	978	197.0	94.0	10.53	(10)
Sun	917	144.8	83.9	6.64	(6)
Star	917	188.3	101.0	9.52	(8)

salient PVC reports. Lowmarket tabloid newspaper PVC reports were, on average, almost twice the size of non-PVC reports, whereas in broadsheets PVC reports are, on average, less than three-quarters of the size of non-PVC reports.

(f) Salience of PVC news reports on front pages The results were very similar to those in Table 15.3....

(g) [...]

(h) Number, size, and relative area of photographs accompanying PVC reports Details of the use of photographs (including sketches, diagrams, and maps) are shown in Table 15.4. Tabloids were more likely than broadsheets to accompany PVC stories with photographs.

Questionnaire survey

The responses to questions 3, 6, and 9 in the questionnaire provided information on a variable which has been related to FOC – personal or vicarious experience of crime itself. ... A total of 226 of the 290 respondents answered question 3 (they could give more than one answer). Twelve (4.1 per cent of all respondents) attributed their unease to personal experience of assault and thirty-one (10.7 per cent) to vicarious experience. Higher percentages of respondents attributed their fear of assault to television or radio coverage (41.4 per cent) and press coverage (39 per cent).

Table 15.4 Photographs accompanying PVC reports

Newspaper	Page area (cm²)	Mean no. of PVC photos	Rank	Mean area of PVC photos (cm²)	Area of PVS photos page area (%)	Rank
Times	1,924	0.79	(3)	103.67	5.39	(4)
Independent	2,038	0.42	(2)	100.48	4.93	(3)
Guardian	1,953	0.36	(1)	125.00	6.40	(5)
Telegraph	1,957	1.46	(4)	81.16	4.15	(1)
Mail	955	2.09	(6)	70.19	7.35	(7)
Express	913	2.38	(8)	40.84	4.47	(2)
Today	936	1.48	(5)	101.49	10.84	(10)
Mirror	970	2.54	(10)	75.83	7.75	(8)
Sun	917	2.33	(7)	66.22	7.22	(6)
Star	917	2.42	(9)	81.94	8.91	(9)

Note: 'Photographs' includes sketches, diagrams, and maps.

Question 6 was answered by 155 respondents. Fourteen (4.8 per cent of all respondents) attributed not feeling 'very safe' in their home at night to personal experience of burglary or assault and thirty-four (11.7 per cent) to vicarious experience. Again, higher percentages attributed their fear to television or radio (24.1 per cent) and press (23.8 per cent) coverage. The discrepancy in attributed source of FOC was more marked in the answers to question 9 of the sixty people who feared being assaulted when driving alone at night. None had personal experience of assault and only three (1 per cent of all respondents) had vicarious experience, while forty-five (15.5 per cent) had seen or heard of such assaults on the television or radio and forty-four (15.2 per cent) had read about them in the press. These results are in keeping with ... findings that the majority of people attribute their knowledge of the risk of crime to information in the mass media.

[...]

Newspaper readership pattern Table 15.5 shows the newspaper readership pattern for the survey respondents. The newspapers are grouped in terms of broadsheets (*Times, Guardian, Independent, Telegraph*), mid-market tabloids (*Express, Mail, Today*), and low-market tabloids (*Mirror, Sun, Star*).

The newspaper readership groups varied significantly in their assessment of victimization risks for the local population. Fig. 15.1 shows that the estimates for both PVCs and non-PVCs of low-market tabloid (LMT) readers were almost twice as high as those of mid-market tabloid (MMT) readers and three times as high as those broadsheet (BS) readers.

Personal worries expressed by respondents followed a similar pattern,

Table 15.5 Newspaper readership pattern for survey respondents

Newspaper 'always' or 'nearly always' read	No.
Broadsheet	49
Mid-market tabloid	80
Low-market tabloid	69
None	28
Others ('occasional' or multiple readers)	64
Total	290

Note: Broadsheet = *Times, Guardian, Independent, Daily Telegraph*; mid-market tabloid = *Daily Express, Daily Mail, Today*; low-market tabloid = *Daily Mirror, Sun, Daily Star*.

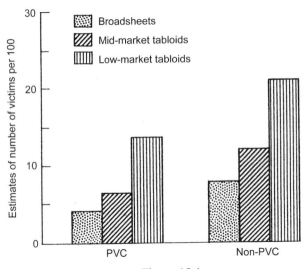

Figure 15.1

but this was significant only in relation to fear of assault, wounding, and car theft. Table 15.6 shows the mean level of worry about personal victimization expressed by the different newspaper readership groups.

The responses to the questions about personal safety when walking alone and in the home at night showed that broadsheet readers felt most safe and low-market tabloid readers least safe (see Figs 15.2 and 15.3) ... However, newspaper readership did not predict how often respondents went out after dark. Broadsheet readers had gone out, on average, 2.53 times in the previous week compared with 2.94 times for mid-market tabloid readers and 2.55 times for low-market tabloid readers.

[...]

Table 15.6 Readers' fears about being a victim of crime

| | Worry about personal victimization (on 1–7 scale) among readers of: | | | | |
	Broadsheet	Mid-market tabloid	Low-market tabloid	F	P
PVC					
Assault/ wounding	2.83	3.03	3.62	3.07 (2,187)	0.05
Sexual assault	2.56	3.25	3.60	2.43 (2,166)	ns
Robbery/ mugging	3.15	3.30	3.86	2.43 (2,187)	ns
Non-PVC					
Burglary	3.61	3.68	4.03	1.04 (2.188)	ns
Property damage	3.00	4.20	3.55	0.70 (2,187)	ns
Theft from car	2.81	3.15	3.91	4.76 (2,138)	0.01

Note: ns = not significant.

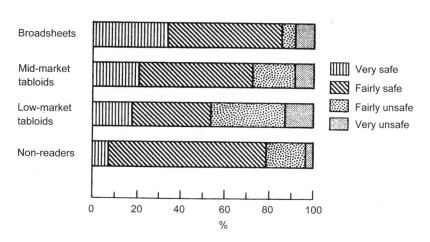

Figure 15.2

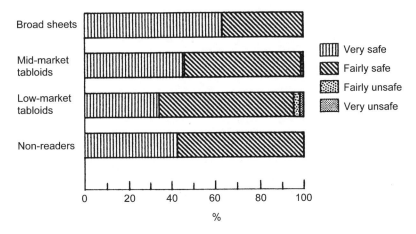

Broad sheets

Mid-market tabloids

Low-market tabloids

Non-readers

|||||| Very safe
▧ Fairly safe
▨ Fairly unsafe
▨ Very unsafe

0   20   40   60   80   100

%

Figure 15.3

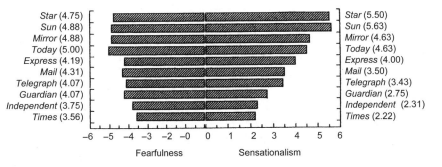

Star (4.75)   Star (5.50)
Sun (4.88)   Sun (5.63)
Mirror (4.88)   Mirror (4.63)
Today (5.00)   Today (4.63)
Express (4.19)   Express (4.00)
Mail (4.31)   Mail (3.50)
Telegraph (4.07)   Telegraph (3.43)
Guardian (4.07)   Guardian (2.75)
Independent (3.75)   Independent (2.31)
Times (3.56)   Times (2.22)

−6 −5 −4 −3 −2 −0   0   1   2   3   4   5   6

Fearfulness   Sensationalism

Figure 15.4

Qualitative analyses

Fig. 15.4 shows the mean judging scores for reports from each newspaper on the 'fearfulness' and 'sensationalism' of the reporting styles. ... The mean scores for each newspaper group are also included. Analyses of variance between the newspaper groups were carried out on the scores for 'fearfulness' and 'sensationalism'. Significant differences were found between the newspaper groups on judgements of 'fearfulness' ... and 'sensationalism' .... It can clearly be seen that broadsheet newspapers were judged to have the least fearful/sensational reporting styles and low-market tabloids to have the most fearful/sensational reporting styles.

Table 15.7 All quantitative and qualitative rankings for all newspapers

Newspaper	Rankings								Mean rankings for newspaper groups
Times	3	3	4	2	4	2	3	4	
Independent	2	1	2	1	2	1	2	3	
Guardian	1	2	1	4	1	4	1	5	
Telegraph	4	4	3	3	3	3	4	1	2.59
Mail	7	7	6	5	6	8	6	7	
Express	6	6	8	9	7	10	8	2	
Today	5	5	5	7	5	5	5	10	6.46
Mirror	8	8	9	10	9	9	10	8	
Sun	10	9	10	6	8	6.5	7	6	
Star	9	10	7	8	10	6.5	9	9	8.42

Overall results

Table 15.7 brings together all of the quantitative and qualitative rankings that have been shown in the newspaper analyses. There is a strong tendency for the broadsheet newspapers to have rankings within the 1–4 range; for mid-market tabloids to rank between 5 and 7; and for low-market tabloids to rank 8–10: 82.5 per cent of all rankings are consistent with this analysis and 92.5 per cent are not further than one ranking away from these ranges.

The survey results showed that broadsheet readers demonstrated lowest and low-market tabloid readers highest levels of FOC on all measures except the behavioural one. While a strong relationship was found between newspaper readership groups and socioeconomic status, there was evidence that newspaper readership was related to FOC independently of socioeconomic status.

Discussion

The results show both that different newspaper groups differ greatly in how they report crime news (particularly news of crimes involving personal violence) and that the corresponding relationship groups vary on most levels of FOC. The variance was in the direction predicted, namely, that people who read newspapers which contain more salient crime reports show more FOC.

[...]

When qualitative aspects of newspaper crime reports were examined, the same pattern emerged: the tabloids (again, the low-market ones in particular) were judged to have the most 'sensationalized' and 'fearful' reporting styles. ... As tabloids, particularly the low-market ones, were judged to have more sensational reporting styles and low-market tabloid readers showed the highest FOC and highest estimates of the likelihood of crime, there is some support for the hypothesis that sensationalized reports increase FOC and raise estimates of the likelihood of crime. However, when the estimates of sensationalism are compared with those of fearfulness, it appears that sensationalism does not bring with it a comparable increase in fearfulness. There appears to have been a dual feeling expressed whereby judges were saying, 'I find this report frightening, but I know that it is sensationalized'. Perhaps this is one aspect of readership 'discernment'. ... Readership gullibility may have been previously overstated.

The questionnaire survey demonstrated that newspaper readership group quite accurately predicts FOC. Using measures of personal safety, worry about personal victimization and estimates of risk, broadsheet readers displayed least and low-market tabloid readers most FOC. Only as a predictor of behavioural differences (measured by how often respondents go out after dark) did newspaper readership fail. This may have been due, however, to the confounding effect of age: broadsheet readers were almost ten years older, on average, than tabloid readers and age was most strongly associated with restrictions in the number of times respondents went out in the evening after dark.

[...]

When the relationships between newspaper readership and the various indices of FOC are considered in detail it becomes clear that newspaper readership was strongly related to feelings of personal safety (whether walking alone at night or while at home at night), if not to behavioural measures. The picture was not so decisive when it came to personal anxiety about being a victim of crime. The variance in respondents' worries about PVC victimization followed the predicted pattern, but worries about non-PVC crime, especially car theft, did not. (Worry about burglary and damage to property was in the expected direction, but not significantly so.) The most striking evidence of the predictive strength of newspaper readership for FOC was displayed in readers' assessments of victimization risks for the local population. For both PVCs and non-PVCs, the readers of low-market tabloids gave estimates that were approximately three times those of the broadsheet readers.

[…]

Despite many significant results, the survey findings must be treated with caution. To categorize respondents solely as young or old, male or female, broadsheet or tabloid reader is tempting but dangerous. Individual FOC results represent an interaction of many factors, of which only some have been measured in this survey. It could be, for example, that newspaper readership and socioeconomic status jointly reflect of some other factor not examined. It may also be that people with high FOC actively seek out newspapers with the most salient crime coverage – either to support their view of reality or for excitement (in the same way that some people often stay up to watch late-night horror movies despite being terrified by them). There is clearly a need for longitudinal studies of the effects of newspaper readership to disentangle the problem of cause and effect.

In conclusion, it can be stated that the reporting of crime by the British daily press varies enormously. Those papers that report most crime (particularly crimes involving personal violence) and in the most salient fashion (visually and stylistically) have readers who have the highest FOC levels. However, the causal link between newspapers and FOC is not clear. In any case, newspapers represent just one source of information that people receive about crime. It may well be the case that newspaper influence interacts with, or is related to, other sources of influence about crime, such as rumour. There is an argument in this paper for some newspapers in particular to report crime in a more dispassionate, objective, and responsible fashion, but there is also clearly a need for further research to pin down more precisely what it is about newspaper reports that is influential and to measure the impact that those features have upon the reader.

References

Fishman, M. (1978) Crime news as ideology, *Social Problems*, 25: 531–43.

Humphries, D. (1981) Serious crime, news coverage and ideology: a content analysis of crime coverage in a metropolitan paper, *Crime and Delinquency*, 27(2): 191–205.

Lester, M. (1980) Generating newsworthiness: the interpretive construction of public events, *American Sociological Review*, 45: 984–94.

Mayhew, P. (1989) *The 1988 British Crime Survey*, London: HMSO.

Moore, M.H. and Trojanowicz, R.C. (1988) Policing and the fear of crime, in *Perspectives in Policing*, vol. 3. Washington, DC: US Department of Justice.

Quinney, R. (1970) *The Social Reality of Crime*. Boston: Little Brown.

Smith, S. J. (1984) Crime in the news, *British Journal of Criminology*, 24(3): 289–95.

Tuchman, G. (1978) *Making News*. New York: Free Press.

16 | THE IMPACT OF KEY EVENTS ON THE PRESENTATION OF REALITY

Hans Mathias Keppllnger and Johanna Habermeier (1995)

Newspaper readers want to know what has been happening. When reading their newspapers they may take four things for granted. First of all, that the events reported did actually occur; secondly, that they happened in the way presented – in these respects most reporting is probably correct; thirdly, that important events are given extensive news coverage – here the amount of coverage is seen as an indicator of the significance of the events; fourthly, that if certain events occur more frequently, more articles will be published. Therefore a great number of reports indicates that a great number of events have taken place. These four notions can be labelled the 'correspondence assumption' of readers, listeners and viewers: the type and frequency of the events correspond to the type and frequency of news coverage.

The correspondence assumption is of concrete significance in the case of a short-term accumulation of reports concerning similar events. Such waves of news coverage signal the existence of political, economic, social and other problems and exert a pressure on authorities to make decisions – governments, administrations, enterprises, etc. They may thus be regarded as an expression of a public crisis. . . .

Communication scholars are eager to know why waves of news coverage arise. In theory there are three possible reasons for this. Firstly, the selection criteria for news remain the same, but the events accumulate. This is in line with the correspondence assumption. Secondly, the frequency of events remains the same, but the selection criteria change for a short term. In this case, events are given news coverage which would otherwise have remained unmentioned. Thirdly, both the selection criteria and the frequency of events change, with three combinations to be distinguished (more events and more attention; more events, but less attention for each; fewer events, but more attention). The second and third reasons raise the question as to why the selection criteria change for a short time. One possible reason for this are key events....

[I]t does not need rare, extreme and thus spectacular happenings for a key event to evolve. In other words, there is only a loose connection between the character of the happenings and their becoming a key event. The fact that an occurrence becomes a key event therefore still gives no information as to why it became one.

The assumption that key events can trigger waves of reporting on similar events, without the events themselves occurring more frequently, is of both theoretical and concrete significance but empirically difficult to prove. Firstly, if the assumption is correct it confirms the theory that the mass media represent a self-referential system which under certain conditions loses contact with the outside world and reacts mainly to its own activities. ... Secondly, if the assumption is correct, it suggests that the increasing number of waves of reports on negative events, e.g. on catastrophes, does not necessarily reflect a deterioration of actual conditions.

Theoretical Assumptions

The assumption that key events might trigger waves of reports about similar events can only be investigated empirically if five conditions are fulfilled. First of all, the existence of a key event must be independently proven and not only concluded from its alleged consequences. A possible indicator of a key event might be an unusual number of reports concerning an exactly defined occurrence. We understand *key events* as spectacular reports about more or less unusual occurrences....

Secondly, the reports about the key events have to be distinguished from reports about similar events. As *similar events*, we regard occurrences of the same type – other earthquakes in our example. Only if key events and similar events are distinguished, can the influence of news coverage on one event upon the reporting of others be determined.

Thirdly, *external data* regarding the frequency of the events in question must be at hand. These data must have been collected independently of news coverage and must reflect the actual development more precisely than the media reports (Rosengren, 1970, 1974).

Fourthly, it must be certain that the events taking place after the key event are not a consequence of previous news coverage. In other words, they must be *genuine events* (Kepplinger, 1990, 1992: 46–59), i.e.

occurrences that happen independent of news coverage. ... Otherwise the impact of the coverage of key events upon the coverage of similar events cannot be distinguished from its impact upon the emergence of subsequent events which might in turn bring about news stories. This would result in a confusion of effects and prevent the unambiguous attribution of effects to causes. Moreover, only the consideration of genuine events allows for testing whether the media can indeed create the impression of an accumulation of events without their true frequency increasing.

Fifthly, similar events have to be distinguished from thematically related events. *Thematically related events* are occurrences factually related with the key event, but not belonging to the same class of events. ... Thematically related events are frequently triggered by the key event or by news coverage. They are, in other words, *staged* or *mediated* events, i.e. incidents either produced only for the purpose of receiving news coverage or adapted to suit the needs of the media (Kepplinger, 1990, 1992: 46–59). ...

Similar as well as thematically related events share a common topic or issue established by the key event. A topic in our context is defined as the sum of all events factually related to the key event or considered to be related to it. Topics are usually identified by key words. ...

The notions 'genuine', 'mediated' and 'staged' indicated the *causes* of events. They signify, respectively, that an event evolved independent of news coverage, was influenced by news coverage or was arranged because of the expectation of news coverage. The notions 'key event', 'similar event' and 'thematically related event' indicate the *communicative function* of events. They signify, respectively, that an event was intensively covered, that it belongs to a certain class (or series) of events, or that there are factual connections between these and other events. ... The notions of causes and functions of events can be used to create a typology of events. It shows that the following analysis is conducted using genuine key events which can be seen as parts of a series of genuine similar events. Together with thematically related events, which can be either genuine, mediated or staged, they constitute a topic which was established by the key event (Figure 16.1).

Key events (and the news coverage occasioned by them) exert influence on readers, listeners and viewers, on journalists, on pressure groups and on decision-makers in politics, administration, business, etc. Firstly, key events focus the attention of readers, listeners and viewers on a certain topic. They make it appear significant and awaken interest in additional information (McCombs and Shaw, 1972; Iyengar and Kinder, 1987). Secondly, key events focus the attention of journalists on a certain occurrence. For them this has the same effect as for readers, listeners and viewers, but it also gives rise to their assumption that the readers, listeners and viewers are interested

Communicative functions	Causes		
	Genuine (independent of the media)	Mediated (influenced by the media)	Staged (for the media)
Key events			
Similar events			
Thematically related events			

Figure 16.1 Typology of causes and communicative functions of events

in obtaining further information. Thirdly, key events stimulate activities of pressure groups who see an opportunity of gaining media attention, since their concerns fit in with the established topic. The consequence is an increased number of mediated and staged events (Molotch and Lester, 1974). Fourthly, key events and the reactions they set off exert a pressure upon decision-makers in politics, business, administration, etc. (Protess et al., 1985, 1987, 1991). In some cases, decision-makers then react on demands possibly based on fictitious developments. As a consequence, decisions in these cases might be objectively reasonable, but are not justified by the course of events in question. ...

Six conclusions may be drawn fromt he theoretical assumptions. Firstly, following a key event, journalists on the whole report more about the topic thus established. ... Secondly, after a key event they give increased news coverage to new similar (genuine) events, even if the number of such events does not increase or if their character does not change. ... Thirdly, after a key event journalists give increased news coverage to past similar (genuine) events, which were given only scant attention before. ... Fourthly, after a key event they emphasize the common qualities of (past and present) similar events and the key event. ... Fifthly, after a key event they more frequently report thematically related events brought about by the key event (i.e. staged) or altered by it (i.e. mediated), e.g. demonstrations and press conferences. Sixthly, the more coverage given to a key event, the more impact it will have upon the future coverage of the topic. This is indicated by the number and length of stories on a topic ..., on similar events ... and on thematically related events. ...

Outline of the Investigation

For the following analysis we identified three key events which fulfilled the conditions mentioned above – a serious traffic accident in Germany involving a petrol tanker [July 1987], a severe earthquake in California [October 1989] and American actor Rock Hudson having the fatal disease, AIDS [October 1985]. These key events were all given intenstive news coverage. The frequency of subsequent events of a similar nature (traffic accidents, earthquakes, AIDS cases) is quite well known from external sources. They are genuine, i.e. not stimulated by the press coverage about the key events. The investigation included all articles in six German daily newspapers and four German weekly papers ... about traffic accidents, earthquakes and AIDS during a period of four weeks preceding and four weeks following the three key events. The analysis is based on a quasi-experimental comparison of the news coverage before and after the key events, which can be regarded as experimental stimuli. After some preliminary steps, all articles concerning the key events were removed. The object of the analysis, therefore, will be the news coverage of three topics before and after a respective key event. The objective of the analysis is to answer the question of whether key events change the news coverage, and if so, how they do it.

[...]

Table 16.1 Number of genuine events four weeks before and after the key events

	Before N	After N	Difference N
AIDS			
Infections	23	20	−3
Deaths	13	11	−2
Traffic			
Accidents	49,325	47,432	−1,893
Deaths	702	649	−53
Earthquakes			
Number	4	3	−1
Deaths	0	53	+53

Sources: AIDS-Zentrum des Bundesgesundheitsamtes (1992) (AIDS); Statistisches Bundesamt (1990) (traffic accidents); Schadensbericht der Münchener Rückversicherung (1990) (earthquakes).

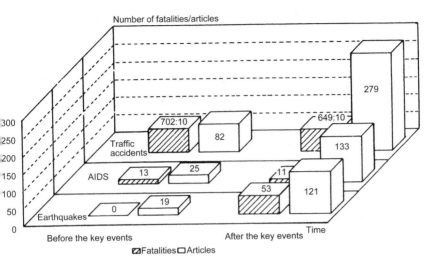

Figure 16.2 Number of fatalities and number of articles on three subjects
Sources: Tables 16.1 and 16.2

Results

Following the key events, the newspapers under investigation reported about four times as frequently than before about the respective topics – traffic accidents, earthquakes and AIDS – including the articles concerning the key events. Figure 16.2 shows the number of genuine events – victims of earthquakes (worldwide), deaths from AIDS (in Germany) and traffic accident fatalities (in Germany) – and the number of articles on these topics before and after the three key events. The number of traffic victims was divided by 10 to fit it into the graphic. To keep the comparison as simple as possible, the number of earthquakes, traffic accidents and AIDS infections (see Table 16.1) are not shown. As Figure 16.2 indicates, the waves of articles after the key events cannot be accounted for by the number of relevant genuine events, which remained more or less stable, while the coverage increased dramatically.

As expected, many of the reports after the key events – 201 out of 533 – devoted their attention to the key events themselves. But it was not primarily these articles which brought about the waves of coverage on the three topics. Instead, by far the larger share of articles after the key events – 332 out of 533 – was occasioned by other events. This suggests that, after the key events, similar and thematically related events were covered more frequently. Against our expectations, there was no linear relationship

Table 16.2 Number of articles before and after the key events – including key events

	Before			After			Difference		
	Key events N	Others N	Total N	Key events N	Others N	Total N	Key events N	Others N	Total N
AIDS	3[a]	22	25	34	99	133	+31	+77	+108
Traffic accidents	0	82	82	100	179	279	+100	+97	+197
Earthquakes	0	19	19	67	54	121	+67	+35	+102
Total	3	123	126	201	332	533	+198	+209	+407

Basis: all articles within a period of four weeks before and after the key events, including articles concerning the key events.

[a] Speculative articles concerning Rock Hudson's AIDS illness.

Table 16.3 Number of articles concerning similar (genuine) and thematically related (mediated/staged) events before and after the key events – without key events

	Before				After				Difference			
	Similar N	Undef. N	Mediat./ staged N	Total N	Similar N	Undef. N	Mediat./ staged N	Total N	Similar N	Undef. N	Mediat./ staged N	Total N
AIDS	2	19	1	22	24	35	40	99	+22	+16	+39	+77
Traffic accidents	61	18	3	82	113	34	32	179	+52	+16	+29	+97
Earthquakes	19	0	0	19	46	3	5	54	+27	+3	+5	+35
Total	82	37	4	123	183	72	77	332	+101	+35	+73	+209

Basis: all articles within a period of four weeks before and after the key events, which did not have the key event itself as the occasion for the news coverage.

between the intensity of coverage about the key events and the intensity of coverage about other events. . . .

We now look at the influence of key events on the coverage of similar (genuine) and thematically related (mediated/staged) events. For this, the stories on the key events are excluded from the analysis (Table 16.3). The following picture emerges: after the key events, considerably more articles appeared on the three topics, even if the reports about the key events are disregarded. This can be attributed in particular to the newspapers reporting on similar (genuine) events – traffic accidents, earthquakes and AIDS cases and deaths. The number of these articles increased by 101. However, the newspapers also increased their coverage of thematically related (mediated/staged) events. The number of articles on these events rose by 73. Finally, there were also more articles on events that could not clearly be classified as genuine or mediated/staged.

As expected, there was a linear relationship between the number of articles about the key events and the number of articles about other similar (genuine) events: the more intensely the papers had covered the key event, the more frequently they published stories on similar events. In contrast, there was no linear relationship between the number of articles about the key event and the number of articles about thematically related (mediated/staged) events. . . .

How was it possible that the papers published more articles on genuine events after the key events although their number actually decreased? Did they give more attention to *new* similar events or did they fulfil the need for information with reports on similar *former* occurrences? The answer to this is two-sided. Firstly, following the key events, the papers mentioned new similar events more often than before. . . . Secondly they gave more attention to new events than before the key event. This cannot, however, explain the large increase in reports about genuine events. Another picture emerges when the coverage of past similar events is considered. Following all three key events, the newspapers and periodicals gave much more attention to events which had occurred some time back in the past. They published a large number of articles about AIDS victims who had died before Rock Hudson's illness became known, about traffic accidents which had occurred before the Herborn accident and about earthquakes which had happened before the Californian earthquake. After the key events, 37 percent of all articles on similar events dealt with past events. . . . We can thus state: while the newspapers had hardly ever dealt with the past before the key events happened, they did so intensively after the key events (Table 16.4).

By definition, key events and similar events belong to the same class of occurrences. . . . Presumably, the same number of very similar incidents

Table 16.4 Coverage of past (genuine) similar events: number of articles and number of past genuine events mentioned before and after the key events (without coverage of key events)

	Before		After		Difference	
	Articles[a] N	Events[b] N	Articles[a] N	Events[b] N	Articles[a] N	Events[b] N
AIDS	0	0	12	17	+12	+17
Traffic accidents	0	0	21	72	+21	+72
Earthquakes	2	2	35	64	+33	+62
Total	2	2	68	153	+66	+151

Notes: [a] All articles mentioning at least one genuine event.
[b] Number of similar genuine events mentioned in all articles.

Table 16.5 Number of articles concerning genuine events very similar to the relevant key event before and after the key events (without coverage of the key events)

	Before		After		Difference	
	Articles[a] N	Events[b] N	Articles[a] N	Events[b] N	Articles[a] N	Events[b] N
AIDS	0	0	7	7	+7	+7
Traffic accidents	10	10	65	136	+55	+126
Earthquakes	16	6	59	91	+53	+85
Total	16	16	131	234	+115	+218

Notes: [a] All articles in which at least one very similar (genuine) event had been mentioned, also coded if the article was not occasioned by the event.
[b] Number of every event mentioned in all articles under consideration.

happened before and after the key events. They were, however, hardly ever covered before the key event, or – if they were covered – aspects resembling the key events were probably not mentioned. . . .

This was very different after the key events. Now the papers focused their attention on genuine events very similar to the key events, or they stressed aspects in a way that events appeared very similar (cf. also Lang and Lang, 1953; Halloran et al., 1970). . . . Again, this change was due to an increased number of articles dealing with similar events as well as to an increased number of similar events mentioned in all the articles investigated. In this way the news coverage conveyed the misleading impression that after the key events the number of very similar events increased (Table 16.5).

On the basis of the data available it is possible to calculate the contribution of the coverage of various types of events on the formation of the respective waves of news coverage after the key events. Between 26 and 55 percent of all articles were stimulated by the key events themselves. Between 18 and 41 percent of all articles were stimulated by similar (genuine) events. This includes both past and new incidents. Between 6 and 56 percent of all articles were stimulated by thematically related (mediated/staged) events.

The large differences between the three topics indicates that the need for additional information, created by the key events, was met in different ways. The availability of information dictated which way was chosen. The more dramatic information about the key event itself available, the more was the coverage concentrated on the key event (earthquake in California more than traffic accident in Hersom, traffic accident in Hersom more than Rock Hudson's illness). The more information on other new genuine events was available, the more coverage concentrated on new rather than past genuine events (traffic accidents more than AIDS and earthquakes). The more information on activities from interest groups was available, the more coverage concentrated on mediated and staged events (AIDS more than traffic accidents, traffic accidents more than earthquakes). Figure 16.3 displays the relative importance of the various types of events for the coverage after the key events. . . .

From a communication scholar's point of view, the causes of the waves of news coverage are now evident. They were not caused by an increased number of similar (genuine) events but by the key events, or respectively, by the coverage which the mass media had given these events. From a newspaper reader's point of view, this looks different. The increase of articles and statements on similar events indicated an increase in the number of such events. Thus the impression of a series of events was created – without the real frequency of events having changed in a significant way.

Summary and Interpretation

The results of this study can be summarized in 10 statements:

1. The papers analysed frequently reported on an earthquake in California, on the news that Rock Hudson was suffering from AIDS and on a serious petrol tanker accident in Germany. The three incidents can therefore be regarded as key events.
2. After the key events there was no accumulation of similar (genuine) events. The number of HIV infections and AIDS fatalities, of traffic accidents and fatalities, and of earthquakes rather remained constant or

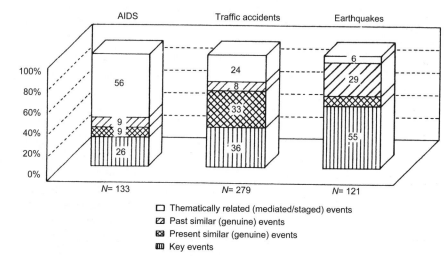

Figure 16.3 Types of events in the news coverage after key events

decreased somewhat. An exception to this is the number of deaths through earthquakes, which increased.

3. After the three key events, the papers analysed covered the respective topics considerably more intensively than before. Subjects of coverage were the key events themselves, similar (genuine) events and thematically related (mediated/staged) events.

4. After the three key events, the papers analysed reported on similar (genuine) events considerably more often than before. As the number of such events largely remained constant, these events cannot be regarded as the cause of the intensive coverage.

5. After the three key events, the papers analysed also reported considerably more often than before on thematically related (mediated/staged) events. These articles can be considered the consequences of occurrences triggered or influenced by the key events.

6. The intensive coverage of similar (genuine) events was largely brought about by articles on past events. After the three key events, the papers investigated first published more articles on past events, and they secondly mentioned more events of this kind. Past similar events can be seen as functional alternatives for new similar events. In the three cases, they filled the gap between the increased interest in the topics and the lack of new events. They were used to satisfy the need for additional information, which had been stimulated by the key events. The news coverage of the key events thus had a paradoxical consequence. The

impression of new and dramatic developments was partly a result of the *instrumental actualization* (Kepplinger et al., 1991) of past events, which now appeared in a new light.

7. After the three key events, the papers investigated reported more often than before on similar (genuine) events which bore a marked resemblance to the key events, and they probably also emphasized those aspects in other events that highlighted the similarity with the key event.

8. The key events had a stronger influence on the coverage of daily newspapers than on the coverage of weekly papers. They influenced the tabloids and regional newspapers more than the national quality papers.

9. The depiction of reality after the key events consisted of stories on three types of events – the key events themselves, similar (genuine) events and thematically related (mediated/staged) events. These three types of events contributed in different degrees to the depciction of reality after the key events. . . .

10. The more intensely a key event had been covered, the more it influenced the subsequent news coverage – with one exception. This holds for the frequency of articles on the three topics as well as for the frequency of articles on similar events. The exception is the frequency of stories on thematically related events, most probably because the number of these stories depended on the activities of interest groups after the key events.

The present results to a large extent confirm the theoretical assumptions. It can therefore be stated: key events focus the attention of readers, listeners and viewers. In addition, they focus the attention of journalists, who wish to satisfy the perceived interest of the public. Since the demand for new information increases more rapidly than the amount of available information on new events of a similar nature, journalists increasingly make incidents from the past a topic, deliberately selecting and tailoring them. In this way, new fears unleashed by new key events are nourished, above all, by reports on past occurences, which appear in a new light.

The results clearly contradict the correspondence assumptions outlined above. After key events the frequency of articles does not reflect the frequency of relevant events. In crises, therefore, it is hardly possible to infer from the frequency of reports about events the actual frequency of these events – unless one filters out from the abundance of articles only those few which report on the new events. This, however, is likely to exceed the capabilities of the normal reader. Therefore it must be taken into account that, especially after key events, the mass media create the impression in the population that events accumulate – although nothing much has really changed. The results suggest an important conclusion for the evaluation of the amount of truth that lies behind news stories implying that a series of similar events has occurred and that the problems related to them have increased. This refers, for example, to the accumulation of specific violent crimes, environmental damage, natural disasters and industrial accidents. ... If series of such events make the media agenda, two possibilities might be distinguished. In cases where the accumulation of news stories was preceded by many and spectacular articles on one specific event, one must assume that in spite of the growing number of stories on similar and thematically related events nothing much has happened – except a key event which has triggered the wave. Here one has to take into account that the news coverage creates a false impression that events accumulate and problems become more urgent. ... In cases where news coverage increased without a preceding key event to be noticed, one must assume that the events were indeed more frequent. There one can suppose that the population's fears, as produced by the coverage, are justified. In the first case, inferring from the depiction of reality on reality itself is fallacious; in the second case it is correct.

References

AIDS-Zentrum am Bundesgesundheitsamt (1992) 'Gemeldere AIDS-Fälle und AIDS-Todesfälle in der Bundesrepublik Deutschland. Verteilung nach Registrierdatum', Berlin (unpublished).

Halloran, James D., Elliott Philip and Murdock, Graham (1970) *Demonstrations and Communication: A Case Study*. Harmondsworth: Penguin Books.

Iyengar, Shanto and Kinder, Donald R. (1987) *News that Matters: Television and American Opinion*. Chicago: University of Chicago Press.

Kepplinger, Hans Mathias (1990) Realität, Realitätsdarstellung und Medienwirkung, in Jürgen Wilke (ed.) *Fortschritte der Publizistikwissenschaft*. Freiburg: Alber-Verlag, pp. 39–55.

Kepplinger, Hans Mathias (1992) *Ereignismanagement. Wirklichkeit und Massenmedien*. Osnabrück: Fromm.

Kepplinger, Hans Mathias, Brosius, Hans-Bernd and Staab, Joachim Friedrich (1991) Instrumental actualization: a theory of mediated conflicts, *European Journal of Communication* 6: 263–90.

Lang, Kurt and Lang, Gladys Engel (1953) The unique perspective of television and its effect: a pilot study, *American Sociological Review*, 18: 3–12.

McCombs, Maxwell E. and Shaw, Donald L. (1972) The agenda-setting function of mass media, *Public Opinion Quarterly*, 36: 176–87.

Molotch, Harvey and Lester, Marilyn (1974) News as purposive behavior: on the strategic use of routine events, accidents, and scandals, *American Sociological Review*, 39: 101–12.

Protess, David, Leff Donna R., Brooks Stephen C. and Gordon, Margaret T. (1985) Uncovering rape: the watchdog press and the limits of agenda setting, *Public Opinion Quarterly*, 49: 19–37.

Protess, David, Lomax Cook, Fay, Curtin, Thomas R., Gordon, Margaret T., Leff, Donna R., McCombs, Maxwell E. and Miller, Peter (1987) The impact of investigative reporting on public opinion and policy making: targeting toxic waste, *Public Opinion Quarterly*, 51: 166–85.

Protess, David, Lomax Cook, Fay, Doppelt, Jack C., Ettema, James S., Gordon, Margaret T., Leff, Donna R. and Miller, Peter (1991) *The Journalism of Outrage: Investigative Reporting and Agenda Building in America*. New York: Guilford.

Rosengren, Karl Erik (1970) International news: intra and extra media data, *Acta Sociologica*, 13: 96–109.

Rosengren, Karl Erik (1974) International news: methods, data and theory, *Journal of Peace Research* 11: 145–56.

Schadensbericht Münchener Rückversicherung (1990) Schadenbeben 1989, Munich (unpublished).

Statistisches Bundesamt (1990) Straßenverkehrsunfälle und Unfallfolgen 1987 nach Tagesdatum, Wiesbaden (unpublished).

THE LENS OF FEAR

David L. Altheide (2002)

Fear of some kind has always been with us. It's the magnitude and nature of fear that is different today. It seems that fear is everywhere. It is as though fear is attached to many activities and issues, and if it is not attached, it is not far removed from them. Part of the reason is due to the context and times of our lives. Two things that make a big difference are the amount of information we have available as well as the mobility we experience. We are aware of more things happening in the world, we expect more, and so more seems to be possible. We also are more mobile, often spending our adult lives in places different from our childhood. So, our grounding isn't as solid and we do not see as clearly.

It is the way we see that matters. I think that using a metaphor of a light-house lens can help us appreciate the role of fear in our everyday lives. The Fresnel lens, developed by Augustine Fresnel in 1822, enabled lighthouse keepers to magnify greatly the focus and power of a candle. This helped ships at sea not only avoid rocky crags, but more importantly, told them where they were in reference to other points of light. Over time, the light and lens became synonymous with lighthouses, and it was this wonderful lens that changed maritime commerce and travel. Most lighthouses were no longer necessary by the 1960s because other technology could provide ships with much better signals about their location and safety. Now associated with another era, most lighthouses, with their Fresnel lenses, are museums that still function, but mainly as demonstrations of the past carried over into the future.

We experience more of our lives through a lens of fear. Concerns, risks, and dangers are magnified and even distorted by this lens. Caution has given way to avoidance. Rarity has been replaced by typicality. And the focus of media attention has taken a toll on our ability to see our way clearly. It is as though the lighthouse keeper and the ship's captain cannot even see one another because of the out-of-control glare coming from a source of light that was once helpful. We must understand this lens in order to help us regain our focus and see more clearly.

The discourse of fear originated in religious beliefs and now pervades a secular society. Fear is an orientation to the world. God and organized religion provided salvation from fear in a sacred society. The state and formal social control promise salvation from fear in our secular society. This remarkable shift has major social implications. Fear of God and sin were normal for me as a small boy since my family and I were 'believers' in a mythology of damnation and salvation. My world was simple as a child: I was taught to seek salvation for my sins in order to be saved from eternal damnation. God could save me, but then again, if I did not do the right thing, God could also damn me. That was the sacred worldview, where faith was the goal and where commitment and 'true belief' were demonstrated to fellow believers on a daily basis, from church service to church service. David Campbell (1998) argues that dangerousness, or the 'evangelism of fear,' with death as its impetus and salvation as its goal, required concern not only with external issues, but with the self as well:

> The church relied heavily on discourses of danger to establish its authority, discipline its followers, and ward off its enemies. ... Moreover, it was this 'evangelism of fear,' that produced a preoccupation with death. ... The required familiarity with death demanded of individuals an eternal vigilance against the self. (1998: 48–9)

Fear is normal in our time. The major point of this book is that fear has become more pervasive in our lives. I have argued that fear is commonly used in public documents and is becoming part of everyday conversation. And I have suggested a mechanism and process by which this has occurred. This process basically involves the mass media and popular culture in general, and the 'discovery' that fear fits rather well with the problem frame, which is a key part of the entertainment format and logic, which, in turn, satisfies commercial demands. Politicians, police, journalists, businesses, and even social scientists have an interest and a stake in fear. Social scientists, for example, monitor it through annual surveys, focusing on indicators of safety and security and examining how people are adjusting their lives. Most of this attention is devoted to fear of crime, but as we saw in previous chapters, fear is not synonymous with crime but rather, travels across topics over a period of time. So what are we to do about fear? What do we know about fear now that we didn't before this and other projects?

A study of fear and popular culture suggests a broader sociology of fear. While such a project is beyond this book, a few key points must be made about the relationship between popular culture and the role and consequences of fear in our lives...

My basic thesis is that fear is contextual and does not exist in a vacuum. The discourse of fear has changed over the last few decades primarily through the work of the mass media and popular culture. Moreover, this culture has pervaded every institutional arrangement in social life. So, a jumping off place for my analysis of how we can avoid negative consequences of the discourse of fear is to simply suggest that popular culture is not just incidental or merely supplementary to other social forces, but, rather, that popular culture has been the key element in promoting the discourse of fear.

Fear is a feature of an ecology of communication that connects information technology to communication formats and social activities and meanings. This requires moving beyond disciplines. Theoretical boundaries are breached when mass media content and forms are part of our everyday lives and contribute to social definitions of self, others, and social issues. I have drawn on work from proponents of symbolic interactionism, structuralism, cultural studies, and poststructuralism who are awash in debates about the origin, nature, and consequences of social interaction, are swimming in mass-mediated symbols, from products to information technology to slogans to political tropes and social issues. Fear is a perspective or an orientation to the world, rather than 'fear of something.' Fear is one of the few things that Americans share. The discourse of fear is constructed through evocative entertainment formats promoting visual, emotional, and dramatic experience that audience members can identify with, live vicariously, and share. However, it is not just 'fear of crime' or a particular thing, but rather a sense or an identity that we are all actual or potential victims held in common by many people. Indeed, studies in other countries (e.g., the United Kingdom) make it very clear that identity, social context, perceptions, and social definitions are very relevant for how safe people feel (Farrall et al. 2000; Van der Wurff et al. 1989). Previous chapters have shown how the object of fear (e.g., crime, drugs, AIDS, children) shifts or travels across topics over time. The sense that something has happened to us, could happen to us, or probably will happen to us connects the present moment with resentments and blame about the past, as well as anxieties about the future.

The most pervasive aspect of this victim perspective is crime. Politicians and state control agencies, working with news media as news sources, have done much to capitalize on this concern and to promote a sense of insecurity and reliance on formal agents of social control – and related businesses – to provide surveillance, protection, revenge, and punishment to protect us, to save us. . . .

It is the fear of the 'other' that we anticipate; we see numerous reports about very atypical occurrences, but we see them night after night. News in the problem frame make commonplace what is very rare. Our worst-case scenarios (e.g., murder, kidnapping, terrorist attacks) are always before us. The news and entertainment industry engulfed in entertainment formats see the world this way and reflect it in their productions (Gitlin 1994).

Cultural and political contexts contributed to the emergence of fear as a perspective that pervades everyday life. A massive expansion of electronic media outlets (e.g., cable TV, videotape rentals, the Internet) overlapped historically with unprecedented consumer growth and Gross National Product, the decline of 'real' international threats (e.g., the fall of the Soviet Union), and conservative political agendas that used crime and especially drug-related issues to gain political legitimacy (Campbell 1998; Garland 2000). The discourse of fear became a key perspective for selecting, organizing, and presenting materials that were consistent with the entertainment formats of popular culture in a secular society. This perspective enables heterogeneous audiences to share a common explanation of what is wrong with the world and thereby provides a way to fix failed expectations that were inspired by awesome social changes, which fractured public life and communities anchoring selves and identities (Hewitt 1989, Holstein and Gubrium 2000; Jacobs 1969; Oldenburg 1989). Commodification of identities fueled consumption and vicarious participation in popular culture as a substitute for leisure time (Bensman and Vidich 1971; Ewen 1976; Ewen and Ewen 1992; Stein and Vidich 1963). More of our experience came from the mass media as popular culture provided more of the style and substance of everyday life. The entertainment perspective expanded (Jackall and Hirota 1999, 2000) as audiences were transformed into markets. Involvement in the public realm increasingly shifted to mass-mediated information emphasizing fear and crises. The security of life in this world became the dominant orientation and informed social concerns and social situations.

Dramatic entertainment emphasis involves salvation; as a secular society, we are less concerned (notwithstanding increases in church attendance) with spiritual development and justice beyond the grave than we are with lifestyle, occupational success, and consumer rights.

Danger (death, in its ultimate form) might therefore be thought of as the new god for the modern world of states, not because it is peculiar to our time, but because it replicates the logic of Christendom's evangelism of fear.

Indeed, in a world in which state identity is secured through discourses of danger, some low tactics are employed to serve these high ideals. These tactics are not inherent to the logic of identity, which only requires the definition of difference. But securing an ordered self and an ordered world – particularly when the field upon which this process operates is as extensive as a state – involves defining elements that stand in the way of order as forms of 'otherness.' ... In this way, the state project of security replicates the church project of salvation. The state grounds it legitimacy by offering salvation to its followers who, it says, would otherwise be destined to an unredeemed death. (Campbell 1998: 50)

The social context of fear reflects the communication order and the dominant modes of information transfer in a historical period. Fear is involved more in public discourse partly because there is such a massive public discourse that can be centrally guided and directed (but not tightly controlled), including setting agendas with news reports passing through the problem frame and media logic that guides news sources representing certain organizational perspectives. Certainly one key factor that led to the news success of the problem frame was news workers' reliance on formal agents of social control (FASC) as news sources. These sources have become the key agents and definers of social issues. Audience familiarity with the general message – because of numerous previous reports – permits short-hand accounts to resonate with the cold shudder of fear. Every atypical and very rare event is presented 'as if' it is but part of a broader sweep of terror.

Fear and victim became linked symbolically through popular culture formats joined in a comprehensive ecology of communication: technology, communication formats, information, concerns, issues, and choices are joined and overlap. The impact is more pronounced when visual representations dominate. Denzin (1995) has shown how visuals are relevant for individual lives and particularly how social context shapes individuals' behavior, expectations, awareness, and reflexive principles or codes for understanding their place in the 'show.' 'The postmodern mediated self ... finds its moral solidarity in those narrative tales that circulate in the cinematic culture' (1995: 265). Countless news reports, entertainment programs, films, and commercials are the symbolic grounding of everyday life, but there are also movies and other visual images. The media images captured by Denzin are consistent with his overall thesis that the post-modern world is characterized by the cultivation of conspicuous consumption, identified by Hollywood genres stressing money, sex, love and intimacy, crimes of violence, passion and greed, race and its repression. 'Gone are the highest ideals of humanity, including freedom, self-respect, open dialogue and honesty' (Denzin 1991: 149).

There can be no fear without actual victims or potential victims. In the postmodern age, victim is a status and representation and not merely a person or someone who has suffered as a result of some personal, social, or physical calamity. Massive and concerted efforts by moral entrepreneurs to have their causes adopted and legitimated as core social issues worthy of attention have led to the wholesale adaptation and refinement of the use of the problem frame to promote victimization. Often couching their causes as battles for justice, moral entrepreneurs seek to promote new social defini-tions of right and wrong (see Johnson 1995; Spector and Kitsuse 1977). Victims are entertaining and that is why they abound. They are evocative, bringing forth tears, joy, and vicarious emotional experience. But victim is more: Victim is now a status, a position that is open to all people who live in a symbolic environment marked by the discourse of fear. We are all potential victims, often vying for official recognition and legitimacy. Much has changed since the Church offered salvation to those who shared a worldview that pitted their immortal souls against eternal damnation. Fear of God was produced by the church's road to salvation; the cure, so to speak, showed the punishment that was being avoided. The Enlightenment and rational thought essentially killed the supporting ontology that made the fear of God an everyday reality. Yet, the contribution to our culture and our collective representations remains:

> The problem was that once the 'death of God' had been proclaimed, the link between the world, 'man,' and certitude had been broken ... an ambiguous situation arose in which there was (and is) a demand for external guarantees inside a culture that has erased the ontological preconditions for them. Modernity is thus an epoch of secret insistence jeopardized by its own legacy of truthfulness and honesty: its bearers demand that every hidden faith be exposed, but faith is necessary to ground the superiority of modern life. (Ashley 1989: 303)

The problem, then, is that we continue to look for salvation but we lack the symbolic means to achieve it.

> However, this ethical impulse cannot be satisfied, particularly when we remind ourselves ... that the culture of modernity necessitates external

guarantees but has erased the ontological preconditions for them. It was this situation, after all, that granted to fear and anger the capacity of securing that which could no longer be reasoned into existence. ... The evangelism of fear centered on death grounded the church's project of salvation; the evangelism of fear articulated in the anxiety about an unfinished and dangerous world secured the state such that security occupied the position of salvation; now the evangelism of fear enunciated by those hoping to ward off 'foreign' intellectual influences works to contain the instability of their representations of the world. (Campbell 1998: 193)

So, we have known for some time that fear is circularly (or reflexively) joined to the 'other,' a role played by the Devil (Antichrist, etc.) for more than two thousand years. Fear was part of the process of protecting us and affording us salvation. This fear was realized in everyday-life terms as people tried to 'be good' in order to avoid damnation, as well as punishing those who violated the sacred rules. (Not keeping the Commandments, for example, also implied that any among the elect who knew about such violations would take steps to prevent their breach, including punishment.) There were, of course, many unintended consequences of this ontology, including the inquisition, the Salem witch trials, and, according to Weber (1954, 1958), the rise of capitalism.

It is apparent then that the origins of a sociology of fear preceded the modern state and crime control efforts. Thus, while it is certainly correct, in my view, that conservative political agendas have benefited from joining fear and victim with crime control agendas, the issue is much bigger, particularly the relationship between fear and everyday-life culture. Crime control efforts contributed to the most recent visual image and identification of the extension of the victim role to citizens. However, this has all been communicated through news reports that have been developed, constituted, produced, packaged, presented, and then reacted to through the evocative problem frame discussed throughout this book. For example, Garland (2000) notes that crime control was a strategy that included the development and linkage of individuals to victim:

The new imperative is that victims must be protected, their voices heard, their memory honoured, their anger expressed, their fears addressed. ... A political logic has been established wherein being 'for' victims automatically means being tough on offenders. A zero-sum policy game is assumed wherein the offender's gain is the victim's loss.

The symbolic figure of the victim has taken on a life of its own, and plays a role in political debate and policy argument that is quite detached from the claims of the organized victims' movement, or the aggregated opinions of surveyed victims. ... This is a new and significant fact of contemporary culture. ... But what is sufficiently acknowledged is the degree to which the figure of the victim has come to have the status of a 'representative individual' in contemporary society. ... Whoever speaks on behalf of victims speaks on behalf of us all. ... Outrage and anger are the culture's antidotes to fear and anxiety, and the open expression of these emotions is part of the consolation and therapy it offers. (2000:351–2)

These concerns lead to a broader formulation of fear that takes into account social and cultural context and the ways in which these are communicated and shared. An ecology of communication is relevant for connecting fear and victim. Both are embedded in evocative visual and dramatic entertainment formats that provide the symbolic direction, meanings and media for shared language, perspective, and topics. Other work has shown that fear and victim are informed by perceived membership (Altheide et al. 2001). Crime and threats to the public order – and therefore all good citizens – are part of the focus of fear, but as noted throughout this book, the topics change over time. What they all have in common is pointing to the 'other,' the outsider, the nonmember, the alien. However, Schwalbe et al. (2000) have shown that 'othering' is part of a social process whereby a dominant group defines into existence an inferior group. This requires the establishment and 'group sense' of symbolic boundaries of membership. These boundaries occur through institutional processes that are grounded in everyday situations and encounters, including language, discourse, accounts, and conversation. Knowledge and skill at using 'what everyone like us knows' involves formal and informal socialization so that members acquire the coinage of cultural capital with which they can purchase acceptance, allegiance, and belonging. Part of this language involves the discourse of fear.

Discourse is more than talk and writing; it is a way of talking and writing. To regulate discourse is to impose a set of formal or informal rules about what can be said, how it can be said, and who can say what to whom. ... Inasmuch as language is the principal means by which we express, manage, and conjure emotions, to regulate discourse is to regulate emotion. The ultimate consequence is a regulation of action....

When a form of discourse is established as standard practice, it becomes a tool for reproducing inequality, because it can serve not only to regulate thought and emotion, but also to identify Others and thus to maintain boundaries as well. (Schwalbe et al. 2000: 433–4)

It is not fear of crime, then, that is most critical. It is what this fear can expand to, what it can become. As sociologist Bernard Beck (n.d.) notes, we are becoming 'armored.' Social life changes when more people live behind walls, hire guards, drive armored vehicles (e.g., sport utility vehicles), wear 'armored' clothing (such as the No Fear brand and 'big-soled shoes'), carry mace and handguns, and take martial arts classes. The problem is that these activities reaffirm and help produce a sense of disorder that our actions perpetuate. We then rely more on formal agents of social control (FASC) to save us by policing them, the 'others,' who have challenged our faith.

References

Altheide, D.L., Gray, B., Janisch, R., Korbin, L., Maratea, R., Neill, D., Reaves, J. and Van Deman, F. (2001) News constructions of fear and victim: an exploration through triangulated qualitative document analysis, *Qualitative Inquiry*, 7.

Ashley. R.K. (1989) Living on border lines: man, poststructuralism and war, in J. and M. Shapiro der Derian (eds) *International/Intertextual Relations: Postmodern Readings of World Politics*. Lexington, MA: Lexington Books.

Bensman, J. and Vidich, A.J. (1971) *The New American Society: The Revolution of the Middle Class*. Chicago: Quadrangle Books.

Campbell, D. (1998) *Writing Security: United States Foreign Policy and the Politics of Identity*. Minneapolis: University of Minnesota Press.

Denzin, N.K. (1991) *Images of Postmodern Society: Social Theory and Contemporary Cinema*. Newbury Park, CA: Sage.

Denzin, N.K. (1995) *The Cinematic Society: The Voyeur's Gaze*. Thousand Oaks, CA: Sage.

Ewen, S. (1976) *Captains of Consciousness: Advertising and the Social Roots of the Consumer Culture*. New York: McGraw-Hill.

Ewen, S. and Ewen, E. (1992) *Channels of Desire: Mass Images and the Shaping of American Consciousness*. Minneapolis: University of Minnesota Press.

Farrall, S., Bannister, J., Ditton, J. and Gilchrist, E. (2000) Social psychology and the fear of crime, *British Journal of Criminology*, 40: 399–413.

Garland, D. (2000) The culture of high crime societies: some preconditions of recent 'law and order' policies, *British Journal of Criminology*, 40: 347–75.

Gitlin, T. (1994) *Inside Prime Time*. London: Routledge.

Hewitt, J.P. (1989) *Dilemmas of the American Self*. Philadelphia, PA: Temple University Press.

Holstein, J.A. and Gubrium, J.F. (2000) *The Self We Live By: Narrative Identity in a Postmodern World*. New York: Oxford University Press.

Jackall, R. and Hirota, J.M. (1999) *Experts with Symbols: Advertising, Public Relations, and the Ethics of Advocacy*. Chicago: University of Chicago Press.

Jackall, R. and Hirota, J.M. (2000) *Image Makers: Advertising, Public Relations and the Ethos of Advocacy*. Chicago: University of Chicago Press.

Jacobs, J. (1969) *The Death and Life of Great American Cities*. New York: Modern Library.

Johnson, J.M. (1995) Horror stories and the construction of child abuse, in J. Best (ed.) *Images of Issues*. New York: Aldine de Gruyter.

Oldenburg, R. (1989) *The Great Good Place: Cafes, Coffee Shops, Community Centers, Beauty Parlors, General Stores, Bars, Hangouts and How They Get You through the Day*. New York: Paragon House.

Schwalbe, M., Godwin, S., Holden, D., Schrock, D., Thompson, S. and Wolkomir, M. (2000) Generic processes in the reproduction of inequality: an interactionist analysis, *Social Forces*, 79: 419–52.

Spector, M. and Kitsuse, J. (1977) *Constructing Social Problems*. Menlo Park, CA: Cummings Publishing Co.

Stein, M.R. and Vidich. A.J. (1963) *Sociology on Trial*. Englewood Cliffs, NJ: Prentice Hall.

Van der Wurff, A., Van Stallduinen, L. and Stringer, P. (1989) Fear of crime in residential environments: testing a social psychological model, *Journal of Social Psychology*, 129: 141–60.

Weber, M. (1954) *Max Weber on Law in Economy and Society; Edited with Introduction and Annotations by Max Rheinstein.*, New York: Simon and Schuster.

Weber, M. (1958) *The Protestant Ethic and the Spirit of Capitalism*. New York: Scribner.

ISSUES

Overview

The moral panic models in Part I and Part II inevitably attracted criticisms in the course of time. A succession of writers identified what they saw as central deficiencies. The first three readings each develop a wider critique of a moral panic model, mainly that of Cohen, from considering a single case study. The last two articles engage in a debate about the general status and relevance of the models.

In *Reading 18*, Simon Watney (1988) argues that the example of AIDS posed a significant challenge to any moral panic model. To simplify his argument somewhat, Watney advances five major criticisms. First, the model tends to portray the state as a prime mover in moral panics when it might more usefully be seen as a site of contestation. Second, a model which separates out individual moral panics cannot appreciate how they may overlap and reinforce each other. Third, the model assumes the crucial legacy of a moral panic to be institutional change when the establishment of a dominant discourse may be equally significant. Fourth, the model does not allow for folk devils resisting this status. Fifth, the model's stress on social anxiety as being projected onto an arbitrary target obscures how folk devils embody the antithesis of conventional values. Watney concludes that, like homophobia, the term moral panic is much too crude to encompass the subtleties of the discourses evident in the AIDS issue.

Watney's is an early and incisive critique of moral panic models raising a wide range of points, few of which have been subsequently debated. His key argument about the serial nature of panics, the focussed targets of social anxiety and discourse as a constitutive element of moral panics have far-reaching implications for the model.

Some of Watney's ideas are taken up in *Reading 19* by Mc Robbie and Thornton (1995), though they use the much later case study of rave culture. They argue a two-fold change since the model's original formulation. First, new kinds of mass media and their relationships with audiences have undermined a centralized media system able to dictate the course of social reaction. Second, the relationship between representation and social reality is now recognized to be much more complex than simplistic ideas about exaggeration or distortion.

They cite the case of rave to show how youth media anticipated a moral panic and thus subverted it. In this and other instances, groups who might be constructed as socially deviant are able to articulate their case through their own organizations and circuits of communication. It is no longer possible to demonize whole sections of the population. The media system itself is now much more diverse and leaky. Even dominant media outlets such as daily newspapers now find they have to accommodate a diversity of views and even entertain self-doubts, for example about national identity, all of which were less evident 20 or 30 years ago.

The model continues to remain relevant but it is showing signs of age. It needs to be rethought in ways which will embrace all the changes in the cultural arena since it was originally composed. There is perhaps some vagueness about the precise changes required and no programme of reform has been devised but, more than any other critique, this one centres on the datedness of the moral panic model.

In *Reading 20* de Young's (1998) analysis of the 1980s' US day care panic produces similar reservations. Her examination of what happened when considerable numbers of day care professionals were accused of sexually abusing children demonstrated that folk devils might have the capacity to fight back. This contributes to a confused and contested pattern of social reaction, as claim is met with counter-claim. de Young wants a more flexible model to allow for these possibilities. Nor are the measures resorted to predictable. In this case the legislative reform was symbolic since the law already covered the alleged offences. The outcome was contradictory in other ways. Though most of the day care cases eventually collapsed, the issue of child abuse was put firmly on the agenda. Like Watney, she sees the focus of the panic embodying wider uncertainties. The safety of childcare related directly to the dilemmas posed by mothers remaining in the workforce.

So once again we encounter feisty folk devils, confused social reaction, symbolic outcomes and a panic which signifies social tensions. Like

Thornton and McRobbie, she feels that Cohen's model is too much a child of its time. The world has moved on while the model has not. It may be that at least some of these criticisms can be incorporated into the model, if it is recognized that each of Cohen's stages is contestable. All the way from the initial definition and labelling through to the measures resorted to, opposition may prove effective. The lack of what Goode and Ben-Yehuda identified as the necessary degree of consensus can derail the whole panic. But such concessions would not rescue the model from accusations that it has been rendered obsolete.

The last two readings constitute a debate between two contemporary authors over the very idea of a moral panic. In *Reading 21* Ungar (2001) accepts that the concept was once an effective way of analysing the sources of collective fear and anxiety but suggests that these are altering in risk society. New kinds of environmental and related issues emerge as the focus of organized concern.

The new issues differ in several ways from moral panics. Compared with moral panics, environmental issues are much more unpredictable. The 'real' extent of the problem is unknown. Nor can the state claim to take effective action when its own negligence is the perceived problem. The threats posed by such issues are also long-term and do not come and go. Mobilizing a social control apparatus targeted at folk devils is not applicable to risk issues, where claims and counter-claims are much more evenly contested.

For Ungar the concept of a moral panic is fundamentally inadequate to account for new risk issues. Even within the narrow range where they can still be applied, the models have several intrinsic deficiencies. Only successful panics have been studied, not failed ones, so the model is bound to be verified. The fundamental argument that moral panics are defined by their disproportionality can only be sustained by more reliable evidence about the 'real' dimensions than is usually produced. The implication is that moral panic models, questionable even in their own terms, have little to offer the analysis of the new types of issues dominant in the risk society.

While efforts have been made to situate moral panic models within the theory of risk society, Ungar interprets the two as mutually incompatible. The kinds of risks identified are not local threats to the moral order: they are global threats to the order of nature. Ungar attempts to promote their significance at the expense of traditional risks represented by moral panics.

The position that moral panic models are inadequate and obsolete is contested in *Reading 22* by Hier (2003). He argues that many of the processes which Ungar sees as differentiating risk issues from moral panics are often similar or becoming so. For example, in both, there may be contestation over the validity of claims made about the threat, whatever it is.

On key issues, moral panic models seem to be more accurate than some risk theory. One instance is that the view of social anxiety held by moral panic models may be more accurate than that of risk theorists. The latter tend to see everyday life as permeated by a sense of global environmental risk, as portrayed by the media, but there is little evidence to support this assumption. By contrast, there are many examples to support the idea that moral panics mobilize a sense of risk and danger at the level of everyday life.

In times of uncertainty people seek to recreate a sense of community and thus of order by redrawing the boundaries between those who belong and those who do not. The stranger is regarded with suspicion, likely at any moment to be redefined as an enemy who threatens the safety of the community and the order which it embodies. Such processes can be mobilized by the state. Extraordinary measures are deemed necessary to preserve order by controlling the enemy within and excluding the enemy without. All this points not to a decline in the rate of moral panics and their cultural significance but to a continuing rise. In the risk society the concept of moral panic is more relevant than ever. Elsewhere Hier (2002: 329) has suggested moral panic analysis might usefully be connected to theories of moral regulation being developed by historians.

Other than those represented here, there are surprisingly few attempts to evaluate moral panic models as a whole. Miller and Kitzinger (1998) and Atmore (1999) may be exceptions but the scope of their critique is limited by their concentration on particular case studies, AIDS and child abuse respectively. This may change as criminologists on both sides of the Atlantic start to take the model seriously. On the other hand, if postmodernist perspectives remain influential, then moral panic concepts may remain peripheral in both mainstream and alternative sociology. Then no notice will have been taken of Ken Thompson's admonition that moral panic 'should be recognized for what it is: a truly sociological concept' (Thompson 1998: 142).

References

Atmore, C. (1999) Towards rethinking moral panic: child sexual abuse conflicts and social constructionist responses, in C. Bagley and K. Mallick (eds) *Child Sexual Abuse and Adult Offenders: New Theory and Research*. Aldershot: Ashgate Publishing.

Hier, S. (2002) Conceptualizing moral panic through a moral economy of harm, *Critical Sociology* 28(3): 311–34.

Miller, D. and Kitzinger, J. (1998) AIDS, the policy process and moral panics, in D. Miller, J. Kitzinger, K. Williams and P. Beharrell *The Circuit of Mass Communication: Media Strategies, Representation and Audience Reception in the AIDS Crisis*. London: Sage.

Thompson, K. (1998) *Moral Panics*. London: Routledge.

Further Reading

Cohen, S. (2002) Introduction to the third edition, *Folk Devils and Moral Panics*. London: Routledge.

Critcher, C. (2003) *Moral Panics and the Mass Media*. Milton Keynes: Open University Press.

de Young, M. (2004) *The Day Care Ritual Abuse Moral Panic*. Jefferson, NC: McFarland and Company Inc.

18

AIDS, 'MORAL PANIC' THEORY AND HOMOPHOBIA

Simon Watney (1988)

AIDS and Discourses About Sexuality

It is a commonplace of medical history that every major epidemic initially appears in a specific localized population. When *The People* reports that AIDS is not 'just a gay disease', and *The Daily Telegraph* conjures up the spectacle of 'rivulets of heterosexual infection snaking out beyond the risk groups', it should be apparent that something very strange and significant is going on. AIDS is being used to articulate modern theories of sexuality, or what Freud called object-choice, as if the virus itself is intrinsically attracted to particular sexual constituencies and not others. We need to establish once and for all, as an urgent priority, that like any other virus. HIV is not a property or respector or persons or of groups of persons. It is simply a blood disease, against which relatively simple precautions are highly effective. That public information campaigns are unable to address this fact remains in need of explanation, together with the whole tendency to either stigmatize or entirely ignore the situation of vast majority of people with AIDS. ... The enormity of the displacement of attention to the situation of non-gay people with AIDS speaks volumes in itself. As one American commentator has pointed out.

> For gay men, sex, that most powerful implement of attachment and arousal, is also an agent of communion, replacing an often hostile family and even shaping politics. It represents an ecstatic break with years of glances and guises, the furtive past we left behind. Straight people have no comparable experience, though it may seem so in

memory. They are never called upon to deny desire, only to defer its consummation.

He concludes that 'for heterosexuals to act as if AIDS were a threat to everyone demeans the anxiety of gay men who really are at risk, and for gay men to act as if we're all going to die demeans the anguish of those who are actually ill ... '(Goldstein, 1983). A media communications industry which can only acknowledge the existence of gay men as a target for contempt and thinly veiled hatred is unlikely to be able to address itself to the issues of sexual diversity which the AIDS epidemic requires us to face as the *sine qua non* of any effective preventative strategies which alone may prevent the spread of the HIV infection, or adequate support measures for the two million gay men in the UK who live from day to day through these terrible times with varying degrees of courage and fear, anger and grief.

The Limits of Panic

Most lesbian and gay commentators on such attitudes have favoured the influential British sociological theory of 'moral panics' for the purposes of explanation and analysis. Drawing on the 'new' criminology developed in the late 1960s, Stanley Cohen (1972) described how societies

> appear to be subject, every now and then, to periods of moral panic. A condition, episode or person emerges to become defined as a threat to societal values and interests; its nature is presented in a stylized and stereotypical fashion by the mass media; the moral barricades are manned by editors, bishops, politicians and other right-thinking people; ... Sometimes the panic passes over and is forgotten, except in folk-lore and collective memory; at other times it has more serious and long-lasting repercussions and might produce such changes as those in legal and social policy or even in the way the society perceives itself.

Subsequent writers, of whom Stuart Hall (1978) is perhaps the most notable, have developed this general picture to embrace the entire process by which popular consent is won for measures which require a 'more than usual' exercise of regulation, particularly in domains which are traditionally understood in liberal philosophy to be private, and especially the home. Hall's work in particular has encouraged a 'stages' view of motal panies, leading to increasingly punitive state control, although it is important to stress that moral panics do not necessarily stem from the state itself, or any of its immediate avatars. On the contrary, what is at stake is the entire relationship between governments and other uneven and conflicting institutions addressing a supposedly unified 'general public' through the mass media. This is particularly important to bear in mind for anyone approaching the question of the representation of homosexuality in this culture, since the entire subject is already and always historically preconstituted as 'scandal'. Indeed, one of the major reasons why lesbian and gay critics were attracted to 'moral panic' theory in the first place was because it offered a corrective alternative to the then dominant school of orthodox sociological 'deviance' theory, which holds, as Jeffrey Weeks (1981) has pointed out, that sexual unorthodoxy 'is somehow a quality inherent in ... individuals, to which the social then has to respond'. For 'deviance' theorists homosexuality is itself a problem, whereas 'moral panic' theory allows us to examine some of the conditions and means whereby homosexuality is problematized.

In his most recent book Jeffrey Weeks (1986) describes how 'one of the most striking features of the AIDS crisis is that, unlike most illnesses, from the first its chief victims were chiefly blamed for causing the disease, whether because of their social attitudes or sexual practices'. He goes on to explain how 'In the normal course of a moral panic there is a characteristic stereotyping of the main actors as peculiar types of monsters, leading to an escalating level of fear and peceived threat, the taking up of panic stations and absolutist positions, and a search for symbolic, and usually imaginary solutions to the dramatized problem'. Gayle Rubin (1984) has also described moral panics as,

the 'political moment' of sex, in which diffuse attitudes are channeled into political action and from there into social change. The white slavery hysteria of the 1950s, and the child pornography panic of the late 1970s were typical moral panics. Because sexuality in Western societies is so mystified, the wars over it are often fought at oblique angles, aimed at phony targets, conducted with misplaced passions, and are highly, intensely symbolic. Sexual activities often function as signifiers for personal and social apprehensions to which they have no intrinsic connection. During a moral panic, such fears attach to some unfortunate sexual activity or population. The media become ablaze with indignation, the public behaves like a rabid mob, the police are activated, and the state enacts new laws and regulations. When the furore has passed, some innocent erotic group has been decimated, and the state has extended its power into new areas of erotic behaviour ... Moral panics rarely alleviate any real problem, because they are aimed at chimeras and signifiers. They draw on the pre-existing discursive structure which invents victims in order to justify treating 'vices' as crimes.

This is how Gayle Rubin, and many other commentators, have qualified what has been going on around AIDS for the last several years. However, the very longevity and continuity of AIDS commentary already presents a problem for a 'moral panic' theory, in so far as this is evidently a panic which refuses to go away, a permanent panic as it were, rather than a 'political moment'. Whilst we may find a certain initial descriptive likeness to familiar events in their description as moral panics, this does not help us to understand the constant nature of ideological supervision and non-state regulation of sexuality throughout the modern period, especially in matters concerning representation. To begin with, the idea of a moral panic may be employed to characterize *all* conflicts in the public domain where stigmatization takes place. It cannot however discriminate between different orders or different degrees of moral panic. Nor can it explain why certain types of event should be especially privileged in this way. Above all, it obscures the endless 'overhead' narrative of such phenomena, as one panic gives way to another, and different panics overlap and reinforce one another. We need to understand how some moral panics may condense a host of anxieties, focusing them on a single target object, whilst others work in tandem to produce a unified effect which is only partially present and articulated in any one of its component elements. Thus for example AIDS commentary tends to draw on a wide range of concerns about childhood sexuality, homosexuality, prostitution, pornography, drug use, and so, which heavily overdetermine all discussion of the virus. At the same time the continual reporting of sexual assaults, murders, debates on sex education in schools and so on all orchestrate the larger question of sexuality itself, as something to be understood as intrinsically dangerous.

Moral panic theory directs our attention to sites of visible intervention concerning, for example, pornography, immigration policy, or abortion, which have strong public profiles. In this respect we might think of a moral panic around AIDS in terms of stories concerning the forcible detention of people with AIDS, or the presence of gay men (by now practically synonymous with the rhetorical figure of the 'AIDS-carrier') on the Royal Yacht *Britannia*, and so on and so forth. But this encouragement to think of AIDS commentary primarily if not exclusively in terms of *excess* does not help us make sense, for example, of government inaction, or the hysterical modesty of politicians from Mrs Thatcher downwards who have been against the provision of explicit safer-sex advice on television or in newspaper 'public information' campaigns. Their actions are far more damaging and dangerous in the long run than all the ravings of Fleet Street, since they effectively condemn thousands of people to ignorance about the very strategies by which lives may be saved. Just as the Centers for Disease Control in the United States have consistently refused to fund sexually explicit educational materials, so until recently the British government is effectively sentencing countless gay to men to death. As Ann Guidici Fettner (1986) concludes, 'AIDS education should have been started the moment it was realized that the disease is sexually transmitted.' In this situation it is difficult but vitally important to recognize that from the perspective of the state gay men are regarded in their entirety as a disposable population.

Classical moral panic theory interprets representations of specific 'scandals' as events which appear and then disappear, having run their ideological course. Such a view makes it difficult to theorize representation as a site of *permanent* ideological struggle and contestation between rival pictures of the world. We do not in fact watch the unfolding of discontinuous and discrete 'moral panics', but rather the mobility of ideological confrontations across the entire field of industrialized communications. This is most markedly the case in relation to those images which handle and evaluate the meanings of the human body, where rival and incompatible institutions and values are involved in a ceaseless and remorseless struggle to discover and disclose its supposedly universal 'human' truth. Hence the intensity of struggle to define the meanings of AIDS, with the virus being used by all and sundry as a kind of glove-puppet from the mouth of which different interest groups speak their values. AIDS, however, has no single 'truth' of its own, but becomes a powerful condensor for a great range of social, sexual and psychic anxieties. This is why it is better to think in terms of AIDS commentary, rather than assuming the existence of a coherent univocal 'moral panic' on the subject. We are here considering the circulation of symbols, of the raw materials from which human subjectivity is constructed. AIDS has been mobilized to embody a variety of perceived threats to individual and social stability, organized around the spectacle of illicit sex and physical corruption. It has been used to stabilize the figure of the heterosexual family unit which remains the central image in our society with which individuals are endlessly invited to identify their collective interests and their very core of being.

The Instrumental Family

As Foucault (1979) and others have argued, we need, however, to recognize that the image of the threatened and vulnerable family is a central motif in a society like ours for which the family is not simply a given object, but is rather an instrument of social policy. What AIDS commentary reveals is the ongoing crisis surrounding the representation of the family in a culture in which only a minority of citizens actually occupy its conventional space at any given moment in time. Familial ideology is thus obliged to fight a continual rearguard action in order to disavow the social and sexual diversity of a culture which can never be adequately pictured in the traditional guise of the family. Those who threaten to expose the ideological operations of familialism will inevitably be castigated as 'enemies' of the family, which is pictured as under constant threat. [...]

[...]

It is clear that the categories which hold together the public profile of familialism – notions of 'decency', 'respectability', 'manliness', 'innocence', and so on – are primarily defensive, in so far as they work to protect individuals from the partially acknowledged fact of diversity. Hence the repetitive nature of moral panics, their fundamentally *serial* nature, and the wide range of tones and postures which they can assume 'on behalf' of the national family unit. The organization of desire in all its forms into the narrow channels of modern sexual identities ensures that the presence of 'enemies' is felt everywhere, within the self, and from without.

This is why there is such a dramatic disparity between the lived experience of people with AIDS, and the model of contagion which they are made to embody. We are not living through a distinct, coherent 'moral panic' concerning AIDS, a panic with a linear narrative and the prospect of closure. On the contrary, we are witnessing the ideological manoeuvres which unconsciously 'make sense' of this accidental triangulation of disease, sexuality, and homophobia. Hence the obsession of AIDS commentary with the distinction between supposedly 'innocent' and 'guilty' victims, and the total inability to distinguish between infectious and contagious illness. AIDS commentary rarely troubles to separate the question of HIV infection from individual opportunistic infection, preferring to talk of 'AIDS-carriers' and an 'AIDS-virus'. What we should recognize is that such telescoping of medical issues indicates a collapsing together of ideological concerns, which transform AIDS into a *malade imaginaire* – the viral personification of unorthodox deregulative desire, dressed up in the ghoulish likeness of degeneracy.

Hence, in the popular imagination of AIDS, we come close to the core of modern familial identities and social policy for which the perverse maps out the boundaries of the legitimate social order. This is why we need to be able to analyze the relations of contingency, analogy and substitution between phenomena which moral panic theory obliges us to think of as discrete and unconnected. Sociology obliges us to think of individual 'moral panics' around drugs, video films, football hooliganism, and so on, because it regards the family as 'a point of departure' rather than a product of complex negotiation between different institutional and discursive formations. Moral panics do not 'reflect' something we should think of as 'the social': on the contrary, they constitute the ground on which 'the social' emerges, in the words of Jacques Donzelot (1979), as 'a concrete space of intelligibility of the family' in which 'it is the social that suddenly looms as a strange abstraction'.

It is thus particularly unhelpful to think of AIDS commentary as a moral panic which somehow makes gay men into monsters, since that is an intrinsic effect of the medicalization of morality which accompanied the emergence of the modern categories of sexuality in the course of the last 200 years. What AIDS commentary does is to elide the virus and its presenting symptoms with the dominant cultural meanings of those constituencies in which it has emerged – black Africans, injecting drug users, prostitutes, and of course gay men. In this manner 'the social' is ever more narrowly confined within familial definitions and values, with the family being scrutinized ever more closely for physical symptoms of moral dissent. The sheer range and variety of AIDS commentary should alert us to the danger of any attempt to explain it in terms of any single, primary and all-determining causes. This however is precisely the tendency of the many lesbian and gay commentators who rely upon the notion of 'homophobia' as if this were an adequate, sufficient, and self-evident explanatory category. The term itself was first defined if not coined by George Weinberg (1973) in the immediate wake of Gay Liberationist politics in the early 1970s as 'a disease' and 'an attitude held by many non-homosexuals and perhaps by the majority of homosexuals in countries where there is discrimination against homosexuality'. For its inception, it uncomfortably straddled both the situation of all social and psychic aspects of attitudes towards homosexuality, as well as both homosexual and heterosexual identities. In effect, the notion simply reversed the sociological and psychiatric tendencies to pathologize all forms of homosexual identity and desire as symptoms of either 'deviance' or 'perversion'.

This confusion of social and psychic factors has dogged the history of the term's usage ever since. Thus Cindy Patton's (1986) recent notion of 'crotophobia' faithfully duplicates all the problems of the original term, being defined as

> the terrifying irrational reaction to the erotic which makes individuals and societies vulnerable to psychological and social control in cultures

where pleasure is strictly categorized and regulated. Each component of sexuality – sexual practice, desire, and sexual identity – constitutes a particular type of relationship between the individual and society, providing gripping opportunities for different forms of erotophobic repression.

Conclusion

Elsewhere (Watney, 1987) I have attempted to separate out some of the central strands within the hysterical dimensions of homosexual stigmatization. In this context though, I would like to return to the question of *systematic misinformation* concerning medical aspects of AIDS with which I began this chapter. Both doctors and journalists share a common professional training which massively privileges the family as the central term of social intelligibility. That doctors should be in the foreground of calls for the mass quarantine of people with AIDS is not in the least surprising, given the 'protective' identity which they are taught in medical school and in medical practice. Medicine remains perhaps the most difficult profession in which to 'come out' in the UK, and many young doctors have been ostracized and held back in their careers for no other reason. Indeed, the National Health Service itself addresses a 'national' population which signally and conspicuously fails to recognize the existence of lesbians and gay men as a fundamental constituency within the nation, let alone our specific medical needs. Effectively, 'national' medicine thereby becomes 'heterosexual' medicine, as is evident from the dramatic under-funding of hospitals and clinics as the AIDS epidemic proceeds to escalate. This is equally apparent from the inability of a medically constituted public information campaign to directly address the actual diversity of sexual practice with the 'public' which they supposedly addressing. Whilst the avoidance of a forbidden object is certainly a sign of phobia, we should remember that phobic avoidance is focussed not on what it is unconsciously afraid, but on displaced symbols of the terrifying object.

Some degrees of phobic response to homosexuality would seem to be the inevitable result of the psychic violence involved in the process which attempts to homogenize all children into the 'correct' identities of adult heterosexuality. But the notion of homophobia precisely avoids the whole question of how desire operates to motivate particular sexual behaviours. At the same time it serves to further regulate and reinforce the workings of modern sexual categories by seemingly forcing together all the varieties of homosexual desire and identity into a monolithic totality, faced by an equally monolithic heterosexuality. Whatever else might be said to characterize homophobia or erotophobia, the fact remains that their signs are understood to be expulsive and aggressive, rather than avertive and defensive.

Thus any approach to AIDS commentary rooted in a critique of homophobia is unlikely to be able to come to grips with subtle questions of metaphor, displacement, repetition, substitutions or absences, privileging instead the most violent physical and verbal abuse of people with AIDS, which in any case is relatively transparent in terms of ordinary liberal 'civil rights' analysis. The questions of why the HIV virus continues to be treated as if it were contagious and transmissable by casual contact, prove stubbornly resistant to the explanatory schemes provided either by 'moral panic' theory, or notions of a unified homophobia. Both in effect offer little more than 'false-consciousness' accounts of how different desiring constituencies perceive and evaluate one another, together with a latent functionalism which glimpses either a unified purposive state or a coherent collectivity of 'hererosexuality' at work behind social and psychic attitudes to AIDS.

Nonetheless, it is probably more helpful than not at this moment in time to retain the notion of homophobia at least as a collective term, referring to the entire range of interacting institutions, discourses and psychic processes which align AIDS with homosexuality as if by essence. This argument is supported by the probability that much hostility towards homosexuality is indeed phobic in origin, in so far as it stems from the threatening return to consciousness of desires and fantasies concerning the human body which can never be completely contained and successfully repressed within the narrow compass of heterosexual identities which defensively equate sexuality with sexual reproduction. The real 'threat' comes not from lesbians or gay men, but from the destabilization of conscious heterosexual identities from within themselves.

In this respect we can recognize that the most frequently encountered characteristic of AIDS commentary is projection, defined by Leo Bersani (1977) as 'a frantic defence against the return of dangerous images and sensations to the surface of consciousness; therefore, the individual urgently needs to maintain that certain representations or affects belong to the world and not to the self. In this manner we can begin to account for the ways in which AIDS is invariably made to carry a fantastic supplement which both precedes and exceeds any actual medical issues. In the same way we can chart the compulsive displacements which add up to the public meanings of AIDS, the scattering of themes and motifs across the entire field of public representation. To fail to notice the systematic connections between contemporary campaigns around sex education, procreation, children's sexuality and AIDS, by classifying them as separate and autonomous 'moral panics' is as dangerous today as any temptation to regard them all as no more than epiphenomena related to a unified and totally recalritrant homophobia.

References

Bersani, L. (1977) *Baudelaire and Freud*. Los Angeles, CA: University of California Press.
Cohen, S. (1972) *Folk Devils and Moral Panics: The Creation of the Mods and Rockers*. London: Martin Robertson.
Donzelot, J. (1979) *The Policing of Families: Welfare Versus the State*. London: Hutchinson.
Foucault, M. (1979) On governmentality, *Ideology and Consciousness*, 6: 5–21.
Giudici Fettner, A. (1986) Is the CDC dying of AIDS?, *Village Voice*, 21(7 October): 40.
Goldstein, R. (1983) Heartsick: fear and loving in the gay community, *Village Voice*, 28(28 June): 26.
Hall, S. et al. (1978) *Policing the Crisis*. London: Macmillan.
Patton, C. (1986) *Sex and Germs: The Politics of AIDS*. Boston, MA: South End Press.
Rubin, G. (1984) Thinking sex: notes for a radical theory of the politics of sexuality, in C. Vance (ed.) *Pleasure and Danger: Exploring Female Sexuality*. London: Routledge and Kegan Paul.
Watney, S. (1987) *Policing Desire: Pornography, AIDS and the Media*. London: Comedia Methuen.
Weeks, J. (1981) *Sex, Politics and Society: The Regulation of Sexuality since 1800*. London: Longman.
Weeks, J. (1986) *Sexuality*. London: Tavistock.
Weinberg, G. (1973) *Society and the Healthy Homosexual*. New York: Doubleday.

19

RE-THINKING 'MORAL PANIC' FOR MULTI-MEDIATED SOCIAL WORLDS

Angela McRobbie and Sarah L. Thornton
(1995)

'Moral panic' is now a term regularly used by journalists to describe a process which politicians, commercial promoters and media habitually attempt to incite. It has become a standard interview question to put to Conservative MPs: are they not whipping up a moral panic as a foil to deflect attention away from more pressing economic issues? It has become a routine means of making youth-orientated cultural products more alluring; acid house music was marketed as 'one of the most controversial sounds of 1988' set to outrage 'those who decry the glamorization of drug culture'. Moreover, as moral panics seem to guarantee the kind of emotional involvement that keeps up the interest of, not just tabloid, but broadsheet newspaper readers, as well as the ratings of news and true crime television, even the media themselves are willing to take some of the blame...

Moral panics, once the unintended outcome of journalistic practice, seem to have become a goal. Rather than periods to which societies are subject 'every now and then' (Cohen 1972/80:9), moral panics have become the way in which daily events are brought to the attention of the public. They are a standard response, a familiar, sometimes weary, even ridiculous rhetoric rather than an exceptional emergency intervention. Used by politicians to orchestrate consent, by business to promote sales in certain niche markets, and by media to make home and social affairs newsworthy, moral panics are constructed on a daily basis.

Given their high rate of turnover and the increasing tendency to label all kinds of media event as 'moral panic', we think it is time to take stock of the revisions, then consider the strengths and weaknesses of this key concept. Although both the original model of moral panics and the reformulations which introduced notions of ideology and hegemony were exemplary interventions in their time, we argue that it is impossible to rely on the old models with their stages and cycles, univocal media, monolithic societal or hegemonic reactions. The proliferation and fragmentation of mass, niche and micro-media and the multiplicity of voices, which compete and contest the meaning of the issues subject to 'moral panic', suggest that both the original and revised models are outdated in so far as they could not possibly take account of the labyrinthine web of determining relations which now exist between social groups and the media, 'reality' and representation.

The Original Theory of Moral Panics

Although the argument that media coverage can have an active role in creating deviant behaviour owes its existence to symbolic interactionist theories of 'labelling' (cf. Becker 1963; Wilkins 1964), it was the pioneering studies of Jock Young (1971) on the social meaning of drug-taking and Stanley Cohen (1972/1980) on the media-inspired confrontations between mods and rockers, and their edited collections (Cohen 1971; Cohen and Young 1973) which developed and effectively launched the concept of 'moral panic'. Not only did their studies explore how agents of social control like the police played a role in 'amplifying' deviance, but they developed a vocabulary for understanding the powerful part played by the media. This meant going beyond the sociological accounts which looked at patterns of ownership and control as signs of complicity between media and government. Attention was now being paid to the ideological role of the media and the active construction of certain kinds of meaning.

In addition, this work explored how deviant behaviour was interactive rather than absolutist. It was more often the outcome of complex chains of social interaction than the product of young people with a predisposition, individually or environmentally, towards crime or rule-breaking behaviour. Finally this approach challenged moral guardians by suggesting that their overreaction was counterproductive. The media coverage of deviance acted as a kind of handbook of possibilities to be picked over by new recruits. Worse still, segregating young people away from the community created a greater risk of long-term social disorder since 'a society can control effectively only those who perceive themselves to be members of it' (Young 1971:39). Overreaction, therefore, contributed to further polarization, though this might have been the desired effect, as Stuart Hall et al. (1978) later argued.

Cohen's *Folk Devils and Moral Panics* is rightfully a classic of media

sociology, embracing a greater degree of complexity than the many summaries of the work indicate. He acknowledges that social control is uneven
and much less mechanistic than the model of deviancy amplification suggests. Indeed one group of respondents (drawn from the non-mod, non-
rocker public) criticizes the media for over-reporting the clashes, while
others describe how they came down to the beach to have a look at the
'fun'. Cohen has a sophisticated grasp of how these events fed into popular
folklore ('Where are the mods and rockers today?' was a question he was
repeatedly asked while carrying out his fieldwork) and when the panic had
finally run its course and de-amplification had set in, the characters in this
drama settled into history as recognizable social types belonging to a particular period, sometimes referred to, even by the agents of social control,
with a hint of nostalgia.

[. . .]

Contesting 'Society' and 'Hegemony'

British society and media, youth culture and 'deviance' have changed
considerably since the 1960s, and these historical transformations bring to
light some of the theoretical and methodological limits of [past] studies. In
original moral panic theory, 'society' and 'societal reactions' were monolithic and, as others have already argued, ultimately functionalist. Similarly,
Hall et al., (1978) Pearson (1983) and Watney (1987) perhaps over-state
hegemony and overlook the counter-discourses from which they draw and
to which they contribute. In the 1990s, when social differentiation and
audience segmentation are the order of the day, we need take account of a
plurality of reactions, each with their different constituencies, effectivities
and modes of discourse.

Given the kinds of moral panic to which they attend, it is problematic
that Cohen's 'society', Pearson's description of collective memory and Hall
et al.'s 'hegemony' exclude youth. Ethnographies of contemporary youth
culture (cf. Thornton 1995) find that youth are inclined *not* to lament a safe
and stable past *but* to have overwhelming nostalgia for the days when
youth culture was genuinely transgressive.

Whether youth cultures espouse overt politics or not, they are often set
on being culturally 'radical'. Moral panic can therefore be seen as a culmination and fulfillment of youth cultural agendas in so far as negative
news coverage baptizes transgression. What better way to turn difference
into defiance, lifestyle into social upheaval, leisure into revolt?

Disapproving mass media coverage legitimizes and authenticates youth
cultures to the degree that it is hard to imagine a British youth 'movement'

without it. For, in turning youth into news, mass media both frame sub-cultures as major events and disseminate them; a tabloid front page *is* frequently a self-fulfilling prophecy. Sociologists might rightly see this in terms of 'deviancy amplification', but youth have their own discourses which see the process as one in which a 'scene' is transformed into a 'movement'. Here youth have a point, for what gets amplified is not only a 'deviant' activity, but the records, haircuts and dance styles which *were said* to accompany the activities.

Knowledge of this youth-culture ethos is such that its exploitation has become a routine marketing strategy of the publishing and recording industries. For example, the 'moral panic' about 'Acid House' in 1988, 1989 and 1990 began with a prediction on the back of the album that launched the music genre. The sleeve notes described the new sound as 'drug induced', 'sky high' and 'ecstatic' and concluded with a prediction of moral panic: 'The sound of acid tracking will undoubtedly become one of the most controversial sounds of 1988, provoking a split between those who adhere to its underground creed and those who decry the glamoriza-tion of drug culture.' In retrospect, this seems prescient, but the statement is best understood as hopeful. Moral panics are one of the few marketing strategies open to relatively anonymous instrumental dance music. To quote one music monthly, they amount to a 'priceless PR campaign' (*Q*, January 1989).

Following London Records' sleeve notes, the youth-orientated music and style press repeatedly predicted that a moral panic about Acid House was 'inevitable'. Innuendo, then full-blown exposés about Ecstasy use in British clubs, appeared in the music press for months before the story was picked up by the tabloids. By the end of August, many magazines were wondering why the tabloids were ignoring the issue, while others, confident of eventual moral panic, imagined possible headlines like 'London Gripped by Ecstasy!' or 'Drug Crazed New Hippies in Street Riot' (*Time Out*, 17–24 August 1988). In September 1988, during the 'silly season', the tabloids finally took the bait and subjected the culture to the full front-page treatment. The government, Labour opposition *and* the police were keen to ignore the topic for as long as they possibly could, only belatedly making statements, arrests and recommending legislation. This moral panic was incited by a couple of culture industries (e.g. recording and magazine publishing) well versed in the 'hip' ideologies of youth subcultures.

In addition to the difficulty we have in excluding rather large social groups and industrial activities from accounts of 'society' or 'consensus', so we can't ignore the many voices which now contribute to the debate during moral panics. In the 1990s, interest groups, pressure groups, lobbies and campaigning experts are mobilized to intervene in moral panics. For example, the spokeswoman of the National Council for One Parent Families, Sue Slipman, played a leading role, on an almost weekly basis over a period of three or six months, in diminishing the demonization by the Tories of young single mothers for having children without being married.

One of the main aims of pressure groups is timely intervention in relevant moral panics – to be able to respond instantly to the media demonization of the group they represent, and to provide information and analysis designed to counter this representation. The effectiveness of these groups and in particular their skills at working with the media and providing highly professional 'soundbites' more or less on cue make them an invaluable resource to media machinery working to tight schedules and with increasingly small budgets. They allow the media to be seen to be doing their duty by providing 'balance' in their reporting. At the same time, they show how 'folk devils' can and do 'fight back'.

This phenomenon of becoming an expert, having been a deviant, has a long history in the field of serious crime, drug abuse and juvenile delinquency. However, the proliferation of groups recently set up to campaign on behalf of or with folk devils and the skill with which they engage with media is an extremely important development in political culture. When Labour and Conservatives take the same line on law and order, arguing for 'effective punishment' and the need for the moral regeneration of society, many media are inclined to give voice to other, sometimes dissenting, groups. In the absence of an immediate and articulate response from Labour, such groups occasionally function as a virtual form of opposition to the government. A new political sociology, taking into account the prominence of the media, might fruitfully explore the precise sphere of influence and the effectiveness of these organizations.

Although moral panics are anti-intellectual, often characterized by a certain religious fervour, and historically most effectively used by the right, only a predominantly right-wing national press arguably stops them from being amenable to the current left. Of course, government is always advantaged, due to higher number of authoritative news sources and to institutionalized agenda-setting. But, there is always the possibility of backfire...

The delicate balance of relations which the moral panic sociologists saw existing between media, agents of social control, folk devils and moral guardians, has given way to a much more complicated and fragmented set of connections. Each of the categories described by moral panics theorists has undergone a process of fissure in the intervening years. New liaisons have been developed and new initiatives pursued. In particular, two groups seem to be making ever more vocal and 'effective' intervention: pressure groups have, among other things, strongly contested the vocality of the traditional moral guardians; and commercial interests have planted the seeds, and courted discourses, of moral panic in seeking to gain the favourable attention of youthful consumers.

This leads us to query the usefulness of the term 'moral panic' – a metaphor which depicts a complex society as a single person who experiences sudden fear about its virtue. The term's anthropomorphism and totalization arguably mystify more than they reveal. Its conception of morals overlooks the youthful ethics of abandon and the moral imperatives of pressure groups and vocal experts. In the 1990s, we need to acknowledge the perspectives and articulations of different sectors of society. New sociologies of social regulation need to shift attention away from the conventional points in the circuit of amplification and control and look instead to these other spaces.

Moral Panics for Every Medium

Not only need the attitudes and activities of different social groups and organizations be taken into account and not subsumed under a consensual 'society', but also the disparate perspectives of different mass, niche and micro-media need to be explored. Britain saw a remarkable 73 per cent increase in consumer magazine titles during the 1980s – the result of more detailed market research, tighter target marketing and new technologies like computer mailing and desk-top publishing. ... Crucially, the success of many of these magazines has been in the discovery and effective representation of niches of opinion and identity...

Despite their proliferation and diversification, however, the media are obviously not a positive reflection of the diversity of Britain's social interests. This is partly because there are large groups of people in which the media are not economically, and, therefore, editorially interested – crucially, the D and E 'social grades' which are categorized by the *National Readership Survey* as the unskilled working class and 'those at the lowest levels of subsistence', in other words, the long-term employed and poorly pensioned. But even here, there are glimmers of hope. The *Big Issue* is now perceived as the newspaper voice of the homeless. Other groups and agencies produce a never-ending flow of newsletters and press releases many of which are written in a house-style customized to the needs of the journalists on national and local media. So-called folk devils now produce their own media as a counter to what they perceive as the biased media of the mainstream...

But one needn't turn to specialist magazines and newspapers to find the plurality and divergences of opinion that characterize today's (and probably yesterday's) 'moral panics'. Even the national dailies have dependably different stances. The paper whose tone and agenda is closest to 1960/1970s-style moral panic is probably the *Daily Mail*. During the Thatcher years, the *Daily Mail* practised and perfected the characteristics of hegemony, in a way which was in uncanny harmony with Thatcherism. It was a daily process of reaching out to win consent through endlessly defining and redefining social questions and representing itself as the moral voice of the newly self-identified middle class as well as the old lower-middle class. The fact that the *Mail* is the only national daily with more female than male readers – if only 51 per cent female – undoubtedly informs its respectable girl's brand of moral indignity. Hence, hysteria about single and teenage mothers is perfect material for a *Daily Mail* moral panic.

Tabloids like the *Sun* prefer to espouse an altogether different brand of moral outrage. With a topless sixteen year old on page 3 and a hedonistic pro-sex editorial line, their moralism need be finely tuned. But that doesn't stop them from being the most preachy and prescriptive of Britain's daily papers, with page after page of the '*Sun* says ...' However, the *Sun*'s favourite moral panics are of the 'sex, drugs and rock'n'roll' variety – stories about other people having far *too much* fun, if only because the paper is set on maintaining a young (and not graying) readership. Moreover, these kinds of story have the advantage of allowing their readers to have their cake and eat it too; they can vicariously enjoy and/or secretly admire the transgression one moment, then be shocked and offended the next. When considering the way moral panics work within different publications, one need keep in mind that *Sun* readers take their paper a good deal less seriously than *Mail* readers take theirs. As Mark Pursehouse discovered in interviewing *Sun* readers, one of the key pleasures in reading the *Sun* is the process of estimating what part of a story is true, what parts exaggerated or totally invented. (cf. Pursehouse 1991)

In the last few years, the broadsheets have not only made use of more visual and colour material, they can also be seen to have adopted tabloid-style headlines to accompany their tabloid supplements. For example, the covers of the *Guardian* G2 section frequently sport exaggerated, sensational headlines. 'BLOOD ON THE STREETS': They're Packing Pistols in Manchester' announces a story about the increasing use of firearms by young drug dealers on mountain bikes in Manchester's Moss Side (*Guardian*, 9 August 1993). Given the more measured copy which follows, the

Guardian would seem to be using this 'shock horror' language to lighten up the story – the capital letters signifying an ironic borrowing of tabloid style. But, as the *Sun*'s language is understood by many of its readers as tongue-in-cheek, the *Guardian*'s irony gives it an alibi, but not absolution. Moreover, these mixtures of outrage and amusement point to the 'entertainment value' of moral panics – something mentioned but not really integrated into previous models....

In considering the *Daily Mail*, the *Sun* and the *Guardian*, we've found that each paper has its own style of in-house moralism. As the British press becomes more competitive, one strategy for maintaining healthy circulation figures is for a newspaper to cast itself in the role of moral guardian, ever alert to new possibilities for concern and indignation. It would seem that professional journalistic style, carefully attuned to the popularity of 'human interest' stories, draws on a moralistic voice which, for the purposes of variety, it is willing to undercut with occasional irony, jokes, etc.

Although the multiplicity of contemporary moral panics is perhaps best demonstrated in relation to print media, the same tendencies can be found in radio and television. Even with only four terrestrial channels, new definitions of youth programming have opened a space for counter-discourses...

Mediated Social Worlds

In addition to unpacking 'society', on the one hand, and the 'media', on the other, the third consideration in updating models of 'moral panic' need be that the media is no longer something separable from society. Social reality is experienced through language, communication and imagery. Social meanings and social differences are inextricably tied up with representation. Thus when sociologists call for an account which tells how life actually is, and which deals with the real issues rather than the spectacular and exaggerated ones, the point is that these accounts of reality are already representations and sets of meanings about what they perceive the 'real' issues to be. These versions of 'reality' would also be impregnated with the mark of media imagery rather than somehow pure and untouched by the all-pervasive traces of contemporary communications.

The media have long been seen to be embedded in the fabric of society. What may be constitutively new is the degree to which media have become something with which the social is continuously being defined. For example, characterizations like '*Mirror* reader' or '*Times* reader' often give us as good an indication of social class as the mention of a particular occupation.

Social age and generation (rather than biological age) are played out in the relation between Radios One and Two or Capital FM and Capital Gold. Subtle differences of gender identity are negotiated when, say, a working-class woman says she dislikes all soap operas, preferring instead news, sport and nature programmes. Similarly, at the risk of being cliché, for a man to admit his devotion to the films of Joan Crawford and Judy Garland is, in some contexts, tantamount to 'coming out'.

At another level, the hard and fast divide between media professionals and media 'punters' seems to have broken down to some extent. The ownership of home video-cameras, the new space for broadcasting home video material on national television ..., the existence of 'right to reply' programmes, the possession of degrees in media studies all point in this direction. Audiences can be credited with possessing a greater degree of 'media literacy' than they did in the past. Also important here is the introduction of a distinctively amateurish (rather than professional) style of presentation.

Finally, the increasing reliance on the audience as a resource for successful television, either as visualized participants or audible internal audiences, seems to give a positive place to the audience in the process of programme production.

The strength of the old models of moral panic was that they marked the connection between 'the media' and 'social control'. But, nowadays, most political strategies *are* media strategies. The contest to determine news agendas is the first and last battle of the political campaign. Moreover, the kinds of social issues and political debates which were once included on the agendas of moral panic theorists as sites of social anxiety, and even crisis, could now be redefined as part of an endless debate about who 'we' are and what 'our' national culture is. These are profoundly 'home affairs'. The daily intensity and drama of their appearance and the many voices now heard in the background but in the foreground, punctuating and producing reality, point more to the reality of dealing with social difference than to the unity of current affairs (cf. Hall, Connell and Curtis 1981).

Conclusion

What has been argued here is that the model of moral panic is urgently in need of updating precisely because of its success. While the theory began its life in radical sociology, the strength of the argument quickly found its way into those very areas with which it was originally concerned, influencing social policy and attitudes to deviance generally. As a result, the police, as agents of social control now show some awareness of the dangers of over-reaction, while sectors of the media regularly remind viewers of the dangers of moral panic and thus of alienating sections of the community by falsely attributing to them some of the characteristics of the so-called folk devils.

Crucially, the theory has, over the years, drawn attention to the importance of empowering folk devils so that they or their representatives can challenge the cycle of sanctions and social control. Pressure groups, lobbies, self-help and interest groups have sprung up across the country and effectively positioned themselves as authoritative sources of comment and criticism. They now contribute to the shape of public debate, playing a major role in contesting what they perceive as dangerous stereotypes and popular misconceptions.

The theory has also influenced business practice, albeit through an undoubtedly more circuitous route. Culture industry promotions and marketing people now understand how, for certain products like records, magazines, movies and computer games, nothing could be better for sales than a bit of controversy – the threat of censorship, the suggestion of sexual scandal or subversive activity. The promotional logic is twofold: first, the cultural good will receive a lot of free, if negative, publicity because its associations with moral panic have made it newsworthy; second, rather than alienating everyone, it will be attractive to a contingent of consumers who see themselves as alternative, avant-garde, radical, rebellious or simply young. In the old models of moral panic, the audience played a minor role and remained relatively untheorized. With few exceptions, they were the space of consensus, the space of media manipulation, the space of an easily convinced public. A new model need embrace the complex realm of reception – readers, viewers, listeners and the various social groups categorized under the heading of public opinion cannot be read off the representation of social issues.

The moral panics we have been discussing here are less monolithic than those the classic model implied. Recent moral panics do remain overwhelmingly concerned with moral values, societal regularities and drawing of lines between the permissible and the less acceptable. However, hard and fast boundaries between 'normal' and 'deviant' would seem to be less common – if only because moral panics are now continually contested. Few sociologists would dispute the expansion over the last decade of what used to be called, quite simply, the mass media. The diversification of forms of media and the sophisticated restructuring of various categories of audience require that, while a consensual social morality might still be a political objective, the chances of it being delivered directly through the channels of the media are much less certain.

References

Becker, H. (1963) *The Outsiders*. New York: Free Press.

Cohen, S. (ed.) (1971) *Images of Deviance*. Harmondsworth: Penguin.

Cohen, S. ([1972]/1980) *Folk Devils and Moral Panics*. Oxford: Basil Blackwell.

Cohen, S. and Young, J. (eds) (1973) *The Manufacture of News*. London: Constable.

Curran, J. (1978) The press as an agency of social control: an historical perspective, in G. Boyce et al. (eds) *Newspaper History*. London: Constable.

Hall, S. et al. (1978) *Policing the Crisis: Mugging, the State and Law and Order*. London: Macmillan.

Hall, S., Connell, I. and Curtis, L. (1981) The 'unity' of current affairs television, in T. Bennett et al. (eds) *Popular Television and Film*. London: British Film Institute.

Pearson, G. (1983) *Hooligans: A History of Respectable Fears*. London: Macmillan.

Pursehouse, M. (1991) Looking at the *Sun*: into the nineties with a tabloid and its readers, *Cultural Studies from Birmingham*, 1: 88–133.

Thornton, S.L. (1995) *Club Culture: Music, Media and Subcultural Capital*. Oxford: Polity.

Watney, S. (1987) *Policing Desire: Pornography, AIDS and the Media*. London: Methuen.

Wilkins, L. T. (1964) *Social Deviance: Social Policy, Action and Research*. London: Tavistock.

Young, J. (1971) *The Drugtakers: The Social Meaning of Drug Use*. London: Paladin.

ANOTHER LOOK AT MORAL PANICS

THE CASE OF SATANIC DAY CARE CENTERS

Mary de Young (1998)

20

The term 'moral panic' was coined by Cohen (1972) to describe a collective response, generated by unsettling social strain and incited and spread by interest groups, toward persons who are actively transformed into 'folk devils' and then treated as threats to dominant social interests and values. Through the use of highly emotive claims and fear-based appeals, a moral panic tends to orchestrate cultural consent that something must be done, and quickly, to deal with this alleged threat. The increased social control that typically follows from such consent ends up preserving and reasserting the very hegemonic values and interests that purportedly are being undermined by the folk devils. A moral panic, then, serves a distinct stabilizing function at a time of unsettling social strain.

Why and how a moral panic arises, the types of people it demonizes, and the methods by which it ends up defining what Durkheim (1938) refers to as the normative contours and moral boundaries of a given society at any historical moment have been of considerable interest to sociologists....

The term also is used to describe the collective response to new folk devils who were demonized in the 1980s – day care providers who, it was claimed, were abusing their very young charges in satanic rituals that included such horrific practices as blood-drinking, cannibalism, and human sacrifices. Between 1983 and 1991, in fact, over a hundred day care centers in major urban areas and small towns across the country were investigated for what quickly came to be known as satanic ritual abuse (Nathan and Snedeker 1995). These investigations created deep and often irreparable breaches in the communities where they occurred and resulted in scores of arrests, often long and costly criminal trials, many convictions despite the

Table 20.1 Day care center, year of investigation initiation, and location

Day Care Center	Year	Location
McMartin	1983	Manhattan Beach, CA
Country Walk	1984	Miami, FL
Small World	1984	Niles, MI
Fells Acres	1984	Malden, MA
Georgian Hills	1984	Memphis, TN
Rogers Park Jewish Community	1984	Chicago, IL
Manhattan Ranch	1984	Manhattan Beach, CA
Craig's Country	1985	Clarksville, MD
Felix's	1985	Carson City, NV
East Valley YMCA	1985	EI Paso, TX
Glendale Montessori	1987	Stuart, FL
Old Cutler	1989	Miami, FL
Little Rascals	1989	Edenton, NC
Faith Chapel	1989	San Diego, CA
Fran's	1991	Austin, TX

absence of any corroborating and material evidence, usually draconian prison sentences and, over recent years, many reversals of those convictions upon appeal (de Young 1994).

The satanic day care scare had all of what Goode and Ben-Yehuda (1994) set out as the defining characteristics of a moral panic: it was widespread, overreactive, volatile, hostile, and largely irrational. But another look at this moral panic, and at the day care cases that are the stuff of it, reveals some interesting refinements that are needed in classical moral panic theory if it is to retain its explanatory and analytical power in the contemporary social world.

It is the purpose of this present article to offer that look. First, the article presents an overview of the satanic day care moral panic. Then, it uses data from a sample of 15 day care cases (Table 20.1), some more notorious than others, to advance and illustrate a discussion of the areas of classic moral panic theory in need of refinement and updating. . . .

The Satanic Day Care Moral Panic

A basic analysis of any moral panic must account for its timing target and trigger, content, spread, and denouement (Goode and Ben-Yehuda 1994). Each of these factors will be examined in turn to provide a necessarily brief overview of the satanic day care moral panic of the 1980s.

Timing of the moral panic

By the 1980s, a number of social, ideological, professional, and political forces had contributed to a growing cultural anxiety about satanic menaces to children (Richardson et al. 1991; Victor 1993). From concerns about demonic influences in heavy metal music, fantasy role-playing games, tarot cards and ouija boards; to urban legends about mysterious satanists abducting fair-haired, blue-eyed children from shopping malls; to rumors of covert satanic cults filming child pornography; to tales about satanic child sex rings, that decade was rife with 'mini-moral panics' about satanic menaces to children, and ripened by them for more.

Target and trigger of the moral panic

Coincident with that concern about the protection of children was another one about their daily care. The economic strains that made participation in the market economy a necessity, and the ideological force of the women's movement that made it an increasingly accessible alternative to unpaid housework, combined in that decade to put more and more women with young children into the labor market. In 1980, in fact, a record 45 per cent of them were working outside of the home and using public and private day care centers for daily child care. . . .

Most working parents were doing so with more than a little anxiety, however, and considered day care centers a change for the worse from the stay-at-home child care of their parents' generation (Hutchison 1992). That anxiety was heightened by the impact of other types of economic strains. Deep cuts in federal funding that over half of the public day care centers had received just a few years before closed down many of them, and left the remaining centers with high enrollment fees, too many enrollees and, because of low wages, too few providers and high staff turnover (Hofferth and Phillips 1987). Trapped as they were between necessity and contingency, working parents reluctantly began transforming the almost sacred covenantal duty of caring for their young children into businesslike contractual arrangements with day care providers.

The tension created by this imbrication of covenant and contract made that most innocuous of social institutions, the local day care center, the target of a moral panic. But a trigger was yet needed, some kind of spark that in the words of Adler (1996) 'would link ethereal sentiment to focused activity' (p. 262).

That spark was lit in 1983 at the McMartin Preschool. A 2.5 year-old enrollee made a statement, vaguely suggestive of sexual abuse, that eventually was worked into an allegation of satanic ritual abuse by social workers who already had some experience as claims makers in the mini-moral panics about satanic menaces to children (de Young 1997).

Content of the moral panic

Eventually, 369 more current and past enrollees of the McMartin Preschool were identified as victims. Their claims, elicited over repeated and sugges-tive interviews by social workers now convinced of a satanic influence in the case, came to define the still unfamiliar term of satanic ritual abuse and, in doing so, gave the ensuing moral panic its content. The children described, among other ghastly things, the ritualistic ingestion of urine, feces, blood, semen, and human flesh; the disinterment and mutilation of corpses; the sacrifices of infants; and orgies with their day care providers, costumed as devils and witches, in classrooms, tunnels under the center, and in car washes, airplanes, mansions, cemeteries, hotels, ranches, neighborhood stores, local gyms, churches, and hot air balloons. In the accusatorial atmosphere of this nascent moral panic, they named not only the seven McMartin day care providers as their satanic abusers, but local businesspeople and city officials, world leaders, television and film stars, and even their own family members (Nathan and Snedeker 1995).

Spread of the moral panic

The same social strains that accounted for the timing of the onset of the satanic day care moral panic also created an engendering environment for its rapid spread across the country. The role of interest, professional and grassroots groups in sustaining both the drama and the exigency of this moral panic, however, cannot be underestimated.

As in all contemporary moral panics, the news media emerged as a major interest group. ... [The cases] had ample complexity to warrant daily coverage from different angles; nearly intolerable horror to evoke and sustain intense emotional responses; enough familiarity in terms of loca-tion, key claims-makers, and even prime suspects to spark interest; real enough folk devils in the roles of day care providers to demonize; and sufficient exigency to elicit feelings that something must be done, and to focus action in doing it.

The news media hardly were monolithic as an interest group, however. While the nearly hysterical tone of reportage set in local coverage of the McMartin Preschool case was mimicked in local news media in other cases across the country, as well as in the mass media, it was tempered considerably in the national press and quelled completely in a few investigative reports in large circulation newspapers. ... And, as both the McMartin Preschool case and many, although certainly not all, of the other satanic day care cases that followed began to fall apart as criminal charges were dismissed, children recanted, or day care providers were exonerated in courts of law, the tone of even local news coverage changed to one of skepticism, criticism, and even excoriation...

One eventual target of that excoriation was the very professionals who, in the role of what Becker (1963: 145) so aptly described as 'moral entrepreneurs,' had triggered and spread the satanic day care moral panic. During its nearly decade-long duration, with many of their activities funded and endorsed by the National Center for Child Abuse and Neglect, these social workers, mental health professionals, attorneys and law enforcement officers acted as the chief claims-makers in not only the local and national news media, but also on network television talk shows and primetime news magazines. The social workers and mental health professionals, in particular, became captains of a burgeoning 'sexual abuse industry,' as Goodyear-Smith (1993) referred to it, and took to the lecture circuit, addressed child protection conferences, conducted workshops, consulted with professionals involved in other cases, and testified as expert witnesses in the criminal and civil trials of the day care providers. Their claims about satanic day care centers also were voiced in sworn testimony in high profile government hearings....

Rhetoric ... may be enough to ignite a moral panic, but rhetoric backed up by 'facts' is more combustible (Best 1990). To make more persuasive claims, both about the satanic day care problem and their expertise in it, professionals developed and widely disseminated a wholly synthetic diabolism out of materials haphazardly borrowed from eclectic sources on satanism, the occult, mysticism, paganism and witchcraft (Mulhern 1991). They constructed 'indicator lists' to assist other professionals, both here and abroad, in identifying child victims, and 'symptom lists' to guide the course of their therapy....

Parents of the allegedly victimized children were unabashed believers, and they constitute the grassroots group that spread the satanic day care moral panic. Like the professionals, and sometimes in conjunction with them, the parents were very vocal and, given their outrage and grief, very pitiable claims-makers. Many of them became keenly politicized as well....

The rapid adoption across the country of ... courtroom innovations, such as shielding child witnesses by allowing them to testify on videotape, closed-circuit television, behind screens, or with their backs to the defendants have not been without legal controversy since they violate the defendants' First and Sixth Amendment rights to a public trial in which accusatory witnesses can be confronted. . . .

Denouement of the moral panic

The satanic day care moral panic effectively ended in 1991 but its denouement is no more a matter of coincidence than was its onset nearly a decade before. Several factors contributed to its demise. The overweening cultural anxiety about satanic menaces to children largely had been debunked and many of its most vocal claims-makers had retreated into silence (Victor 1993). Changing economic conditions over that decade only increased the number of women in the labor force and the concomitant increase in the use of day care may have worked to integrate this service even more thoroughly into the culture, thus reducing the conflict associated with its use (Hofferth and Phillips 1987).

Changes in day care over the decade of the moral panic, and largely in reaction to it, also acted to pare down any residual conflict about its use. State licensing agencies tightened day care regulations and by legislative fiat were given more teeth to enforce them. As a result, allegations of any kind were promptly, even aggressively, investigated and the licenses of day care centers in noncompliance were suspended or revoked. . . .

In the accusatorial atmosphere of the moral panic, day care providers also took measures to protect themselves from false allegations. . . . They installed video cameras to record their activities, opened up private spaces to public view, and kept physical contact with their young charges to a necessary minimum. They adopted open-door policies and invited parents to drop in without notice to talk with staff, observe their children or even spend time with them. The net effect of these and other changes was not only to make day care centers more accessible to worried parents, but more like families, thus further minifying the anxiety about their use (de Young 1997).

What also certainly played a role in the denouement of the moral panic was the fact that the satanic day care cases, so reprehensible in the court of public opinion, nonetheless did not fare well in courts of law. As Table 20.2 shows, in many cases in the sample charges were dropped against day care providers and convictions eventually overturned. . . .

Finally, the schism within the claims-making professional groups that widened over the years of the moral panic also played a role in its demise. The satanic day care center was the site upon which an almost gothic professional struggle for social, political, and moral meaning had taken place, yet no consensus about that meaning was ever reached. The

Table 20.2 Disposition details for 38 defendants in the sample of 15 day care cases

Day Care Center Defendant	Verdict	Sentence
McMartin Preschool		
Raymond Buckey	Not Guilty	–
Peggy Buckey	Not Guilty	–
Virginia McMartin	Charges Dropped	–
Peggy Ann Buckey	Charges Dropped	–
Betty Raidor	Charges Dropped	–
Babette Spitler	Charges Dropped	–
Mary Ann Jackson	Charges Dropped	–
Country Walk		
Frank Fuster	Guilty	6 life terms
Ileana Fuster	Pled Guilty	10 years
Small World		
Richard Barkman	Guilty	50–75 years. Conviction overturned, pled guilty to lesser offense in lieu of re-trial, 5 years probation
Fells Acres		
Gerald Amirault	Guilty	30–40 years
Violet Amirault	Guilty	8–20 years. Conviction overturned, re-trial ordered. Superior Court denied re-trial and reinstated original sentence; that ruling overturned by state Supreme Court which overturned conviction and ordered re-trial
Cheryl LeFave	Guilty	8–20 years. Conviction overturned, re-trial ordered. Superior Court denied re-trial and reinstated original sentence; that ruling overturned by state Supreme Court which overturned conviction and ordered re-trial
Georgian Hills		
Betty Stimpson	Charges Dropped in Trial	–
Jeff Stimpson	Not Guilty	–
Frances Ballard	Guilty	5–35 years. Conviction overturned; charges dismissed
Paul Shell	Charges Dropped	–
Rogers Park Jewish		
Deloartic Parks	Not Guilty	–
Manhattan Ranch		
Michael Ruby	Not Guilty	–
Craig's Country		
Sandra Craig	Guilty	10 years. Conviction overturned; charges dismissed
Jamal Craig	Charges Dropped in Trial	–
Felix's		
Martha Felix	Guilty	3 life sentences. Conviction overturned; charges dismissed
Francisco Ontiveros	Guilty	Life. Conviction overturned; charges dismissed

Table 20.2 *continued*

Day Care Center Defendant	Verdict	Sentence
East Valley YMCA		
Michelle Noble	Guilty	Life plus 311 years. Conviction overturned; retried, not guilty.
Gayle Dove	Guilty	20 years. Conviction overturned, charges dismissed
Glendale Montessori		
James Toward	Pled Guilty	27 years
Brenda Williams	Pled No Contest	10 years
Old Cutler		
Bobby Fijnje	Not Guilty	–
Little Rascals		
Robert Kelly	Guilty	12 life sentences. Conviction overturned, re-trial ordered; charges dismissed
Betsy Kelly	Pled Guilty	7 year suspended sentence
Dawn Wilson	Guilty	Life. Conviction overturned, re-trial ordered; charges dismissed
Willard Privott	Pled Guilty	10 year suspended sentence
Shelly Stone	Charges Dropped	–
Darlene Harris	Charges Dropped	–
Robin Bynum	Charges Dropped	–
Faith Chapel		
Dale Akiki	Not Guilty	–
Fran's		
Fran Keller	Guilty	48 years
Dan Keller	Guilty	48 years

intra-professional dispute about the satanic day care cases, the inter-professional criticism of how they were handled, coupled with the growing public discontent with the expansion of clinical authority into families, institutions, and courts of law very well may have led to the construction of a new folk devil – the overzealous, short-sighted professional, bent on proving sexual abuse of any kind – and a new moral panic, colloquially known as 'the backlash,' now being directed against them (Myers 1994).

Rethinking Moral Panics

The classic theory of moral panic has enjoyed a quite long and lively tenure in the discipline of sociology, but the satanic day care moral panic of the 1980s reveals that some refinement and updating of the theory is needed. Specifically, another look has to be given to folk devils, the societal reaction to a moral panic, and the social ends it serves. Each of these will be examined in turn with data from the sample of 15 satanic day care cases used for illustration.

Folk devils

Every moral panic needs folk devils, those individuals or groups who, in the inflammatory rhetoric of the various claims-makers, are held responsible for the very social strains and concerns that fomented the moral panic in the first place. Their alleged deviance, amplified by repeated claims that divest them of any positive characteristics and invest them with negative, folk devils become in the cultural imagination 'quintessentially evil' (Cohen 1972: 43).

What makes their demonization so nearly effortless is that the folk devils of classic moral panic theory tend to be already marginalized individuals and, as such, have neither the credibility nor the resources to counter the claims against them. . . .

Not so with the day care providers who were the folk devils of the satanic day care moral panic. As surrogate parents to the country's youngest children, they not only provided a much in demand service but in other senses of the term were well integrated into their communities. . . .

Demographically, the day care employees were unremarkable. The 16 men and 22 women criminally charged in the 15 satanic day care cases in the sample ranged in age from 14 to 77 years, with a mean age of 38 years (SD 14.77). Thirty-one were White, 4 Latino, and 3 African American; 24 were married at the time of their arrest, 10 single, 3 divorced, and 1 widowed.

Far from being the defenseless, ineffectual folk devils of classic moral panic theory, many of the 38 day care providers in the sample took active measures not only to assert their innocence, but resist their demonization. Their integration into their respective communities afforded them access to the kinds of resources that made it possible to do so. . . .

The lack of marginality of the satanic day care folk devils has two implications for an updated theory of moral panic. First, it suggests that the targets of moral panics may not be just the expediently constructed folk devils of classic theory, but also those akin to what Watney (1987: 41) once described as 'monstrous representations,' those whose appearance of conformity and normalcy is believed to hide more than it reveals. The creation of such monstrous representations seems to be more a process of pathologizing then demonizing and certainly would be enhanced if, as in the case of the satanic day care moral panic, the primary claims-makers are well versed in the language of psychology and their claims are made in a culture that is as well.

[...]

Second, the lack of marginality of the targets of the satanic day care moral panic suggests that a refined theory must take into account how the empowerment of folk devils impacts the course of the moral panic over time, shapes public discourse about the strains and concerns that engendered it, and challenges efforts at social control. An updated theory also would bring more analytical focus to the interactions between empowered folk devils and those interest groups, particularly the media and the courts, that are resources for presenting and defending their interests even while they play a major role in spreading the moral panic.

Societal reaction

In classic moral panic theory, the societal reaction to a moral panic generally is described as invariable. Indeed, this allegedly monolithic response is a theoretical necessity in that it helps explain both how and why a moral panic tends to spread with such alacrity. Yet this assumption that societal reaction is hegemonic, to borrow a term from Hall et al. (1978), certainly also has led theorists to overlook counterclaims and counter-narratives, and to underestimate their role in shaping the course of the moral panic....

The satanic day care moral panic was rife with those very counterclaims and counternarratives. They took the form not only of the protestations of innocence by the accused day care providers, but of the views of skeptics that were juxtaposed with those of the primary claims-makers routinely in the national media and occasionally even in the local media. Within the professional groups, claims and counterclaims were so vociferously and angrily made that Putnam (1991) urged mental health professionals to resolve their conflict over satanic ritual abuse in day care or risk stalling the considerable progress they already had made in the area of sexual abuse. In the criminal trials of the day care providers, counter-claims and counternarratives not only were offered by expert witnesses for the defense, but by community people personally touched by the moral panic....

The assumption of classic moral panic theory that societal reaction is hegemonic is called into question by the satanic day care moral panic. Rather than opting for theoretical convenience, an updated theory needs to take into account the plurality of reactions that inevitably will arise in a complexly differentiated society, and to assess the impact of those counterclaims and counternarratives on the course and content of the moral panic.

Social ends

In classic theory, moral panics are described as working on behalf of the dominant social order. Through their use of emotive rhetoric and fear-based appeals, and their demonization of folk devils, moral panics tend to orchestrate social consensus that something must be done, and quickly, to deal with the imminent threat. The increased social control that usually follows not only is aimed at the threat, but also acts to preserve and reassert those very values and interests that purportedly are being undermined. . . .

Although it also is true that some moral panics never achieve any discernible social ends and, in the words of Cohen (1972:28), just devolve into 'folklore and collective memory,' an updated theory must consider the possibility that the ends achieved are more symbolic than real. Consider the satanic day care moral panic's legacy in law. Like every moral panic, this one needed the authority of the law to legitimate its claims and activities and restore the social order so threatened by its folk devils. Over the 1980s, the satanic day care moral panic provoked a dozen states to either revise existing criminal codes to include references to ritual abuse, or propose new legislation that specifically criminalizes the ritual abuse of children. Although at first blush all of this appears to be in service of increased social control, the irony is that the very behaviors that are alleged to comprise satanic ritual abuse – sexual assault, kidnapping, torture, murder – already are prohibited by criminal and child protection laws (Ogloff and Pfeifer 1992). These reiterative new laws, then, have more symbolic than actual value, and it is symbolic social ends such as this that an updated theory of moral panic must anticipate and analyze.

On an ideological level, the satanic day care moral panic actually achieved contradictory social ends. By the early 1980s an emerging feminist ideology of sexual abuse was shaping discourse on this once taboo topic and setting out a controversial agenda for sexual politics. Noting the stark asymmetry in gender in its perpetration and victimology, the feminist ideology redefined sexual abuse in terms of male dominance and contextualized it within the routinized, culturally sanctioned interactions between men and women, parents and children, fathers and daughters. And by situating childhood within a moral and political frame, the feminist ideology gave voices to once culturally silenced children and treated them as credible witnesses to their own victimization.

The satanic day care moral panic, on the one hand, served as a courier for dominant interests and values that were threatened by this emerging feminist ideology (de Young 1996). More of its folk devils were women than men, thus weakening the link between sexual abuse and male dominance, and forging a new one between bizarre and sadistic sexual abuse and women as perpetrators. It loosened the embeddedness of sexual abuse within the routine and the familiar by mystifying its context with claims that children were being abused not only in their day care centers but in other unusual or unrecognizable places, during the course of meaningless rituals and incomprehensible ceremonies performed not only by their day care providers but by robed and hooded strangers. The moral panic also delegitimated the voices of children. Their allegations of satanic ritual abuse most often were the products of months, even years, of such relentless interrogation by therapists, police, prosecuting attorneys, and parents that it is impossible to discern just whose voice really is telling the tale....

On the other hand, the satanic day care moral panic had the antithetical effect of actually advancing the feminist ideology of sexual abuse, and it is the possibility of this kind of achievement of contradictory social ends that an updated theory must anticipate. In response to counterclaims critical of their decorum in the satanic day care cases, professional organizations developed standards of practice for interviewing, evaluating, and treating any child or adult with a history of sexual abuse (American Academy of Child and Adolescent Psychiatry 1988). These not only serve as a check and balance against the beliefs, values, and assumptions of professionals that in the case of the satanic day care moral panic so obviously occluded the assessment process, but act to bring more common, albeit prosaic, cases of sexual abuse into the public realm. In doing so, these standards of practice lead to the identification of cases that lend some legitimacy to the still emerging, but no less controversial, feminist ideology about sexual abuse.

[...]

Conclusion

In his groundbreaking study, Cohen (1972) concluded that moral panics reveal something of interest about social structure, social process, and social change. The satanic day care moral panic of the 1980s certainly is no exception. From its origin in the structurally generated strains and anxieties peculiar to that decade, to its emotive rhetoric that transformed day care providers into folk devils, to the social processes of its spread by varied interest groups, and finally to its denouement and institutional and ideological legacy, the satanic day care moral panic is, in every sense of the term, a revealing moral panic.

One of the things this moral panic also reveals is that the classic theory of moral panic is in need of updating and refinement. First, an updated theory must anticipate that the folk devils of some moral panics may be as empowered as the day care providers were in the satanic day care moral panic. With access to a variety of resources that will allow them to protest their innocence and resist their demonization, such empowered folk devils inevitably will impact the course of the moral panic, shape public discourse, and challenge efforts at social control in ways that an updated theory must take into account and analyze. Second, an updated theory also must anticipate that in a complex, differentiated society, reactions to a moral panic may be far from uniform. That certainly was the case in the satanic day care moral panic. Throughout its nearly decade-long course, its claims were criticized, belittled, and rejected, and the impact of such counterclaims on the course and the content of the moral panic must be considered. Finally, an updated theory must bring some analysis to the possibility that the social ends achieved by a moral panic may be as institutionally symbolic and ideologically contradictory as those achieved by this one.

If the satanic day care moral panic is at all predictive of what future panics will resemble, then it also suggests a future approach to sociological analysis. That analysis must take careful consideration of the multi-mediated nature of the complexly differentiated social worlds that will be the contexts of future moral panics. The intricate web of relations between various interest groups, the kinds of claims they make, and the media that present and contest them, must be part and parcel of future analysis. And so must be the many audiences that receive them. Either overlooked completely or treated as little more than passive dupes in classic analysis, these audiences must be seen and appreciated for their imaginative and active roles in moral panics. Whether as actors, observers, readers, or listeners, audiences actively appropriate and decode the 'facts' of the claims of moral panics and act in relation to them. They do so as well with the ideological underpinnings of those claims. Future analysis, therefore, must include a critical examination of the ideology of moral panics, how it resonates with the lived experiences of those audiences, how it acts to recruit them, and how it retains them often long after the 'facts' of the claims have been disputed and debunked.

The satanic day care moral panic is a fascinating slice of American cultural history. It was as widespread, overreactive, hostile and irrational as any moral panic that preceded it, but a great deal more revealing than most. What it reveals is that it is time to take another look at classic moral panic theory.

References

Adler, J.S. (1996) The making of a moral panic in 19th century America: the Boston garrotting hysteria of 1865, *Deviant Behavior*, 17: 259–78.

American Academy of Child and Adolescent Psychiatry (1988) *Guidelines for the Clinical Evaluation of Child and Adolescent Child Abuse*. Washington, DC: Author.

Becker, H. (1963) *Outsiders*. New York: Free Press.

Best, J. (1990) *Threatened Children: Rhetoric and Concern about Child-Victims*. Chicago: University of Chicago Press.

Cohen, S. (1972) *Folk Devils and Moral Panics*. London: Paladin.

de Young, M. (1994) The face of the Devil: the satanic ritual abuse crusade and the law, *Behavioral Sciences and the Law*, 12: 389–407.

de Young, M. (1996) Satanic ritual abuse: exploring the controversies. Paper presented to the 11th International Congress on Child Abuse and Neglect, August, Dublin, Ireland.

de Young, M. (1997) The Devil goes to day care; McMartin and the making of a moral panic, *Journal of American Culture*, 20: 19–26.

Durkheim, E. (1938) *The Rules of Sociological Method*. Chicago: University of Chicago Press.

Goode, E. and Ben-Yehuda, N. (1994) *Moral Panics*. Oxford: Basil Blackwell.

Goodyear-Smith, F. (1993) *First Do No Harm: The Sexual Abuse Industry*. Auckland, NZ: Benton-Gay.

Hall, S., Critcher, C., Jefferson, T., Clarke, J. and Roberts, B. (1978) *Policing the Crisis: Mugging, the State and Law and Order*. London: Macmillan.

Hofferth, S.L. and Phillips, D.A. (1987) Child care in the United States: 1970–1995, *Journal of Marriage and the Family*, 49: 559–71.

Hutchison, E.D. (1992) Child welfare as a women's issue, *Families in Society*, 73: 67–77.

Mulhern, S. (1991) Satanism and psychotherapy: a rumor in search of an inquisition, in J.T. Richardson, J. Best and D.G. Bromley (eds) *The Satanism Scare*. New York: Aldine de Gruyter.

Myers, J.E.B. (1994) *The Backlash: Child Protection under Fire*. Newbury Park, CA: Sage.

Nathan, D. and Snedeker, M. (1995) *Satan's Silence: Ritual Abuse and the Making of a Modern American Witch Hunt*. New York: Basic Books.

Ogloff, J.R.P. and Pfeifer, J.E. (1992) Cults and the law: a discussion of the legality of alleged cult activities, *Behavioral Sciences and the Law*, 10: 117–40.

Putnam, F. (1991) Commentary: the Satanic ritual abuse controversy, *Child Abuse and Neglect*, 15: 175–80.

Richardson, J.T., Best, J. and Bromley, D.G. (eds) *The Satanism Scare*. New York: Aldine de Gruyter.

Victor, (1993) *Satanic Panic* Chicago. Open Court

Watney, S. (1987) *Policing Desire: Pornography, AIDS and the Media*. London: Methuen.

21

MORAL PANIC VERSUS THE RISK SOCIETY
THE IMPLICATIONS OF THE CHANGING SITES OF SOCIAL ANXIETY

Sheldon Ungar (2001)

Moral panic has enjoyed a good run in the sociology of deviance, where it acquired a special affinity with youth-related issues. This paper suggests that the sociological domain carved out by moral panic is most fruitfully understood as the study of the sites and conventions of social anxiety and fear. Researchers select particular crises to investigate, and thereby ignore others. But societies change, as do the phenomena associated with outbreaks of public concern or alarm. As new crises accumulate and become more visible, they are likely to find their way on to the research agenda. This paper examines new sites of social anxiety that have emerged along-side moral panics. These are best captured by Beck's ... concept of a 'risk society'. The paper, then, compares the elements and conditions of moral panic with those of the *political potential of catastrophes* bred in a risk society (1992: 24; italics in original). The aim of the comparison is three-fold: 1, to establish the position of risk society threats alongside more conventional moral panics; 2. to examine the conceptual shifts that accompany the new types of threats; and 3. to outline the changing research agenda, including the identification of gaps characteristic of moral panic research.

The Idea of Moral Panic

...Cohen's classic definition is cited so frequently that readers are apt to skip it! Careful perusal of the text reveals that it allows for but does *not* necessitate most of the presumptions and concepts that have accrued to the study of moral panic. Consider the concept of folk devil, which is typically identified with the evil doings of an individual or group of individuals. Cohen's definition, however, encompasses not only 'person or groups of persons' but also 'condition' and 'episode.'

Similarly, nothing in this text necessitates the idea of disproportionality, although the exaggeration, of the threat has been a key concern of moral panic researchers (e.g., Jenkins 1998, 1999) and of social constructionists generally (Ungar 1998a).

Since most of the ostensibly critical elements of moral panic are not stipulated by definition, they apparently flow from the (more contingent) procedures and details of Cohen's classic study. In this context, it is probably a sterile exercise to ask what moral panic is 'really about'. ... Instead, the aim here is to open space for the consideration of other social anxieties that do not quite fit the moral panic paradigm. Then these new anxieties will be used to reflect on the nature and limits of the moral panic research.

Social Anxiety in the Risk Society

Starting from the mid-1980s on in particular, new social anxieties in advanced industrial societies have built up around nuclear, chemical, environmental, biological and medical issues.

Pertinent examples of these anxieties include the threat of nuclear winter, Three Mile Island, breast implants, various forms of reproductive technology and biotechnology, the ozone hole, the 'greenhouse summer of 1988,' the Exxon Valdez, Ebola Zaire, and Bovine Spongiform Encephalopathy (BSE). These new risks have steadily gained greater prominence and created their own issue-attention cycles. ... Not surprisingly, ecological concerns rose to the top of the public agenda by the late 1980s (Dunlap and Scarce 1991).

Beck (1992, 1995) subsumes these new sites of social anxiety under the concept of a risk society. While risks are an inevitable consequence of industrialization, Beck claims that the 'side effects' produced by late modernization are a new development. As compared to the recent past (and especially prior to the Second World War), these risks have novel impacts that are: 1) very complex in terms of causation; 2) unpredictable and latent; 3) not limited by time, space, or social class (i.e., globalized); 4) not detectable by our physical senses; and 5) are the result of human decisions. Essentially, the economic gains following from the application of science and technology are increasingly being overshadowed by the unintended production and distribution of 'bads'. These have gone from being unrecognized, to latent, to globalized, as new types of technology and processes of production, new chemicals, drugs and so on, and new scales of activity combine to accentuate the risks.

According to Beck (1992: 24; italics in original), 'In smaller or larger increments – a smog alarm, a toxic spill, etc. – what thus emerges in risk society is the *political potential of catastrophes* ... Risk society is a *catastrophic society*.' The catastrophic potential of the risk society gives rise to a reflexive orientation, whereby new technologies are subject to increasing scientific scrutiny and public criticism. But despite the greater public involvement and accountability implied by 'reflexive modernization' (Beck et al. 1994), side effects remain for the most part unpredictable and incalculable. They are akin to normal accidents, where what has been scientifically ruled out (as either impossible or extremely improbable) predictably occurs ... With new technologies such as genetic engineering, the scientific procedures for monitoring risks and protecting the public shift from the security of the laboratory to the real world. As society is rendered into a social laboratory, accidents not only come as a surprise but also can provide a crash course in institutional failings.

[...]

Coexisting Anxieties?

How will the rise of such risk society issues affect the occurrence and development of moral panics? A difficulty in addressing this question is a lack of agreement about what is happening with moral panics. McRobbie and Thornton (1995) argue that panics are harder to constitute than they once were. Citing the failed effort to construct a moral panic around single mothers in Britain, they suggest that the proliferation of mass media and the attendant capacity of folk devils to fight back (they are 'less marginalized than they once were') have sharply curtailed the potential for moral panics. In contrast, Thompson (1998: 2) refers to the 'increasing rapidity in the succession of moral panics' and 'the all-pervasive quality of panics that distinguish the current era'.

Fear of crime remains high and seems to be immune to data indicating that crime rates have been falling throughout the 1990s. If fear of crime in particular suggests that panics are not about to be displaced by risk society threats, it may be better to speak of a complementary relationship between the two types of anxieties. Thus Hollway and Jefferson (1997: 258) suggest that fear of crime and risk of victimization must be considered in light of Beck's argument that risk is 'pervasive in late modernity'.

[...]
Fear of crime may be a relatively reassuring site for displacing the more uncertain and uncontrollable anxieties of a risk society.

Jenkins' (1999: 8–9) study of designer drugs locates a substantive realm where there are elements of convergence between the two types of social anxiety. What he calls 'synthetic panics' are linked to new technologies and human ingenuity, scientists cast as Dr. Frankenstein, a loss of control, and the creation of 'forbidden knowledge' – all common elements of risk society issues. The latter has also brought a reflexive orientation whereby victims challenge authorities and fight back. Since McRobbie and Thornton (1995) observe a similar resistance by folk devils in moral panic, it appears that relationships between authorities and their publics are becoming more open and less manipulative regardless of the type of social anxiety involved.

Comparing the Old and the New

To compare the two types of social anxiety, this paper draws on analyses of moral panic because it is a more seasoned concept whose antecedence has allowed time for the systematic formulation of criteria. The most systematic (if at times plodding) historical and theoretical account of moral panic is provided by Goode and Ben-Yehuda (1994a, 1994b). They list 'five crucial elements or criteria' of moral panic: 1. Concern; 2. Hostility; 3. Consensus 4. Disproportionality; and 5. Volatility. The ensuing comparison is guided by their five crucial elements, though the organization of the discussion departs from theirs.

The present analysis focuses on the conceptual shifts that accompany emerging risk society threats and the changing research agenda implied by them. Conceptually, moral panic is linked to a social constructionist perspective. The main issues addressed in this research concern the exaggeration of the actual threat and the use of panics to engineer social consensus and control. With risk society accidents being highly unpredictable and uncontrollable, the social constructionist concern with exaggeration is largely undermined as an analytic strategy. The roulette dynamics of risk society accidents are also at variance with the model of social control and folk devils used in moral panic research. Instead of authorities and other institutional actors using social anxieties to impose moral order, they can find themselves as carriers of 'hot potatoes'. Methodologically, the risk society points to an array of new questions and throws into relief some faulty research assumptions and procedures found in moral panic studies.

The Issues of Concern/Consensus

That heightened concern is a prerequisite for panic is true by definition. Beyond this truism lies a morass of problems. These are rendered manifest through an examination of changes in the types of social issues that form the sites of social anxiety (cf. McRobbie 1994: 216). Moral panic has always been conceptualized narrowly (as seen in the five criteria listed above), and thereby encompasses only a small number of the subset of social problems that fall in the domain of deviance – and even more specifically, youth deviance. Hence panics could be designated as 'time-to-time' events, something, like witch hunts, that are more exceptional than ordinary. In contrast, claims about the potentially fearful events associated with a risk society are far more ubiquitous.

The risk society is characterized, in other terms, by a stream of emergencies and would-be emergencies. ... The dissimilar sites and pools of issues affect all elements of the analysis of social anxiety. Moral panic is constituted by a relatively small pool of mostly familiar threats, or variations on a theme. The risk society is constituted by a vast number of relatively unfamiliar threats, with new threats always lurking in the background. When occasional problems are supplanted by a burgeoning pool of contending 'catastrophes', all aspects of claim-making are rendered more open, variable, and problematic. In this section I discuss two conceptual issues – models of panic creation and the status of failed panics – and one methodological issue – questions about the depth and extensiveness of public concern.

Models of panic creation

Research on moral panic generally takes a top-down approach to claims-making. ... Theoretical sociological interest in the concept, ... devolves around notions of social regulation, manipulation by the powerful, and deviance amplification.

Risk society issues do not generally fit a top-down model. If responses to nuclear reactors are prototypical, panics appear to require some catalytic real-world event that is given direction by interest groups and carried forward by elements of the informed public, often as part of social movement organizations (Ungar 1990, 1992). Significantly – this will be elaborated below – political authorities and large actors often find themselves the target of such activities and have encountered strong resistance in their efforts to influence long-term public opinion (e.g., Rothman and Lichter 1987).

From a social constructionist perspective, claims making pertaining to moral panics can derive more from a shift in moral boundaries than either the objective standing of a condition or new evidence. ... Moreover, claims may be about valence issues (these are one-sided issues, as in hard drug use) or involve relatively disproportionate power on the contending sides, as folk devils are pitted against better-organized and more powerful groups. With the risk society, issues tend to be warranted more by scientific findings or claims, with scientists, for all their public liabilities, playing a central role in the cast of claims makers. Given scientific uncertainties, the likelihood that the media's attempt to strike an equilibrium will be greater for 'factual' than for moral claims ... and the chance that the powerful will find themselves targeted, a more equal balance of power between rival claims makers is anticipated with risk issues.

In short, moral panic has conventionally focused on social control processes aimed at the moral failing of dispossessed groups. Risk society issues tend to involve diverse interest groups contending over relatively intractable scientific claims. However, the former have come closer to the latter as diverse media and attention to a broader range of voices allow folk devils to contest the setting of moral boundaries. Social regulation processes, in other words, have become less predictable and more fractious.

Failed panics

At the extreme, one could contend that knowledge about moral panics is fundamentally tainted. Virtually all of the research involves retrospective studies of panics which were 'deemed' authentic. But in the absence of comparable examples of unsuccessful efforts, conclusions about key variables and processes amount to asserting that what transpired (more or less) had to. Thus it is usual to attribute panics to broader social, economic or political strains, but no effort is made to determine whether these subterranean dissatisfactions have existed for extended periods of time without provoking panics. ...

Claims making to no effect is much more transparent for risk society issues. In this case, the pool of potential catastrophes closely mirrors Hilgartner and Bosk's (1988) ecology of competition for scarce attention in different public arenas. Given scientific uncertainty, frequent invisibility, and the rival claims making about issues that are often unfamiliar and complex, it is very difficult to bring attention to many issues. A key process here involves crossovers, where issues jump from one arena to another and potentially create a 'whirlwind' of attention (Ungar 2000)...

Until recently, methodological problems made it extremely difficult to follow the passage of issues across different arenas. Thus claim making at community levels or at the base of social movement organizations remains relatively invisible to most social research, especially when data are collected from the national mass media or conventional polling samples used by Gallup and the like. But since risk issues are usually articulated first (or very early on) by scientists, both jumps and blockages at crossover points can be systematically studied with the use of computer indexes and the Internet.

Tapping into public concerns

One key crossover involves the spread of fear among broad elements of the general public. Definitions of moral panic all stipulate that 'overheated periods of intense concern' or 'explosions of fear' must be relatively widespread among the public. A surge of public concern implies that an issue is 'in the air' ... This metaphor suggests that the 'attentive' public is not only aware of the issue but is sufficiently alarmed that they discuss it. However, personal worries and agitated conversations leave few traces. Even community meetings tend to be invisible a step beyond their immediate venue. An issue may be percolating among members of the public, but the concerns are still more likely to fizzle than to foam upwards.

... Overall, behavioural indicators – anti-nuclear demonstrations, community protests against the release of convicted child abusers, or the drop in British beef sales during the BSE scare – are preferred. Unfortunately, direct behavioural evidence is often lacking or difficult to come by.

Here again there appears to be an important difference between the two types of social anxieties. While research on moral panics infrequently draws on poll results (Beckett 1994; Thompson 1998; 121–2), some risk society threats like Ebola and nuclear reactors have generated more specific data on public reactions (e.g., Moeller 1999: 80–95; Rothman and Lichter 1987).

[...]

With moral panic in particular, researchers have finessed the problem by employing indirect and questionable indicators of public concern. Most common is the use of coverage in the mass media as a surrogate for public concern. Yet a large number of studies of agenda-setting report weak effects that are consistent with Gamson and Modigliani's (1989) conclusion that media attention and public opinion constitute parallel but *distinct* systems of meaning. Another ostensible measure of public concern is legislative activity on an issue (Goode 1989). However, research on agenda setting indicates that the relationship between political activity and public concerns is weak and contingent (Kingdon 1995). That is, both policy proposals and policy changes are largely determined by institutional contingencies and activities specific to the policy domain.

Both media coverage and legislative activity involve actors several steps removed from the general public. While public opinion polling would appear to furnish more direct and cogent measures of public concerns, polls typically occur too infrequently to catch the dramatic soar and slump cycles of issues that make it in the air (Ungar 1994). Moreover, the questions used in polls tend to be too limited to tap into intense outbreaks of concern that verge on or encompass fear. . . .

Catching waves of public concern remains a difficult task. However, researchers can get closer to the action. Over the last decade, at least two alternative media have emerged through which public concerns can be accumulated and amplified. The first is talk radio.

[. . .]

The second alternative medium for voice amplification is the Internet.

[. . .]

Finally, it may be possible to use extant findings about media practices to locate a 'signature' of public concern. According to Sandman (1994: 254; italics in original), '*Alarming content about risk is more common than reassuring content or intermediate content – except, perhaps, in crisis situations, when the impulse to prevent panic seems to moderate coverage.*' Since this moderation effect has been found for AIDS, nuclear accidents, and Ebola (Ungar 1998b), evidence of media moderation appears to afford a better indicator of outbreaks of public concern that simple counts of media coverage.

Tracking public concerns by means of the methods listed above willynilly is more difficult than counting media coverage or relying on poll results. Rather than drawing inferences from a single source or indicator, investigators are asked to look for clusters of cohering evidence. . . .

The Issues of Hostility/Volatility

According to Goode and Ben-Yehuda (1994a: 33; italics in original), 'not only must the condition, phenomenon, or behaviour be seen as threatening, but a clearly identifiable group or segment of society must be seen as *responsible* for the threat'. . . .

For the most part, folk devils have been identified as youth or other dispossessed groups who are the target of moral outrage due to their 'evil activities' that threaten core values of society. But instead of regarding folk devils as givens, a risk society perspective suggests that their creation is best seen as a *foraging* process, an essayed induction that must take hold. As unforeseen side effects, manufactured hazards seem to generate a greater diffusion of blame, with multi-faceted targets that can include governments, corporations, and other institutions.

[...]

Conceptually, the shift in social control processes and in the nature and targets of social reactions are probably the most significant sociological developments associated with the risk society. With moral panic, authorities either play a central role in initiating panics or are likely to join ongoing proceedings and derive some benefit from legitimating and perhaps directing them. In the roulette dynamics characteristic of manufactured accidents – 'accidents' is used as a shorthand to cover actual mishaps, as well as claimed mishaps or claims about potential mishaps – authorities typically forfeit their commanding role and may become the target of moral outrage. Rather than amplifying the threat, they usually try to dampen it.

[...]

The exposure and accumulation of oversights, ineptitudes, and violations tends to engender a marauding sense of disbelief and anger. But this is generally different to moral panics, where evil folk devils are usually a 'distinguishable social type' (such as the Mod or the Rocker) whose visibility is the basis of his or her expurgation (Hay 1995: 198) With risk society accidents, the violators are more institutionally-based and somewhat invisible. It is often their routine rather than deviant actions that underlie the problem. ... The targets of public anger are as likely to be seen as perplexed, vacillating and inept as evil or malign, especially as beleaguered experts search for immediate answers to complex questions in what amounts to a media fish tank. That is, accidents give rise to a need for 'science-on-demand', something that the deliberate process of science can rarely supply. ... Rather than serving as a force of social control or cohesion, risk society accidents tend to create 'corrosive communities' as the different actors try to deny their culpability and pass the hot potato. ... In this foraging process, public trust is the ultimate victim.

The impacts of manufactured accidents also tend to be more severe and chronic than those associated with moral panics. According to Altheide (1997), the 'problem frame' that has emerged in the media to deal with moral panic-related issues implies that there is 'An Answer' to the problem. The system may be overburdened, but at least something can be done about the situation. Such formulistic solutions, rendered familiar by past variations on the theme, rarely apply to risk society accidents. That is, contamination by modern hazards tends to be more insidious and unbounded. There is an irreducible ambiguity to the harm, as toxic effects can be difficult to identify, take years to manifest themselves, or not appear until the next generation. The ambiguity not only means that it is extremely difficult to sound the 'all clear,' but that 'toxic tort' cases stretch conventional rules of evidence and liability (Grambling and Krogman 1997). The upshot is to create corrosive communities, as demands for admissions of blame and compensation are thrown into the political arena with, all too often, explosive effects.

The Issue of Disproportionality

Disproportionality has undoubtedly been the central problematic of the moral panic literature. For one, it encapsulates the political agenda motivating this research domain: specifically, the power of moral entrepreneurs to exercise social control by amplifying deviance and orchestrating social reactions so that the panic becomes a consensus-generating envoy for the dominant ideology. Disproportionality is also at the core of the social constructionist approach. According to this perspective, social reactions have little relationship to the ostensible threat or condition (it may be improving even as the panic gets underway), but are largely determined by claims making activities (Ungar 1998a). Finally, exaggerating the threat has also became a reflexive tool, as the media have come to habitually ask whether politicians are seeking to incite panic or question their own culpability in generating outbreaks of panic (Hay 1995, McRobbie and Thornton 1995).

Disproportionality also commands the bulk of empirical activity, as researchers make. Herculean efforts to find the elusive grail of 'objective reality.' Whereas public concern is too often inferred from media coverage, Goode and Ben-Yehuda (1994a: 36–7) 'want to be very careful' and 'acknowledge that determining and assessing the objective dimension is often a tricky proposition'. Hence they go to great lengths to salvage disproportionality and thus save the field from those who suggest that the concept is too value-laden and polemical to be scientifically useful (e.g., Waddington 1986)...

Not surprisingly, perhaps, their efforts to shore up disproportionality lead them into an objectivist position. When they assert that incalculability is not true for 'possibly most' problems, they are implying the existence of a set of known and agreed on threats. But what is at issue is not the quantity of 'real' threats, but those specific conditions that successfully emerge as sites of social anxiety...

If the intractable scientific uncertainties of risk society issues mostly obviate the central moral panic/social constructionist concern with exaggerated threats, the volatility of the former puts a further dent into the idea of disproportionality. Since a hot potato can be handed off several times before it securely befalls a specific target, there is the question of whether the hostility directed against particular groups or institutions is in fact warranted...

Beyond disproportionality – an idea that has long been problematic – risk society issues pose a challenge to the sanctified status of claims making in the creation of social problems. Programmatically, social constructionists prefer to regard all issues as intrinsically the same and to attribute differences in outcomes *primarily* to variations in claims making activities (Koopmans and Duyvendak 1995). Pragmatically, risk society issues tend to acquire a scientific trajectory and accident history that are 'sticky', and thereby constrain the claims that can be viably made by issue entrepreneurs (Ungar 1998a). While a trajectory still allows operatives *some* choices in running a problem, their claim making activities are not nearly as malleable as social constructionists claim, and can engender resistance or turbulence if they try to ignore the sticky history of the problem. ... In short, claims making on risk society issues is, in comparison with conventional moral panic issues, hedged in by more apparent and sticky issue trajectories, by a more equal balance of power on the part of rival claim makers, and by a comparative absence of distinguishable types of folk devils that evoke deep-seated hostility and fear.

Conclusion

The present analysis uses the developments associated with a risk society to throw into relief some blinkers surrounding the moral panic-deviance nexus. For all its pitfalls, one cannot wish away the reality that many sociologists *want* a concept like moral panic as a tool to debunk particular social claims or reactions. Taking a critical posture is not inherently unscientific. Rather, it depends on whether or not observers have sufficiently rigorous evidence to support the contention that *particular* reactions are *patently* unwarranted. For most issues, the requisite evidence has been lacking, and hence sociological pronouncements have not been particularly authoritative.

Social anxieties raise the basic issue of safety. Moral panics, along with earlier industrial risks, were largely contained in a discourse of safety. Moral deviants could be identified (there were 'tests' for witchcraft, with an embedded ambiguity that always rendered it possible to 'find' deviants).

The deviants were then, at least theoretically, subject to social control. Indeed, even if social reactions were more symbolic than practical, they could still serve to affirm moral boundaries. And the latter could be effectuated regardless of whether the claims exaggerated the nature of the threat or not.

A safety discourse faces rupture in the risk society. Invisible contaminants, intractable scientific uncertainties, unpredictable system effects, the almost tragic calls for 'science-on-demand' at the height of an accident, the prying open of standard operating procedures, efforts to pass off the hot potato, and potential latency effects that hinder closure of the threat – these all suggest that planning and pre-market testing have been replaced by post-market coping, as things are wont to go boom in the night.

Hindsight notwithstanding, it can be presumed that British authorities had no idea that announcing a tentative link between BSE and 10 possible cases of CJD would touch off a marauding storm. As previously noted, the public wants unambiguous answers pertaining to risk and safety, especially for phenomena that are involuntarily imposed on them. A safety model that boils down to the post-market coping with accidents is not readily sold to a public whose demands for a yes/no risk evaluation hardly countenances a cost-benefit analysis.

With this case and the accumulation of other comparable manufactured risks, the idea that institutions connote safety is severely challenged. According to Beck (1995: 128)

> The political dynamism of the ecological issue is not a function of the advancing devastation of nature; rather it arises from the facts that, on the one hand, institutions claim to provide control and security falls short and, on the other hand, in the same way, devastation is normalized and legalized.

The gap between a safety discourse and the emergent discursive formations and practices built around post-market efforts to cope with emergencies opens up key questions for sociology. These include issues of trust, expertise and authority, the fallibility of science, the nature of (once hidden) institutional practices, the threat of immobility and, ultimately, the affirmation of social order.

References

Altheide, D.L. (1997) The news media, the problem frame, and the production of fear, *Sociological Quarterly*, 38(4): 647–68.

Beck, U. (1992) *Risk Society: Towards A New Modernity*. trans. M. Ritter. London: Sage.

Beck, U. (1995) Ecological Enlightenment: Essays on the Politics of the Risk Society. New Jersey: Atlantic Press.

Beck, U., Giddens, A. and Lash, C. (1994) *Reflexive Modernization: Politics, Tradition and Aesthetics in the Modern Social Order*. Cambridge: Polity Press.

Beckett, K. (1994) Setting the public agenda: 'street crime' and drug use in American politics, *Social Problems*, 41(3): 425–46.

Cohen, S. (1972) *Folk Devils and Moral Panics*. St Albans: Paladin.

Dunlap, R. and Scarce, R. (1991) The polls – poll trends: environmental problems and protection, *Public Opinion Quarterly*, 55(4): 651–72.

Gamson, W.A. and Modigliani, A. (1989) Media discourse and public opinion on nuclear power: a constructionist approach, *American Journal of Sociology*, 95(1): 1–37.

Goode, E. (1989) The American Drug Panic of the 1980s: social construction or objective threat? *Violence, Aggression and Terrorism*, 3(3): 327–48.

Goode, E. (1990) The American drug panic of the 1980s: social construction or objective threat? *The International Journal of the Addictions*, 25(9): 1083–98.

Goode, E. (1994) Moral Panics: culture, politics and social construction, *Annual Review of Sociology*, 20: 149–71.

Goode, E. and Ben-Yehuda, N. (1994a) *Moral Panics: The Social Construction of Deviance*. Oxford: Blackwell.

Goode, E. and Ben-Yehuda, N. (1994b) Moral Panics: culture, politics and social construction, *Annual Review of Sociology*, 20: 149–71.

Grambling, R. and Krogman, N. (1997) Communities, policy and chronic technological disasters, *Current Sociology*, 45(3): 41–57.

Hay, C. (1995) Mobilization through interpellation: James Bulger, juvenile crime and the construction of a moral panic, *Social and Legal Studies*, 4(2): 197–223.

Hilgartner, S. and Bosk, C.L. (1988) The rise and fall of social problems: a public arenas model, *American Journal of Sociology*, 94(1): 53–78.

Hill, C. (1996) World opinion and the empire of circumstance, *International Affairs*, 72(1): 109–31.

Hollway, W. and Jefferson, T. (1997) The risk society in the age of anxiety: situating a fear of crime, *British Journal of Sociology*, 48(2): 255–66.

Jenkins, P. (1998) *Moral Panic: Changing Concepts of the Child Molester in Modern America*. New Haven, CT: Yale University Press.

Jenkins, P. (1999) *Synthetic Panic: The Symbolic Politics of Designer Drugs*. New York: New York University Press.

Kingdon, J. (1995) *Agendas, Alternatives and Public Policies*. New York: HarperCollins.

Koopmans, R. and Duyvendak, J. (1995) The political construction of the nuclear energy issue and its impact on the mobilization of anti-nuclear movements in western Europe, *Social Problems*, 42(2): 235–52.

McRobbie, A. (1994) Moral panics in the age of the postmodern mass media, in A. McRobbie *Postmodernism and Popular Culture*. London: Routledge.

McRobbie, A. and Thornton, S.L. (1995) Re-thinking 'moral panic' for multi-mediated social worlds, *British Journal of Sociology*, 46(4): 559–74.

Moeller, S. (1999) *Compassion Fatigue: How the Media Sell Disease, Famine, War and Death*. London: Routledge.

Rothman, S. and Lichter, S. (1987) Elite ideology and risk perception in nuclear energy policy, *American Political Science Review*, 83(2): 383–404.

Sandman, P. (1994) Mass media and environmental risk: seven principles, *Risk: Health, Safety and Environment*, Summer: 251–60.

Thompson, K. (1998) *Moral Panics*. London: Routledge.

Ungar, S. (1990) Moral panics, the military industrial complex and the arms race, *Sociological Quarterly*, 31(2): 165–85.

Ungar, S. (1992) *The Rise and Fall of Nuclearism: Fear and Faith as Determinants of the Arms Race*. Pennsylvania: Pennsylvania State Press.

Ungar, S. (1994) Apples and oranges: probing the attitude-behaviour relationship for the environment, *Canadian Review of Sociology and Anthropology*, 31(3): 288–304.

Ungar, S. (1998a) Bringing the issue back in: comparing the marketability of the ozone hole and global warming. *Social Problems*, 45(4): 510–27.

Ungar, S. (1998b) Hot crisis and media reassurance: a comparison of emerging diseases and Ebola Zaire. *British Journal of Sociology*, 49(1): 36–56.

Ungar, S. (2000) Knowledge, ignorance and the popular culture: climate change versus the ozone hole, *Public Understanding of Science*, 9(3): 297–312.

Waddington, P.A.J. (1986) Mugging as a moral panic, *British Journal of Sociology*, 37(2): 245–59.

22

RISK AND PANIC IN LATE MODERNITY

IMPLICATIONS OF THE CONVERGING SITES OF SOCIAL ANXIETY

Sean P. Hier (2003)

Introduction

...Ungar (2001) argues that new sites of social anxiety emerging around nuclear, chemical, environmental and medical threats have thrown into relief many of the questions motivating moral panic research. Drawing from the writings of Ulrich Beck, he conceptualizes the risk society in terms of changing sites of social anxiety which '... have steadily gained greater prominence [compared to moral panics] and created their own issue-attention cycles' (2001: 273). Attempting to explicate the purported differences between the two types of threats – exaggerated deviations germane to moral panics and the potential emergence of catastrophes in the risk society – Ungar privileges anxieties associated with the latter to assess the implications of the *changing* sites of social anxiety...

This paper charts an alternative trajectory, asserting that analytic priority rests not with an understanding of the implications of changing but converging sites of social anxiety...

The purpose of the analysis, then, is three-fold. Concerned that Ungar has established a dangerous benchmark in the sociology of moral panic, the paper first challenges his endorsement of the ontology of contemporary risks. It is shown how his reliance on the constructs of scientific rationality and reflexive modernization culminate in a narrow conception of folk devils, claims making and general perceptions of public safety. This critique is used, secondly, to explicate how Ungar's selective treatment of the risk society theory flows into an (inadvertent) alignment with Anthony Giddens's conceptualization of social anxiety. This is revealed as problematic in that it leads to an over-socialized conception of individual choice, failing to consider seriously how people deal with contingency. Using Zygmunt Bauman's work as a point of departure, the final portion of the paper demonstrates how, in sharp contrast to Ungar's model, the affirmation of social order is situated in the realm of locality, forged through the production of everyday living. As the intangibility of contemporary anxieties are reduced to the level of personal safety, far from rendering moral panics obsolete, it is concluded that the emergence of the risk society presents fertile ground for moral panics.

Moral Panic Versus the Risk Society

... For Cohen, every moral panic requires the delineation of a scapegoat or 'folk devil', an identifiable object onto which social fears and anxieties may be projected. As the personification of evil, he conceptualizes folk devils as susceptible to instant recognition as 'unambiguously unfavourable symbols' (1972: 41) which are stripped of positive characteristics and endowed with pejorative evaluations. Cohen is clear that moral panics come about through a complex chain of social interactions involving claims makers, moral guardians and the media, set in the context of socio-political change and an ensuing climate of 'cultural ambiguity'. ... Although moral panics centre on a particular folk devil, the locus of the panic is not the object of its symbolic resonances, not the folk devil itself. ... Folk devils serve as the ideological embodiment of deeper anxieties, perceived of as 'a problem' only in and through social definition and construction.

By contrast, anxieties subsumed under the concept of the risk society are purported to emanate more from an historical conjuncture rather than localized sites of social/moral disruption. According to Beck (1992), whereas the modernization process served to dissolve the structure of feudalism in the nineteenth century in the wake of the emergence of the industrial society, modernization is now dissolving the industrial society as we ascend 'towards a new modernity'. Concomitantly, while the preoccupation of the early modern industrial society was centrally concerned with the production and distribution of 'goods' – wealth, income, education, etc. – the late modern risk society is principally consumed by the conflictual distribution and political [re] allocation of 'bads' – the industrial fall out and latent side effects produced in the period of early modernity. Hence, in contrast to the limited spatial and temporal threats intrinsic to moral panics, hazards confronting the risk society '... are revealed as irreversible threats to the life of plants, animals, and human beings' (1992: 13).

... [T]he proliferation of risks in late modernity gives rise to an acute awareness of monumental uncertainties and anxieties, as '... the unknown and unintended consequences [of modern industrial production] come to be a dominant force in history and society' (1992: 22). Simultaneously, society becomes an issue and problem for itself, precipitating a confrontational reflexivity and a 'globalization of doubt' concerning the degree of faith instilled in science and technology. Yet, this skepticism, captured by the notion of 'reflexive modernization', is inherently paradoxical. Although characterized by a new form of political and cultural relations whereby non-expert voices emerge to contest the uncertainties manufactured by the techno-scientific complex, oppositional parties' dependence on techno-scientific knowledge remains two-fold: first, to understand and comprehend what degree of risk exists; and second, to understand what the risks are. In contrast to the standard path for moral panics, then, where folk devils are of a ' "distinguishable social type" ... whose visibility is the basis of his/her expurgation' (Hay 1996: 198), the delineation of 'folk devils' in the risk society is understood as a 'foraging process' involving the search for some liable party or parties (Ungar 2001: 281). Such a process unfolds in the context of actors struggling to come to terms with the tensions ensuant between the techno-scientific rationalities of the expert world and the social rationalities produced in the domain of everyday living.

Social Versus Scientific Rationality

Ungar contends that, while moral panic is linked to a social constructionist approach which places an explanatory premium on the exaggeration of the actual threat posed by some condition, episode, person or group of persons, risk society accidents are highly unpredictable and uncontrollable, essentially neutralizing the constructionist approach as an analytic strategy ... [T]he issues addressed by moral panic research primarily involve exaggerated representations of only a small number of temporal anxieties that are manipulated to subdue otherwise marginal and dispossessed populations. Risk society accidents, on the other hand, eschew the temporality of moral panics, '... characterized by a stream of emergencies and would-be emergencies' (2001: 276) which are confronted by reflexive social agents as institutional failings in a politically fomented public arena.

Ungar's epistemology corresponds to a realist or materialist perspective, proponents of which not only endorse the view that the risks of late modernity stand as objective conditions of an unprecedented magnitude, but which presents '... an understanding of the human actor in which there is a linear relationship between knowledge of a risk, developing the attitude that one is at risk and adopting a practice to prevent the risk happening to oneself' (Lupton 1999: 21). Whilst it is true that Ulrich Beck, as the main expositor of the risk society thesis, holds that the threats and dangers confronting populations around the globe are only too real, it is important to recognize that he demonstrates a significant degree of restraint concerning his endorsement of the ontological certainty of the until-recent invisible side effects of industrialization...

Far from the conceptual foundations of a peremptory realism, however, Beck's contributions are more accurately characterized as 'weak social constructionism': risks which represent objective hazards and dangers, amenable to rationalistic calculation and assessment, but which are additionally '... mediated, perceived and responded to in particular ways via social, cultural and political processes' (Lupton 1999: 28)...

Thus, it follows from the invisible character of contemporary risks that the processes and mechanisms involved in the 'unveiling' of risks to the wider public are neither able to achieve sociological focus independent of a constructionist approach, nor are they available for full elucidation by adopting a linear model of simple reflexivity.

Claims making and social control

Seeking to corroborate his problematization of the social constructionist approach in the risk society, Ungar affirms that '... the roulette dynamics of risk society accidents are also at variance with the model of social control and folk devils used in moral panic research' (Ungar 2001: 276). In moral panics, he contends, governing authorities channel existing social anxieties towards a specific target (folk devil) in a fairly direct fashion for the purpose of imposing a sense of moral order or social control on situations or events that are perceived to lack such a property. Successively, '... claims making, pertaining to moral panics, can derive more from a shift in moral boundaries than either the objective standing of a condition or new evidence (2001: 277). The unfolding of risk society accidents propels institutional actors confronted with the political aftermath of 'catalytic real world catastrophes' to distance themselves from the identified location(s) of institutional failings in an attempt to displace imputations of liability and blame...

[R]isk society issues have given rise to a reflexive process of confrontation/refutation, rendering all aspects of claims making more open to discussion and criticism and, by corollary, exposing the conceptual limitations of claims making in moral panic research.

A degree of caution is warranted. Recent innovations in the sociology of moral panic have not only called attention to the increasingly eclectic character of the mass, niche and micro media, but to the enhanced degree of social leverage exhibited by folk devils McRobbie and Thornton, 1995). . . .

[C]laims making activities and processes of social control are far from self-evident through the duration of the construction – and contestation – of moral panics.

The Ecstacy panic in Toronto [Hier 2002] exemplifies the convergence of the sites of social anxieties purported to reside within the risk society . . . with more traditional formulations of moral panic. . . . As Jenkins (1999) explains, a great deal of anxiety surrounding synthetics such as Ecstacy stems from fact that they are manufactured scientific processes, drawing on fears concerning the fearsome potential of unchecked experiments. Not only did the risks and synthetic uncertainties constructed around Ecstacy-intake serve as a strategy to incite moral panic in this case, but as the weeks wore on a number of organizations representing Toronto's rave communities emerged to subvert the discourses designed with the intention of characterizing Toronto's rave communities as being 'at risk'. They did so by amplifying and accentuating the risks associated with forcing raves into locations containing substandard facilities (running water, adequate ventilation, supervisory presence, etc.), finding their interests defended in the same media outlets that only weeks earlier had run a scrupulous campaign against them. In this regard, whereas a risk discourse was utilized with the intention of serving as a *mechanism of social control* by authorities to subdue ravers, the same discursive technique was subverted as a mechanism of resistance apropos a *reflexive [rule-altering] confrontation*, as blame itself became a moral technology.

. . . [M]uch of Ungar's argument is contingent on what assumptions are made about the 'reality' of contemporary risks – at least a partial reflection of the theoretical slippage inherent in Beck's work (see Cottle 1998). If risks are understood as objective conditions confronting contemporary societies, it is only in the realm of *scientific rationality* that the 'invisibility' of contemporary risks can be understood techno-scientifically along a theoretical plane through the 'claims making' activities of experts. Conversely, it is within the realm of *social rationality* that 'risks' become 'visible' as lay knowledge, and in this respect contemporary perceptions of risk necessitate understanding along an epistemological plane through social, political and cultural channels. Processes of claims making in risk society issues should be understood to parallel claims making activities involved in moral panics in that they set the context for, but do not directly dictate what, the public perceives as a threat.

Anxiety and Risk in late modernity

It is now necessary to explore in greater depth the constructs of anxiety and risk in late modernity. Whilst intuitively attractive, the invocation of 'social anxiety' as an explanatory technique capable of capturing the essence of the late modern experience should neither be accepted uncritically nor without pause. As is evidenced in Ungar's analysis, the explanatory power of such an account rests on the a priori assumption that, confronted with the objective, catastrophic conditions of the risk society, social actors adjust their thought patterns and behavioural routines according to a rationally calculated, collectively shared, sense of existential insecurity. ... [F]aced with the objective conditions of the now-prevalent manufactured uncertainties brought about through industrialization, individuals collectively enter into a state of 'anxiety' emanating from the catastrophic potential of the risk society. ... [S]uch an account contains the seed of its own demise, as it is bound to spiral into an over-socialized conception of individuals as mere 'risk actors' playing a predetermined role in a culturally prescribed risk-narrative.

Hollway and Jefferson (1997) problematize 'the missing subject' in overly socialized conceptions of late modern living. They envision anxiety as a complex dimension of the human psyche rooted in the dynamic unconscious, which only secondarily assumes the form of historically and culturally specific, shared anxieties.

Although manifesting differently across time, space and place, anxieties are understood to derive from a more deep-seated intersubjective human condition which is not etiologically social in the last instance.

Of particular importance is Hollway and Jefferson's conceptual stipulation that social-psychological explanation must theorize the passage of risk discourses through individual psyches. ... It is not that social anxiety as an explanatory concept is superfluous in their view, but rather that the analysis of anxiety and everyday responses to it requires consideration of the experiential forms of anxiety, in addition to the social conditions that serve to generate it. ... Giddens (1990, 1991) explains the contours of late (or high) modernity as consisting of ambivalence and existential anxiety, characterized by the 'distanciation' of time and space and the 'disembedding' of social relations. Such an ambivalence ... arises from the intersection of social events and social relations 'at distance' with local contextualities. ... [L]ate modernity involves a radical realignment of how individuals 'live in the world' in the sense that time-space distanciation and the disembedding of social relations (i.e. 'abstract systems') renders human experience increasingly susceptible to the actions and agency of 'absent others'.

Yet, anxiety in Giddens's assessment does not emerge unilaterally from the mechanisms of distanciation and disembedding – ... not directly from social change via globalization. Rather, Giddens understands anxiety as an existential feature of the human condition that must be understood in relation to the overall security system that individuals develop...

In the face of future threats or dangers, the ability to trust, developed in childhood, acts as a 'protective cocoon' permitting the continuity of routine daily functioning, relatively free of what would otherwise be debilitating anxieties. Considering that at any given time individuals could conceivably be overwhelmed by anxieties which are implied by 'the very business of living' (1991: 40), the protective cocoon acts to provide a sense of 'unreality', a relative feeling of invulnerability to the contingencies of the risk society.

Experiential Lifeworld versus the mediated world of risk

Giddens declares that 'although everyone lives a local life, phenomenal worlds are for the most part truly global' (1991: 187). He contends that distant/global relations increasingly enter into, and influence, the everyday phenomenal worlds of social actors. Such an intrusion of the distant into the local is purported to disrupt familiar life patterns and give rise to a form of 'life-politics' (Giddens) or 'sub-politics' (Beck) which signifies a phenomenal attachment that individuals develop with global affairs through mediated experience(s). ... [T]he experience of individualization, set within the context of globalization, gives rise to a phenomenal attachment with distant others, culminating in a moral responsibility for solving planetary problems.

... Giddens understands the functioning of risk discourses as socializing individual choice and positioning social actors in certain specific ways (cf. Lupton 1999) by ascribing predominant explanatory importance to the trust relations that actors develop with expert systems. But Tomlinson (1994) questions the extent to which people have an on-going, phenomenal experience with global affairs. Taking particular issue with Giddens's claim that distant events have permeated the experiential lifeworld to the extent that remote influences may have become more familiar than proximate affairs, he insists on preserving the distinctions between distant/local and mediated/immediate experience. To be sure, Tomlinson contends, most people are aware of global affairs through their engagement with the mass media, but this form of mediation is encountered as a distinct mode of experience, separate from immediate experience and the contextuality of the familiar.

Phillips (2000) goes some distance to substantiate empirically Tomlinson's theoretical postulate in her study of how people understand, talk about and respond to ecological risks via the mass media...

Phillips contends that political consumption only provides people with a limited sense of agency in global political affairs, as they discursively differentiate eco-politics as a *mediated public realm* separate from the *realm of everyday experiential reality*. ... Individuals are shielded from a sense of blame or anxiety, not from trust relations embedded in expert systems, but from a sense of order or control achieved in the realm of everyday living through routinized patterns of responsible living.

Hence, implicit in the refutation of the socializing character of contemporary risks is the problematization of the mass media as a discursive space which functions to shape public discourse and popular consicousness of late modern conditions.

Tomlinson and Phillips argue that the mediated experience of risk leaves individuals with only a weak sense of global unity. Rather than culminating in the formation of a kind of 'transnational citizenship' based on a concern for distant others, individualization is understood as socially atomizing, reflected in the discursive distinction people make between the mediated world of global risks and the experiential reality of everyday life. This is not to suggest, of course, that people are immune to the influence of mass mediated risk knowledge formats circumscribed largely by experts, but simply that peoples' perceptions of risk are situated within the context of routinized and normalized local order and the production and functioning of everyday living.

Locality and Order in an Age of Contingency

It follows from the foregoing discussion that, if anxieties continue to build up around the *invisibility* of risk, the production of order should be expected to play out on the quotidian front, situated in the immediate realm of everyday living. Given that individuals have no means available to them to determine the uncertainties which place them 'at risk', all aspects of life represent a potential source of anxiety. If, in the face of pervasive and yet unknown 'threats', we are witnessing not the resolute triumph of risk (i.e. probabilistic analyses) over uncertainty ... but the divisive character of the political distribution of risk, understanding how individuals (and groups) are dealing with indeterminacy is of foremost importance. Accordingly, this final section offers one explanation for how a sense of social order is forged and maintained in an age of contingency.

Community and security

... [S]ocial theories of late modernity have generally agreed that the concept of risk serves as an epistemological resource which is regularly invoked to explain or account for manufactured *uncertainty*. In this sense, risk represents a discursive technique which implies faith in the *controllability* of social phenomena.

... [R]isk has come to signify danger. ... [T]he conflation of risk and danger stems largely from the perception that the consequences or side-effects of human actions are unknowable, and a heightened sense of 'risk consciousness' serves to normalize collective feelings of suspicion and fear (Furedi 1997). The latter creates the illusion that life's contingencies are susceptible to human calculation and, ultimately, human control.

At the forefront of this body of knowledge is Bauman's (1991) argument that one of the principal, though impossible, tasks that modernity sets for itself is the production of order and the quest to extinguish existential uncertainty.

... [T]he production of order establishes the limits to incorporation; it comes together under the pretense of an inclusive community founded on the precepts of mutual understanding and common unity.

... [T]hroughout modernity the quest to establish a sense of existential security – community – has come at the expense of the de-legitimation of the Other: the criminalized, racialized, gendered or stigmatized. ... Existential insecurities find a tangible target in the pursuit of 'community' through the expurgation of the Other. ... [A]lthough the 'communitarian' aspect of community appears to social actors as antithetical to 'the modern', it is in actuality firmly immersed within the confines of modernity: divisive, exclusionary and protectionist. ... [F]ar from delivering the existential comforts imagined to reside with a state of 'community', the ways in which community is pursued serves only to contribute to an extended range of uncertainty.

From strangers to enemies

... [T]he attainment of community remains contingent on reducing the complexity and intangibility of late modern conditions to the *discernible level of personal safety*. It involves, as Simmel (1950) saw it, the production of the stranger: s/he who is brought into existence through various forms of sociation involving both proximity and distance, neither near nor far. The stranger is 'one of us', an element of the group itself, situated somewhere between familiarity and remoteness, but never close enough to fall within the established order of what is understood to constitute 'sameness'. . . . [T]he category of the stranger stands in opposition to the notion of community; the stranger represents the categorical incomprehensibility of ambivalence.

. . . Under conditions of reflexive modernity, Beck [suggests], the 'ordering categories' reminiscent of industrial society are changing (or have changed) by way of the tripartite influence of individualization, globalization and manufactured uncertainty.

> Individualization . . . means that own-group identity becomes blurred. Globalization means, among other things, that the walls of distance break down and that strangers and strangeness are increasingly caught in the horizon of one's own life. Manufactured uncertainty means danger lurks everywhere and no one does anything about it. . . . It boils down to a question of concern to all of society: the *politicization of the question of security*. (Beck 1998: 133, 134)

. . . [A]s people continue to lose their unambiguous social positions in a world where everyone is in a sense 'strange', collective identities become permeable and the barriers reminiscent of simple modernity grow pale. . . . [P]eople no longer feel obliged to develop ways to deal with strangers per se, but rather various sorts of strangers are forced to develop ways to deal with one another in a social environment where the category of the stranger has become generalized.

Confronted with conditions of universal estrangement brought about through advanced modernization, Beck (1997) concedes that the culmination of these processes may not lead to a reflection on modernity and its consequences, but could alternatively assume the form of 'counter-modernization'. . .

As an active and conscious *component of modernity*, counter-modernization transforms modernity's questioning of doubt and uncertainty into trust and certitude, simplifying as emotive that which is infinitely complex by the very standards of modernity. The necessity therefore presents itself to distinguish between the production of everyday stereotypes of the stranger on the one hand, and enemy stereotypes on the other. In contrast to the construction of the categorically incomprehensible 'cultural stranger', enemy stereotypes are decisive temporal constructions which are understood to present an immediate affront to both personal and group safety. As the antithesis to 'security', the threat posed by 'the enemy' abolishes all individuality and lends itself to the construction of a defensive ascription under the guise of communal security. What this signifies for Beck (1998: 136) is that '. . . the models of perception and action in risk society are transferred to the risk of civilization'. Or, to put this contextually, as a general suspicion of anomie takes the place of the contingencies of the risk society, people will invariably be drawn to practices and discourses that offer the promise of social order and social control in the face of existential uncertainties (cf. Hollway and Jefferson 1997)...

Importantly, while appearing on the surface to be constructions of the state, enemy stereotypes must be understood to originate with, or emerge from, everyday cultural stereotypes of the stranger. As Beck explains, enemy stereotypes represent a form of 'bureaucratic stranger' which is brought into focus through the institutions of civil society. That is, the categorically decisive bureaucratic construction of the enemy emerges to replace the categorically incomprehensible cultural construction of the stranger, as discourses centering on cultural differences are transferred to safety discourses focusing on the 'risk factors' ingrained in enemy stereotypes. In the Canadian [boat people] example, so powerful was the discourse constructed around the risks posed by the migrants' presence that the coverage, hinging on a narrative of personal safety, articulated a politics of security and a discursive interrogation of the legitimacy of the state's protective capacity (Hier and Greenberg 2002). Successively, the state responded by housing the migrants in a make-shift prison for nearly a year before deporting them, set against the backdrop of a national debate on the country's immigration and refugee policies. ... The state is able to draw on existing anxieties as '... cultural difference is energized into a discourse about enemy stereotypes intended to legitimize the construction and reinforcement of the preventative security and protective state' (Beck 1998: 139).

Therefore, the presence of the enemy as the antithesis to security stimulates the pursuit of a sense of community – a subjectively unambiguous distinction between 'self' and 'others' – that precludes any spatial allowance for alternative identities. In turn, reducing the complexity and intangibility of existential insecurity to that of communal belonging satisfies two purposes. First, it confronts directly the individuating tendencies of late modernity, turning them into immediate matters of communal safety and collective security. Subsequently, and second, it affirms a sense of fleeting community in a world of generalized strangers, contributing to the consolidation of a sense of own-group identity. 'Identity' then emerges as the surrogate for 'community' as an ordering practice in late modernity, contributing to the tempering of the precariousness of 'community' (Bauman 2001). In a culture of suspicion and fear, characterized by an individuated, distanciated, uncertain world, the context in which everyday *cultural stereotypes* of the stranger present themselves as ambivalent becomes increasingly more differentiated in the form of bureaucratic *enemy stereotypes* signifying *risk factors* to be avoided.

Whither Moral Panic?

What, then, can be said for the fate of moral panic in a risk society? Recall that Beck forecasts a 'commonality of anxiety' that will give rise to a solitary politics in the face of global contingency. ... [T]his will come in the form of global solidarity based on the reflexive confrontation/refutation of modernity, cutting through traditional boundaries of social segmentation. ... [S]uch a projection should be received with caution. The commonality of anxiety – or rather the perception of risk – does draw people together, but it does so at the level of quotidian order. ... Beck's notion of counter-modernization, as a more specified form of reflexive modernization, offers greater analytic promise.

Counter-modernization as an analytic concept is particularly useful in that it allows for the fusion of two seemingly disparate issues: the need to impose order at the level of everyday life and the ordering practices of the state. Contrary to Ungar's contention that the catastrophic potential of the risk society has rendered subsidiary the more mundane, locally situated, iterative disruptions in daily living, it is a more fruitful analytic endeavour to understand the politicization of risk as contributing to an extended level of disruptions in the routine functioning of everyday living which are subsequently incorporated by the state under the pretense of 'law and order'. ... [A]s Furedi (1997: 147–68) argues, set against the backdrop of a heightened sense of risk consciousness, 'the new etiquette' of caution, fear and danger has distanced itself from judgments about what is morally proper or acceptable, becoming transposed into discourses of safety, security and communal living. ... [A]lthough the utilization of a risk calculus has arisen to transform many social problems into a set of risks and dangers, post-moral techniques and discourses of risk-management have ended up doing old moral regulation work (Moore and Valverde 2000). To put this succinctly, as anxieties endemic to the risk society converge with anxieties contained at the level of community, we should expect a proliferation of moral panics *as an ordering practice* in late modernity.

References

Bauman, Z. (1991) *Modernity and Ambivalence*. Cambridge: Polity Press.
Bauman, Z. (2001) *Community: Seeking Safety in an Insecure World*. Cambridge: Polity Press.
Beck, U. (1992) *Risk Society: Towards a New Modernity*. trans. M. Ritter. London: Sage.

Beck, U. (1997) The construction of the other side of modernity: counter-modernization, in U. Beck, *The Reinvention of Politics: Rethinking Modernity in the Global Social Order*. Cambridge: Polity Press.

Beck, U. (1998) How neighbours become Jews: the political construction of the stranger in the age of reflexive modernity, in U. Beck, *Democracy Without Enemies*. Cambridge: Polity Press.

Cohen, S. (1972) *Folk Devils and Moral Panics*. St Albans: Paladin.

Cottle, S. (1998) Ulrich Beck, 'risk society' and the media: a catastrophic view?, *European Journal of Communication*, 13(1): 5–32.

Furedi, F. (1997) *Culture of Fear: Risk-taking and the Morality of Low Expectation*. London: Cassell.

Giddens, A. (1990) *Consequences of Modernity*. Stanford, CA: Stanford Press.

Giddens, A. (1991) *Modernity and Self-Identity*. Cambridge: Polity Press.

Hay, C. (1996) Mobilization through interpellation: James Bulger, juvenile crime and the construction of a moral panic, *Social and Legal Studies*, 4(2): 197–223.

Hier, S.P. (2002) Raves, risk and the ecstacy panic: a case study in the subversive nature of moral regulation, *Canadian Journal of Sociology*, 27(1): 33–57.

Hier, S. and Greenberg, J. (2002) Constructing a discursive crisis: risk, problematization and 'illegal' Chinese in Canada, *Ethnic and Racial Studies*, 25(3): 490–513.

Hollway, W. and Jefferson, T. (1997) The risk society in the age of anxiety: situating a fear of crime, *British Journal of Sociology*, 48(2): 255–66.

Jenkins, P. (1999) *Synthetic Panic: The Symbolic Politics of Designer Drugs*. New York: New York University Press.

Lupton, D. (1999) *Risk*. London: Routledge.

McRobbie, A. and Thornton, S.L. (1995) Re-thinking 'moral panic' for multi-mediated social worlds, *British Journal of Sociology*, 46(4): 559–74.

Moore, D. and Valverde, M. (2000) Maidens at risk: 'date rape drugs' and the formation of hybrid risk knowledges, *Economy and Society*, 29(4): 514–31.

Phillips. L. (2000) Mediated communication and the privatization of public problems, *European Journal of Communication*, 15(2): 171–207.

Simmel, G. (1950) *The Sociology of Georg Simmel*, ed. K. Wolff. New York: Free Press.

Tomlinson, J. (1994) A phenomenology of globalization? Giddens on global modernity, *European Journal of Communication*, 9(1): 149–72.

Ungar, S. (2001) Moral panic versus the risk society: the implications of the changing sites of social anxiety, *British Journal of Sociology*, 52(2): 271–92.

INDEX

MORAL PANICS AND THE MEDIA

Chas Critcher

"Chas Critcher's study is doubly welcome as it discusses theoretical underpinnings thoroughly, and also provides a set of illustrative case studies ... This is an important and stimulating book for a range of audiences." – VISTA

- How are social problems defined and responded to in contemporary society?
- What is the role of the media in creating, endorsing and sustaining moral panics?

The term 'moral panic' is frequently applied to sudden outbreaks of concern about social problems. Chas Critcher critically evaluates the usefulness of moral panic models for understanding how politicians, the public and pressure groups come to recognise apparent new threats to the social order, and he scrutinizes the role of the media, especially the popular press.

Two models of moral panics are identified and explained, then applied to a range of case studies: AIDS; rave culture and the drug ecstasy; video nasties; child abuse; paedophilia. Examples of moral panics from a range of countries reveal many basic similarities but also significant variations between different national contexts. The conclusion is that moral panic remains a useful tool for analysis but needs more systematic connection to wider theoretical concerns, especially those of the risk society and discourse analysis.

224pp
0 335 20908 4 (EAN: 9 78 0335 209088) Paperback
0 335 20909 2 (EAN: 9 78 0335 209095) Hardback

Critical Readings
VIOLENCE AND THE MEDIA

C. Kay Weaver and Cynthia Carter (eds)

The relationship between media representations and real acts of violence is one of the most contentious and hotly debated issues today.This book is the first to bring together a selection of highly influential readings that have helped to shape this area of research. It includes key investigations of how, and with what implications, the media portray violence in the twenty-first century.

Critical Readings: Violence and the Media contains sections examining how media violence and its 'effects' have been theorized; how media production contexts influence the reporting and representation of violence; and how audiences engage with depictions of violence. Violence is analysed in different media formats, including television, film, radio, the news, public information campaigns, comics, video games, popular music, photography and the internet.The readings cover a range of perspectives, including social learning, desensitisation and cultivation theories,'no-effects' models, sociological, feminist and postmodern arguments. An editor's introduction and section introductions serve to contextualise the readings.

Providing a detailed and theoretically grounded consideration of the cultural and social significance of media violence, *Critical Readings: Violence and the Media* is an essential resource for students of media studies, cultural studies, sociology and communication studies.

Contributors: Alison Adam, Albert Bandura, Martin Barker, Eileen Berrington, Douglas R. Bruce, David Buckingham, David Campbell, Jay Dixit, Lisa Duke, Molly Eckman, David Gauntlett, George Gerbner, Henry Giroux, Jack Glaser, Donald P. Green, Kellie Hay, Annette Hill, Birgitta Höijer, Derek Iwamoto, Ann Jemphrey, Christine L. Kellow, Jenny Kitzinger, Magdala Peixoto Labre, Catherine Amoroso Leslie, Debra Merskin, Jennifer Paff Ogle, Mary Beth Oliver, Valerie Palmer-Mehta, Julian Petley, Charles Piot, Srividya Ramasubramanian, Dorrie Ross, Sheila A. Ross, Medhi Semanti, H. Leslie Steeves.

400pp
0 335 21805 9 (EAN: 9 78 0335 218059) Paperback
0 335 21806 7 (EAN: 9 78 0335 218066) Hardback

DATE DUE
